THE DESTRUCTION
OF LORD RAGLAN

THE DESTRUCTION
OF LORD RAGLAN

A Tragedy of the Crimean War 1854–55

Christopher Hibbert

WORDSWORTH EDITIONS

FOR TOM

First published in 1961 by Longmans

Copyright © Christopher Hibbert 1961

This edition published 1999
by Wordsworth Editions Limited
Cumberland House, Crib Street, Ware,
Hertfordshire SG12 9ET

ISBN 1 84022 209 3

© Wordsworth Editions Limited 1999

Wordsworth® is a registered trade mark of
Wordsworth Editions Limited

Printed and bound in Great Britain
by Mackays of Chatham plc, Chatham, Kent.

*'Every whale must
have a Jonah
when the sea runs high'*

LORD STRATFORD DE REDCLIFFE
2 FEBRUARY 1855

CONTENTS

NOTE

When Lord Raglan died on the plateau before the still untaken Sebastopol, his sister-in-law the Countess of Westmorland, whose husband was British Ambassador in Vienna, received a letter of sympathy from Prince Metternich. 'Time and the secrets which it still holds,' Metternich wrote, 'will establish amply the historical truth concerning the character and conduct of Lord Raglan.'

No biography of Lord Raglan has yet been published. And his private papers have lain in boxes at Cefntilla Court for more than a hundred years. These papers contain not only Lord Raglan's own personal correspondence but a great number of papers and letters written by his family and friends, A.D.C.s and staff. They also contain numerous papers which were sent to Lady Raglan after her husband's death.

Lord Raglan's great-grandson has been good enough to allow me full access to these papers and has put no restrictions upon my use of them. He has also kindly given me permission to consult the Field-Marshal's military papers which he deposited some years ago in the Royal United Service Institution.

In these two collections most of Lord Raglan's correspondence is contained. There are, however, various other letters and papers of his elsewhere. I have, accordingly, to acknowledge the gracious permission of Her Majesty the Queen to make use of material in the Royal Archives, Windsor Castle. I must also express a debt of gratitude to the Duke of Norfolk for allowing me access to the Arundel Castle Archives; to the Duke of Wellington for allowing me to make use of the Wellington papers at Stratfield Saye and Apsley House; to the Earl of Halifax for letting me use the Hickleton papers; to Mrs. Leopold Lonsdale for permission to quote from Lord Raglan's letters to the Countess of Westmorland; and to the Trustees of the Newcastle Estates for permission to study and quote from Lord Raglan's letters to the 5th Duke of Newcastle.

NOTE

For helping me find the relevant papers, or for making copies of them for me, I want to thank Mr. Robert Mackworth-Young, librarian at Windsor; Mr. J. H. Hodson of the Department of Manuscripts, Nottingham University Library; and Mr. Malcolm Cole; Mr. Francis W. Steer, the County of Sussex Archivist; Mr. Francis Needham, the Duke of Wellington's librarian; Mr. T. L. Ingram, Lord Halifax's archivist; and Mr. R. E. Freeman, Mrs. Lonsdale's agent.

The Verney Papers at Claydon House contain several letters from Florence Nightingale about Lord Raglan, and I am grateful to Sir Harry Verney for allowing me to see them and to quote from two of them.

For permission to quote from the correspondence of Lord Burghersh, one of Lord Raglan's A.D.C.s in the Crimea, I am indebted to the Earl of Westmorland. Mr. P. I. King and the staff of the Northamptonshire Record Office have kindly helped me with these letters; and my father has made copies of them for me.

For permission to make use of the Crawford Muniments containing letters from Ensign Robert Lindsay of the Scots Fusilier Guards, I am grateful to the Earl of Crawford and Balcarres.

The letters of Private George Conn of the 79th Highlanders, from which I have quoted, were first printed in the *Aberdeen University Review* in 1959, and I am indebted to Miss Nan Shepherd, the editor of the *Review*, and to Mr. William Weir, who edited the letters, for drawing my attention to them.

The letters of Colonel William Tomline form part of the Pretyman Collection in the Ipswich and East Suffolk Record Office, and Mr. D. Charman, the joint archivist, arranged for copies of these to be made for me.

The letters of Captain F. C. Elton of the 55th Regiment form part of the Elton Papers at Clevedon Court, and I must thank Sir Arthur Elton for permission to make use of them.

I want also to thank Mr. D. W. King, the War Office librarian; Miss W. B. Coates and the staff of the National Register of Archives; the staffs of the British Museum and the Public Record Office; Professor Robertson of the John Rylands Library, Manchester; Brigadier John Stephenson and the librarian's staff at the Royal United Service Institution; Miss Susanna Fisher of the Manuscript Department of the

National Maritime Museum; Mr. B. M. G. Butterworth of Messrs. Robson Lowe Ltd; Mr. M. Davies, Librarian of the Royal Army Medical College; Mr. F. J. Tyzack; and Miss Frances Ryan.

I owe a particular debt of gratitude to Dr. Douglas Simpson of Aberdeen University, who has been generous enough to place at my disposal the fruits of his research into Lord Raglan's early life and record; to Mrs. Cecil Woodham-Smith and Mr. C. E. Vulliamy, who have given me much useful information; and to Mr. W. Baring Pemberton and Major Freddie Myatt who have been good enough to read the proofs.

A great number of family papers, letters and diaries have been lent to me, and I want especially to thank Mrs. E. Ashton for letters written to her grandfather, Captain Stephen Lushington, R.N.; Mrs. Balfour of Balfour and Trenabie for letters from her father, Midshipman Evelyn Wood; Miss Joanna Barnard for letters from Major-General Henry Barnard; Mrs. L. J. Bickford for letters and the diary of her grandfather, Captain C. M. J. D. Shakespear, R.H.A.; Miss F. M. Biddulph for letters from Captain Henry Duberly of the 8th Hussars and Major-General J. B. Estcourt; Mr. J. A. Biddulph for letters and a diary of his grandfather, Captain M. A. Biddulph, R.A.; Major-General Harold H. Blake for letters and a manuscript medical history of his regiment written by his grandfather, Dr. Ethelbert Blake, surgeon to the 55th Regiment; Mrs. Joyce Carlton for letters from her great-great-uncle, Corporal John Spurling of the 63rd Regiment; Mrs. Alma Chadburn for copies of letters from her father, Sergeant Chadburn of the Coldstream Guards; Mrs. L. M. Chesterton for letters from Captain The Hon. Henry Neville, Grenadier Guards, and Cornet the Hon. Grey Neville, 5th Dragoon Guards; Mr. Guy Cracroft for letters from the Rev. the Hon. Sydney Godolphin Osbourne and Major Charles Naysmyth; Mr. F. R. Crozier for letters from his great uncle the Rev. James Alexander Crozier; Mrs. Violet Dickson for letters from her late husband's great-uncle, Colonel H. Dickson, R.A., and from the Duke of Cambridge; Mr. and Mrs. F. H. Dorling for letters from Captain Lyon and Colonel the Hon. George Cadogan; Mrs. Diana Drummond for letters from her great-great-uncle Dr. Joseph Skelton, Surgeon to the Coldstream Guards; Major R. S. Dyer Bennet for letters from Captain William Powell Richards, R.A.; Mrs. Eveleen Fisher-Rowe for the privately printed letters of

NOTE

her father-in-law, Cornet E. R. Fisher of the 4th Dragoon Guards; Mr. W. H. S. Godfrey for the diary of Captain A. W. Godfrey of the Rifle Brigade; Lieutenant-Colonel J. N. W. Hearn for the diary and order book of Brigadier-General J. G. S. Neill; Mrs. M. Heaton-Armstrong for letters from her husband's great-uncle, Lieutenant G. W. Stacpoole; Brigadier L. F. R. Kenyon for a copy of a letter from Mr. Roger Fenton; Mrs. Janet King for letters from Captain Charles Hay and the Rev. J. C. Hulbert; Canon W. M. Lummis for letters from Mr. W. H. Pennington; the Lady Constance Malleson for the diary of her father, Lieutenant the Hon. Hugh Annesley of the Scots Fusilier Guards; Mr. Peter Metcalfe for letters from General Sir George de Lacy Evans; Mrs. A. E. Pearson for letters from her great-uncle, Captain E. B. Maunsell of the 69th Regiment; Sir Francis Portal, Bart., for the privately printed letters of his great-uncle, Captain Robert Portal of the 4th Light Dragoons; the Hon. Lady Raglan for letters from her great-uncle, Colonel Frederick William Hamilton of the Grenadier Guards; Mrs. Geraldine Roberts for letters from her father, Major H. R. Roberts, R.M.A.; Mr. Charles W. Rogers for letters from his great-uncle, Paymaster Henry Dixon of the Royal Fusiliers; Brigadier G. MacLeod Ross for letters from Dr. John Lizars; Major F. H. W. Ross-Lewin for letters from his great-uncle, Captain J. D. Ross-Lewin of the 30th Regiment; Colonel C. A. L. Shipley for letters from his grandfather, Captain R. Y. Shipley of the Royal Fusiliers; Mr. V. A. Spinks for letters from his wife's grandfather, Private Thomas Bishop of the Grenadier Guards; Mr. R. A. Swinmoe for the autobiography of his grandfather, William Cattell; Mrs. B. Walker-Heneage-Vivian for letters from her father-in-law, Major Clement Walker-Heneage of the 8th Hussars; and Mrs. Mary Woodhouse for letters to her grandfather, Captain Purcell Woodhouse of the 90th Light Infantry.

For drawing my attention to their family papers or other sources which I might well have missed, and for answering questions concerning them, I want to thank Mr. David Balfour of Balfour and Trenabie; Major-General R. E. Barnsley; the Duke of Beaufort; Mr. F. H. Blake; Mrs. E. H. Campbell; Mrs. Olive Clarke; Viscount Colville of Culross; Mr. Roger Coxon; Mr. F. R. Crozier; Lieutenant-Colonel H. S. Flower; Mr. James Gauntlett; Mr. Helmut Gernsheim; the Rev. W. S. H. Hallett; Lieutenant-Colonel F. C. Hitchcock; Mr. Arthur

Knight; Mr. K. Macrae Moir; Lieutenant-Colonel A. G. F. Monro; Mrs. L. A. McGuy, Mr. Andrew Melville, Mrs. C. W. Pollock-Gore, Mr. Martin H. Press, Mr.W. A. Ramsay, the Rev. J. M. B. Roberts, Mr. Norman Scarfe, Miss Joan Wake and Sir John Wheeler-Bennett. The letters of Henry Clifford of the Rifle Brigade were published by Michael Joseph in *Henry Clifford: his Letters and Drawings from the Crimea* (1956) and extracts from them are given with the kind permission of Michael Joseph Ltd. and Mr. Nicholas Fitzherbert; G. Bell & Sons Ltd. have let me quote from the letters of Colonel George Bell in *Soldier's Glory* (1956); the Folio Society Ltd. from those of Sergeant-Major Timothy Gowing in *A Voice from the Ranks* (1954).

For helping me with Russian and German books, I am grateful to Miss Phyllis Auty and Fräulein Hannalore Preywisch. Mrs. Richard Owen has read several French authorities for me and where quotations from these are given in English the translations are hers.

Although I have made Lord Raglan the central figure of the tragedy, I have tried at the same time to write a military history of the war from primary sources. This has not been done in this century. It was, of course, done in the nineteenth. And no one who writes of the Crimean War can fail to be indebted to the man who spent more than thirty years doing it. Kinglake's *Invasion of the Crimea* is extravagantly elaborate, highly idiosyncratic, often prejudiced and sometimes wrong. But it is a work of art; and, I think, the greatest military history written in English. No book could pretend to take its place. This one, however, has had the benefit of some sources which were not available when Kinglake's book was written; and it has, at least, the merit of being more compact.

CHRISTOPHER HIBBERT

1

LORD FITZROY SOMERSET

You are aware how useful he has always been to me
The Duke of Wellington

I

In the second week of the hot July of 1808, the British cruiser *Donegall* sailed out of the Cove of Cork and set course for Corunna. Aboard her were Lieutenant-General Sir Arthur Wellesley and a nineteen-year-old lieutenant of Dragoons. They bore so marked a resemblance to each other that men took them for father and son. It was an understandable mistake.

They had the same penetrating eyes, the same healthy complexion, the same high-beaked nose. They shared too the same sort of patrician handsomeness. But the General's expression in repose was proud, austere and somewhat remote; the young Lieutenant's gentler, warmer and less self-assured. Despite the twenty years' difference in their ages, by the time their ship docked in Corunna harbour they were already friends.[1] The friendship was never to be broken.

The young man was Lord FitzRoy Somerset, the youngest of the Duke of Beaufort's eleven children. His commission as a cornet in the 4th Light Dragoons had been bought for him when he was still a fifteen-year-old schoolboy at Westminster, and he had already shown himself to be an officer of great enthusiasm and promise. On Christmas Day 1810 Sir Arthur Wellesley chose him to succeed Colonel Bathurst as his Military Secretary.

Colonel Bathurst had been obliged to retire from this envied appointment, as he had been driven by his master's difficult temperament to a nervous breakdown. Captain Lord FitzRoy Somerset, however, was not likely to suffer a similar collapse; for he had the ability of preserving in the midst of confusion, irritation, danger or abuse a quite astonishing serenity. He was also extremely tactful, industrious and discreet. He promised, indeed, to be an ideal Military Secretary; and Wellesley found him to be one.

Already he had proved himself a brave officer. A month after his

I

arrival in the Peninsula, he had asked for a transfer to an infantry regiment, and had served in the 42nd Regiment of Foot. He had seen action at Roliça, at Vimiero and at Talavera. He had been slightly wounded at Busaco. And everywhere he fought, he showed that complete indifference to danger which forty-five years later was to impress a whole army.

As Military Secretary he performed many more active duties than were usually expected of men in that appointment. When, for instance, the first attempt to carry the breaches at Badajoz was repulsed with terrible slaughter, he formed one of a heroic party which climbed by escalade into the bastion of San Vicente and helped to bring about the surrender of the fortress, which opened the way for the victorious British army to stream across Spain and then into a France weakened by the Grande Armée's retreat from Moscow.

Lord FitzRoy was twenty-three now and a Lieutenant-Colonel in the 1st Foot Guards, at the newly created Lord Wellington's request. His future seemed bright and assured. He was hitched to Wellington's star and he was rising with it.

In 1814, when for that one 'year of revelry' the war with Napoleon was over, he married his master's beautiful niece.* He had met her the year before and had fallen in love with her within a few days of first seeing her. As the Duke's A.D.C. he had gone with him to Spain on a diplomatic mission for Castlereagh, and Emily Wellesley-Pole had travelled with them. She was, her sister afterwards wrote,

> so much struck with the entire confidence and high opinion with which the Duke regarded him, that when, soon after their return to England he proposed for Emily, my father at once and with joy consented to the match, though some of our relatives considered that being a younger son with but a small annuity . . . it was not 'so good a match' as the young lady, who was very much admired and courted, might look to. I remember hearing my father say, 'I had rather see my daughter married to him, than to the richest Duke in the Kingdom, so admirable do I think his conduct and disposition. Besides which, with his talents, and industry and high character, he is quite sure to become a most distinguished man.'[2]

* The Hon. Emily Harriet Wellesley-Pole, the second daughter of the Duke's brother William, Lord Maryborough, who afterwards became the 3rd Earl of Mornington. She married Lord FitzRoy at her father's house, 3 Savile Row, on 6 August 1814.

He was certainly at this time a happy and successful one. When Wellington returned to Paris as Ambassador at the end of the year, Lord FitzRoy remained with him as his secretary and acted as Minister Plenipotentiary during the Duke's absences at the peace conference in Vienna. He spoke French fluently, with a strong and disarming English accent, and he and his lovely and vivacious wife were both admired and envied. But it was a period of their lives which was to end abruptly.

In February 1815 Napoleon escaped from Elba. The next month he entered Paris in triumph and the war had started again.

Lord FitzRoy took his pregnant wife to Brussels and on 18 June was at Wellington's side at Waterloo. They had left Brussels together at eight o'clock in the morning of the 16th and for three days he had acted once more as the Duke's principal A.D.C. Towards the evening of the third day a musket-ball from a sniper on the roof of the farmhouse of La Haye Sainte smashed his right elbow. He walked back to a cottage used as forward hospital and showed his lacerated arm to the surgeon in charge. The surgeon told him to lie down on a table and then he cut the arm off between the shoulder and the elbow. Lord FitzRoy did not even murmur. The Prince of Orange, lying wounded in the same small room, was unaware that an operation had been performed, until the arm was tossed away by the surgeon and the Colonel called out, 'Hey, bring my arm back. There's a ring my wife gave me on the finger.' [3]

On the following day Wellington wrote to the Duke of Beaufort:

> I am very sorry to have to acquaint you that your brother FitzRoy is very severely wounded, and has lost his right arm. I have just seen him, and he is perfectly free from fever, and as well as anybody could be under such circumstances. You are aware how useful he has always been to me, and how much I shall feel the want of his assistance, and what a regard and affection I feel for him, and you will readily believe how much concerned I am . . . I hope he will soon be able to join me again. [4]

It was not long before he did. As soon as he was well again, he returned to Paris as Secretary of Embassy while the Duke was there as Commander of the occupation forces. He accompanied him on diplomatic missions to Vienna and Verona, and when in 1819 the Army of Occupation was withdrawn and Wellington returned to London as

Master-General of the Ordnance, Lord FitzRoy came home with him as Secretary. In 1827 the Duke of York died and Wellington was appointed Commander-in-Chief at the Horse Guards in his place. Lord FitzRoy was once again called upon to follow him as Secretary.

He was thirty-nine and already a Major-General. He was a Knight Commander of the Order of the Bath, a Knight of the Order of Maria Theresa of Austria, of St. George of Russia, of Maximilian Joseph of Bavaria, of the Tower and Sword of Portugal. He was an A.D.C. to King George IV, a Freeman of the City of Gloucester, Member of Parliament for Truro. He had been to Madrid on an important diplomatic mission for the Government and was soon to go to St. Petersburg with Wellington on another one. He was greatly respected and greatly liked. At Oxford, where he accompanied Wellington for his installation as Chancellor, he himself received the honorary degree of D.C.L. In bowing his gown slipped off his shoulder, revealing his empty sleeve.' It acted like an Electric Shock,' his brother wrote proudly, 'and there was such a peal of applause as was hardly ever heard before.' [5]

His private life too was happy and successful. He was devoted to his wife and to his four young children.* He was not rich, but he had enough to spend between three and four thousand a year.[6] And he enjoyed spending it. He had a pleasant town house and many good friends in the country. He stayed often with his brother, now Duke of Beaufort, at Badminton, with the Duke of Richmond and Gordon at Goodwood, with the Wellingtons in the over-heated rooms at Stratfield Saye which were reserved for his use. He loved hunting and shooting and good food and the company of good-looking women and the pleasures of society. And like so many of the members of that society he cared little for the changing world outside it. Science and mechanics, which were beginning already to change the whole life of Europe, meant nothing to him. Nor did painting, nor music; nor did books. In fact in the great mass of his private correspondence only once does he mention having read one. It was *The Count of Monte Cristo*. 'So far as I have got in it,' he confessed, 'I find it is tiresome—very poisonous.' [7]

* These were Arthur William FitzRoy (born in 1816 and died of wounds received in the first Sikh War of 1845); Richard Henry FitzRoy (born in 1817 and later to become the 2nd Lord Raglan); Charlotte Elizabeth (born in 1815 at Brussels); and Katherine Anne Emily Cecilia (born in 1823). Both the girls died unmarried.

Even politics interested him only when they impinged upon the Army. In the six years that he sat as a High Tory Member for Truro he never spoke once in the House. But in private conversation he was eloquent in defence of the Army's rights and privileges and scathing in his condemnation of Joseph Hume and Cobden and Bright, the Benthamites and the Manchester School and all those who, as Florence Nightingale afterwards said, 'made a deity of cheapness' and who seemed to wish to cut down the Army both in size and influence. In public, remembering perhaps the Duke's advice not to bring up the question of the Army as some politician would be sure to ask for a reduction in its estimates, he rarely spoke of it. But he kept a careful eye on it from his office at the Horse Guards. He worked long hours there and knew the business of his profession as well as any man in it. He was unashamedly against any change; he had few original ideas of his own, but he protected the Army and guarded it as best he could. He knew, however, that no man in an England which was so confident of peace, so careful of public money, so jealous of the Army's privileges and power and so constitutionally nervous of its capacity for evil, could stem the growing desire to weaken it. Wellington had not been able to; and if Wellington could not, no one could.

Sir Francis Head called one day at the Horse Guards to show Lord FitzRoy a memorandum he had prepared on the fine training methods of the Prussian Army, and he asked why the British Army could not adopt a similar system. 'For some seconds,' Sir Francis remembered, 'Lord FitzRoy appeared unwilling or unable to answer my plain question; at last, calmly shrugging up his left shoulder and the stump of his right arm, he replied, "Joseph Hume".'[8]

Sometimes, as he later confessed to his elder daughter, he felt so irritated and dismayed by the economies which were being continually forced upon the Army that he contemplated handing in his resignation. But he knew that when it came to the point he could never do it. He could never leave the Army and he could never leave the Duke. In 1845 he was offered the Governor-Generalship of Canada. Wellington, of course, knew of the offer but refused to give him any advice as to whether or not he ought to accept it. Lord FitzRoy's sister-in-law, the Countess of Westmorland, went to see the Duke at Apsley House the day after the offer had been made. 'Well,' Wellington said as soon as she entered the room, 'he has declined.' His face was 'lit up with pleasure'. 'I was sure he would not leave you,' Lady Westmorland said. And the Duke replied that he did not know what he would have done if he had.

When Lady Westmorland told her brother-in-law what the Duke had said she saw 'tears start to his eyes'.[9]

For the Duke was growing old and weak and absent-minded, and Lord FitzRoy was obliged to do most of his work. He would fall asleep in the middle of a discussion, and men would have to tiptoe from the room and ask his Military Secretary what should be done. In 1852, sitting by a window in his room at Walmer Castle, the old man died in a high-backed chair. For more than forty years Lord FitzRoy had served him. For the rest of his life he remembered this with pride.

II

Lord FitzRoy had hoped to succeed the Duke as Commander-in-Chief, but the appointment was given to Lord Hardinge, and he himself was made Master-General of the Ordnance. It was a disappointment and something of a slight, for Lord Hardinge, although the older man, was a junior officer. 'The appointment of FitzRoy Somerset', Charles Greville thought, 'would have been more popular than that of Hardinge to the command of the Army, especially with the Army, but I have no doubt the Court insisted on having Hardinge, who is a great favourite there.'[10] As if to compensate him for his discontent, in October Lord FitzRoy was offered a peerage. He was not immediately sure that he would accept it. He did not know that he particularly wanted to be a peer, or that he could afford it. But the Queen was insistent. The Prince Consort wrote from Balmoral to the Prime Minister:

> It would be a great pity if Lord FitzRoy were to be obliged to decline the peerage on account of poverty; at the same time it may be difficult to relieve him from the payment of fees by a public grant. Under these circumstances, rather than leave Lord FitzRoy unrewarded, and a chance of him feeling mortified at a moment when his cheerful cooperation with Lord Hardinge is so important to the public service—the Queen would *herself* bear the cost of the fees.[11]

And so on 10 October 1852 Lord FitzRoy Somerset became the first Lord Raglan.

The fear that his mortification might make his dealings with Lord Hardinge strained was unjustified. He entered upon his new appointment, as he entered upon everything, with enthusiasm and industry. He 'liked the work so much', he later told his son, 'and got on so well with everybody there', that he could not have been happier at the Horse Guards.[12]

It was fortunate that he enjoyed the work, for there was much to do. Most nights he was obliged to take a mass of papers home with him.[13]

It is difficult now fully to understand exactly what his duties were. No less than seven more or less independent authorities shared in the organisation of the Army, and helped in reducing it, as Prince Albert aptly said, to a mere 'aggregate of battalions'. The complication, the muddle, the duplication, the mutual jealousies, the labyrinthine processes of supply and control, were astounding.

The Commander-in-Chief at the Horse Guards was a sort of Chief of the Imperial General Staff. But although he was in command of all troops in Britain, he did not command those overseas. His power was derived from the Crown and not from Parliament.

The Master-General of the Ordnance was in charge of equipment, fortifications and barracks. That much was certain. He exercised also an indeterminate power over the Royal Artillery and Royal Engineers, particularly in respect of pay and discipline.

A Board of General Officers took charge of clothing.

The Commissariat, which was a civilian authority and a department of the Treasury, took charge of supplies and supposedly of transport, but in fact it had little effective means of moving its supplies, Wellington's baggage-train established in the Peninsular War having long since been disbanded on the grounds of economy.

The Medical Department was largely independent of any of the other departments, except that of the Secretary-at-War which financed it and the Purveyors Department which, as a kind of subsidiary of the Commissariat, supplied it with some but not all of its requirements.

The Secretary-at-War, who looked after the pay and finance of the Army—except the Artillery and Engineers—and its arrangements with civilian contractors, was not responsible for the size and cost of the Army, which came within the province of the Secretary of State for the Colonies.

It was impossible even then for most people to comprehend this jungle.

Further entanglements arose through the tendency of many commanding officers to consider their regiments as their own personal property and to ignore or evade the instructions and rules which came from Whitehall. This attitude was, of course, entirely understandable. The Army List printed a scale of regulation 'Prices of Commissions', which showed, for instance, that a lieutenant-colonelcy in a regiment of the line was worth £4,500, in a cavalry regiment £6,175, in the Household Cavalry £7,250 and in the Foot Guards £9,000. Every officer knew, however, that Commissions were usually sold for prices considerably in excess of these; and there was talk of regiments changing hands for as much as £40,000 and even on one occasion £57,000.[14] Having paid so much to command a regiment, an officer did not feel inclined to stand too much interference in his running of it. He was, in any case, allowed by Queen's Regulations a remarkably free hand.

Many commanding officers, indeed, openly resented suggestions that their regiments should join in the large-scale manoeuvres which were held with disastrous infrequency. They knew how to move their regiments about in drill formation, how to set them up for a parade. And if they weren't quite sure, their adjutants were bound to know; and if it came to a war, well, their 'men had guts and they'd never lost one yet'.[15]

Soon after Lord Raglan took over at the Board of Ordnance, a training camp was established at Chobham for 8,000 men. The manoeuvres which took place on the Common were embarrassing to watch. The men were splendidly clothed, but they were led by officers who had no conception of military tactics. Units frequently got lost, were found by distracted staff officers advancing with smart determination and affected grimness on men of their own side, were taken off the field altogether by commanding officers who thought the 'whole damned thing' was 'a waste of time'. 'This Army,' remarked an officer in the Royal Artillery with angry exasperation, 'is a shambles'.[16]

A few months later, with hope and confidence and the cheers of an admiring people, it was sent to war.

2

THE FINEST ARMY

We were going out to defend a rotten cause
Sergeant Timothy Gowing, Royal Fusiliers

I

Few soldiers in the Army could say for sure what the war was about. There was some talk about the Holy Places and the defence of the Turks threatened by the Russians; but for soldiers, of course, reasons should not matter.

Remembering his march down to the dockyard at Portsmouth, cheered by an enormous and enthusiastic crowd, Timothy Gowing of the Royal Fusiliers gave expression to a general opinion. 'We were going out to defend a rotten cause,' he wrote, 'a race that almost every Christian despises. However, as soldiers we had nothing to do with politics.'[1]

But even the politicians were not aware of all the 'various and many coloured strands' which wove themselves into this vast tragedy.[2] They knew something of the independence, the influence and the anti-Russian feeling of the arrogant, temperamental, clever Ambassador to Turkey, Lord Stratford de Redcliffe; they knew something too of the Czar's propensity for conversational indiscretions, of his references to Turkey as the 'sick man' of Europe, whose immense and crumbling empire stretching from the Adriatic to the Persian Gulf, from the Black Sea through Syria and Palestine to the deserts of Arabia, was ready for conquest and division; they knew that neither Lord Aberdeen the Prime Minister, nor Lord Clarendon, his Foreign Secretary, had wanted war but that Palmerston, the Home Secretary, was a more powerful man than either of them and as strong a Russophobe as any of those Englishmen who three years before had cheered themselves hoarse for Kossuth, the Hungarian patriot and victim of Russian imperialism; and they knew that the upstart Napoleon III, as unpopular with many Englishmen as the Czar Nicholas I himself, wanted a military alliance with Britain, not least for its implication of respectability, and that Britain with her sea power threatened by Russia's

9

yearning for Constantinople, the gateway to the Mediterranean, could not refuse him. There was much else, of course, that they could not know. And it did not greatly matter.

For there were terrifying stories of the growing strength of the Black Sea Fleet and its mighty base at Sebastopol, only two hundred and fifty miles north of the Bosphorus. And some day soon the battle for the Bosphorus and the Sea of Marmara would have to be fought.

The first blows were struck with predictable fury in the Holy Land, where a festering quarrel between the monks of the Roman Catholic Church supported by France and the monks of the Orthodox Church supported by Russia had reached a new bitterness. For years the claims of one side to rights and privileges at the Holy Places, and particularly in the church of the Nativity and the church of the Holy Sepulchre, had been greeted by contradictions and cries for protection. In June 1853 a riot took place in Bethlehem, where the Roman Catholic monks who had been handed a front-door key to the church of the Nativity placed their own silver star over the Manger. The Orthodox monks tried to stop their rivals fixing it there and in the struggle some of them were killed. The Turkish police, the Czar protested, had connived at their murder. Within a matter of days a Russian army was marching towards the Danube on a crusade to protect the Holy Places from Islam.

They were marching for the Principalities of Moldavia and Wallachia, which now form part of Rumania and which were then under the joint protectorate of Turkey and Russia. War might still have been avoided. The Czar felt hopeful that Britain would not fight. Notes, memoranda, threats, despatches, flew from St. Petersburg to Paris, from Constantinople through Vienna to London, and crackled uncertainly over the electric telegraph. But as the weeks went by there became fewer and fewer men who doubted that war was coming.

By October Turkey was at war with Russia. England for the moment still remained neutral. And then on 30 November the Russian Black Sea Fleet under Admiral Nachimoff sailed out of Sebastopol, found a Turkish flotilla off the south shore of the Black Sea at Sinope and sunk its every ship. Nearly 4,000 Turkish sailors were lost, and many of them, so it was widely reported in the Press, were shot by Russian gunners as they floundered in the water.

British opinion was outraged by what was commonly referred to as a 'massacre'. And those voices previously crying caution and restraint were stilled by the shouts for the destruction of Sebastopol. No one listened any more to talk of Turkish atrocities. Aberdeen was forced to give way to the views of Palmerston. *The Times*, which had previously supported Aberdeen, now decided that war must come. And the Queen, who a few weeks before had doubted whether 'England ought to go to war for the defence of so called Turkish independence', now concluded that she was bound to do so.[3]

On 6 March Gladstone as Chancellor of the Exchequer raised the income tax from 7*d*. to 1*s*. 2*d*. in the pound. 'The expenses of War,' he reminded the House, 'are a moral check, which it has pleased the Almighty to impose upon the ambition and lust of conquest that are inherent in so many nations.'[4]

On 27 March 1854 England declared war on Russia. France had already done so the previous day.

And so the soldiers went marching down to Portsmouth with their bands playing, the shouts and cheers of the crowd in their ears and the memory of the Queen with the Prince and their children standing on the balcony at Buckingham Palace in the morning sunlight, appearing 'much affected', bowing and smiling 'most graciously', waving them good-bye.[5]

II

There seemed an enormous number of them as they marched through the streets and the dockyard gates, but it was, in fact, a small army of less than 30,000 men which was being sent to Turkey, a smaller army than the French. With large establishments in India, in Africa, in the Western Hemisphere, all over their vast Empire, it was always a problem for the officers at the Horse Guards to find enough men to form a powerful force in Europe, which was indeed something that for many years they had not been called upon to do. During the first year that Lord Raglan was Master-General of the Ordnance a Militia Bill had been passed providing for the embodiment of 80,000 men. These militiamen were to receive three weeks' training annually, but they were not available for overseas service unless they volunteered. And now that an expeditionary force was required for service in Europe, the Government were able to send no more than ten brigades of infantry, two brigades of cavalry and the complementary numbers of artillery and engineers. The brigades of infantry were each of three regiments, and two brigades formed a division.

To find sufficiently capable and adequately experienced officers to command these five infantry divisions presented an even greater problem than finding the regiments to form them. And, as it happened, only two of those officers chosen had experience of commanding in action, against trained troops, anything larger than a battalion; and only one of them was under sixty, and he had never been in action before.

He was the thirty-five-year-old Duke of Cambridge. A grandson of George III, a cousin of the Queen, a colonel of the Hanoverian Guards at nine and a major-general at twenty-six, his name was immediately suggested as commander of the 1st Division, comprising three battalions of Foot Guards and the Highland Brigade. He was a good-natured man, industrious, well-liked and affable. That he could lead men under fire was yet to be disproved.

Sir George de Lacy Evans, appointed to command the 2nd Division, was almost twice his age. He was the most experienced of the divisional commanders and, in the later opinion of the French Commander-in-Chief, the best.[6] He had been born in Ireland in 1787 and had joined the Army as a volunteer in 1806. As a young man he had fought in the Peninsula, in India and in America, and had commanded with some success the British Legion in Spain during the fight against the Carlists. Knighted for his services in Spain in 1837, he had since then been interested more in politics than in the Army. First as Member for Rye and then for Westminster, he expressed views unusually radical for a soldier. But then he was an unusual man. Moody, intelligent, rather remote and extremely brusque, his thin head with its long, curling hair and black eyes peers out of his photographs with an air at once theatrical and accusatory.

Sir Richard England, commanding the 3rd Division, was another Irishman. His father, a general, had been one of the first English-speaking Canadian colonists, and Sir Richard had been born in Canada in 1793. He had been at Walcheren, seen service in the Kaffir War and in India. Knighted in 1843 and promoted major-general eight years later, he was a man of meagre talent and reputation.

In command of the 4th Division was a better-known figure. The

Hon. Sir George Cathcart was at sixty the youngest of them all, apart from the Duke of Cambridge. He had been bought a cornetcy in the Life Guards when he was fifteen by his father, General Earl Cathcart, at that time Ambassador at St. Petersburg; and by a succession of purchases and exchanges found himself a lieutenant-colonel in the 7th Hussars in 1826. He had not distinguished himself since; but he was granted a 'dormant commission' by the Government, which provided for his succession to the command of the army in the event of the death of the Commander-in-Chief in the Field. Touchy, inexperienced, stubborn and tactless, he was an unfortunate choice. But the idea that the senior of the divisional generals, Sir George Brown, should succeed to the command was unthinkable.

Sir George Brown was, perhaps, the most unpopular infantry officer in the Army. The 'old wretch is more hated than any man ever was', one of his young officers thought. 'He blusters and bullies everybody he dares and damns and swears at everything an inch high'. 'An old imbecile bully' another of his subalterns called him, expressing a widely held judgment.[7] He was a fierce martinet who had fought under Moore at Corunna as an ensign in the 43rd Foot, and his men were not allowed to forget it. He was a firm believer in the leather stock that soldiers still wore, constricting their throats like a garrotter, in the salutary effects of pipe-clay and flogging, in the necessity for the rejection of all suggestions about Army reform. Lord Panmure said that 'he never knew a man who so cordially hated all change'. It was, in fact, in protest against some minor reforms introduced into the administration of the Army the year before that led him to retire. He thought also that the Prince Consort, a young civilian, meddled a great deal too much in military affairs. Although almost as cordially disliked by his superiors as by his men, he was known to be a brave and resolute soldier, and as this was something which in so many other cases had to be taken on trust, he was given command of the Light Division.

The Cavalry Division was given to the fifty-four-year-old Earl of Lucan. He was a military maniac. Like Sir George Cathcart, by numerous exchanges and purchases he got himself the command of a regiment without ever having done much to prove himself worthy of it. In the same year that Cathcart bought the command of the 7th Hussars the Earl of Lucan bought that of the 17th Lancers for £25,000. He

turned it into 'Bingham's Dandies'. But it was more than a toy; it was
an obsession. He rose before dawn, worked unceasingly. He was conscientious, prejudiced, vindictive, brave, narrow-minded and violently
unpopular.

His brother-in-law, the Earl of Cardigan, commander of the Light
Brigade in his division, possessed most of his faults and few of his
virtues. He was as heartily disliked as Lucan and even more arrogant.
They hated each other.

The Hon. James Scarlett, who was given command of the Heavy
Brigade, was, however, quite unlike either of them. Sensible, pleasant, easy-going, his was a character everyone liked and admired. Men
hoped that his sound common sense would do something to help hold
the cavalry division together.

Finding officers for the staff was as great a problem as finding competent generals. Lord de Ros, who was appointed Quartermaster-
General of the army and thus made responsible for a variety of duties
far more extensive than the name of the appointment would seem to
imply, was 'an extremely curious fellow'. He was 'very eccentric,
both in his habits and dress; very amusing, too'.[8] But a more unsuit-
able officer for a position which combined the present-day duties of
Chief of Staff with those of Quartermaster-General it would have been
difficult to find. He not only lacked experience but did not seem in the
least anxious to acquire it. He was very fond of sunbathing.

Brigadier-General James Bucknall Estcourt, appointed to be
Adjutant-General, was more industrious. But he also had little experience. He had never been to war and was, in fact, more interested in
exploration than in the Army. While sitting as M.P. for Devizes he
had gone on the Euphrates Valley Expedition to find a route to India
from the Persian Gulf. He was a man, one of his officers thought, 'of
remarkably kind and courteous disposition'. But these are not qualities much required of an adjutant-general, responsible for the discipline of an army. General Estcourt was 'too kind and too forgiving'.[9]
He was, however, a great deal more efficient than most officers who
were given appointments on the staffs of the various divisional headquarters.

The real trouble was, of course, as the Secretary-for-War was later
to observe, there was 'no means of making General Officers or of
forming an efficient staff'. The Senior Department of the Royal

Military College had been in existence for many years, but few officers thought it worth while to attend it. That sort of thing was all very well for Frenchmen and Germans and even for those officers who were unfortunately obliged to think of the Army as a career and to serve in India, but it did not do for gentlemen.

Indeed, the less exciting departments of the Army were handed over altogether to civilians. And no one had yet had cause to doubt the wisdom or convenience of leaving the humdrum matters of supply and transport almost entirely in the hands of a department of the Treasury. Administered by bureaucrats, many of them grotesque in their pedantry and ineptitude, the Commissariat Department was hopelessly ill-equipped to move and supply an army of 30,000 men, and Lord Raglan at the Ordnance Office had frequently complained of its insufficiency and its lack of any reserve of trained officials. Appointed to run it was Mr. James Filder, a man of sixty-six called from an already lengthy retirement.

To hold this muddled assembly together and, what was perhaps of more importance, to hold the allies together, there were fortunately a few men who appeared at first sight to have some qualifications. Lord Hardinge, Lord Gough, Lord Combermere and Lord Raglan were all distinguished officers, and the names of all of them were mentioned as suitable commanders. But when their records were examined it was found that Lord Raglan was the only one under seventy. On reflection it seemed that there could only be one choice.

Lord Raglan had been taught the business of war by the Duke—and this in itself was considered by a trusting country as almost a guarantee of success—he had been in the Army for nearly half a century, he had earned great respect and great affection, he was strong and healthy, he was a trained diplomat and spoke excellent French. There were, of course, those who wondered whether a man who had spent the last forty years behind a desk and who had never commanded so much as a battalion in the field was an ideal man to command an army, but when asked to point out another officer more suitable they could not. And so, less than three weeks after war was declared, General Lord Raglan, P.C., G.C.B., found himself sailing for a conference in Paris and then on to Turkey in command of what was proudly called in *The Times* 'the finest army that has ever left these shores'.

3

SCUTARI

The Russians have made regular fools of us, brought us out here and
then cut away. Too bad!
Captain Nigel Kingscote, Scots Fusilier Guards

I

The troops disembarked on the shores of the Dardanelles and entered
a new and strangely bewildering world. Gallipoli was 'filthy in the
extreme'; a higgledy-piggledy, 'ugly, Irish-looking town' where the
houses were mere clay-walled sheds; where savage, hairy dogs and
screaming children rushed in hundreds up and down the narrow,
stinking streets; where Armenians and Jews, and Greeks in fezes and
baggy blue trousers, and Turks with pistols and knives stuck in their
sashes, pushed past each other on their interminable errands. And
sometimes 'a bundle of clothes in yellow leather boots' might be seen
moving about 'which you would do well to believe', as the correspondent of *The Times* put it, contained 'a woman neither young nor
pretty'. At the side of the streets, on wooden stages raised two feet
from the ground, elderly Turks in shawls and flowing coats, and
descendants of the Prophet in their green turbans, sat smoking silently,
puffing great clouds of smoke through their dirty-looking beards as
they stared with a kind of impassive suspicion at the red-coated English
soldiers, the menacing French Spahis and the chattering Zouaves. Only
occasionally, when an English lady passed delicately by, or the tough-
looking wife of a soldier or a pretty *vivandière* moved across their static
line of vision, did the Turks seem to evince a momentary interest.[1]
    The French and English, allies after years of enmity, liked each other
much better than anyone had dared to hope. 'The French and ourselves got on capitally,' a corporal in the 7th wrote, 'particularly the
Zouaves whom we found a very jolly set.'[2] The difficulties of conversation seemed no barrier to friendship. Groups of French troops
talking as fast as possible could be seen chatting excitedly to British
soldiers, who answered them with cheerful animation, neither understanding a word that the others said.[3]

17

There were, of course, jealousies and difficulties. The British advance parties were annoyed with the French for having got to Gallipoli first and for having made the best part of the town a French quarter with offices, shops, stores and an officers' restaurant already comfortably established. So much, indeed, were the British quartermasters' preconceptions upset by their allies' unconcerned selfishness that by the time the rest of the troops arrived very little had been prepared for their reception.

The French, on the other hand, were annoyed with the British for treating the inhabitants with such *naïveté*. Everyone agreed that the Turks were 'a lazy, dirty, ungrateful lot' and that the Greeks were 'much worse' and 'the greatest cheats going'.[4] And yet the British insisted on spoiling the market by paying much too much, and sometimes even what was asked, for food and drink and horses. Wine which could be bought during the first few days for 4*d*. or 5*d*. a bottle went up to 2*s*.; Dutch cheeses were sold for 8*s*. each; hard old hams cost £1; and bad foreign beer was sold as English ale for 1*s*. 6*d*. a bottle. The French soon lost their patience and, with less concern for the susceptibilities of their unwilling hosts, issued a fixed tariff and so arranged a system of compensation rather than of purchase. An English officer haggling with a Greek over the price of a horse would fail to come to terms, and later the Greek would find himself being forced to part with the horse to a Frenchman for a good deal less than the Englishman had offered.[5]

The impressively superior equipment of the French army was another source of friction. French wagons, ambulances, crates of medical supplies and comforts, heaps of tents and planks for hutting were seen in neat rows along the harbour walls, making an English officer demand in envious exasperation if the French had come to colonise the country.[6] For the British army was supplied with few, if any, of these things and was happily unaware of their necessity. The only modern and completely effective equipment that it shared with the French were the Minié rifles which were soon to be supplied to almost the whole army with the exception of some regiments of the 4th Division.[*]

[*] Captain Minié of the Chasseurs d'Orléans had invented his blunt lead bullet in 1847 and his rifle two years later. Prompted by Lord Raglan, the British Government extended a factory at Enfield where rifles incorporating the best features of the Minié were made, but there were other factories making modified types all over Europe, and by one of these the

The whole attitude of the English to war seemed indeed to the general commanding the French 1st Division that of enthusiastic but inexperienced amateurs. It was as if they were sportsmen who had come to the East to enjoy some new form of blood sport. He felt as he looked at their army that he had been taken back a hundred years.[7] The English officers, he noticed, came out loaded with luggage.* They brought with them their country suits, their Kaffir servants, most of them brought their favourite horses, some of them brought their wives. The soldiers too brought women—an average official allowance was six wives for every hundred men—but although they were supposed to do duty as washerwomen and nurses they were never as amenable to discipline as the strictly controlled *vivandières* and *cantinières* of the French army.

The fundamental difference between the French and English approaches to the military life was epitomised at the beginning of May when the commander of France's 3rd Division arrived at Gallipoli. He was Prince Napoleon, the Emperor's cousin. Tall, stout, and fussy, nicknamed 'Plon-Plon', but with an unmistakable Buonaparte face and a lock of hair carefully trained in the Buonaparte manner, his sabre clattering grandly, giving 'you the idea of an actor', he came proudly on to the jetty, in his gold lace and plumes. He was greeted by a guard of honour and the Imperial salute from the guns of the five French battleships in the harbour.[8]

A few days earlier Lord Raglan had stepped ashore. He was, as usual, wearing a plain blue frock coat and there was no one to meet him. He walked up to the town with Mrs. Estcourt, the Adjutant-General's wife, and his four A.D.C.s, all of whom were also his nephews, like a tourist on an Oriental cruise with a few young friends.

A week later the Duke of Cambridge arrived, 'a quiet looking gentleman in a tweed jacket'.[9]

II

On the evening of the day that Lord Raglan arrived in Gallipoli he sailed up the Bosphorus for Constantinople.

Russian army was also supplied with rifles. The Russians, however, had not ordered them in large quantities and most of their regiments still used smooth-bore muskets.

* According to Hugh Annesley of the Scots Guards the Duke of Cambridge's luggage filled seventeen carts.

Seen from the sea it was, one of his officers thought, a place 'of exquisite beauty'. Against their background of cypress-covered slopes, minarets and the domed roofs of mosques glittered in the sunlight; the garden of the Sultan's palace fell in a cascade of flowers and exotic creeper to the water's edge, and across the blue sky, above the masts of the ships, storks flew with silent grace and plovers swept in droves, like the souls of the damned that the living called them. Around the ships, dolphins splashed in and out of the waves and frail caïques, intricately carved, floated with graceful aimlessness. Looking down into the caïques, officers saw with pleasure that the women lying on cushions spread all over the floor were not so carefully concealed by their yashmaks as they had been in the streets of Gallipoli. The old women smoked; the young ones ate sweets, sipped lemonade and looked back, smiling and fluttering their henna-tinged eyelids, glancing into hand mirrors and smoothing their robes over their large and sumptuous breasts, their dyed nails red against the white silk.[10]

But once in town, Hugh Annesley, of the Scots Guards, regretfully wrote, 'we were certainly disillusioned. The streets are filthy beyond description, and very difficult to walk over, as the stones are all nohow, so that you can hardly look up off the ground without danger of falling.'

Porters rushed headlong through the narrow alleys with enormous bundles on their heads, sending the sharp stones flying, giving an occasional shout but never stopping, knocking people against the walls with wonderful unconcern. If you stepped aside to avoid a dead dog, you were likely to step on a dead rat. 'The Stench' beat anything Captain Clifford had 'ever smelt'. You rarely saw a pretty 'she-Turk', another officer complained. All you could see of most of them was their ankles, which were 'for the most part decidedly bad, thick and clumsy; feet ditto'. In the back streets soldiers soon discovered dark cafés and darker brothels where the wine and the women were cheap; where Armenian girls performed 'feats of astonishing agility'; where you could get drunk for sixpence, and syphilis for a shilling. In the 55th Regiment its surgeon reported venereal disease as his major problem, and the 55th was one of the army's most disciplined regiments.[11]

The amount of drunkenness, one of Lord Raglan's four A.D.C.s thought, was 'frightful. The other night 2,400 men were reported drunk.' 'The army gets drunk,' Colonel Sterling was 'sorry to say.

We have nothing to complain of in the conduct of the men when they are sober; when drunk they knock the Turks about, so we flogged a man the other day to make an example.'

Lord Raglan decided that the sooner he could get the army moved farther north the better. His own headquarters were in a stuffy, low, red-painted, wooden building on the beach at Scutari. The small courtyard in front was crowded with the horses of A.D.C.s and visitors and surrounded by little stone boxes for sparrows and swallows to build in. Through the eleven windows of his room, where he was 'always at work morning, noon and night', he could see the sea and the stagnant sludge at the water's edge where dogs prowled amidst the sticks and the motionless birds and the rotting flotsam. At the side of the house was a wooded knoll, topped by gravestones, white above the long green grass; and here, by a fountain, water-carriers and groups of Turks and Armenians and Greeks peered down into the courtyard speaking monosyllabically as they leaned against the sad cypresses and puffed at their pipes.[12]

Behind the house was the camp of the Guards and beyond that the Turkish barracks, soon to become the most notorious military hospital in the world, and beyond the barracks the camps of the Light Division. And all around the camps the Jewish money-changers with their jingling leather purses and their cries of 'Change de monnish, John. I say, Johnny, change de monnish'; and the Greek sutlers in their squalid huts of plank and canvas; and the horse-copers leading bony animals blown up with fresh grass; and the boys selling sweets, lemonade, sherbet and cigars, and the other boys trying to sell their sisters, roamed and shouted and pleaded and got kicked and made money.

All May was spent here and the weather got hotter, and Lord Raglan, in the words of one of his A.D.C.s, the cheerfully irreverent Captain Nigel Kingscote, became 'a little seedy'. He was doing 'enough work for a dozen men' and the climate was wearing him down. 'The fact is ,' Lord Raglan told his elder daughter Charlotte, his beloved 'Puggums', 'my house is furiously hot. It is built of wood and has windows in every room in unusual numbers. The situation is low and on the beach where all the filth of Constantinople is driven either by the wind or the current and so great is the abominable smell thereof that for the last ten days I have been driven from the room I used to sit in and have been forced to receive and transact business in my bedroom.'

His unaccustomed depression was brought about not so much by the heat and the diarrhoea which he, like almost everyone else in the army, was suffering from, but by his concern for the army's welfare and his disagreements with the French command.[13]

III

The first difference of opinion with the French had arisen over the way in which the Turkish army should be employed.

Marshal St. Arnaud, the French Commander-in-Chief, decided that being the senior officer in the allied armies he should command the Turks.[14] He was both ambitious and determined. 'A strange, flighty fellow,' Sir George Brown thought him, 'and one it will not do to take at his word.'[15] When as a young man he had joined the Foreign Legion in Algeria, he had announced 'I will be remarkable or die' and he had spent the rest of his life in pursuit of this passion for fame. Brave, gay, unscrupulous and resourceful, he had helped the Emperor to seize power in his savage coup in 1851 and had been rewarded by the baton of a Marshal of France and now by the command of the French expeditionary army. But the Emperor was not a man to leave the commander of his army a free and unwatched hand. St. Arnaud's constant adviser and usual companion was a Colonel Trochu, the Emperor's confidant and the Marshal's senior A.D.C. It was widely believed by the British staff that he and not St. Arnaud was the real commander of the French Army.[16]

With Lord Stratford's help, however, Lord Raglan was able to persuade St. Arnaud to abide by the tripartite agreement, which provided that each army should be separately commanded.[17] Changing tack, St. Arnaud then suggested that when French and British troops were acting together the ultimate authority ought to lie with the French. Lord Raglan politely answered that he could take no orders other than those from his own Government.[18]

At eleven o'clock one night during the following week, Colonel Trochu came to Lord Raglan's house and demanded an immediate interview. A few days before, St. Arnaud, Raglan and Omar Pasha, the Turkish commander, had agreed that the allies should cross the

Black Sea to Varna, a small port in the Bulgarian provinces of the Turkish Empire near which the Russians were laying siege to the fortified town of Silistria. Colonel Trochu now announced that the French army was not ready to move and that the English should immediately stop any further embarkations for Varna, for which the Light Division had already sailed.

Lord Raglan, patient, courteous, but firm, said that he could not agree. An undertaking had been given to the Sultan and he could not see his way to breaking it. After two hours of fruitless persuasion Colonel Trochu left.

The following day Marshal St. Arnaud himself arrived. He had, he said, devised an entirely new plan for the French army. He was going to send only one division to Varna. The rest of the army was to move to a defensive position south of Bourgas with the whole of the north-eastern range of the Balkans between it and the scene of the fighting. He invited Lord Raglan to conform to this movement. In any case the French would carry it out. The troops in fact were already on the move. Once again Lord Raglan listened politely, and once again courteously but firmly regretted that he could not agree to the French suggestions and gave his reasons for refusing to do so. St. Arnaud then behaved in a curious way. He asked for a piece of paper and wrote down his grounds for altering the plan which a few days before had had his approval.[19]

Lord Raglan, as St. Arnaud was discovering, was an extremely difficult man to argue with. He imposed, as his Quartermaster-General put it, a powerful ascendancy over all who came into contact with him. He did this not by a forceful manner of disputation, nor by evasion, nor even by any particular skill as an advocate; but partly by a calm and persuasive confidence in the merits of his case, and mainly by his extraordinary ability to arouse in those who disagreed with him an urgent wish not to displease or upset him. 'I believe,' Lieutenant Somerset Calthorpe, his youngest A.D.C., wrote in his diary, 'his influence is great with both Marshal St. Arnaud and Omar Pasha.'

And so, without attempting to explain it, the Marshal handed the paper to Lord Raglan and then immediately left the house.

'It is important,' the brief document insisted, 'not to give battle to the Russians, except with all possible chances of success, and the certainty of obtaining great results.' If the allies only had one division each at Varna, no one could blame them for not marching to the relief of Silistria. But if they had more, they might be forced into a battle with the Russians which they were not yet sufficiently well organised to win.[20]

It was true, of course, that so far the allies had no firm and fully equipped base of operations. But it is known now, and it was apparent to Lord Raglan then, that Russia was unprepared for war in Bulgaria; that threatened by an ungrateful Austria, already thrown out of the Black Sea by the allies' fleets, and checked by a strong Turkish army, her unsupported divisions at Silistria were in no position to resist a determined attack. Besides, the move had a political importance and a psychological advantage, which could not possibly be said of the suggested cautious approach towards the southern slopes of the Balkans. Finally, and for Lord Raglan it was the reason which should outweigh all others, the Sultan had been given the allies' word.[21]

The morning after St. Arnaud's visit Colonel Trochu came to the British headquarters. Unmoved by further pleas, Lord Raglan declined to place any part of his army in the position proposed. Three days later General Rose, chief British liaison officer at French headquarters, called to say that the French had given way. They would go to Varna.[22]

The decision was taken on 9 June. A fortnight later, at dawn on the 23rd, the British troops in camp near Varna heard the distant roar of the Russian siege guns suddenly stop. They all thought that Silistria had fallen.

Nigel Kingscote had had a feeling for some days that 'something was up'.

On 24 June he was enjoying a 'capital dinner' in the Duke of Cambridge's tent. The Duke's French cook was 'positively *cordon bleu*. The entrées were just as good as if they had been prepared in St. James's Palace.' There was no news from the Turkish army to interfere with the quiet enjoyment of the guests. But the following night when the invitation was returned and the Duke was not faring quite so well at Lord Raglan's, where the German cook was less impressive, an officer came in with urgent news from Silistria. The guests looked at him nervously. The news, however, was good.[23]

The siege had been raised. The Russians were retiring across the Danube.

SCUTARI

A few days later at Giurgevo the Turks crossed the Danube after
them. The Russians attacked their pursuers but were defeated. By 11
July Prince Gortschakoff was in full retreat towards Bucharest. The
Principalities of Moldavia and Wallachia were abandoned. The
Turkish Empire, for the moment, was saved and the declared object
of the war was achieved. 'The Russians have made regular fools of
us,' Nigel Kingscote said, 'brought us out here and then cut away.
Too bad!'

But he need not have worried, for the war went on. Everyone realised now that Britain and France were fighting against Russia, and not
for Turkish independence. In London, and to a lesser extent in Paris,
the enthusiasm for the war was becoming almost feverish. No one
could stem it. Those who spoke against its further prosecution on the
reasonable grounds that it was no longer necessary were shouted
down. The cautious, peaceful Lord Aberdeen was shown in *Punch*
blacking the Czar's boots. 'The grand and political objects of the war
could not be obtained,' *The Times* declared, 'so long as Sebastopol and
the Russian fleet' were in existence. A successful expedition against the
place was the 'essential condition of permanent peace'. In the House
of Lords when Lord Lyndhurst 'unhesitatingly' declared that 'in no
event, except that of extreme necessity ought we to make peace', he
was loudly cheered. 'I believe', he added to even louder cheers, 'that
if this barbarous nation, the enemy of all progress . . . should once
succeed in establishing itself in the heart of Europe, it would be the
greatest calamity which could befall the human race.' Crowds in full
agreement with these sentiments marched through the streets with
banners, shouting patriotic slogans, singing jingoistic songs. Anyone
who wasn't for war was no patriot. War would 'sweep away at once',
the Rev. Charles Kingsley said, 'the dyspeptic unbelief, the insincere
bigotry, the effeminate frivolity which paralyses our poetry as much
as it does our action'. The war, the Queen told the King of the Belgians, 'was popular beyond belief'. Gladstone was concerned by the
inexorable drift of emotion. He had made it clear that he could only
support the war so long as the public law of Europe remained in danger. But he stayed in office as Chancellor of the Exchequer. Disraeli
said he supposed we were going to fight the Czar to stop him protecting the Sultan's Christian subjects. But then wasn't that just the
sort of thing that damned fellow would say?

At Pembroke Lodge, Richmond, on the hot summer's evening of 28 June, the Duke of Newcastle, formerly Secretary of State for the Colonies and now provided with a new department as Secretary-for-War, read out a despatch he had written to Lord Raglan authorising the invasion of the Crimea. Other long and boring papers had been read out beforehand and all the members of the Cabinet thought they could take the despatch for granted. The draft of a private letter which was to accompany it they had in any case already seen. The room was stuffy, the Duke's voice went droning on. Before he had finished reading most of his listeners had, to his understandable irritation, fallen asleep. The sudden rattle of a chair woke them up. But only momentarily. Soon the irresistible urge to doze overcame them again, and once more their eyelids closed. Later on, in another room, they confessed themselves wholly satisfied with a document with which most of them were only superficially familiar.[24]

4

VARNA

*No one seems to care whether we go to Sebastopol or South America,
or stay as we are or do nothing*
Major Clement Walker-Heneage, 8th Hussars

I

The armies had gone to Varna assured by Omar Pasha of the 'salu-
brity' of that part of the Bulgarian coast. It was, they were told, 'a very
healthy spot'.[1]

It was certainly beautiful. The little town itself, an irregular clump
of houses, minarets and dusty squares, was enclosed by a white wall
flanked by forts at the side of a sandy bay. The camps were placed on
higher ground outside the town in a rolling, mainly uncultivated
country where flowers and fruit grew in wonderful profusion in the
meadows and on the wooded slopes of the hills. It reminded a lieutenant in the Artillery of his native Glamorgan. 'It produces corn, grapes,
melons, cucumbers (which the people eat raw by a dozen a day without injury), Indian corn, barley, oats, in fact with proper cultivation
you may grow anything.' Strawberries and cherries, even potatoes,
grew wild for the taking. And everywhere there were birds—night-
ingales and eagles, blackbirds and jays, doves and storks and herons
flying across the unclouded sky.

The Bulgarians seemed a friendly and likeable people. Occasionally
one of them—or perhaps a Greek—disliking any ally of their hated
Turkish masters would take a shot at an officer bathing in the sea or
riding alone through the long grass and thistles. He would be handed
over to the Pasha, who would trim his ears and nose and give him
'200 blows on the feet'.[2]

But for the most part the inhabitants gave no trouble. Offered the
generous sum of 3s. 8d. a day by an army disastrously short of transport, they were pleased to bring their carts and oxen and buffaloes
and work for the Johnnies. Eating their coarse brown bread covered
with grease and rice and garlic, they sat in their conical sheepskin
caps, waiting patiently for orders, staring at the women of the army

washing their husband's clothes as if watching witches. There were not so many women with the army as there might have been, for Lord Raglan had made it clear that he did not care for their presence on active service and had advised officers to discourage their men from bringing their wives or supposed wives with them. And a shipload of ninety-seven wives sent to Gallipoli from Malta were immediately sent back again by Sir George Brown. There were, nevertheless, far more women with the army than Lord Raglan would have liked. Men had insisted on their right to bring them, and officers had looked the other way when wives in excess of the permitted numbers were smuggled aboard the transports. Their numbers led the Turkish soldiers politely to enquire if each general had his own harem. '*Mashallah!*' they exclaimed as they sat for hours staring at them and at the Highlanders, who wore skirts too. '*Mashallah!* By God's permission!' The French *vivandières* were not so great a curiosity, as there were fewer of them, and many of them were so tough that they could easily be mistaken for men. They wore the facings of their respective regiments on their jackets, and spurs on their well-polished boots. 'They are very ugly,' Captain Henry Neville of the Grenadiers thought, 'but pronounced by our men to be stunning.'[3]

The friendliest relations existed between French and British troops and between the three allied commanders. Marshal St. Arnaud loved riding through the English camps, where he was received with 'thunders of cheering in the British style' and replied with happy contentment, 'England for ever!' Omar Pasha, a clever, pale, worried-looking man who spoke a mixture of French, German and Italian with an extraordinary accent was quite as popular.* 'It is well known,' he told Lord Raglan once during a review of British troops at Varna, 'that the Emperor of Russia is mad, but surely he cannot be mad enough to fight against troops like these.' He liked the look of them so much, he told Somerset Calthorpe, that after the war was over he would visit England and marry 'une Miss Anglaise'. Calthorpe wondered what would become 'of the present Mrs. O.P.'†

---

* 'He is a capital fellow,' Nigel Kingscote told Lord Raglan's son Richard. 'Quite different to the Turks in general, hates all display and the energy he must have is wonderful. . . . He is a sporting looking fellow and sits well on his horse in a plain grey frock coat and long jack boots, he is very fond of horses.'

† At a previous review of British troops the atmosphere was more strained. The Duke of Cambridge had asked General Canrobert to review the Guards Brigade on 18 June. Neither

But much as Omar Pasha confessed he liked the look of the British troops, Lord Raglan felt unable to return the compliment. As for the Bashi-Bazouks, the ferocious 'cut-throat looking crew' of Turkish irregulars, he would have nothing to do with them, despite the Duke of Newcastle's frequent suggestions that Colonel Beatson, an officer experienced in the training of Indian cavalry, should organise some squadrons for service with the British army. They behaved towards the Bulgarians with apparently unchecked cruelty and they reminded him of the Spanish guerillas whose treatment of French prisoners had so horrified him as a young man. He never even considered the possibility of employing them. It was, perhaps, a pardonable prejudice. And Omar Pasha, grateful for Lord Raglan's easy friendship, never pressed him to accept their services.[4]

Nothing, indeed, during these few weeks of early summer overshadowed the allies' mutual understanding and respect. For the British army certainly, it was a happy, friendly time. Rations of salt meat and biscuits were good. Some officers complained of black and acid bread, swarming with ants. Others, more fastidiously, wrote of the privations of having to use pewter plates, 'to drink out of a single mug and to sit on pack saddles to eat—onions!' But most of them, and all of their men, considered themselves well fed. Beer, sugar, tea, rice and preserved potatoes could all be bought from the Commissariat at wholesale prices. The Bulgarians offered fowls for 1s. 2d., turkeys for 2s. 6d., milk for a penny a quart, eggs for twopence a dozen. And the country wine, a Guards officer thought, was 'really not bad when mixed with sugar and a little of the Burrage' that grew all around the camp.[5]

Sport was good too. Men swam in the sea; fished in the lakes for huge carp, bream and pike; hunted in the woods for buffalo and wild boar.

But there were other animals too in the weeds and the long, lush grass—snakes and thousands of frogs, insects two inches long, slugs and immense leeches. And these were more characteristic of a

of them had remembered that the date chosen was the anniversary of the Battle of Waterloo, and General Canrobert found himself saluting flags which bore the names of great English victories, 'the most disastrous days in the history of France'. Although nothing was said, General Canrobert felt that the Duke realised the mistake he had made. In future when French Generals reviewed British regiments, their colours remained in their cases (Bapst, *Maréchal Canrobert*, II, 131).

country which as the hot, stifling summer wore on, the British army learned to hate and to fear.

The valley round the lake at Alladyn, eight miles inland from Varna, where the 1st Division was camped, looked lovely and healthy by day, but at night you could 'see the damp and miasma rising from the place like a white cloud'.[6] Men began to suffer from diarrhoea and a feeling of constant lassitude and nausea, and there were occasional cases of cholera. The camp, like that of other divisions, was moved, but the sickness increased. A hot wind blew almost daily from the west, covering the grass and the tents and the food with a white limestone powder and a clutter of dead flies. And then on 19 July it was known that a serious epidemic of cholera, prevalent all over the south of Europe that summer, had broken out in the French camp. Three days later the British camps were infected. Once more the tents were moved, but the sickness followed them.[7]

A ghastly lethargy settled down upon the army. Men walked about, languid, gloomy and pale, like ghosts. Lord Raglan himself, although it was still 'wonderful how hard he worked', looked 'pale and worn'. Lord de Ros, the Quartermaster-General, was a 'complete wreck'.[8] 'All seem,' a surgeon in the Guards Brigade noted in his diary, 'as if a dozen years of hard suffering had been added to their lives.' Seeing a group of officers in his own regiment on 31 July, he scarcely recognised their sunken faces.[9] Flies and gnats and brown beetles swarmed in the camps and settled in millions on bits of meat which the men, too exhausted to eat, threw away into the dust. The elementary rules of sanitation were disregarded. Latrines were filled, but the men had no energy to dig more; carcasses lay about putrefying in the sun. In the large barracks used as a general hospital in Varna, exhausted orderlies watched the writhing, sweating bodies of the sick with a kind of dazed indifference, while the lice and fleas and rats, 'great big grey fellows' that made you shudder, crawled over the mouldering floors.[10] Along the two white walls of that part of the building used by the French, Mr. Russell, the principal correspondent for *The Times*, saw on a moonlit night in early August a long train of carts full of sick French troops sent in from the camps. A number of soldiers were sitting silently down by the roadside, 'and here and there the moonbeams flashed brightly off their piled arms. . . . The quiet that prevailed was only broken now and then by the groans and cries of pain of the poor sufferers in the carts.' Russell saw that about fifty carts were empty and he asked a *sous-officier* 'for what purpose they were required. His answer, sullen and short, was *"pour les morts"*.'[11]

It was generally believed that no one came out of this packed hospital alive, and men did what they could to conceal their sickness for fear of being sent there. 'Cholera increasing,' the commanding officer of the 1st Regiment noted with his usual graphic brevity, 'and men dying fast. Every case taken in at the General Hospital in Varna has gone to the grave. 15 dead last two nights. The old pensioners sent out with the ambulance wagons are dropping off fast. I expect they will all be buried at Varna. Worn out before coming here, they get drunk when they can, and die like dogs.'[12]

The old ambulance-drivers were not the only men to get drunk. A belief had grown up that the French had first succumbed to cholera because they drank so much bad red wine, and that a good preventive was the coarse strong brandy which could be bought from the sutlers' shops for 3s. 6d. a large bottle. By the middle of August French and English soldiers lying dead drunk and covered with flies under the blazing sun were a common sight.[13]

Despite the increasing number of restrictions and the flow of new orders both as to behaviour and to dress, discipline was loosening fast. After a man of the 88th had broken into a house and smashed its contents, looting in his division was made a capital offence. Straying a mile from the camp was to be punished by flogging. Officers were forbidden to wear civilian clothes, but many of them still slouched about with their buttons undone, turbans round their forage caps, and nothing round their open necks; 'a great many having nothing perceptible but their noses which appear from a dense forest of beard and whiskers'.* They were all 'bored to death, longing to go anywhere'.[14]

On 7 August, the hot weather broke and it became cold and windy; but there was no change in the health of the troops. Three days later on a cool, fine day when a furious fire at Varna destroyed thousands of pounds' worth of stores, including 16,000 pairs of boots and over

---

* Lord Raglan had given in to the Duke of Newcastle, who, prompted by *The Times*, had suggested that the men might be allowed to wear beards. He had resisted the suggestion at first on the grounds of cleanliness, but now the sun had 'made inroads on the faces of the men', and, to Sir George Brown's horror, he had allowed them to imitate 'the hairy men amongst our allies' (Raglan Crimean Papers).

150 tons of biscuit, eighty men of the Coldstream Guards died from cholera.*[15] 'It is time we were going from this,' Colonel Bell protested, 'burying the dead is our chief employ.' 'No doubt we shall go soon,' a major in the 8th Hussars wrote home without interest. 'But such is the state of apathy that we are reduced to, that no one seems to care whether we go to Sebastopol or South America or stay as we are or do nothing.'[16]

II

Lord Raglan's instructions to take the army to Sebastopol had already arrived. They placed him in a difficult position. There could be no doubt, he decided when he had read them, how determined the Government were that he should invade the Crimea.

I have on the part of Her Majesty's Government [the Duke of Newcastle had written] to instruct your lordship to concert measures for the siege of Sebastopol, unless, with the information in your possession but at present unknown in this country, you should be decidedly of opinion that it could not be undertaken with a reasonable prospect of success. The confidence with which Her Majesty placed under your command the gallant army now in Turkey is unabated; and if, upon mature reflection, you should consider that the united strength of the two armies is insufficient for this undertaking, you are not to be precluded from the exercise of the discretion originally vested in you, though Her Majesty's Government will learn with regret that an attack, from which such important consequences are anticipated, must be any longer delayed.

The difficulties of the siege of Sebastopol appear to Her Majesty's Government to be more likely to increase than to diminish by delay; and as there is no prospect of a safe and honourable peace until the fortress is reduced and the fleet taken or destroyed, it is, on all accounts, most important that nothing but insuperable impediments—such as the want of ample preparations by either army, or the possession by Russia of a force in the Crimea greatly outnumbering that which can be brought against it—should be allowed to prevent the early decision to undertake these operations.[17]

The private letter which accompanied this despatch informed Lord Raglan that its instructions were unanimously approved by the

* The fire at Varna was believed to have been started by Greeks. 'Five Greeks were caught setting fire to buildings by the French, who immediately bayonetted them', Lord George Paget told his wife. 'They do things better than we do in this army.'

Cabinet, and that the Emperor of the French had expressed his entire concurrence with them.[18]

Having read the despatch, Lord Raglan asked Sir George Brown to come to the headquarters in Varna, as he wanted to discuss it with him. Sir George read it, while Lord Raglan finished writing a letter.

What, asked Sir George when he had read it, do we or the French know of the strength of Sebastopol and of the number of the Russian forces in the Crimea?

Lord Raglan replied that they knew practically nothing. The Foreign Office believed that Russia had a million men under arms, but that the numbers in the Crimea were not more than 45,000, including 17,000 sailors. These numbers could perhaps be reinforced fairly quickly by a few infantry battalions from the Caucasus and by units from the army which had retreated from the Principalities. No British or French ambassador seemed able to add anything more definite to this. Neither Lord Stratford nor Lord Raglan himself had any faith in the information supplied by spies, and both shared their contemporaries' emotional antipathy to the use of them.[19] St. Arnaud had heard a rumour that the Russian forces in the Crimea amounted to 70,000. Vice-Admiral Dundas, commander of the English fleet, had received a statement that they numbered 140,000.[20] But the Duke of Newcastle believed that the Foreign Office figure of 45,000 was about right and had pressed Lord Raglan to accept it.

When Lord Raglan had explained how little he knew of Russian strength in the Crimea, Sir George Brown said, 'You and I are accustomed, when in any great difficulty or when any important question is proposed, to ask ourselves how the Great Duke would have acted.' The Great Duke, Brown thought, would not have undertaken such an enterprise without more certain information. Nevertheless, he added, Lord Raglan had better accede to the proposal, as the Government had made up their minds to it; and if the present commander would not agree to it, they would send out someone who would.[21]

This was not an argument much to Lord Raglan's taste. But there seemed to him more cogent reasons why he should do what the Government wanted. The armies were sick, but the Medical Department assured him that a sea voyage was as good a way of improving their health as any other.* They were becoming undisciplined, but this was because they were bored by their long inactivity. The British army, now of about 27,000 effective men, was admittedly small, but the French had another 30,000 and Omar Pasha had agreed to contribute 7,000 Turks. If the Foreign Office figures were right, these 64,000 men would be more than a match for the Russians at present in the Crimea. And Lord Raglan did not intend, once the armies had landed, that any time should be given to the enemy to reinforce their troops before Sebastopol was taken. The British transport system was indeed lamentable; and the Commissariat responsible for it, like other departments of the army, was, as he frequently warned the Duke of Newcastle, overworked and inefficient. But he had already asked the Government to organise a land transport corps, and the officers of the Quartermaster-General's office were collecting together in Bulgaria as many horses, oxen and carts as they could find. He hoped that these, together with others they would be able to buy in the Crimea, would be enough until his repeated requests for further transport and more commissariat officers were complied with. Finally and most importantly, he believed, as the Duke himself had taught him, that he must consider the Government's wishes as if they were commands.

By 19 July he had made up his mind and wrote to Newcastle to tell him that 'more in deference to the views of the British Government' and to the 'known acquiescence of the Emperor Louis Napoleon in those views' than to their own judgment, he and Marshal St. Arnaud were preparing to invade Russia.[22]

'I cannot help seeing,' the Duke replied, 'through the calm and noble tone of your announcement of the decision to attack Sebastopol, that it has been taken in order to meet the views and desires of the Government, and not in entire accordance with your opinions. God grant that success may reward you, and justify us! . . . I will not believe that in any case British arms can fail.'[23]

III

By the time Lord Raglan received the Duke's reply his men were on the march to the transports waiting for them at the scarred and

* 'A night on board ship,' Lord George Paget had already decided, 'adds a week to one's life.'

34

blackened port of Varna. A few units were under the impression that they were going to Odessa, but most of them had been making gabions and fascines and scaling-ladders for weeks and thought that they would be more likely to be using them against Sebastopol. That the armies were being sent to the Crimea had, in fact, already been announced in the Press in London. 'I am grieved beyond measure,' the Duke of Newcastle told Lord Raglan, 'at the unpatriotic conduct of *The Times* in . . . proclaiming to the Emperor the attack on the Crimea. . . . I believe it is a mere guess on its part but every sovereign nation thinks *The Times* is in the confidence of the Government.'[24] But even if it had been a guess, no great intuitive powers were needed to forecast an attack on the base of the Black Sea Fleet. And the disastrous march of the cholera-struck French 1st Division to the Dobrudja had not misled the Russians into believing anything else.[25] 'We are going to the Crimea,' Lord Burghersh said. 'I only hope we have strength enough to get there.'

For the British army, although having generally recovered from cholera, was still pitifully weak and seemed unable to throw off the debilitating effects of diarrhoea and dysentery. Some regiments were reasonably fit, but others were a pathetic sight. 'Any person who saw us at Manchester last winter,' an officer in the Royal Fusiliers wrote, 'would not know us now. The men are all gone as thin as they well can be.'[26] The Guards were so weak that they were unable to carry their packs and even without them could march only five miles a day.[27]

There was, however, a general thankfulness that at last the army was on the move. 'Hurrah for the Crimea!' Cornet Fisher exclaimed in relief. 'We are off to-morrow. Take Sebastopol in a week or so, and then into winter quarters.' The news that the army was moving at last made Captain Biddulph 'drunk with excitement'. Although when he saw the flat-bottomed boats which were intended to serve as transports for his guns, he began to have doubts about the success of the landing. They looked unwieldy and gimcrack as they swayed heavily in the bay, lashed together with ropes, their uneven decks formed by roughly matched planks. 'These great boats will make pretty targets,' he thought, 'if the fleet cannot silence the guns on shore.'

It was an apprehension which few men shared. The fleets in the bay were an inspiring spectacle. 'Such a sight,' a surgeon wrote excitedly to his sister when he had got aboard the *Sonning*, 'was never seen since the foundation of the world—magnificent—impossible to describe. . . . How they can resist such a force as ours I know not. Failure seems impossible.'[28]

There was 'a perfect forest of shipping of every kind'. Bobbing about between the ships and the shore were hundreds of small boats carrying troops to the transports and the men of war, and returning again to the newly-built stone jetties where soldiers covered in white dust and women hiding amidst the baggage awaited their turn to embark.[29] By the evening of 6 September most of the men were aboard and many of the women too. Standing in hysterical groups along the jetties, however, were many women who had not managed to smuggle themselves aboard, but at the last minute they too were taken to the transports, as there was no way otherwise of caring for them.

At dawn on 7 September Admiral Dundas gave the signal to weigh anchor. There was a gentle breeze and a fine morning sky. Flags flew bravely and bands played with cheerful determination as the long lines of sailing-ships were towed by steamers out to sea.

Marshal St. Arnaud, tired of waiting for the English, who had been held up by having to embark their far more numerous horses, had already set sail in the *Ville de Paris*.[30] On 8 September the steamship *Caradoc*, with Lord Raglan aboard, caught up with him at the agreed rendezvous. St. Arnaud was, however, too ill to leave his cabin and sent an invitation to the British commander to come aboard the *Ville de Paris*. But Lord Raglan could not, with his single arm, climb aboard the French three-decker sailing-ship tossing in a rough sea and sent Colonel Steele, his Military Secretary, and Admiral Dundas, the naval commander, instead.[31]

Colonel Steele found St. Arnaud sitting up in his bunk, so ill that he could scarcely speak. But Colonel Trochu was there, of course, to speak for him and so was Admiral Hamelin, the French naval commander. A discussion took place as to a suitable landing-place on the Russian coast, and three places were suggested. It was an indeterminate discussion and no decision was taken. At length St. Arnaud found strength to say that he would agree to anything Lord Raglan suggested.

The discussion was, therefore, continued aboard the *Caradoc*, where Lord Raglan, to a French suggestion that the landing should take place on a beach a hundred miles from Sebastopol and thus postpone the forthcoming clash with the enemy, replied with characteristic restraint that a reconnaissance of the coastline nearer the town might not be a waste of time. And so at four o'clock in the morning of Sunday 10 September the *Caradoc* with General Canrobert, Marshal St. Arnaud's second-in-command aboard, steamed away to Sebastopol.[32]

The domes and cupolas of the town and the masts of the ships under the guns of the high forts could be seen a long way off. But the only sound was the ringing of church bells. As the *Caradoc* steamed closer, the officers on board could see that 'the fortifications looked of immense strength and appeared to bristle with guns'.[33] Steaming north along the coast-line, the *Caradoc* ran up a Russian flag and people rushed down to the beaches to look at the big iron ship of a kind that they had not seen before. At the mouth of the Katcha the *Caradoc's* noisily vibrating engines clattered away into silence, as this was the place that General Canrobert and Sir George Brown had chosen on a previous reconnaissance.[34] But neither Lord Raglan nor the naval officers considered it suitable; the beach was narrow and since its advantages as a landing-place had been advertised in the newspapers, a cluster of tents had appeared on the cliffs.[35] The engines were started up and the ship steamed on again. South of Eupatoria, about thirty-five miles north of Sebastopol opposite a long sandy beach where naked men and women were happily bathing together, the *Caradoc* slowed down, then stopped. Lord Raglan had found the place that he was looking for. He did not invite discussion. He asked the admirals a few questions, then announced his decision. The armies would land there within the next few days.[36]

When the *Caradoc* rejoined the fleets it was late evening. 'Hundreds of boats were going about' between the ships, and 'you could have fancied yourself in port'. As the *Caradoc* steamed slowly to its anchorage past the *Orinoco* the men standing on deck in the warm sunlight raised their hats in the air and cheered lustily.[37]

During the next three days both armies enjoyed a period of happy confidence which not even the regular splash of French corpses, sewn up in blankets and dropped into the sea, could dispel. The men had been at sea a week now and 'had been feeding like fighting cocks'; and most of them, as the doctors had forecast, felt well again.[38]

On 12 September, a calm almost windless day with a burning sun, 'a long range of barren low land' came into sight. That night as the ships lay once more at anchor, the men looked towards the Crimean shore and at the countless flickering lights of the ships shining on the dark water, wondering why it was so quiet.[39]

The following morning the coast-line still appeared barren and deserted. A peasant with a cart, a horseman riding across the cliff top, were the only figures in sight, and neither showed any curiosity in the armada closing in upon their homeland. During the afternoon Colonel Steele and Colonel Trochu landed at Eupatoria and handed the mayor a summons to surrender. Before accepting the summons, the mayor fumigated it in accordance with the health regulations of the town. Then, having read it, he politely informed the visitors that they might land at the lazaretto, provided they considered themselves in strict quarantine.[40]

5

CALAMITA BAY

We made fires the best way we could, with broken boats and rafts
Sergeant Timothy Gowing

In the morning the sun rose in a cloudless sky. Looking ashore from their transports the soldiers could see the waves lapping gently on a long and sandy beach, broken here and there by shallow cliffs of red clay and sandstone. It was very quiet. Opposite them the beach narrowed to a thin strand of shingle, and behind this strand were the calm, unruffled waters of a salt-water lake. To their right was another smaller lake and beyond this a lonely crumbling fort with a half-ruined white tower. The countryside inland was as peaceful and untroubled as the shore. Through their telescopes the officers watched cattle grazing in their silent pastures and flocks of sheep ambling over the green turf. They saw stacks of grain and hay against the white walls of farmhouses, and stubble fields covered with wild lavender. It was an idyllic scene—with no figures.

And then just as a post-carriage came into sight rattling along the rough road to Simpheropol, a troop of Cossacks trotted over the crest of a hill and presented themselves for the first time to their enemies. They rode ill-assorted shaggy horses which were made to look taller by curiously high saddles. Their bulky coats, sheepskin caps and roughly laced leggings were in striking contrast to the elegant green frock-coat, trimmed with silver lace, and the slender riding-boots worn by their officer, who sat astride a bay charger making notes in a pocket-book. They carried enormous lances, fifteen feet long, and menacingly heavy sabres.[1]

The French were the first to land. Their small war steamers, closer to the shore than the British fleet, let down their first landing-craft a little after seven o'clock. As the leading boat beached, its crew leaped out and formed a knot on the shore. Spadefuls of sand and shingle flew into the air, and it seemed to *The Times* correspondent that they were digging a grave. Then above the sailors' heads a flag-staff appeared, and a moment later the tricolour uncurled against the sky. An hour later several French regiments were already on shore with advanced posts as far as four miles inland. By midday a whole division was firmly established in a defensive position.[2]

The British, however, were not able to follow this impressive example. They were already in something of a muddle. It had been intended that a buoy should be placed opposite the old fort to mark the dividing line between the French and British disembarkation points. But during the night the buoy had been moved some way to the south. No one knew who moved it. The French, who by its removal enjoyed the use of the whole of the intended landing-place, were naturally blamed. And the British, now left facing a sandstone cliff, had to move south to a point where the beach began again.

It was not, then, until nine o'clock that a gun was fired on the *Agamemnon* drawing attention to the signal for the landing-craft to come alongside the transports. A few minutes later rope ladders were flung over the sides of the ships and hundreds of soldiers clambered down, helped from rung to rung by roughly sympathetic sailors who treated them 'like stupid children', patting them on the back and telling them 'not to be afeerd on the water'.[3] On a mile-wide front the small boats rushed inshore. Ahead of the others a gig with Sir George Brown and Captain Dacres, the beachmaster, raced a boat from the *Britannia* carrying a party of Royal Welch Fusiliers, the passengers in each boat cheering excitedly, and then vociferously claiming the victory as both of them grounded almost in the same instant. Soon afterwards Lord Raglan landed and 'wherever he went the troops cheered him'.[4]

All morning the landing continued. The black and tranquil sea of the night before was now alive with colour and movement as the rowing-boats, plying back and forth between the ships and the shore, carried thousands of troops towards the arms of swearing, laughing sailors, who lifted them with good-natured insults on to dry land. 'Come on, girls,' they shouted at the kilted Highlanders, throwing their arms wide open, and the Highlanders, accepting remarks which would have earned a Guardsman a broken jaw, improved on them and then held hands to skip with elaborate delicacy up the beach.[5]

But these high spirits and gaiety were far from common. The faces of many of the men, as they fanned out over the beach between the coloured marking-posts and filed up the hill beyond, were white and drawn in weakness and pain. All the infantry were weighed down with a mass of cumbersome equipment. In addition to his rifle, to which his bayonet was now fixed, each man carried fifty rounds of ammunition; his blanket and greatcoat folded up into a sort of knapsack with an extra pair of boots, socks, a shirt and forage cap inside; a canteen of water; part of his unit's cooking apparatus; and three days' rations comprising 4½ lb. of meat and 4½ lb. of biscuit. There was no transport. Even the ambulance wagons had been left behind, as they had proved 'very rough' in Bulgaria and were considered too rickety to be of any use in the Crimea.[6]

Soldiers struggled under their burdens to reach the hill beyond the beach, only to collapse in exhaustion or agony on reaching it. By noon, when the sun had disappeared behind threatening clouds and a drizzle of rain had begun to fall through the sea breeze, several men were being carried back to be buried under the sands they had marched across so short a time before. The desperately sick were carried back also and next morning were put aboard the *Kangaroo*, a ship with accommodation for 250 sick into which more than four times that number were crammed. When signalled to proceed to Scutari, her Captain reported back, 'It is a dangerous experiment.' An officer from the *Agamemnon* went on board and 'found the decks covered with dead and dying men; he described the scene as one of the most horrible he had ever witnessed; he could scarcely walk the decks for the dead'. Lord Raglan when he heard of it made some 'very strong remarks', but he could not alter a system which acquitted the responsible officer at a subsequent court-martial because he had complied with the regulations of his department.[7]

Most of that first afternoon the fine rain fell steadily down, and the tentless troops looked disconsolately back at the ships riding at anchor against the blackening sky. Some of them tried to make fires, Timothy Gowing remembered, 'the best way we could, with broken boats and rafts'. At nightfall the storm broke, and the men huddled together on the beach and on the plateau above it, crowding miserably in the few places of shelter or lying in the open, resignedly trying to sleep in the wet and cold and waiting for the morning. Officers did their best to protect their full-dress uniforms; Colonel Bell of the Royals lamenting his 'expensive nightdress' of gold-embroidered scarlet with its epaulettes that cost him twenty guineas, wet through under a 'scotch plaid and a six foot square of waterproof'; Lieutenant Hugh Annesley of the Scots Fusilier Guards deriving some comfort from the adequate pillow he discovered his bearskin to be, when placed on a haversack full of biscuit.

The rain stopped before dawn, and once again the sun rose in a cloudless sky. All the infantry and some of the artillery had been dis-embarked the day before, but the cavalry was still aboard and it was more difficult to get one horse on shore than a hundred men. Some officers could not bear to watch their strapped and frightened animals, most of whom had had a fearful crossing, being lowered into the boats, where they stamped and snorted in terror. Several boats were overturned at the water's edge and their horses were tipped out to flounder in the sea 'with their heads in the air and the surf driving into their poor mouths'. At length it was decided that the landings would have to be discontinued until the sea became calmer.[8]

By the evening of the following day, however, all the remaining horses and most of the army's stores had been got on shore. But the problem now was to move these enormous piles of biscuits, barrels of salt meat, tins and sacks, ammunition boxes and equipment which lay in dumps all along the beach. Already it had been necessary to re-ship the tents, which had been unloaded after the first night's storm and which there now seemed to be no possibility of carrying.

General Airey, who had taken over from the invalided Lord de Ros as Quartermaster-General, was aware that this lack of transport was a major concern, and had been doing all he could to collect to-gether as many carts and bullocks as possible before the army moved on to Sebastopol. He was a man of wonderful energy and talent. He was fifty-one, but looked much younger. For several years he had lived on his cousin's vast tracts of land in Upper Canada, where he had hacked down pines to build himself a house, earning the obvious respect of men peculiarly reluctant to show it. At the outbreak of war he had been Military Secretary to the Commander-in-Chief, Lord Hardinge, and had been asked by Lord Raglan to become his Quartermaster-General. Preferring duty in the field, however, he had been given a brigade in the Light Division. But now that Lord de Ros had gone home he had accepted the appointment which Lord Raglan had again pressed upon him. On landing he had sent Major Lysons with a company of the Royal Welch Fusiliers to advance quickly on a long string of wagons winding its way inland under a Cossack escort. The Cossacks had pricked the bottoms of both bullocks and drivers with the tips of their lances and then, as the Fusiliers drew closer, unyoked the animals and tried to drive them off. But when the Fusiliers opened fire the Cossacks trotted away, leaving the frightened Tartars to bring back their carts and animals as an offering to the red-coated foreigners, whom they clasped round the knees in supplication.[9]

It was a beginning; and during the next two days officers of the Quartermaster-General's department were sent deep inland to bring in all the wagons, baggage animals, drivers and supplies they could find. An expedition led by Lord Cardigan was a sad failure—'the most absurd expedition it has ever been my ill luck to be engaged in', Arthur Godfrey called it—but others were more successful, and by the time the army and its equipment had been completely disembarked 350 wagons with their teams and drivers had been collected, together with 67 camels, 253 horses, 45 cartloads of poultry, corn and flour and 1,000 head of cattle and sheep. The figures looked impressive in the returns, but to move and feed an army of 27,000 men it was a good deal less than enough. And Lord Raglan told Airey that he must have more.[10]

The French, whose army at this time was slightly smaller than the British, were more fortunate. Not only did they have an adequate transport corps but they had no scruples about taking what they wanted. Sometimes money was offered, but there was no bargaining. A Tartar learned to feel himself lucky if he was offered compensation at all and was glad to get money out of a French soldier who was just as likely to take his goods for nothing. There was nothing they could do to prevent this plunder, the French officers complained. The spirit of the army was 'so revolutionary' that they had 'not control over their men' and were 'much surprised at the discipline of our troops'.[11]

Camels loaded with grain and country carts packed with vegetables soon became a common sight in the French camps. Spahis, flourishing their lances 'in high delight', drove hundreds of sheep and cattle towards their lines, the cattle tossing their horns and bellowing as they lumbered over the shingle.[12]

This attitude towards plunder was one which Lord Raglan was anxious his own troops should not develop. During the afternoon of 15 September he called a meeting of the headmen of the surrounding villages. The old Tartars came up to his tent, dignified, polite and apprehensive, their wide-set little eyes warily cunning; and Lord Raglan greeted them with gentle courtesy. They wore long robes and fez-shaped hats of black lambskin, and he a civilian frock-coat which seemed to emphasise the polite and gentlemanly atmosphere. 'I never met a man,' Somerset Calthorpe said admiringly, 'who had so completely the power of pleasing whomever he chose'. The army would regretfully have to take all their carts and animals, Lord Raglan told them, but they would receive adequate payment. Responding to the deference of his manner some of the headmen, implying that they had no affection for the Russians of the North, said that the British were welcome to borrow the carts and their teams for as long as they liked without compensation. The offer was accepted, but Lord Raglan added that his officers had instructions to ensure that all cattle, food and corn supplied to his army must be paid for.* When the meeting broke up the headmen were assured that their people had nothing to fear from the allied armies, which would treat them with consideration and respect. A few hours later Lord Raglan heard that in a nearby village a Tartar woman had been raped by Zouaves, and an A.D.C. afterwards remembered how the calm, controlled face of his general for once betrayed his emotion and became suddenly red in anger and shame.[13]

His own troops were not, of course, blameless. Two days after this meeting with the village headmen an immense flock of sheep came scurrying into the camp of the 3rd Division during a church parade. The open-air service was interrupted as men rushed at the sheep with their bayonets. The voice of the chaplain was drowned in the shouts of the men and the clattering baaing of the terrified sheep, and soon the field was spattered with the animals' blood.[14] This was, however, an unusual windfall. The French had made good use of their two hours' start on shore. Dr. Robinson, assistant surgeon to the Scots Fusilier Guards, watching Zouaves staggering under the loads of captured calves and sheep, disappointedly noted in his diary: 'Very little livestock has escaped the hands of our allies.' It was a common complaint.

On the 18th Lord Raglan decided it was futile to wait any longer. The men were growing restless and impatient. 'What the devil are

---

* Standard prices were, for instance, established at 6d. for 25 eggs; 6d. for fowls; 1s. each for turkeys and sheep.

we waiting for?' one of them asked in angry frustration. 'Has the Czar caved in?'[15] The army must move on, and the stores and equipment it could not carry must be put back on board the ships. The next day the advance on Sebastopol was to begin.

The French, who had had far fewer horses to disembark and a much better transport system than the British, had been ready for two days, and St. Arnaud had not troubled to disguise his impatience with the muddle and slowness of his allies. On at least two occasions he had clattered into their headquarters, surrounded by his aides and the Spahis of his escort, to ask when they would be ready and to remind Lord Raglan that both his own army and that of the Turks were waiting for them.

Reveille was sounded in the camps on the 19th at three o'clock in the morning, but it was six hours later before the advance began. For most of these six hours the French were bugling and drumming impatiently as the English in an agonising muddle, first of all in darkness and then in the early morning light, swarmed all over the beach, digging graves, carrying stretchers, dragging back to the boats the equipment and supplies they were unable to carry with them,* There was no time to cook their meat, which they had to carry raw; there was no time even for some of them to fill their canteens with water at the single well.

By nine o'clock, when at last they were ready, the armies marched off to the south in brilliant, hot sunshine. The French, claiming the side of precedence, were on the right between the British and the sea, and were thus largely protected from attack. The British, on the other hand, were exposed on three sides to an unknown country; and a more experienced general than Lord Raglan would have had cavalry patrols and contact squadrons well out in his front and on his flank to guard against surprise. His army marched, however, in a dangerously compact mass.

Lord Cardigan led the way with the 13th Light Dragoons and the 11th Hussars; Lord Lucan was on the exposed left with the 8th Hussars followed by the 17th Lancers; Lord George Paget with the 4th Dragoons brought up the rear. Between them, protected at front and back by companies of the Rifle Brigade in extended order, the five

---

* Many supplies were thrown away. Hugh Annesley filled a stocking with tea-leaves from one of six chests that the Commissariat had decided to abandon.

infantry divisions marched in solid phalanxes with the sixty guns of the artillery rumbling along in neat groups of twelve on their right.[16] Behind the 3rd Division a ragged herd of cattle and sheep, and the bullocks, camels and horses pulling the creaking country carts, tramped over the soft turf, 'as green and smooth as a racecourse'.[17]

It was a lovely undulating countryside. In places the ground was covered with fern and lavender and some strange herb which no one recognised. Crushed under thousands of heavy boots it gave up a curious smell, strong and bitter.

At the head of each division, regimental colours fluttered proudly from their corded staves and regimental bands played cheerful marching songs to which the men supplied their own obscenely humorous verses.

But neither the gaiety nor the energy lasted long. The sun grew hotter as the sea breeze dropped, throats became dry with thirst, the bands stopped playing and parties had to be sent back to bring up stragglers, trailing wearily, hundreds of yards behind the marching columns. Although everything not needed on the march—including, by Lord Raglan's order, their leather stocks—had been sent on board the ships, which followed the army like shadows up the coastline, even their unaccustomedly light loads were more than many of the troops could bear. Men talking happily with their neighbours would suddenly fall silent and then their throats would choke with vomit, their faces blacken and they would stumble out of the ranks in the agonies of cholera. The most frightening thing about this cholera, Captain Biddulph told his father, was the suddenness with which it attacked you. A man might be cheerful, healthy and contented, taking a sip from his canteen, perhaps, during a rest on the march; and then a few minutes later the cholera would be on him and four hours later he could be dead.

The farther south the armies marched the more deserted the landscape became. All the cattle had been driven off by the Cossacks, and even the hares which before had leapt out of the paths of the advancing columns in every direction were now few and far between. Smoke poured from burning villages and the once white walls of farmyards were scorched and blackened. Soldiers entering farmhouses to enjoy a rest out of the glare of the sun found them empty and silent. Even the furniture had gone. Hanging from the ceiling beams were perhaps a few bundles of dried herbs or a row of saucepans and on the walls the gaudy pictures of saints.[18]

The worst ordeal was the thirst. Many of the troops had been thirsty for days. Water was scarce on the transports and even scarcer ashore. The rain which fell during the storm of the 17th had soon soaked away into the dry, cracked earth, and the wells which had been dug produced only brackish water. What water the troops could now find on the march was undrinkable. The rims of their mouths became alarmingly tinged with blue. By midday the army was unable to march for more than half an hour at a time without a rest. When the men were ordered to fall in again many of them fell to their knees, begging for water and close to delirium. They dropped their great-coats in the blazing heat and threw away their shakos, and the columns behind tramped wearily over them; and then unable to bear the agony of marching any longer the men themselves crumpled to the ground until bodies and accoutrements of all sorts lay about in such confusion that it was difficult for the regiments at the rear to thread their way through them. Men of the 3rd Division threw their rifles on to the tops of the baggage carts and clung to the sides like drowning men to lifeboats. Lady Errol on her mule, and her French maid on another mule behind her, were almost concealed by the rifles of sick men from Lord Errol's regiment.[19]

With the sound of their boots muffled by the fern and thyme and lavender, the army now marched in foreboding silence. The rumble of the gun-carriage wheels, the creaking of the country carts, the groans and wearily muttered curses, the chink of the cavalry, were the only sounds that were heard above the ceaseless chatter of the larks that sang and fluttered happily against the bright blue sky as if in cruel mockery.[20]

Well in front of the leading columns and followed by his staff, Lord Raglan rode anxious and silent. When an A.D.C. suggested he was too far in advance, he replied with unaccustomed curtness, 'Do not speak to me now: I am busy.'[21] He had cause to be. Somewhere ahead of him in this quiet, unknown country was an enemy whose strength he could only guess at. Behind him was an army on the verge of collapse. Occasionally he caught sight of a Cossack patrol watching his advance and then galloping back with the news of it across the softly undulating plain. This plain was, he recognised, perfect cavalry country; and yet his cavalry was not only wholly inadequate in numbers but had as its most senior officers two men who knew practically nothing of war and whose loathing for each other had been increased by the events of the past few weeks.

As soon as the Earl of Cardigan had arrived at Varna with the Light Brigade the trouble had begun. Lucan, the divisional commander, had been left behind outside Scutari with the Heavy Brigade and then, after its departure, by himself. He was furious with Cardigan for issuing orders to the cavalry without consulting him, and he was furious with Raglan for permitting it. Lord Raglan was undoubtedly in the wrong in dealing direct with Cardigan in Bulgaria and was not much surprised when Lucan was violently provoked and 'quarrelled with everyone'. But he believed that the only hope for the cavalry was to keep the two men apart. Certainly as soon as Lucan had arrived at Varna he had gone for Cardigan 'hammer and tongs' and they had been at it ever since.[22]

But a greater problem than the dissensions of the cavalry commanders was the terrifying problem of supply. Those overladen carts, those horses and melancholy camels trailing along in the rear of his straggling columns, were his only means of transport. Weeks before he had written to the Government to suggest the organisation of a Land Transport Corps, but nothing yet had been done. His frequent complaints about the lack of transport which formed his 'principal want and a most serious one' remained, so far, unacknowledged.[23]

At two o'clock he came up to the crest of another ridge, and below him in a gentle valley sparkling out to the sea was the Bulganak river. The men when they saw it were uncontrollable. Breaking ranks they rushed down the slope to plunge their burning heads into the cool water and gulp it, choking and spluttering, down their throats.[24]

Beyond the Bulganak the land rises in steps and then dips out of sight into hollows before rising again. And Lord Raglan decided that before taking his army up that treacherous far bank of the river he must send a reconnaissance patrol ahead of him. Already he had noticed the sheepskin caps of a squadron of Cossacks bobbing and dipping in and out of view behind the highest ridge. While the infantry were still splashing the water over their heads, he sent Lord Cardigan to reconnoitre the ground beyond the southern bank.

Lord Cardigan trotted off with the four squadrons of the advance guard towards the top of the first ridge. Lord Lucan, anxious not to leave the matter in the hands of his brother-in-law, galloped after him and joined him on the crest. From here the two generals, looking towards the next slope, saw their danger and their opportunity. Moving slowly towards them across the gently sloping turf was a massive Russian cavalry force, two thousand strong. This was the moment Cardigan had been waiting for. He knew just what to do and how to do it. As calmly as if he were supervising a musical ride at Deene Park he ordered his men to form line. The movement was performed with magnificent precision. The Russians halted, threw out skirmishers and opened fire with their carbines at long range. The advance guard remained motionless and waited.

But Lord Raglan, not so close to the next overhanging ridge as his cavalry commanders, could see farther than they could, and the sight was alarming. Behind the Russian cavalry, drawn up on the higher ridge where the advance guard could not see it, was a dense grey mass. The air above this long dark smudge seemed to glitter and flash like the light of a thousand sparks. It was the glint of the sun on bayonets. 6,000 men of the Russian 17th Division were barring the way to the south.[25]

It was too late now to turn the flank. Cardigan must be withdrawn before the presence of his four squadrons in so vulnerable a position brought on a general engagement. Fortunately the confidence and strength displayed by his rigidly unwavering lines seemed for the moment to be keeping the enemy from further movement. Provided he did not move precipitately either in retreat or attack he might be saved.

To increase the show of confidence and power so effectively given by his four isolated cavalry squadrons, Lord Raglan ordered the 2nd and Light Divisions to cross the river and form in line on the southern bank, while the 8th Hussars and 17th Lancers were sent forward to take position behind the advance guard. As the men came wearily forward, Raglan anxiously watched the enemy for any sign of movement. But the solid masses remained as before.

As soon as his other troops were in position, Lord Raglan sent General Airey galloping across the open ground to deliver to Lucan an order to retire. Airey found the two generals in the middle of a quarrel. Lucan had been nagging Cardigan to make some minor alterations in the disposition of his men; Cardigan, disdainfully ignoring the unnecessary advice, had been heatedly urging a disastrous charge. When Airey reined up the two men were both still arguing.[26]

The order which Airey carried to them was polite and imprecise. It was one of the tragedies of Lord Raglan's command that his orders were often to be so. The politeness was fashionable, expected and perhaps unavoidable in an army in which staff officers and commanders were chosen with more regard to their family than their merit. But the imprecision was based on a false conception of the duties of an army commander. In the face of the enemy Lord Raglan was much too ready to think of himself as an adviser rather than a leader. He was often too willing to leave a decision in the hands of junior commanders merely because they were more closely in touch with their particular problem than he was, because they were, as he himself once put it (as if that settled their capacity to make the right decision), 'on the spot'. So relaxed and tentative a hold on the direction of a military engagement might well have been effective had the officers in whose hands Lord Raglan was content to leave it been men, not only as intelligent as he was, but also with as much opportunity of understanding what effect their decisions might have on the battle as a whole. Lord Raglan's readiness to give his officers credit for more intelligence and foresight than they possessed, and his assumption that they could see and understand as much of the battle as he could, were serious weaknesses and were to contribute to at least one disastrous result.

On this occasion at the Bulganak, however, General Airey saved what could have become a dangerous situation by re-forming the Commander-in-Chief's order in far more categoric terms. Needing no particular insight to recognise that Lucan and Cardigan were both about to lose their temper, he commanded them in Lord Raglan's name to retire.

Still unaware of the immense force confronting them, the four squadrons of the advance guard trotted away in sulky reluctance with the Russian cavalry jeering at their retreating backs. It seemed to them that they owed their humiliation to the interference of Lord Lucan, who had prevented Lord Cardigan from leading them in a glorious charge. An officer unjustly commented that Lord Look-on would be a more appropriate title, and the nickname stuck.[27]

The infantry were delighted. Already furiously resentful at having to watch those complacent horsemen trotting along so comfortably on that terrible march, they were glad to be given fresh evidence that when there was real fighting to do, it was the foot regiments that had to do it. 'Serve them bloody right,' a private in the 41st told his brother with malicious pleasure, 'silly peacock bastards.' [28]

The withdrawal was carried out with calm efficiency. As the cavalry fell back, the two artillery batteries which Raglan had ordered up opened a covering fire. Almost immediately the fire was returned, but it was a half-hearted response. The Russians, now that the English cavalry had extricated themselves, saw no point in further action here, for behind them, only a few miles away, was a position of enormous strength. It might be possible to hold this position indefinitely. Certainly Prince Mentschikoff, the Russian commander, confidently assured the Czar that there was no doubt it could be held for three weeks while the defences of Sebastopol were made impregnable; and even his less assured officers believed they could hold their ground for at least a week.[29] So in accordance with this plan the Russians withdrew from the ridges of Bulganak, and the British army came up on to them to bivouac for the night in order of battle. When darkness came the men, most of them too exhausted even to eat, fell to the ground, permitted at last to sleep. Some of them, too cold or too tired to go to sleep, looked across the plain towards the Alma river. Beyond the river, on the steep ridges which rise there to a formidable height, an untouched Russian army lay encamped. And all night long, as far as the eye could stretch, hundreds of watch-fires twinkled in the darkness.

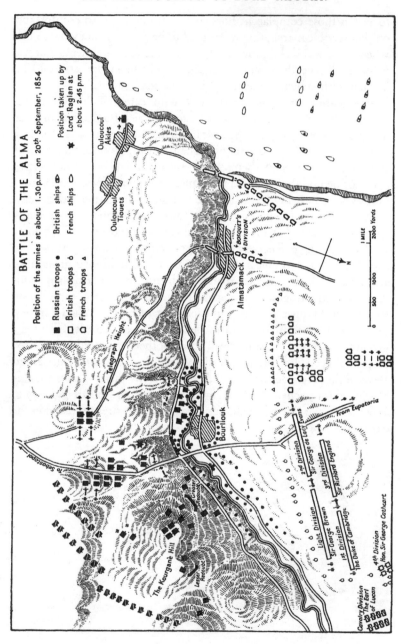

BATTLE OF THE ALMA

Position of the armies at about 1.30 p.m. on 20th September, 1854

Russian troops ■   British ships ⊂⊃
British troops □   French ships ○
French troops △

Position taken up by
Lord Raglan at
about 2.45 p.m. ✦

6

ALMA

Up the hill we went, step by step, but with a fearful carnage
Sergeant Timothy Gowing

I

On the morning of the following day Lord George Paget rode past Lord Raglan's cottage and saw him outside it talking to Airey and Estcourt. 'He looked anxious,' Paget remembered afterwards. And the staff officers around him were all wearing their cocked hats, which 'meant business'.

It was a lovely morning with a gentle, refreshing sea breeze, and Midshipman Evelyn Wood on board the *Queen*, lying at anchor at the mouth of the Alma river, thought how strangely peaceful and quiet the landscape looked from the sea. To his left, on the British side of the Alma, the ground rose gently from the river bank. It was a green, soft countryside broken here and there by vineyards enclosed by low stone walls and the gardens and orchards of small white houses. But to his right, where the Russians watched and waited on the far side of the river, the land rising sharply to a high plateau was in striking contrast. Here the steep, ridged slopes were barren and stony and, as if to emphasise their harshness, a wall of rock 350 feet high cut them off at the sea like a massive book-end of granite.

Seen from the front, the Russian position appeared quite as formidable. About three miles inland from the sheer West Cliff was another hill, which became known as the Telegraph Height. It occupied the centre of the position, and although it was not as precipitous as the West Cliff it was quite as high. To the left of it was a third hill, and this was by far the most important of all. Prince Mentschikoff, standing there a few days before, had proudly shown General Kiriakoff its wide field of fire. 'Isn't it a grand place?' he had said. It was in fact, as Lord Raglan immediately recognised, 'the key of the position'.[1]

It was known as the Kourganè Hill. On its forward slope a swelling rib of land jutted forward towards the river, and here a breastwork

53

had been formed to give protection to a battery of twelve guns. Soon to be the scene of violent fighting the breastwork, although not much more than a shallow ridge of earth designed to prevent the guns from running down the slope, became known throughout the British army as 'the Great Redoubt'. Higher up the hill, the guns of 'the Lesser Redoubt' commanded the eastern flank.

Between Kourganè Hill and Telegraph Height the thin white road to Sebastopol cut its way up through a narrow col and disappeared out of sight behind the hills. On either side of the road, the first of them less than five hundred yards from the wooden bridge at the riverside village of Bourliouk, were several further batteries, each of them supporting the one below, and between them covering every inch of the road as it climbed between the hills towards the pass.

In September the Alma is not deep and can be forded in several places, even towards its mouth; so Mentschikoff's task was not so much to watch the bridge at Bourliouk, and a second one at Almatamack, but to cover those places from which, having crossed the river, the allies would find it most easy to reach the pass. And all these places were covered by guns from the heights, the ranges carefully marked out by stakes. The ground below was bare and open. Even the few willow trees by the river bank had been cut down so that the assaulting troops should have no shelter. Prince Mentschikoff had reason to feel secure.

He was by nature a confident man. Arrogant and autocratic, he was not popular with his men; and his officers had long since learned not to offer him any advice.[2] In a previous campaign he had been castrated by a round shot from a Turkish gun, and he hated the Turks, and all their allies, with a hatred pathological in its intensity. His headquarters on Kourganè Hill overlooked what he hoped would be the scene of their slaughter.

To his left Prince Gortschakoff, with General Kvetzinski as his second-in-command, commanded the troops of the centre, and General Kiriakoff those on Telegraph Height. West Cliff, that wall of rock overlooking the sea, he considered quite inaccessible and left its defence to a single battalion of the Minsk Regiment.[3]

II

At seven o'clock the British army was woken from its crumpled sleep and got up silently. No drum or bugle sounded. Here and there a body huddling under its coat or blanket did not respond to the sergeant's kick, and, when the clothes were pulled roughly away from the neck, the head slumped back to the ground and open eyes stared sightless at the sky.[4]

And so down the course of the Bulganak, its banks now churned to mud, the procession of the dead and dying once again began. By eight o'clock three hundred men, more than half of them dead from cholera, lay on the shore at its mouth waiting to be buried or to be taken aboard the fleet.[5]

Already it was hot and the men moved about the camps in heavy lassitude. Many regiments whose duty it had been to bivouac in line facing east, as a protection to the army's flank, had a long march to make before being able to wheel into line with the others. Consequently the French, for the second day in succession, were kept waiting. At nine o'clock General Bosquet's division had been in battle formation for four hours and were now making their morning coffee, grumbling at the English for being late as usual. At last, two and a half hours later, the English were in position and the advance could begin.[6]

Now that they were on the move again, their commander was in a less anxious mood. He spoke almost gaily with his staff. He 'might just as well have been riding in Rotten Row in Hyde Park'. Suddenly a 'handsome little grey pony' dashed past them and through the line of skirmishers in their front, throwing its civilian rider headlong to the ground. They all roared with laughter, but when Lord Raglan caught up with the rider he offered him one of his own horses and told his orderly to put the pony's saddle to rights. He had been introduced to the unfortunate horseman an hour or two before, when his pony had drawn attention to itself by neighing and screaming so loudly that Lord Raglan had said, 'I never heard a pony make such a row; does anyone know who the gentleman is?'

'I think he's one of the newspaper reporters, my Lord,' a staff officer said. 'Shall I send him away?'

Lord Raglan laughed and said, 'If you do, he will show you up, you may depend on it.'

Someone then recognised the gentleman and told Lord Raglan that it was Mr. Kinglake, the author of *Eothen*.

'Oh,' said Lord Raglan, 'a most charming man.' And he went over to talk to him.[7]

The army was now marching steadily forward on a front nearly five miles wide. The sea breeze had lulled to a breath, and the sun shone fiercely down. The British were still on the left, the French on the right by the sea. And this customary precedence ensured for the larger French army a position of relative security. For not only could it enjoy the protection of the fleet, already firing in support across the Russian lines, but it was advancing on a part of the front almost completely bare of Russian troops. Whereas in the path of the British advance was the whole force of the Imperial army. For this dangerous situation Lord Raglan was partly to blame.

The night before, an excited St. Arnaud had ridden to his cottage with Colonel Trochu. The Marshal was not in pain, and Lord Burghersh, noticing his unnaturally glinting, almost feverish eyes, wondered whether his state of high animation was due to drugs. Speaking sometimes in French, sometimes in English, he suggested that the French army should attack on the right, cross the river at Almatamack and roll up the Russians from their left flank. While this operation was in progress the English should attack the centre and the other flank. The Russians would be caught in a pincer and be forced to retire. It was quite simple, St. Arnaud assured his allies, taking a map from his pocket and putting it on the table. The map, drawn with the many flourishes of an excited hand, showed the Russian army so completely occupied with the French that it was apparently unaware of the English forces creeping round its side. The production of the map brought from the Marshal a fresh flood of rhetoric. Lord Raglan sat watching him, listening with a politeness so gravely attentive that those who knew him well felt that he was trying not to smile, but making no comment. Anxious at all costs to avoid a strained relationship with St. Arnaud, he thought it better not to risk a discussion which might turn into an argument. After saying that the French could rely on the full co-operation of the British army, he scarcely spoke another word. He believed that no workable plan could be made until the allies had discovered the extent of the Russian position.[8] But St. Arnaud cannot be blamed for supposing that the principle of his plan had been accepted; nor for believing that Lord Raglan's silence indicated the necessity for more elaborate and more vehement explanation.

Colonel Trochu, perhaps in an attempt to stem the flow of enthusiastic explanation which he knew the English officers were beginning to find rather embarrassing, interrupted St. Arnaud to ask him when and where the French troops were to be relieved of their packs. That, answered St. Arnaud, angrily dismissing a matter which was later to assume a profound importance, was a question of mere detail. A few minutes later the Marshal left. He was still in an elated mood. But he was not at all sure what the English intended to do.[9]

By noon the next day, when the advance was already in progress, he was still not sure. It did not seem greatly to disturb him. He felt confident of victory. A little while before he had ridden across the front of an English regiment and the men had cheered him loudly, and he, excited and touched by this display of friendship, had raised his hat in the air to return the compliment, shouting back with only a slight accent, 'Hurrah for old England!'[10] A little later, riding in front of the Connaught Rangers, he called out to them, 'I hope you will fight well to-day.' 'Sure, your honour, we will,' one of them shouted back. 'And don't we always fight well?'[11]

Now he was riding across the front of his own men, being cheered by them, his guidon fluttering proudly above the heads of his escort. As he reached a mound on the steppe, Lord Raglan came up to meet him, and the two men rode alone to the crest of the mound to get a more distinct view of the Russian position. For several minutes the two commanders stayed there together, St. Arnaud apparently talking constantly, Lord Raglan looking by comparison in his civilian coat 'as unlike a commander-in-chief as more like a gentleman', both of them staring across the river through their field-glasses. An English soldier saw Lord Raglan show his glass to St. Arnaud.[12] It had been specially made for him, so that, fitted on to a leather-bound gun-stock, he could hold it effortlessly in his one hand.

As the two commanders sat in their saddles in amiable conference, the armies halted and waited. Several men in different parts of the field remembered afterwards the sudden silence that followed this halt. It was as if for that moment all sounds were washed from the air. There was an unaccountable feeling of timelessness. Then small noises began to disturb the silence and seemed curiously loud. A man's cough sounded like a cannon-shot. The 'mere neighing of an angry horse seized the attention of thousands'. At last Sir Colin Campbell, commander of the Highland Brigade, practical and down-to-earth, said to one of his officers, 'This will be a good time for the men to get loose half their cartridges.' And the noise of the Highlanders clattering their equipment and tearing open their cartridge packets broke the unnatural silence and brought the soundless scene to life again.[13]

The commanders were still on the knoll. No one overheard their conversation. But certainly even now St. Arnaud had not discovered what Lord Raglan intended to do, for when Sir George Brown rode up to join them the Marshal snapped his telescope shut and said to Raglan, 'Do you intend to turn their flank or attack in front?' Looking at the wide plains rolling away to his left Lord Raglan said that the extra miles of marching necessary for a flank attack would take too much out of his men, and that in any case with his hopelessly outnumbered cavalry he could not possibly turn the position. Further than that he would not commit himself until the battle had begun. And so St. Arnaud rode away, still in doubt, leaving the English with a plan to be decided by events.[14]

At one o'clock the advance was sounded and the British army moved forward again. In front of the compact marching columns, companies of the Rifle Brigade under Colonel Lawrence and Major Norcott ranged across the plain in uneven skirmishing formation, looking to the Russians like green flies moving over the paler green ground in unrelated groups.[15] Soon the guns of Kourganè Hill opened fire, and the leading divisions spread out into line to make a less concentrated target. The Light Division was on the left in the front line, the 2nd Division on its right. The 3rd Division followed the 2nd, and the 1st Division supported the Light. The 4th Division was slightly to the left and rear of the 1st. So far all had been carried out perfectly in accordance with the rules of military handbooks. But now those unpredictable human factors, for which the manuals cannot allow, interfered with the neatly contrived arrangements and brought them almost to chaos.

Sir George Brown was extremely shortsighted. This was part of the trouble. A man with keener eyes, or one who did not disdain the use of spectacles, would have seen much sooner that the Light Division was not nearly far enough extended to its left and was also advancing at an oblique angle to the rest of the army, so that the men of its right-hand regiment, the Royal Fusiliers, were getting squeezed up against the left-hand brigade of the adjoining division. Soon the flank regiments of these two divisions were inextricably muddled and marching bad-temperedly on each other's heels. 'By God,' Sir Colin Campbell exclaimed as he watched them, 'those regiments are not moving like English soldiers.'[16] No one on his staff dared point this out to Brown or suggest how it might be remedied. He was a man who hated advice. He 'always', an officer in his division wrote of him, '*pooh, poohs* anything that may be told him'.[17]

Lord Raglan saw the danger and sent Colonel Lysons to warn Brown to move farther over to his left. Raglan watched for the order to take effect, but it did not do so. So he decided to go over himself. When he arrived, however, he could not find Brown and instead gave the order to General Codrington, in command of Brown's 1st Brigade. But having spoken to Codrington, Lord Raglan immediately wished that he hadn't. Knowing that the touchy Sir George might well resent, or at least be embarrassed by, an order being given to a subordinate officer, he withdrew it.[18] Frequently throughout the campaign Lord Raglan's excessive sensitivity and concern for the feelings of others were to lead him into similar errors. On this occasion the mistake was never rectified, and the two divisions marched on towards the river increasingly entangled.

Behind them the Duke of Cambridge was determined not to make a similar mistake and when his 1st Division came under fire it spread out into line in rear of the Light Division on so wide a front that its left stretched well beyond the Light Division's left and its right so far into the ground which the neighbouring 3rd Division would need when it deployed that Sir Richard England, its commander, was left with hardly any room in which to manoeuvre. Lord Raglan was thus obliged to withdraw the 3rd Division from that part of the field altogether and place it in support.

The British army was now in nothing like the order in which it had begun the advance half an hour before. To the Russians watching from across the river it looked comfortingly like a rabble. Near the sea the dense columns of the French, followed by the close-packed Turkish battalions, presented the expected appearance of power and force; but these straggling lines of red-coated men opposite seemed strangely weak and uncontrolled. The Russian troops had been told that they would be fighting sailors and, having so poor an opinion of their own Marine battalions, they were not so surprised as they might have been to see the English in these absurdly thin, unmilitary lines.[19] They were not even advancing now but inexplicably lying down in dotted red streaks across the plain below, under a heavy fire.

To have come so far forward and then lie down to rest or wait under this unremitting barrage seemed, to the British officers too, a curious military move. But you could not but admire, one of them thought, the coolness of Lord Raglan himself, whose surrounding group of mounted staff officers in white plumed hats was drawing upon himself a particularly fierce but apparently disregarded fire. Earlier the group had included numerous 'amateurs' and newspaper correspondents. An A.D.C. had asked Lord Raglan if these hangers-on bothered him, as if they did he would send them away. 'No, let them stay,' Raglan said, and then added, 'You know, directly we get under fire, those not obliged will depart, you may rely upon it.' Two minutes later the first shot was fired against them. It fell short and bounced over their heads. 'You should have seen the hangers-on scatter in all directions.'[20]

Lord Raglan remained completely unruffled, 'taking no more notice of the firing than if he had been at a review'.* Turning to give an order to a junior officer, who excitedly and noisily whirled his charger to carry it off, he rebuked him gently: 'Go quietly. Don't gallop.'[21] Careful always to present an appearance of unhurried calm in the face of the anxious stares of his own soldiers, he was as concerned to keep from Russian observers any indications of a flustered command. But there was cause nevertheless for anxiety.

He had, there was no doubt, come too far forward. The leading regiments of Bosquet's division on the French right wing were only now approaching the river around the village of Almatamack, and it would be a long time yet before they had crossed it and clambered up the steep slopes beyond to reach a position from which they could threaten the Russian flank and draw troops away to defend it. In the meantime the British soldiers, lying down on the soft turf, had to

---

* 'Lord Raglan's behaviour,' the Queen afterwards told the King of the Belgians, 'was worthy of the old Duke's—such calmness in the midst of the hottest fire' (MARTIN, III, 136).

endure the fire of the Russian guns without being able to reply to it. They had watched with angry disappointment as artillery teams had unlimbered their guns and unsuccessfully tried to reach the Russian redoubts.[22]

For most of the troops this was their baptism of fire, and they bore it with their special inherited form of courage, resigned, grimly humorous and stoical. They picked out the Russian guns and gave them names—'Bessie', 'Maggie' and 'Annie'—after unpopular wives of sergeants or officers; they shouted obscene insults at the round shot as they came rushing and bouncing over the plain, advising their mounted officers behind them which way to ride to avoid them; sometimes they would have no warning of a shot's approach until, too late, they felt the rush of air and then perhaps a sickening thud as a man was hit and the life crushed out of him. At intervals men could be seen all along the line, dragging still quivering bodies to lay them down in rear of the ranks and then, returning to the front, to lie down themselves once more and wait.[23]

And now, as they waited, their attention was suddenly wrenched away from the rush and thud of the cannon-balls and the shells exploding in the air above their heads by an explosion of infinitely vaster force down by the river. As if it were one enormous powder-barrel the whole village of Bourliouk leapt into flames. The empty houses, packed to the windows with loose, dry hay, were covered in the instant by fiercely crackling fire and billows of smoke. Within minutes the whole village and the bridge to the east of it were hidden. The dense black screen of smoke lay there for hours, unmoving, and obscuring the view like a pall.

The choking fumes and intense heat made the village unapproachable; and De Lacy Evans, whose 2nd Division lay opposite it, realised that when the time came to move he would be unable to advance in extended order, but would have to send in one brigade in front of the other, thus further cramping the line.

At two o'clock an officer rushed up to Lord Raglan and shouted in great excitement, 'My Lord, the French are warmly engaged.' And certainly down by the river's mouth could be heard the quick crackle of rifle-fire. But Lord Raglan, knowing the French skirmishers' habit of shooting as they advanced through thick country to keep their spirits up and to let their commanders know where they were, listened for answering shots. After a moment or two he turned to the breathless officer. 'Are they engaged?' he said softly with that almost extravagant politeness of tone in which he answered officers who displayed a lack of control. 'Are they? I cannot catch any return fire.'[24]

Indeed there was none. Bosquet's division, and the Turkish battalions attached to it, were fording the river unopposed. The fire of three French steamers had already driven the Minsk Regiment inland from the village of Ouloucoul Akles, and Kiriakoff's artillery was not yet in action.[25] Prince Mentschikoff himself remained on Kourganè Hill, still in the happy belief that the left flank where the French were closing in on him was inaccessible. When informed of the startling news he at first refused to believe it. Finally persuaded, he rode off angrily towards the sea, ordering seven battalions of infantry, four batteries of artillery and four squadrons of hussars to follow him. He galloped away more than four miles to the village of Ouloucoul Tiouets, where the horsemen of his escort were seen and fired on by the French fleet.[26]

Bosquet's men were now also being fired on by four guns brought out of Ouloucoul Akles, and when the batteries ordered up by Mentschikoff came on to the field they too opened fire. But the Russian gunners were no match for the French, who had to Mentschikoff's amazement already dragged twelve guns up the hill-side. These guns were at one time engaging nearly forty of the enemy's and slowly overpowering them.[27]

Prince Mentschikoff by now was in a state of mind close to hysteria. Feverishly impatient for the arrival of his seven battalions of infantry, he could think of nothing else and sat watching the artillery in restless anxiety. At last the infantry arrived. But no sooner had they done so than he decided he could do nothing with them after all and ordered them to march back again to Kourganè Hill. He galloped away after them, leaving Bosquet in secure possession of the ground.[28]

But although Bosquet was firmly established there he had neither enough men nor enough guns to advance. He was accordingly obliged to wait on the plateau until he was reinforced. And reinforcements were slow to arrive.

Marshal St. Arnaud, apparently feeling that he had discharged his duty by so doing, had divested himself of two magnificent and heroic sentences. Waving his arm towards the river, he said to General

Canrobert in command of his 1st Division and Prince Napoleon in command of his 3rd, 'With men such as you I have no orders to give. I have but to point to the enemy.'[29]

Canrobert, in brave compliance with these implied instructions, led his men straight ahead, crossed the river and began to climb the steep cliffs now facing him. He was soon in difficulties. The infantry found the going hard enough; for the artillery it was impossible. He was obliged to call a halt; for it was, and is, an axiom of French infantry tactics that massed troops shall not advance across open ground without artillery support.

The men lay down beneath the plateau, those in front protected to some extent by the still sharply rising cliffs, but those in the rear exposed to the full blast of the Russian batteries now firing fiercely from Telegraph Height. And while the men waited there under fire, as the British had been waiting for an hour, the artillery rumbled back down the slope and across the river again and then a mile away downstream to the place where Bosquet's leading brigade had crossed.

Meanwhile Prince Napoleon's division had also come under heavy fire from Telegraph Height and remained amongst the vineyards to the right of the burning village of Bourliouk. The Prince attempted to get neither infantry nor artillery across the river, and his men crouching behind the vineyard walls began to complain that they were being 'massacred'. To add to their confusion and fear, St. Arnaud chose this unlikely moment to call up his reserve division under General Forey and sent one brigade in support of Bosquet, the other in support of Canrobert. The troops came through the smoking, blood-splashed vineyards, increasing the muddle and congestion on an already narrow front.[30]

For half an hour frantic officers, both English and French, had been riding up to tell Lord Raglan of the French army's predicament. He had listened to their pleas and warnings with polite concern. And then a French A.D.C. came up to him with a message to the effect that unless something were done immediately to relieve the pressure on Bosquet's troops they would be 'compromised'. Lord Raglan, disliking the vague word, asked the A.D.C. to be so kind as to express himself in plain French. They would, the officer then said, putting St. Arnaud's fear more clearly, retreat.[31]

By the time the French officer had left him Raglan had come to a decision. As he told Kinglake that evening he could no longer bear the sight of his soldiers lying down so patiently under fire. He had waited a long time for the French movement to take effect, and now it seemed that he should wait no longer. When he decided to give the order to advance he was riding alone at the head of his entourage. He stopped and his staff closed up to him. He spoke a few words to General Airey, whose face suddenly lit up in happiness and relief.[32] A moment later Captain Nolan was galloping towards the front. And then at last, one after the other, the regiments rose to their feet, and the men walked down towards the river.

III

It was hotter than ever now, and the sun shone fiercely down. Some men, already weak from months of intermittent dysentery or diarrhoea and now parched with thirst and exhausted by the heat, faltered uncertainly as they took their first steps. Within minutes the turf was littered with discarded knapsacks and shakos, and here and there the advancing troops had to step over the prostrate body of a man who had fallen fainting to the dizzily swaying ground. When they reached the bottom of the slope the going was harder. Here the smooth turf of the steppe was broken up by walls and fences, orchards and vineyards, and the long, narrow gardens of the scattered houses by the river's edge. The gunfire too was now closer and more intense and, as well as the thud of round shot, they could hear the soft but unmistakable whistle of musket-balls, easily distinguishable from the singing whine of the Minié bullet.[33] Looking up beyond the river they saw the mouths of the heavy guns revealed for a moment through the smoke by short red bursts of flame. Some of the men began to feel that faintness and nausea which comes over imaginative soldiers going into battle for the first time. 'I know that I felt horribly sick,' one of them remembered, 'a cold shivering running through my veins . . . the sights were sickening.'[34]

A few of them got no farther than the unburned outskirts of the village. The tempting comfort of open doors or windows drew them away to the dark safety of cottages and cowsheds, where they crouched shivering with fever and fear, hoping for nothing but oblivion.[35]

The line of advance, never orderly, was now completely broken up, and battalion commanders had to abandon all hope of leading on their men in those neat, parade-ground formations which constant practice had made so apparently simple to achieve.

With the burning village in his front, De Lacy Evans had been obliged to send two regiments under General Adams round to the right of it while he and the rest of the division had to scramble forward as best they could over the ground to the left under a storm of musket-balls, canister and grape. The walls and isolated buildings afforded little shelter, and the men rushed forward in groups from cover to cover in full view of the Russian gunners on the other side of the river. It was a painful and slow advance. Before they reached the Alma, the regiments in the 2nd Brigade alone had lost nearly a quarter of their men, many of them crushed under the ruins of walls tumbled down by round shot.[36]

Farther to the left the Light Division was dashing forward over ground somewhat less exposed, and was making faster progress. General Buller on the far left had been sent off by Sir George Brown with the single laconic order: 'Advance in line. And do not stop till you have crossed the river.' To his right General Codrington with the Light Division's other brigade was almost in the river.

As shortsighted as Sir George, Codrington had the good sense not to despise the use of an eye-glass and kept one securely tied to his forage cap. He had never been in action before, but those who saw him this afternoon could not doubt that he was a soldier. He spoke little and to the point and when he was not talking his teeth were clamped tightly shut behind straight firm lips. He rode unhesitatingly into the river on his small grey Arab horse, and the men behind followed him without question.

But the river was in places much deeper here than nearer the sea where the French had crossed. Part of Bosquet's force had crossed at its very mouth and had forded it by a ridge of sand where the waves rose no higher than the men's knees. Here the current was swift and the bed uneven. Some men crossed without trouble, scarcely getting their socks wet; others fell into pot-holes up to their necks, or were suddenly swept downstream as their feet slipped on a loose stone. Where Codrington crossed, the water rose no higher than his horse's fetlocks, but close to him a horse was swimming in deep water.

'A number of poor fellows were drowned,' a sergeant in the Royal Fusiliers reported. 'Or shot down with grape and canister—which came amongst us like hail—while attempting to cross. Our men were falling now very fast.'[37]

For almost two miles of its length the river was full of troops, holding their rifles and ammunition above their heads as they waded and ran, choked and splashed, through the fast flowing water. All around them the surface plopped and sputtered as musket-balls cascaded down from the steep bank opposite, or flew downstream from concealed positions behind the twisting curves.

On the far bank of the river the land rose slightly for a few yards to form a ledge beneath the steeply rising bank, and it was on this ledge that the officers tried to reorganise their men into some sort of order. It was a virtually impossible task. The scramble through the vineyards and the dash through the river to this narrow ledge of dried mud had mixed them up irretrievably. Men shouted for their officers and officers for their men; sergeants got hold of groups of men of different companies and even of different regiments and offered their services to any officer who would take them over. The bends in the bank cut off the view both upstream and down, so that it was impossible to see what was happening farther along the front. And all the time the Russians at the top of the bank shot down at the easy targets below, unhindered and undisturbed, for Colonel Lawrence had been induced by the suffocating and blinding smoke from the village of Bourliouk to take his skirmishing riflemen far away to the left.[38]

Sir George Brown, whose life for so many years had been spent in the pursuit of discipline and order, was almost distraught at the sight of such chaos. Finding a foothold for his horse, he stumbled up on to the top of the bank, his always red face scarlet with anger, and stared shortsightedly about him; while a group of Russian soldiers stared back, too surprised to fire.[39]

On his left General Buller had crossed the river and formed up on the plains to defend, so he afterwards said, the flank of the army against an expected cavalry attack. He had carried out his vague orders to advance and not to stop until he had crossed the river,·and no more orders came to him. He took no further part in the Light Division's attack. By this time, however, he only had two regiments with him, the 88th and 77th, as nearly all the men of the 19th had got mixed up with General Codrington's brigade.

And General Codrington himself was in no doubt what should be done with them, or with any others who would follow him. Shouting at the top of an unusually loud voice to everyone on the ledge who could hear him, he gave an order at once encouraging and un-ambiguous. 'Fix bayonets,' he bellowed. 'Get up the bank and advance to the attack.'[40]

There could be no doubt about this. The men rushed eagerly at the bank, thankful at last to be led out of so unpleasant and constricting a position, and climbed up on to the top.

About five hundred yards in front of them, on either side of the Great Redoubt, the two dark masses which some of them had noticed from across the river were now seen to be squares of densely packed Russian troops, their long, sombre yellowish-grey overcoats reaching almost to the ground. Behind them, partly concealed by a dip, rows and columns of bayonets glinted in the sunlight. It was a forbidding and menacing sight. And the men now coming up by scores to the top of the river bank had ample opportunity of studying it, for the guns in the Great Redoubt, which the unmoving ranks of grey-coated troops seemed to be guarding as they might have guarded a sacred temple, were silent. The only movement came from the Russian skirmishers withdrawing quickly up the slope.

But no one could doubt that as soon as the skirmishers were safely out of the way the guns would begin firing again. And officers and sergeants did all they could by frantic shouts and gestures to spread the men out quickly into the long, thin lines which would be their only hope of survival. Colonel Lacy Yea of the Royal Fusiliers and Colonel Blake of the 33rd shouted themselves almost hoarse as they urged the men to open out from the congested clumps in which they stood. 'Never mind forming, for God's sake!' Yea yelled at a group of his men who were being made to perform some wholly inappropriate drill. 'Come on! Come on, men! Come on, anyhow!'[41]

And they did. Accepting at last the impossibility of finding their own friends, corporals or officers, they moved out into extended order next to men they scarcely knew or had never seen before at all.

'Up the hill we went,' Timothy Gowing said, 'step by step but with a fearful carnage.... The smoke was now so great that we could hardly see what we were doing, and our fellows were falling all round; it was a dirty, rugged hill. . . . My comrade said to me, "We shall have to shift those fellows with the bayonet, old boy!" '42

Almost as he finished speaking, Gowing's friend was shot in the mouth, and the massive Russian column on his left came slowly lumbering down the slope like a gigantic monster. A Russian observer on the hills above watched it as it seemed to slide slowly and inexorably down the slope towards the thin, ragged line of red-coated soldiers nowhere more than two deep. He 'did not think it possible for men to be found with sufficient firmness of morale to be able to attack, in this apparently weak formation, our massive columns'. But impressionability is not one of the British soldier's faults. And the Russian on the heights continued to watch, 'astonished at the extraordinary firmness with which the red jackets having crossed the river opened a heavy fire'.43 They fired into the mass, calmly reloaded and fired again. Many of them had grabbed handfuls of grapes as they dashed through the vineyards and now held big bunches which they had not yet been able to eat, clenched between their teeth.

Too rigidly drilled or unskilfully led, the Russian column, although not much injured by this peppering, stopped in its tracks and then retired to its original position at the side of the Great Redoubt. And the soldiers who had brought this about seemed as little affected by its retreat as they had been unconcerned by its advance. They closed the gap between themselves and the other advancing troops and went up the slope as before.

There were still not many of them. On the left were the 19th Regiment, which had got swept away from General Buller's brigade, some men of the Rifle Brigade under Colonel Lawrence, who had now found his bearings again, and most of the Royal Welch Fusiliers from Codrington's brigade in the Light Division. One of the other two regiments in his brigade, the 33rd, was in the centre; and on the right were some companies of the 95th, drawn away from the 2nd Division, and the Royal Fusiliers under Lacy Yea. Major Norcott with four companies of the Rifle Brigade was closing in from the left flank, giving a determined covering fire.44

For the first hundred yards the Russian guns remained silent, gently smoking in the sunlight, and the blocks of infantry on either side of the Great Redoubt stood impassive and motionless. As they got nearer the British soldiers could see, above the thick and clumsy greatcoats, the wide, strangely white faces of the Russian soldiers taking shape, and their spiked helmets with the small brass badges glinting in the sun.

And then at last the order was given and the guns opened fire again and for a moment the advancing line hesitated. But then it came on again, backed up now by more men clambering to the top of the river bank and urged on by officers shouting above the rising din. Some groups of men were thrown back into the river by blasts of round shot, others were delayed by drill-conscious officers who thought it advisable to get them into some sort of formation before advancing, but others followed Colonel Yea's advice and came on as they were.

Straight up towards the mouths of the guns the straggling, irregular line of soldiers hurried and scrambled. Too breathless to return the fire, they went on through the shattering noise of exploding shells, the whistle of grape and canister and musket-balls, and the round shot bouncing with irresistible force along the turf. Many men fell, wide gaps appeared, but the rest came on. On the right Colonel Yea was hit on the buckle of his belt by a musket-ball. 'Damn you!' he shouted at an officer who was shot through the foot. 'Damn you! Why don't you come? I've got a bullet in my guts, but I'm going on.'[45] Soon the remains of his regiment came up against the enormous Russian column standing beside the Great Redoubt and began a heroic fight which was to last almost as long as the battle.

In the Redoubt itself, protecting the gaily coloured ikon of St. Sergius blessed by the Archbishop of Moscow, the soldiers of Holy Russia tended their guns with the expert ease that comes from long practice: loading, firing, sponging down and loading again with a quick but unhurried rhythm. But fast as they fired, however well they aimed, the tenuous, dispersed line of advancing men was too elastic to break.

Suddenly through the drifting smoke the British soldiers nearest the Redoubt heard the jangle of artillery teams and the screech of wheels twisting on stony earth. Someone shouted, 'They're taking away the guns.' A moment later, after an almost simultaneous blast from all the guns had torn even wider holes in the British line, the firing stopped. The Russians, imbued with the knowledge which was now almost a tenet of faith that on the Czar's own orders they must on no account lose a gun, were taking good care not to risk doing so. The soldiers spared by the Russians' final blast ran on towards the parapet walls.[46]

A young and boyish officer in the Royal Welch Fusiliers, carrying the Queen's Colour of his regiment, planted it in the loose earth of the parapet. No sooner had he turned round in proud and childlike pleasure than he fell dead, shot through the chest, and the silk, dragged down with him, covered his body like a crimson shroud. A sergeant quickly took the stave from him and, although wounded, held it aloft as a rallying signal for the men behind him.[47]

The earth of the Great Redoubt now swarmed with excited soldiers cheering and shouting, some of them scratching names and initials or the number of their regiment on the brass barrel of a howitzer which the Russians had not had time to take away; others sitting exhausted in temporary safety behind the shallow walls trying to get their breath. Outside the Redoubt Captain Bell of the Royal Welch Fusiliers caught sight of a Russian gunner frantically whipping three horses, which were struggling to drag the wheels of a gun out of a rut. He jumped out of the Redoubt and ran towards the gunner, and pointing his pistol at his head he signalled at him to get down. The gunner jumped off the carriage and ran away. Sir George Brown then came up, still scarlet with rage, and ordered Captain Bell to return immediately to his company. Before he did so Bell quickly pulled round the horses' heads and sent them rattling with the gun down the slope.[48]

The Great Redoubt was captured. But although Codrington and Brown instantly set about placing the men in positions from which it might be defended, the chances of successfully doing so, unless reinforcements came quickly, seemed remote. And as if to add to their fear that the capture was only a minor and costly victory temporarily allowed, there came from the vast numbers of Russian soldiers on the slopes outside a 'long, sorrowful, wailing sound' at once piteous and alarming.[49]

IV

In the two directions from which supporting troops might have been expected, the slopes up to the Great Redoubt were bare of movement except where wounded men struggled and stumbled amidst the debris of battle.

To the left General Buller had watched the progress of Codrington's brigade and had realised he must help it. He sent a message to Colonel Egerton in command of the 77th ordering him to advance, and he prepared to do so with the 88th himself. Unfortunately, Colonel Egerton did not think highly of his Brigadier-General's capacity and, seeing on his own front further Russian battalions supported as he knew by cavalry, he decided to ignore the order and stay where he was.[50]

Now General Buller suffered from the same affliction as his fellow brigade commander Codrington and his divisional commander Sir George Brown. He was very shortsighted. And like most shortsighted men he was ready to believe that men with good eyes saw much farther than they did. So not only did Buller condone Colonel Egerton's refusal to obey his orders, but he also decided to keep the 88th where it was. Indeed, so alarmed had the Colonel made him that, not content with keeping it there, he ordered it to form square to repel cavalry, although no cavalry was either in his sight or in anyone else's.

The other supports which the men in and around the Great Redoubt looked for in vain were from the 1st Division. But neither the Highland Brigade nor the Guards had yet crossed the river.

The Duke of Cambridge, in fact, was being very slow and very cautious. The orders he had received from Lord Raglan were indeed somewhat vague. He had been told to advance in support of the Light Division. That was all. What, he would like to know, exactly did it mean? The Duke was not a man of great initiative and with more definite orders or stronger guidance would have done better than he did, for he was by no means unintelligent. But overcome by the fear of making a mistake and near to losing his nerve he decided, like General Buller, to stay where he was. At one time he rode up to Buller and said, 'What am I to do, Buller?' 'Why, your Royal Highness,' Buller replied, 'I am in a little confusion here—you had better advance, I think.' He decided, however, not to take the advice that he had asked for.[51]

His division at this time was on the far side of the vineyards, and it was here that General Airey rode up to him and found him anxiously wondering what to do. It was Lord Raglan's intention, Airey said in that categoric tone of voice that brooked no denial, that his Royal Highness should instantly continue his advance in support of the Light Division. So eventually the 1st Division moved on again. But in the vineyards it came under fire and stopped once more. After a few minutes, however, a breathless rider from General De Lacy Evans's staff galloped up to the Duke and told him to advance. And so at last, with the Highland Brigade on the left and the Guards Brigade on the right, the 1st Division marched down to the Alma.

It moved in splendid order. Seven of the officers in the Grenadiers had been adjutants, and the precision with which their regiment marched through the gardens and vineyards towards the river was magnificent. The men walked into the river as if they were about to cross a road, unhesitating, not moving a yard to right or left to find a better crossing-place. Some walked easily across; others waded in water up to their cross-belts; a few swam, the weight of their enormous bearskins forcing their heads down into the water; one or two were drowned.

But when the survivors of the 1st Division reached the far bank of the Alma, they had come too late. The troops in the Great Redoubt were now under so heavy a fire from the batteries higher up Kourganè Hill that many of them had jumped out of the battery and refused to follow Codrington when, urging them to come after him, he had ridden back over the parapet on his still unharmed grey horse. No one could blame them. The place was an 'inferno of exploding shells' and if they were to hold it, they could best do so by defending the ground outside.

There was another danger now too. For advancing on them from the right was an immense square mass of infantry. Hidden by a dip in the ground the men themselves could not be seen. But a forest of bayonets glinted above the line of turf which marked the edge of the hollow. Then the spikes of the helmets appeared, and then the flat white faces and soon the whole long first rank could be seen tramping forward in silence.

The muskets were dipped now, the fixed bayonets pointing towards the Great Redoubt. Suddenly a voice which no one recognised shouted: 'The column is French! Don't fire, men! For God's sake don't fire!'[52]

The order not to fire was passed along from man to man and from group to group all along the straggling ranks lying around the Redoubt. And despite the urgent efforts of several officers to correct the mistake, the order was at first obeyed. Colonel Chester of the 23rd rode up and down the lines where his men lay clustered, shouting at them that the column was not French but Russian and commanding them to fire. But as soon as he fell from his horse, shot twice through the chest, another mounted officer went up to a bugler of the 19th and ordered him to sound the 'Cease fire'. The bugler did not recognise the officer, who, he said afterwards, was certainly not in his regiment, but nevertheless he did as he was told.

A few moments later another mounted officer—or it may have been the same one, as he was never identified afterwards—came up to another bugler and told him to sound the 'Retire'. Many other buglers on the field who heard the call took it up and repeated it. But by this time a shower of musket-balls was whipping into the ground behind them, and the men thought it safer to stay where they were.[53]

In this confusion of bugle-calls, contradictory shouts and lack of known orders, several junior officers, mainly of the 23rd, collected together to decide what to do. Disdaining the relative safety of the parapet walls, behind which they might have crouched in conference, they conducted their discussion with cheerful bravado standing up in full view of the enemy, who took good advantage of the opportunity so recklessly presented and shot nearly all of them. Those who escaped decided that they must hold the ground at all costs.

There were few men left disposed to agree with them. One of their sergeants stood up and insisted that the repeated bugle-calls must surely be obeyed. Like his colonel a few minutes before, he was shot and killed as soon as he had spoken.[54]

By now the men were edging back of their own accord. Around them and behind them, sprawled all over the slopes of the hill, were nine hundred killed and wounded bodies; and the survivors knew that they could not hope to hold back the oncoming hordes unaided. Taking advantage of a slackening in the enemy's fire they fell back towards the river, leaving to the enemy the ground they had so dearly won.

The heavy Russian column came slowly on as far as the Redoubt, but there it halted, waiting for the support of another column marching down from the crest. But as the distance between the two columns narrowed Prince Gortschakoff and General Kvetzinski saw something which so much alarmed them that any thought of pursuit was rejected. Already anxious about the fate of Prince Mentschikoff, they looked across the heights towards the sea in the direction he had taken and from which he might soon return. Instead of seeing him they saw, standing on the top of a high ridge jutting out from Telegraph Height, a group of officers who should not have been there. These officers, calmly conferring so far behind the Russian lines, wore the flowing white plumes of the English General Staff.[55]

V

Lord Raglan, on issuing his divisional commanders with their brief orders, had decided to ride on ahead to get a good view of the battle. Leaving his staff to follow him and his army behind him, he trotted off towards the river, downstream from the village of Bourliouk where the flames leapt fiercely to the sky and bullets knocked showers of sparks out of burning hay-ricks. With the quick and practised eye of a keen field sportsman, Lord Raglan found a track and a ford, and was soon amongst the French skirmishers clearing the way for the advance of the left wing of Prince Napoleon's division.[56]

The skirmishers looked in amazement at the extraordinary English general riding past them in his blue frock-coat, white shirt and black cravat, like a country gentleman out for an hour or two's exercise on his estate. They paused in their loading to stare at him, their ramrods half-way down their barrels, as if they were wondering what on earth he was up to, passing through them into the heart of the enemy's position.[57]

Soon he was beyond them and amongst the Russian skirmishers on the higher ground. A well-aimed shot hit one of his gaily plumed staff in the shoulder, and then another officer was knocked from his horse. But the remainder trotted on higher and higher up the slope, between the high hedges where the shot whistled over their heads.

Lord Raglan, dipping down into a gully on his right, now found the going rather hard and Lord Burghersh called to him: 'This seems a better way, my Lord.' So Raglan turned Shadrach's head to the left and joined the others on the easier path they had found. The bay horse had become infected by his master's excitement, and although he had been calm enough before he was now so restless and eager it was impossible to keep him still. And when at last Lord Raglan reached the top of the ridge he could only use his telescope with the greatest difficulty.

But even without it the view commanded from this position was magnificent and revealing. Below him on his left he could see the batteries in the valley and beyond them the whole of Kourganè Hill and the upturned soil of the Great Redoubt; behind him to his right great columns of Russian infantry were drawn up in reserve. Not many hours previously one of these battalions had been posted on ground close to where he sat, but now no troops were near enough to threaten him and no guns in the battery could reach him. He might have been drawn to the spot by divine guidance.

It needed no second glance to realise the possibilities of this commanding position. Immediately Lord Raglan sent back Airey to bring up General Adams's brigade from De Lacy Evans's 2nd Division.

'Our presence here,' he said, knowing that the Russians could not fail to be alarmed by the sight of his clustered staff, 'will have the best effect. Now, if we only had a couple of guns.'[58]

Overhearing his words Colonel Dickson, attached to his staff as interpreter, and Captain Adye, both of the Royal Artillery, turned their horses round without further orders and galloped back as hard as they could towards the river. Lord Raglan awaited their return with characteristic patience and restraint, talking about his horse as if for the moment Shadrach held more interest for him than the battle, then watching silently as the men of Codrington's brigade came up from the river and captured the Great Redoubt, only to be beaten back again for lack of support. So far away he could do nothing to help them.

Much sooner than anyone might reasonably have expected them, Dickson and Adye came back again and soon two guns were firing enfilading shots at the batteries in the valley below. The first two shots went wide, but the third hit a wagon drawn up behind the guns and the fourth went raking through the battery itself. Suddenly a staff officer shouted: 'Look! They're carrying off their guns.'

The two nine-pounders now turned to fire on the infantry battalions drawn up in reserve, and here again only two shots were needed to find the range. The third and subsequent shots ploughed through the dense masses, laying open great gaps in them, until they gave way and retreated out of sight.[59]

Once more the guns turned, and this time tried to reach beyond the valley to the columns by the Great Redoubt, and again they were successful, for although they were out of range General Kvetzinski believed his men would come under fire if they advanced down the slope in pursuit of Codrington's broken brigade and therefore held them back.

And thus it was that a few well-placed shots from two nine-pounder guns had given the British a short respite from further slaughter, and a temporary advantage.

VI

For the French, however, there was no such comfort. Bosquet was still isolated on the heights waiting for reinforcements; Canrobert, also across the river, was waiting for his artillery to come up; while Prince Napoleon remained in the vineyards.

Napoleon indeed had been put in an acutely difficult position by the defection of more than a quarter of his force. His best regiment, the 2nd Zouaves, had decided they could be kept waiting no longer and they marched across the river to join forces with the 1st Zouaves in Canrobert's division. This was only part of his trouble. The reserve brigade which St. Arnaud had called up to support Canrobert now blocked the narrow pass in front of him for more than a mile. It remained there in a long, snake-like, immovable formation throughout the battle. Apart from being a hindrance to Prince Napoleon it was, of course, no help to Canrobert. And Canrobert without the benefit of its assistance, and without artillery, did not feel in a position to resist a Russian counter-attack should one be made.

One soon was made. Prince Mentschikoff on his way back to Kourganè Hill hesitated, and for a moment considered leading the attack himself, but eventually he decided the threat to the Great Redoubt was more worthy of his presence and he left the problem in the hands of Kiriakoff, who professed himself confident that his own brigade alone was more than a match for two enemy divisions.[60]

With eight battalions Kiriakoff marched across Prince Napoleon's front, where the reserve brigade lay out of view congested in the pass, and prepared to attack Canrobert. And Canrobert, as he had expected he would have to do, withdrew to lower ground.

The sight of these eight battalions marching so determinedly in front of them made Prince Napoleon and St. Arnaud extremely nervous, and they sent an *aide-de-camp* with an urgent request for help from the English, who, so far as they could find out, had done nothing yet to help in the attack.[61] The *aide-de-camp* galloped up the slope towards the English staff, dismounted at the bottom of a ridge too steep for the horse to climb, clambered up on foot, lost his hat, and arrived in front of Lord Raglan so agitated and breathless that at first he could not speak. Lord Raglan was one of those men who find the embarrassment of others highly infectious. He also blushed readily. The French officer stood in front of him panting and gasping for words, and as Lord Raglan politely leant over in his saddle towards him his face flushed hotly under his sunburn.

'Milord, milord,' the young Frenchman eventually managed to say, 'nous avons devant nous huit bataillons.'

'Je puis,' Lord Raglan replied comfortingly, prepared to let him have one of the two which Adams had been asked to bring up, 'je puis vous donner un bataillon.'

The *aide-de-camp* rushed back to his horse, evidently astonished at the *tranquillité* of the English staff, and carried the promise to St. Arnaud.[62] But by the time he arrived Canrobert had already given way, and the English army needed all the battalions it could muster.

VII

Colonel Lacy Yea's single battalion of the Royal Fusiliers was at this time the only infantry unit still heavily engaged with the enemy. Outnumbered more than two to one by the massive Regiment of the Grand Duke Michael it had been losing men steadily for an hour, and at last, but scarcely perceptibly, was beginning to lose ground.

Yea himself, shouting and swearing as obscenely as the most foul-mouthed of his sergeants, was still there, riding his cob in and out of his ranks, spreading his men out, encouraging them, now galloping back to bring up a few lagging stragglers, now rushing forward again, seeming to enjoy himself as much as if he were in the midst of the Wall Game at Eton which as a boy he used so much to relish.

Although he was hated in peace time as a brutal martinet, his men could not but admire him now. Constantly in the sights of the Russian marksmen, the nearest of whom were less than fifty yards away, he rode up and down his ranks as the musket-balls whipped by him ·but miraculously left him unharmed, except the one which neatly cut off his moustache. Once saved by a corporal who shot one of his would-be assassins, he turned in his saddle and said with a gruff, unaccustomed condescension: 'Thank you, my man. If I live through this you shall be a sergeant to-night.'[63]

Encouraged by his recklessly heroic example, men would rush forward from the scattered ranks firing their rifles hysterically at the dense mass of maddeningly uniform white-faced troops. 'Come on, Eighth Company,' an officer shouted, infected by this mood of desperation, and dashing up to the front rank ran one Russian through with his sword and knocked another down with his fist before a third shot him dead.

In the Russian ranks too there was an officer who encouraged them with the same energy that Yea himself displayed. Presumably he was an officer—although men and leaders alike wore that same long drab grey overcoat, and it was difficult to tell—but certainly he behaved like one. Immensely tall, he strode about between the ranks, until his towering head and shoulders became objects of respect not only in the eyes of his own men but also in those of the Fusiliers, who seemed reluctant to shoot him. Their colonel had to order one of them to do so.[64]

With his death much of the spirit went out of his men, who by now had lost many of their other officers as well. Prince Gortschakoff himself rode up to them in an effort to encourage them to make a bayonet charge, but they were too demoralised and he had to leave them to carry on the fight in their own, increasingly reluctant way.[65]

Prince Gortschakoff had seen that the Royal Fusiliers also were on the point of collapse. Twelve officers were either killed or wounded and more than two hundred men. A determined bayonet charge could not have been withstood. A few minutes after he had given up trying to bring it about, however, the situation had completely altered.

De Lacy Evans, with the two regiments of Pennefather's brigade and the remaining one from General Adams's, had at last been able to get across the river. As soon as Lord Raglan's two guns had opened the mouth of the pass by forcing the batteries in the valley to limber up and retreat, he had seized his opportunity. Sir Richard England, whose 3rd Division was still in reserve, had come up to him and offered him all his artillery; and he had been able to cross not only with three battalions but also with several guns.

Evans and England had thirty guns between them. But several teams had difficulty in dragging guns across the river and at least two got inextricably stuck in it. Others were delayed by misleading or contradictory instructions. Captain Biddulph, the intelligent adjutant to the 3rd Division's artillery, was furious with the 'shocking old woman' Sir Richard England for giving him such vague orders.

We were [he indignantly wrote to his father] in a very ambiguous way told to go there or there with a pointing attitude—no place or position selected. I believe if it had not been for me the battery would have been entirely cut up. We advanced and found no opening in the line and the line not by any means far enough in advance for us to open with 9 prs against guns of such calibre as 18 or 24 prs. We were soon in the thick of it. A shot passed like the devil under my horse's belly, one across my bows, one knocked off a gunner's head, another went through a horse.

Two guns came rattling back past him, as it was 'too hot' for them. He told his colonel that it was 'a shame and a ruin to keep his battery under such a fire when nothing could be done'.

When the battery seemed on the point of destruction, however, one of De Lacy Evans's three infantry battalions, the 55th under Colonel Warren, arrived in a position up the valley where it could support the Royal Fusiliers by firing on the left flank of the Russian column. The 55th opened a heavy fire, and immediately the column wavered. Officers with drawn swords walked about between the ranks, threatening, shouting, pleading. Sometimes one of them could be seen going up to a frightened soldier and shaking him by the throat. But shout and threaten as they did, it was too late. Slowly the mass began to move back and soon it was in full retreat; with the British artillery 'banging away at it'.[66]

And now at last the Guards had come up. Major Sir Thomas Troubridge of the Royal Fusiliers galloped back to the Grenadiers behind him and told them that the Russian column was in retreat but that his own regiment was in no state to pursue them. The Grenadiers agreed to pass through the ranks of the Royal Fusiliers in pursuit.

But the Regiment of the Grand Duke Michael was already re-forming in line with the Great Redoubt. Supporting it, in and around the Redoubt itself, were other immense Russian battalions stolidly watching and waiting. None of them had yet been heavily engaged. They numbered in all not less than 15,000 men. The Guards Brigade, confident, proud and immaculate, marched up the slopes of Kourganè Hill against them.

VIII

The Grenadiers, on the right, although now under heavy fire, came on in that same exemplary formation in which they had advanced to the river. They passed through the Royal Fusiliers, met a few strag-gling groups from the 95th on their way back from the Great Re-doubt and, in the words of their commanding officer, Colonel Hood, 'opened out to let them pass, and closed up as coolly as if in Hyde Park'. A few paces more and they came upon other remnants of the force that had retreated from the Great Redoubt. There were about three hundred men in all, and Codrington was doing his best to re-form them under the colours of the Royal Welch Fusiliers. Now that the Guards had come it would be a good opportunity, Codrington thought, to re-form them on the left of the Grenadiers and advance up the slope with them. But he was a Guardsman himself and re-membered his protocol. The Grenadiers might not like being so closely associated with a regiment of the line, and he thought it best to ask permission before embarrassing them. Would the Grenadiers mind having a line regiment on their left? Yes, the Grenadiers would mind, they said, and went on alone.

Not all of them were so particular. When Major Hume of the 95th asked permission for himself and eight of his men to join the Grenadiers in their advance, Colonel Frederick Hamilton, who com-manded the left wing, consented. It would have been as well, he thought afterwards, if Codrington's offer of a considerably larger force had not been rejected, as now there was a wide gap on the Grenadiers' left, where the Scots Fusilier Guards, who had marched from the Alma a few minutes before them, had met with a terrible reverse.[67]

At first, although under heavy musket-fire, they had advanced in excellent order. But a short way up the slope they had come across a number of men of the Royal Welch Fusiliers who had rallied and were holding their ground as they fired back at the Great Redoubt. The Scots Guards came up to them just as an enormous number of Russian troops swarmed on to the parapet walls of the Redoubt and fired a shattering volley into the Royal Welch, who consequently retired with such speed and violence that several Guardsmen were knocked over, one with such force that he broke his ribs. The previously neat line was now ragged and faltering. Several officers, led by Hugh Annesley until a musket-ball tore out part of his tongue and twenty-three of his teeth, shouted: 'Forward, Guards! Forward, Guards!' Young Robert Lindsay carrying the colours was pushed so far forward that the line began to resemble an arrow-head, with Lindsay at its point, facing the very centre of the Great Redoubt.

Men fell on all sides in the ferocious musket-fire, but on the others rushed until they came to within less than forty yards of the redoubt, when, with a sudden roar, the Russians jumped out of it with their bayonets at the charge.

Hoping it was not too late to save the men from massacre, General Bentinck ordered them to retire.

'The battalion will retire,' Captain Hugh Drummond, the adjutant, yelled, waving his pistol in the air as he galloped up with the order to the front. But the battalion did not feel inclined to do so. Indeed it was difficult to see how the leading men could retreat without being cut down by Russian bayonets before they had forced their way back through the congested ranks behind them.

'The battalion will retire,' Captain Drummond ordered again, and then a third time, and at last in a frantic shout, 'The battalion *must* retire.'

Obeying this final appeal, the Scots Guards fell back. But the Russians were now so close that several of them were slashed in the back and killed as they ran away down the slopes. They did not stop until they reached the river line, where their pursuers left them and allowed them to re-form.[68]

It was a horrifying humiliation. A hundred and seventy-one men had been killed or wounded, including eleven officers. And a huge hole was torn in the middle of the Guards Brigade.

Prince Gortschakoff was quick to seize his opportunity. Leading them in person, he brought down two Russian battalions in a furious bayonet charge towards the left flank of the Grenadiers and into the gap between them and the Coldstream. Colonel Hood brought his battalion to a halt. The Coldstream were too far away to be of any help. He was about to give the necessary instructions to prepare his men to meet the charge as best they could when one of those mysterious mounted officers, who rode up from no one knew where, came on to the scene and gave a baffling order:

'Retire!'

'Retire!' Colonel Henry Percy, one of the left-wing company commanders, repeated. 'Retire! What the devil can they mean?'

The anonymous officer had now ridden off to give the same order to the equally indignant Coldstream and so could not be questioned.

'I suppose,' Colonel Percy decided, 'they must mean "dress back".'

And in accordance with this generous but brave and sensible interpretation the left wing of the battalion fell back to form a right angle with the remainder.[69] As soon as they had completed the movement, the Grenadiers opened fire on the Russians charging down through the gap. One of the first bullets killed Prince Gortschakoff's horse. The Prince himself was thrown violently on his head to the ground and, confused and slightly concussed, walked disconsolately back up the hill leaving General Kvetzinski in command. The success of the left wing's accurate fire encouraged the men in the centre and on the right to wheel round and join in the firing. They did this 'instinctively', Colonel Hood reported, and 'the effect was instantaneous'. The Russians 'checked perceptibly with astonishment at the telling nature of our flank-fire'. The value of the Minié rifle in the hands of men well trained to use it was being amply proved.

Seeing the havoc which they were causing in the dense masses, the Grenadiers began to cheer with excitement. For several minutes they cheered and fired by turns, and then the Russian column began to hesitate on its ground. Colonel Hood saw his chance. 'The line may advance by the centre. The men may advance firing.' Later he wrote home of the great effect of 'this common-sense manoeuvre of a line against a dense column. I hope due credit will be done to my fine fellows, for it was a proud sight to see them behave so well. . . . In five minutes the Russian column faltered, then turned, then ran.'

General Kvetzinski, supervising its retreat, had his horse shot under him. Then he was shot in the leg, so that he had to be carried on a litter by the men of his rearguard, then in his other leg and then in his side. Despite his wounds he continued to give orders and encouragement to the men around him, as the Grenadiers, with the Coldstream on their left, and the Scots Fusiliers, who had reformed with remarkable speed and courage, came after him.

The Duke of Cambridge, riding with the Coldstream, trotted over the parapet wall and into the Great Redoubt, deserted except for the wounded, groaning and bleeding into the churned-up earth.

IX

The Guards had broken the Russian defences on the right, but on the left there were still twelve untouched Russian battalions. And there were only three battalions left on the field to contend with them.

But these three were the Cameron Highlanders, the 93rd Highlanders and the Black Watch, three of the finest regiments in the whole army. And they had as their brigade commander a soldier with as much experience of fighting as anyone on the battlefield that day.

Sir Colin Campbell had served under both Moore and Wellington. He had fought all over the world, in Spain, in America, in China. He had been wounded four times. He was both brave and talented. Twice he had commanded a division in India. But he had no influence and little money, and when war with Russia had been declared he was, after forty-four years' distinguished service, still a colonel. No other brigade commander was as highly respected by his men.

Before leading them on he said to them:

Now men, you are going into action. Remember this: whoever is wounded—I don't care what his rank is—whoever it is must lie down where he falls till the bandsmen come to attend to him. No soldier must go carrying off wounded men. If any soldier does such a thing his name shall be stuck up in his parish church. Don't be in a hurry about firing. Your officers will tell you when to do so. Be steady. Keep silent. Fire low.[70]

The brigade had moved off in echelon, the Black Watch slightly ahead on the right, the 93rd in the middle, the Cameron Highlanders somewhat withdrawn on the left. Like many Highland officers Sir Colin held most other regiments in a disrespect which was close to contempt. On passing the 88th, still standing patiently in square to repel the invisible cavalry, he angrily told them to get into line. 'Let the Scotchmen go on,' a man cynically retorted. 'They'll do the work.' And on being told that the Guards, advancing under a ferocious fire, would be destroyed and ought to fall back, Sir Colin turned furiously in his saddle. 'It is better, Sir,' he said, 'that every man of Her Majesty's Guards should lie dead upon the field than that they should now turn their backs upon the enemy.'[71]

That was something he was determined his own men would never do. They might die, but they would never retreat. They went on, sweeping round the back of the Great Redoubt, into an increasing musket-fire. Men fell all around him, but the ranks never wavered. Sir Colin himself, riding with the Black Watch, had given them orders to advance firing, which was something only controlled and steady troops could do without more danger to themselves than to the enemy. They were performing the exercise perfectly. But behind him on his left the 93rd were being too restless and eager, and he had to ride back to them to calm them down. He halted them, made them dress their ranks, although they were under heavy fire, and would not let them advance again until they were once more in unbroken lines. While supervising the operation Sir Colin's horse, already twice wounded, was shot in the heart and sank slowly to the ground. No sooner had Campbell taken the horse of his A.D.C. than his English groom came up; touched his cap politely, more in deference to an employer than in a military salute; and apologised for being so forward, but the musket-balls were falling so heavily on the ground in the rear that he felt Sir Colin's chestnut would be safer up in front. The brigadier mounted his other horse and the 93rd moved on again.[72]

The silent, determined advance of the tall, improbable-looking soldiers seemed to the Russians, so the wounded prisoners afterwards confessed, both irresistible and unearthly. From left to right the line extended for more than a mile, and, unused as they were to seeing the formation, they had no reason to suppose that behind the screening wreaths of smoke it was only two ranks deep.

Out of the whorls of smoke figures would appear tramping towards them in deathly silence, across the soundless turf. Only the sharp crack of their rifles was real. They wore dark chequered skirts and curious bonnets with high plumes. The smoke twisted them into strange shapes. Folds in the ground hid their legs, so that some of the enemy thought they were horsemen and others not men at all but ghosts.[73]

The Russian columns were firing still, but fear was getting a hold on them and officers once more were moving about in the ranks, their swords flashing in the air, as the rifle-bullets whined and thudded about them.

Soon that strange, hollow wail as of a dying animal again filled the air. But by this time the menace had gone out of it. It seemed a cry of agony and despair. And as it died away the columns broke and fled.[74] Sir Colin Campbell raised his hat in the air, and the Highlanders around him, given permission at last to shout, cheered so loudly their voices were heard two miles away. Sir Colin, himself, went over to report to Lord Raglan. His chestnut horse had now been shot and he was on foot. When he found Lord Raglan, there were tears in his eyes. As his Highlanders had done so well could he, he asked, have permission to wear a Scottish bonnet? Lord Raglan smiled and nodded.[75]

All over the battlefield men walked about congratulating each other. 'There was such a shaking of hands,' Somerset Calthorpe said, 'one felt very choky about the throat and very much inclined to cry.' Colonel Lacy Yea was crying. The tension was over, and he had broken down. A colour had been lost. 'A colour gone!' he sobbed. 'And where's my poor old Fusiliers? My God, my God.' He 'cried like a child wringing his hands'.[76]

X

Prince Mentschikoff came back in the very moment of disaster. Riding across the valley towards Kourganè Hill he met Prince Gortschakoff, still muddled from his fall, on the ground where so short a time before the Russian reserves had proudly stood. Mentschikoff fired at Gortschakoff a series of angry questions: 'What's this? What's the matter? Why are you on foot? Why are you alone?'

Gortschakoff wearily replied, 'My horse was killed near the river. I am alone because all my aides and staff officers have been killed or wounded. I myself,' he added, holding out his tattered coat, 'have received six shots.'[77]

As he spoke two English guns, dragged up quickly into commanding positions, roared at the disordered masses of his retreating soldiers. Taking no steps to prevent the withdrawal becoming a rout, Mentschikoff rode away up the hill. He joined a group of his men and, after riding for a minute or two in silence, he exclaimed with the sudden anger of despair, 'It is a disgrace for Russian soldiers to retreat.' A nearby officer turned on him, furious and drunk. 'If you had firmly told them to stand, they would have held their ground.'[78]

It was too late now. Behind them on the knolls, where the English staff had stood, there were now red lines of troops; and in the valley several heavy guns fired unceasingly with round shot, canister and rockets up the pass, scattering the Russian infantry 'like sparrows, and doing great execution'.[79]

Lord Raglan, having placed Adams's two battalions on the knoll and pushed forward his guns, rode over towards the Great Redoubt to join the Duke of Cambridge. From here he saw that the Earl of Lucan had brought up the Horse Artillery and had placed it in battery on the right of the Highland Brigade, where it was firing on the retreating army.

Lucan and Cardigan impatiently awaited orders to take their cavalry in pursuit. But Lord Raglan, anxious, in his own phrase, to keep his small cavalry force 'in a bandbox', and not to risk it for the sake of a few enemy guns or prisoners, sent the Adjutant-General over to Lucan with orders for the cavalry to escort the guns farther forward. 'The cavalry,' Estcourt added of his own accord, seeing the irritation in Lord Lucan's face, 'are not to attack.'[80]

The cavalry refrained from attacking, but they did gallop forward of the guns to take some stragglers prisoner. Twice Lord Raglan, watching his activities apprehensively, sent an A.D.C. forward to Lucan to call him back to his escort duty. Lord Lucan sulkily complied with the order, setting his prisoners free.

On the right Kiriakoff was withdrawing before Canrobert's guns, which were now across the river and in battery. For a time he stood his ground on Telegraph Height despite heavy gunfire, but his depleted eight battalions were no match for the mounting force of the French army. He too joined in the general retreat, and the Zouaves led the way to the summit of Telegraph Height, ruthlessly bayoneting the few Russians who had been left there either by mistake or as a pathetically inadequate rearguard. French regimental colours were tied to the scaffolding of the unfinished pillar of the Telegraph building to provide a welcome for Marshal St. Arnaud, who rode up to the summit of the hill in the belief that a ferocious fight had just taken place there. 'I thank you,' he said in a voice which could make the simplest phrases sound dramatic, 'I thank you, my Zouaves.'[81]

So far as he was concerned it was the end of the battle. He had been in his saddle since early morning, and it was now half-past four. The excitement of the day had filled his dying body with a nervous energy, but now all was spent.[82] When a message came to him from Lord Raglan asking him to join the English in pursuing the enemy, he refused. It was 'impossible' for the French to go on, Lord Raglan was told. In any case their knapsacks were still in the valley, and they would have to go back for them.[83]

Lord Raglan himself wanted to pursue the enemy with Sir Richard England's 3rd Division, the cavalry and the horse artillery, but he did not feel justified in doing so without the French, so orders were given for the army to bivouac for the night on the ground where it stood.[84]

Disappointed and saddened by St. Arnaud's lack of co-operation, Lord Raglan trotted back through his army down towards the river. He was cheered vociferously by the men and even by the wounded lying on the slopes. Scarcely acknowledging the cheers, which always filled him with an embarrassment so sharp it was close to anger, he went down to Bourliouk, where in the charred and smoking buildings the surgeons were at work amongst the wounded. For an hour he went from house to house, talking to the men lying patiently in rows against the walls. One of his A.D.C.s was with him and wrote home in horror of the surgeon's 'arms covered with blood, the floors strewed with limbs just amputated and slippery with gore'.[85]

On the slopes above the village and on the plains behind it the wounded lay groaning and crying piteously for water. The surgeons, still wearing their full-dress uniforms, their instrument cases slung across their shoulders, worked in the fading light, going from man to man, operating on the bare ground or on doors wrenched from barns and cottages.[86] 'There are far too few of us,' Dr. Skelton said. 'I performed all the operations in my power for Russian and English indiscriminately.' But there seemed no end to the numbers. The dead and wounded lay in piles together. 'Here Russian, there English—in one spot lay five officers of the 23rd dead. One of them the Colonel—they suffered very severely.'

The Russians, unlike the British, had kept their fire low, and most of the wounds were dangerous and painful ones in the stomach and lower part of the lungs.[87] Soon after six the sun went down, and the surgeons did their best to carry on with their work in the dark. There was no room left in the houses. On the cold and open ground figures crouched over suffering bodies in the flickering light of fires. There were hardly any lamps, few instruments, almost no drugs. All night the screams and groans and whispered pleas for water filled the air with an agony of sound. Sometimes a musket-ball went whistling across the slopes as loaded Russian musket barrels, used by soldiers as grates for their fires, exploded in the heat, or a wounded Russian fired on an English soldier crawling towards him in the darkness.[88] Even the surgeons and the soldiers who spent the whole night carrying water to friends and enemies alike were not spared by these Russian prisoners, who fired on anyone who approached them and sometimes on the English wounded lying near them. 'My attention was drawn to one nasty case,' Timothy Gowing wrote. 'A young officer of the 95th gave a wounded Russian a little brandy out of his flask and was turning to walk away when the fellow shot him mortally.' On the beach a wounded Russian shot a sergeant in the back when he was giving another Russian soldier a drink of water.[89]

Several similar outrages were reported. 'The Russian officers were gentlemen, but their men were perfect fiends.'[90]

The feeling was reciprocal. 'We expected to have to fight soldiers,' the wounded A.D.C. of a Russian general said when he was taken prisoner, 'not red devils.'[91] Any hope that the war might be conducted with chivalrous respect was gone now. Already each side thought of the other with hatred and bitterness. Wounded prisoners were treated with scant care by guards and orderlies, and sometimes forced to recite 'Nicholas! no bono' at the point of the bayonet.[92] As soon as they died their bodies were as likely as not to be stripped by French soldiers. The Zouaves, indeed, hardened by years of savage Algerian warfare, were inured to the sight of mutilation and death. They could be seen happily chatting and eating their meals surrounded by neat rows of wounded men and corpses. Their burial parties were conducted in the most haphazard way and with a grisly humour. Midshipman Wood was shocked to see a Zouave shovel a corpse into a grave and then pick up a loose leg and stick it in the corpse's crutch.*

The British burial parties too were mostly carried on without the pretence of ceremony, the dead being tipped wholesale into long and shallow pits. 'A trench was dug a certain length and six feet wide. The bodies were collected and laid in a row beside this long grave. Then fifty or sixty of them were dragged up by the heels into the pit, packed side by side in their bloody uniforms and covered up.'⁹³ And as the soil was shovelled over them, the vultures flapped their wings and flew away to fresh prey.

Bad as things were on shore, the filth and chaos on board the hospital transports at sea was appalling. On some ships the only medical attendants were a few soldiers' wives. On others the surgeons could scarcely move about the decks for the piles of sick and wounded.

Already the sickening smell of putrefaction filled the air, and ordure and vomit covered the decks and the lice-ridden clothes of the dead and dying. Flies and beetles crawled across the slime into the food. Maggots swarmed in festering wounds. A staff surgeon climbed on board the transport *Caduceus*, where there were more than four hundred men with cholera, chronic diarrhoea or dysentery, and found 'no medical appliances of any kind were on board', and yet the 'crew were busily engaged in receiving more sick men, or tying up and throwing overboard men who had been lifted on deck dead, or had died shortly after leaving the boats'.⁹⁴ When the *Caduceus* eventually sailed for the hospitals at Scutari there were 430 men still alive on board. By the time she arrived more than a quarter of them were dead. The horrors and mismanagement of a war which even now brings tears of rage and pity to the eyes had begun.

For two days the army collected together the wounded and buried the dead; parties of marines and sailors endlessly went up and down between the heights and the mouth of the river carrying sick and crippled men on bits of canvas slung between wooden poles. And high up on the hill, where disappointed soldiers opened hundreds of

* Captain Clifford's Kaffir servant, with a kind of macabre innocence, rushed excitedly about the battlefield inspecting the armless and legless corpses and thinking they looked 'like apples in an orchard'. He came back to his master loaded with Russian swords and helmets. 'This is very beautiful,' he said, 'so plenty men dead. Legs and arms all over. All Sir's enemies.'

knapsacks to find nothing more exciting than a few lumps of black bread and broken biscuit, a luckier one than the rest found a picnic basket with six cold chickens and two bottles of champagne inside. Scattered around the basket were several shawls and parasols, a 'lady's bonnet very nicely trimmed', and, unaccountably, a petticoat. Here on a platform, specially erected for their benefit, had sat 'many Russian ladies' invited by Prince Mentschikoff to watch through pearl-handled opera-glasses the defeat of the invading armies.[95]

7

FLANK MARCH

Land the siege trains! But, my dear Lord Raglan, what the devil is there to knock down?

Major-General the Hon. Sir George Cathcart

In the early afternoon of the day after the battle Admiral Lyons called on Lord Raglan and found him 'in low spirits'. During the morning Raglan had had two interviews with Marshal St. Arnaud and at both of them had failed to get the French to agree to the plan of following the success up rapidly, and trying to 'take the Northern Forts [of Sebastopol] by a *coup-de-main*'.[1]

The French troops were too tired to move on immediately, St. Arnaud said. They must have rest and time to reorganise themselves. Besides, he had heard that the passage of the next river, the Katcha, would be strongly resisted and that the one after that, the Belbec, was defended not only by great numbers of Russians but also by enormous earthworks. The allies could not afford the loss of life which would be involved in forcing them. Lord Raglan confessed himself 'disappointed' by the Marshal's attitude, but did not press his point further for fear of disrupting an alliance for which he felt the Government held him personally responsible.[2]*

For the second time now in two days St. Arnaud had behaved in a way which Raglan considered incompetent and feckless, but the English general remained as calm and polite, reasonable and accommodating, as the French had learned to expect him to be. Indeed, on this occasion—and there were to be others—Lord Raglan's unemphatic expressions, his immediate willingness to understand the French point of view, were positively misleading. St. Arnaud seems to have been genuinely unaware of his anxiety to push forward; and because Lord Raglan carefully avoided comment on his disagree-

---

* The Government, in fact, gave him full credit for the difficult preservation of the alliance. In the enthusiasm which followed the news of the victory on the Alma the Duke of Newcastle wrote to assure the Queen that 'never since the days of the Great Duke has any army felt such confidence in and love for its leader, and never probably did any general acquire such influence over the allies with whom he was acting'.

ments with his allies in his official communications with the Government, the French were subsequently able to present themselves as held back from following up the victory on the Alma by Lord Raglan's *'lenteur'*. A few months later Raglan was to confess that the maintenance of the French alliance weighed on his mind with the heaviness of an obsession, and he regretted that he had always conformed with their ideas. For the moment, however, he believed the preservation of an *entente cordiale* to be essential, and understood how dangerous might be the political repercussions of an open breach. In any case, to act alone might prove a military as well as a political disaster, for he had lost more than 2,000 of his best men killed and wounded in the battle; and although the Russians had lost 5,500, their army still numbered well over 40,000 and was constantly being reinforced. Russian regiments were marching to the Crimea from all over the south of Russia.[3]

Lord Raglan was convinced that he should not advance without the French. And those who have criticised him for not doing so have not always been aware of the emphasis laid upon the necessity for joint action by the British Government. 'It is not intended,' his original instructions read, 'that in every operation of a minor character an equal number of the two armies must be jointly employed. This might sometimes be inconvenient, but you will take care that, even in such cases, previous concert shall be secured.'[4] In any event he needed the French. They had lost 1,600 men and officers, St. Arnaud had told him. But he put the figure himself at 560 at the most.[5] They now had more men than he had, and hardly any of them had yet been heavily engaged with the enemy. To hear their officers talking, though, Lord Burghersh thought, you might have been forgiven for supposing that they had won the battle single-handed. St. Arnaud, indeed, made no bones about taking a lion's share of the credit. 'Victory! Victory!' he wrote to his wife. 'Yesterday I beat the Russians completely. I took their formidable positions which were defended by more than 40,000 men. They fought bravely but nothing could resist the impetuosity of the French.' 'I lost fewer men than the English did', he told his brother in another letter, 'because I was quicker. My soldiers run; theirs walk.'[6]

It was a form of vanity which sometimes made Lord Raglan lose his usual calm and understanding tolerance. That night at dinner, when a trumpet sounded shrilly from the French camp, he said quite petulantly, 'Ah! there they go with their infernal *toot-toot-tooting*; that's the only thing they ever do!'[7]

By the evening of the next day still nothing was decided. The French refusal to advance quickly on Sebastopol had given Lord Raglan an opportunity to get his wounded aboard the fleet. Without adequate facilities for doing so this was necessarily a lengthy process, and St. Arnaud was now able to complain that it was the English who were holding up the advance and not himself. 'It is quite true,' he told his brother, '*qu'ils ont plus de blessés que moi, et qu'ils sont plus loin de la mer.*' But there it was, once again, '*les Anglais ne sont pas encore prêts*'.[8]

At last both armies were ready, and on the warm and sunny morning of 23 September 1854 they marched down from the heights above the Alma into the lovely valley of the Katcha. The scent of thyme and lavender filled the air, and the soldiers were able to pick huge bunches of grapes and fill their pockets and knapsacks with melons and onions, apricots and pears. Occasionally the cackling of hens could be heard over the garden walls, and there would be a shout and a squawk and a flurry of feathers as the men leapt upon their prey. The cottages were neat and attractive and the people who lived in them, when they could be persuaded to approach the strangely clothed foreigners, pleasantly shy and friendly. For the first time the men saw that not all the inhabitants of the Crimea were peasants. They passed several large country-houses. 'You never saw such plunder,' Lieutenant William Richards told his aunt, 'as some of the men got [from these] villas of the Russian nobility and the rich people of Sebastopol. . . . The houses were very magnificently furnished, pier glasses 7 feet high, beautiful china, gilt furniture, etc.' The ground was littered with Russian equipment dropped during the headlong flight of the army into Sebastopol. Broken wagons, knapsacks, blankets, hats, kitchen utensils, boxes of ammunition, parts of Prince Mentschikoff's elaborately fitted field-kitchen, were spilled and scattered everywhere. But of the army itself there was no sign. Nor was there any sign of the earthworks on the Belbec which St. Arnaud had mentioned with such respect. The report of a strong battery at the mouth of the river and heavily armed ships in the Sebastopol roadstead brought the armies to a halt for two hours, but it proved to be false, and when they moved on they were not molested.[9] The Russians

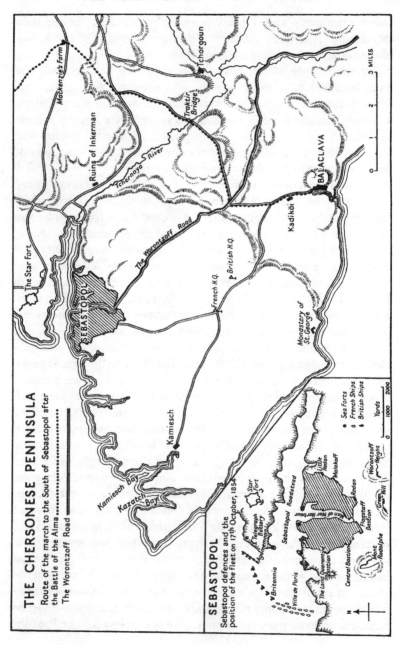

THE CHERSONESE PENINSULA

Route of the march to the South of Sebastopol after
the Battle of the Alma ....
The Worontzoff Road _____

SEBASTOPOL
Sebastopol defences and the
position of the fleet on 17th October, 1854

had, in fact, been in such haste and disorder during the retreat that not even the bridges over the river had been destroyed, and the buckets still hung undamaged at the well-heads.[10]

Although several more cholera cases had to be left behind on the Belbec, the health of the army was generally improving despite the vast quantities of fruit, much of it unripe, which the men could not be prevented from eating. And morale had never been higher. There was a feeling that the war was as good as won. A rumour went round the army that Mentschikoff had cut his throat and the gates of Sebastopol were to be opened.[11]

And so in a mood of new confidence the allies marched up the far side of the Belbec valley, and came on to the crest of another hill. But it seemed a special hill marking the end of a journey, for now at last below them, its dazzling white buildings, steep streets and green copper domes beautiful and quiet in the sunlight, was the town of Sebastopol.

A long, deep stretch of sparkling blue water, on which many ships rode peacefully at anchor, cut the town in two. On the far side of this roadstead were the main buildings of the town, the naval barracks, the arsenals, the dockyard installations, the handsome churches, the Admiralty building with its curious onion-shaped tower, the classical library and the Temple of the Winds. The far side of Sebastopol was also cut in two from north to south by the wide Man of War Harbour, which ran right through the town from the forts overlooking the roadstead to the southern walls. On the north or nearer side there were several storehouses and a naval barracks but little else. Above them, however, and not far below where the allies now stood, was a star-shaped fort of obvious strength. It stood on a spine of raised ground with gun embrasures facing north and south as well as out to sea. Numerous other gun emplacements on the steep cliffs jutting out over the sea guarded the entrance to the roadstead.

As he looked down on the town and at the massive solidity of the Star Fort, St. Arnaud became suddenly weak and tired. He got off his horse and lay face downwards on the ground. Too ill to join them, he left the English to discuss the problem of attack. He had already said that it should be made from the south.[12]

Lord Raglan himself still favoured an attack on the north side backed, as it could be, by a fierce bombardment of the south side by the fleet.[13] He was inclined to agree with a naval captain who had lain at anchor in the harbour before the war and had subsequently reported that 'on carrying the position of the [Star] fort on the north, the place would fall immediately'.[14] Todleben, the most able Russian officer in Sebastopol, also subscribed to this view and so did Prince Gortschakoff.[15] On the north side of the harbour there were at this time only eleven thousand men, most of them sailors and some of them armed only with pikes and cutlasses.*

A successful attack on that side would have inestimable advantages even if the south side did not immediately fall, for a sustained operation against Sebastopol from the north would bring the allied armies across the roads leading out of the town towards the isthmus at Perekop, the only line of communication between the Crimean peninsula and the Russian interior.

St. Arnaud, however, was not the only senior officer who advised against an attack from the north. Accompanying the British army as an expert adviser was a wizened seventy-two-year-old general of the Royal Engineers, whose experience was unsurpassed and whose advice was considered invaluable. The illegitimate son of the popular singer Susan Caulfield and the General Burgoyne who had allowed himself to get surrounded by the American rebels at Saratoga, he had passed out of Woolwich before the end of the eighteenth century. He had been a practising engineer ever since and enjoyed an international reputation.

General Burgoyne gave several cogent reasons why a march inland and around Sebastopol to its south side would be preferable. He argued that an attack from the north was obviously now expected, and that by attacking from the south the allies would not only enjoy the advantage of surprise, but also the advantage of assaulting what, from all reports, was still an imperfectly entrenched position; for of the several redoubts along the southern edges of the town not one was yet complete. Furthermore, the ground from which the allies would operate on the south side afforded much better cover than on

* Despite the opinion of some later writers it is difficult to believe that Todleben and Gortschakoff were wrong. Russian prisoners certainly felt that had the victory on the Alma been followed up Sebastopol would have fallen. 'A Polish marine came in to-day from Sebastopol,' Hugh Annesley wrote in his diary on 23 September, 'and he says if we had followed them up on the 20th we might have entered the forts along with them, they were so done and dispirited.'

the north; and, in the event of a protracted siege operation, Balaclava afforded a better harbour for the fleet than any that could be used within reasonable distance of where the allies now stood.[16] In spite of Burgoyne's arguments Lord Raglan still preferred an immediate attack before the Russian army had time to reform. He thought constantly of the danger of losing contact with the fleet, while he took his army through an unknown and wooded country with inadequate maps. He felt, nevertheless, that a delayed attack would suit the mood of the French staff better, and asked Burgoyne to go to their headquarters and propound his views. Burgoyne did so, and the French staff, reluctant at first but afterwards persuaded by the tired St. Arnaud, who did not want to argue any more, agreed in principle.[17] Close at last to agreement with them, Raglan himself went to see St. Arnaud the following day. By now it was known that the Russians had sunk several block-ships across the entrance to the Sebastopol roadstead, and there consequently seemed less likelihood than there had been immediately after the Alma that Sebastopol could be quickly taken. And even if it could be, the problem of supplying the army until the block-ships were raised would be a very real one. Lord Raglan, who had in any event preferred the idea of an attack from the south when still in England, was now persuaded that the allies had left it too late to attack from the north and asked St. Arnaud if he were now in a position to commit the French to Burgoyne's plan. St. Arnaud nodded. There was something vaguely alarming in the Marshal's stiff formality, the way he sat rigidly in his chair with his hands gripping the arm rests. As they left one of Lord Raglan's staff said how regally he had behaved. 'Didn't you see,' Lord Raglan answered him, 'he's dying.'[18]

A few hours later St. Arnaud was in the agonies of cholera. The next morning he was too ill to see Lord Raglan when he called on him. But at half-past eight the march around Sebastopol began.

The English led the way, and the French cheered them as they passed.

II

So as to leave the forest track clear for the artillery and cavalry, the infantry had to march south-south-east by compass. The route led through the thick brushwood of a dense oak forest, and the men stumbled along, pushing the tangled branches aside, swearing as they sprang back to sting across their cheeks, hot, bad-tempered and still parched with thirst.

Ahead of them on the track was Lord Lucan with the cavalry and horse artillery. His orders were to reconnoitre with a battalion of the Rifle Brigade as far as a group of buildings, once the home of a Scottish admiral who had supervised the construction of the naval defence of Sebastopol at the end of the eighteenth century, and now accordingly marked on the map with the unlikely but friendly-sounding name of Mackenzie's Farm. The track ended by these buildings and came out on to the main road leading from Sebastopol to Simpheropol. He was not to move out of the wood but to maintain a careful watch on Mackenzie's Farm and on the road leading past it. With him, acting as guide, was Major Wetherall of the Quarter-master-General's staff.

It proved an unfortunate choice. For in the middle of the wood the track forked. Major Wetherall, after a moment's hesitation, led the cavalry up the right-hand fork. The track became rougher and rougher, every few hundred yards it became more and more difficult to discern, and then it petered out altogether. Major Wetherall was lost.

The horse artillery had not been able to move as fast as the cavalry, and when it came to the fork a lone hussar told them which way Lord Lucan had gone. The artillery officers looked at it in amazement. It was, one of them decided, 'a mere wood-cutting road'. They could not take their guns up there. It was evidently a mistake.[19]

They were standing there wondering what to do when Lord Raglan with his staff and a cavalry escort trotted up to join them. Lord Raglan was at first annoyed to see the artillerymen apparently halting for an unauthorised rest, but when shown the track the cavalry had taken, he realised their officers were right; and leaving them at the fork, he led the way up the other track.

A little way beyond the fork General Airey came up beside him. They talked softly as they trotted together down the track. Just before they came in sight of Mackenzie's Farm, Airey noticed a gap between the trees in front and asked if he might ride on ahead to investigate. He galloped up the track towards the opening and then suddenly reined up. It was as if his horse had abruptly shied at a jump. Quickly he raised his hand above his head, and there was no mistaking in the gesture the urgent warning to be quiet and to halt. Just in time he had stopped the horse from taking him out of the wood and on to the road from Sebastopol. For on the road, strolling about, talking, smoking and leaning against the sides of wagons which stretched in a long line down the hill and out of sight, were scores of Russian soldiers. For a moment Airey sat still watching them. They were obviously the rearguard of a large force resting on the march. But the wagons, Airey noticed in surprise, were facing away from Sebastopol. Mackenzie's Farm was a charred and smoking ruin.[20]

Lord Raglan, realising that Airey had reached the edge of the wood, turned round in his saddle and in a 'low, tranquil voice' told two staff officers to find out what had become of the cavalry. Another officer was sent back to the fork to fetch up the horse artillery. Then Lord Raglan moved slowly forward to join Airey.[21]

Some Russian soldiers, lying on the verge of the wood in front of him, looked up and caught sight of his blue coat between the foliage. They were so surprised they stared at him for several seconds without moving. Even when they had gone, presumably to report the presence of two enemy generals calmly watching them through the branches, the Russian column neither moved on nor showed any signs of entering the wood. Lord Raglan sat firmly in his saddle, contemplating the enemy, as if their total destruction was about to take place.[22]

The staff officer had now got back to the horse artillery and told them what had happened. 'Instantly,' Captain Shakespear wrote in his diary, 'the words—Get Lord Raglan out of the way—were said by everyone as we got our guns on the move.'

But Lord Raglan had no mind to be got out of the way. He was sitting in his saddle where he liked to be—at the very head of his army. He was in perfect control both of the situation and of himself. Although when Captain Chetwode, the officer commanding his escort, at last galloped up to him, followed by a breathless and red-faced Lord Lucan, he controlled his anger with evident difficulty. 'Lord Lucan,' he said in an ice-cold voice, 'you're late!'

Even now the cavalry moved slowly. The 8th Hussars were so long in coming up that the horse artillery would not wait for them, and dashed on by themselves, 'impetuous for the fight'. The guns wheeled out into the road and in less than a minute, Shakespear wrote, had come into action, blasting round shot down the hill, 'the enemy flying before us. We limbered up and pursued as hard as our guns would go for 10 minutes. Suddenly the road turned to the right and to our astonishment a regiment of infantry was formed across the road, front ranks kneeling within 30 yards of us. They fired a volley but were so bewildered *nothing* touched us, except two horses were slightly wounded in the legs. Then they bolted into the bush.'

The cavalry came galloping past in pursuit. But true to his often protested design of keeping them for an emergency or for when a real advantage could be gained, Lord Raglan called them off. They must at all costs, he had told one of their colonels a few evenings before, be 'shut up'. The men, understanding little of the reasons for this apparently excessive caution, were furious with disappointment.[23]

But the loot was fascinating. In the carts were crates of food, wigs, long sheepskin coats, hussars' fur-lined pelisses, women's under-clothing, bottles of coarse and ferocious brandy, pornographic novels in French. Sitting incapably drunk in one cart was a Russian artillery officer. He had an empty champagne bottle in his hand and was singing happily. He greeted his English captors with protestations of everlasting devotion, pressing them to have a drink from his bottle, which proved, on his offer being accepted, to be empty.[24]

He seemed to have been the only officer present with this part of the rearguard and was brought to Lord Raglan to explain why his men were moving out of Sebastopol and how much of the Russian army was doing so.

Far from being able to give any intelligible information, he could scarcely stand on his feet. English soldiers laughed at him, with that sort of amused, contemptuous affection which they usually feel for the paralytically drunk. Lord Raglan looked at him in disgust and appalled embarrassment. Unable to bear the sight of a drunken officer being ridiculed, he turned his back on him, the hot flush he could never hide on such occasions reddening his sunburned face like a crimson mask.[25]

The encounter appeared to have upset him much more than his near escape from walking into the hands of the enemy. When Lord Cardigan came up to him at this moment he said to him sharply,

'The cavalry were out of their proper place. You took them much too low.'

'I am, my Lord,' Cardigan replied in the injured but self-satisfied tones of one who knows he is in the right, 'no longer in command of the cavalry.'[26]

Cardigan was annoyed, Lucan was furious, Raglan and Airey were irritated by both of them. Everyone seemed to be in a bad temper. The men, thirsty and tired, their faces and hands scratched by the thorns of the brushwood, were now given the added frustration of finding that the well in the yard beside the still smoking ruins of Mackenzie's Farm had been filled in by the Russians.[27]

The army moved down the steep road into the valley of the Tchernaya River in sulky silence.[28] Later on that night, in a thick fog, the French followed them. At eleven o'clock they stumbled into the British rearguard at Mackenzie's Farm and there they camped. It was always afterwards known as *le camp de la soif.*[29]

III

Lord Raglan established his headquarters for the night in a little stone hut where the Traktir Bridge crosses the Tchernaya. The baggage of the staff had not arrived by nightfall, and they would have had nothing to eat had not Captain Thomas of the Royal Horse Artillery shot a wild boar, a leg of which he sent to Lord Raglan with his compliments.

Lord Raglan's German servant cut the leg in slices and grilled them over a bright and crackling fire. The spirits of the staff began to improve. The pork was excellent. Someone lent Lord Raglan a tin plate and a fork, but the others ate their pieces in their fingers, sitting cross-legged round the fire, talking cheerfully.[30]

Only the Commander-in-Chief seemed quiet and anxious. Soon after supper he went to the stone hut; but not to sleep. When Nigel Kingscote, with the rest of the staff, lay down for the night by the banks of the river, a light was still shining through the hut's single window.

'We were,' Lord Raglan wrote afterwards, 'in a dangerous situation.' Cut off now from the fleet, still waiting at anchor at the mouth of the Katcha, his army lay in a valley in the heart of an unknown and scarcely reconnoitred countryside, an ideal object for attack. Many of its best men lay sick, wounded or dead behind him, with one of his five infantry divisions as their only protection.[31]

He never felt more relieved, he told his wife a few weeks later, than when he saw the sun come up the following morning to shine on an army rested and not attacked. Before the troops had finished their breakfast of salt meat and biscuits, he was in his saddle and crossing the Tchernaya. He had sent back a message through the forest to the fleet with instructions for it to be brought round to Balaclava, and he wanted to lose no time in getting there himself.

About four miles from the Traktir Bridge is the little village of Kadiköi. It stands on the plateau above Balaclava, which is hidden from it by the sharply falling cliffs. It was a pretty village with grapes hanging in clusters round the cottage porches, and when Lord Raglan entered it with his staff he was greeted by its few remaining inhabitants as a hero and conqueror. They told him that Balaclava below was undefended.

He went on down the track towards it. Near the bottom of the slope the track turned sharply, and he came upon what appeared to be an inland pool, enclosed on all sides by high cliffs. As he looked down into the water a single mortar began to fire from an ancient castle above him. A bomb exploded near his feet and was followed by two or three more. Balaclava seemed to be defended after all, and he sent back for the Light Division to occupy the heights behind him. No sooner had the officer galloped off with the message than a boom of heavy guns was heard from the still hidden sea behind the cliff. The fleet had already arrived. The Commandant of Balaclava, Colonel Monto, left his mortar and came down from his castle, with the four or five Greeks who formed the local militia, to surrender. And Lord Raglan went on beside the water until the road turned again round the corner of the cliff, and he came out into the village and saw suddenly the open sea. The people knelt in the streets and held up trays loaded with fruit and flowers towards him and pieces of bread sprinkled with salt, as a sign of hospitality and friendship.[32]

It seemed, at first sight, with its green-tiled cottages smothered in honeysuckle and clematis, a charming little fishing-village, understandably a popular summer resort for the people of Sebastopol. But it had a vaguely menacing air. The houses and sheds by the water's edge were clustered under steep cliffs of dark red stone which rose steeply and massively, 'perpendicular and tremendous', to the high, undulating plateau far above.[33] The harbour was long and twisting, almost landlocked between its high cliffs of overhanging rock that cut off the view of the open sea and gave it that curious and somehow alarming impression of an inland lake which Lord Raglan had noticed. The waters were undoubtedly deep, so that big ships could come and moor right alongside the harbour walls, but they were also extremely narrow. It was obvious that Balaclava could not serve as a base for both the allied armies.

The English were there first, but the French could consider themselves entitled to it, as when the armies turned about to face Sebastopol it would be on the right of the line. The French staff told Lord Raglan that he could choose between keeping it and staying on the right, or moving over to the left and using the shallower harbours at Kamiesch and Kazatch. Lord Raglan consulted Rear-Admiral Sir Edmund Lyons, who gave it as his opinion that the British army should hold on to Balaclava, which would provide them with the most satisfactory means of communication with their fleet along the whole coastline.[34]

The decision was a grave mistake. Both Kamiesch and Kazatch proved more adequate bases than Balaclava, and the French, by using them, once more enjoyed the protection of the sea on their left flank and that of the British army on their right, whereas the right of the British was open to attack. The problem of finding enough men to defend this flank while at the same time laying siege to Sebastopol was one which was never to leave Lord Raglan's mind.

At the time, of course, no one supposed that the capacities of Balaclava would ever be fully tested. In a week or two, perhaps in a few days, Sebastopol would be stormed and taken. Indeed, both Sir Edmund Lyons and Lord Raglan advocated an immediate assault before the Russian defences could be strengthened. And the Russian commanders believed if an assault had been made with determination and spirit at that time Sebastopol would have fallen. But once more the French did not agree.[35]

It was not St. Arnaud now. For St. Arnaud had been told by Colonel Trochu that to give himself a chance to recover he must be free from worry. 'I understand you,' the Marshal had said after a moment's silence. 'Send for General Canrobert.'[36] St. Arnaud's cholera was almost better, but his heart was failing him. He was taken on board the French ship *Berthollet* to die in peace. Lord Raglan had been to say good-bye to him and had left him with tears in his eyes.[37] 'Although he occasioned me many difficulties,' Lord Raglan afterwards told the Duke of Newcastle, 'I must say I deeply regret him.'[38]

In time General Canrobert was also to arouse in him the same sort of affection. A small but impressive-looking man with a high, domed head, stiffly waxed moustache and piercing eyes, Canrobert, although only forty-five, had been chosen by the Emperor himself to succeed St. Arnaud.[39] He had served with distinction in Algeria and had carried out his unpleasant orders during the December massacres without complaint. A few weeks after Napoleon's *coup d'état* he had been appointed *aide-de-camp* to the President. Despite a misleadingly theatrical manner, he was a brave and popular officer with a high sense of duty and of military discipline. When recommended for promotion to General, his papers described his military qualities as being 'quite out of the ordinary'. He was not, however, suited to high command. 'A commander-in-chief', he wrote himself, 'must not be sensitive on the battlefield. An officer who is tender-hearted in everyday life must become indifferent to the point of hardness in battle.' This indifference was something Canrobert could never achieve.[40]

The thought of an immediate assault, he told Raglan, appalled him. He could not ask his men, whose obedience to such orders was not as unquestioning as that of English soldiers, to walk across open ground in the teeth of guns firing at them both from the redoubts and from the ships in the harbour. Besides, there was the danger of a flank attack to be considered. Prince Mentschikoff had obviously taken his army out of Sebastopol to be in a position to attack the besieging armies from the hills on their right. An assault without the support of heavy guns, he said, would be a crime.[41]

General Burgoyne, for the second time that week, agreed with the French view. Preferring a less dramatic phrase than Canrobert's, he said an unsupported assault before siege-guns had got down the enemy fire would be 'utterly unjustifiable'.[42]

In face of this opposition Lord Raglan gave way. Well aware of its political effect, he immediately rejected a suggestion that the British should assault alone. Anxious above all things to keep the friendship

of the allies free from strain, he not only accepted the French decision
without further argument, but did not even give the impression in his
despatches that any serious conflict of opinion had taken place. Orders
were given for the siege-guns to be landed.

General Cathcart, whose 4th Division was on high ground facing
down towards the very centre of the Russian defences, was horrified
when he learned of the commanders' decision. Ever since the Alma
he had been happily insisting that the Russians would not give any
more trouble. 'He makes rather light', Lord Raglan confided to a
friend with characteristic understatement, 'of what we have before us
now.' He was so convinced of the advisability of an immediate assault
that he had sent a private note to Lord Raglan telling him that he was
'in the strongest and most perfect position I ever saw. 20,000 Russians',
he thought, 'could not disturb me in it. . . . They are working at 2 or 3
redoubts but the place is only enclosed by a thing like a low park
wall, not in good repair. . . . I am sure I could walk into it with
scarcely the loss of a man at night or an hour before daybreak.' So
sure was he of this, and so ready to take offence at what he took to be
the wilful refusal of Lord Raglan to consider the advice of a man
whom the Government had decided should succeed to supreme
command, that when Lord Raglan rode up to him on the evening of
28 September to tell him what had been decided, he exploded with
indignation.

'Land the siege-trains! But, my dear Lord Raglan, what the devil
is there to knock down?'[43]

At this time indeed there was little; but with every hour that
passed there was more. Looking through their glasses at the growing
mounds of earth outside the town, English officers on the heights
above could not but marvel at the determination and industry of the
swarming figures of men, women and children who worked all day,
and then through all the night by the light of lamps and flares, to save
their houses from attack.

8

SEBASTOPOL

If I myself give the order to retreat, kill me with your bayonets
Vice-Admiral Korniloff

The people of Sebastopol were being inspired in their determined resistance by two remarkable men.

Vice-Admiral Korniloff, chief of staff of the Black Sea Fleet, a deeply religious as well as a stirringly patriotic man, had the intense, romantic appearance of the young Napoleon. Energetic and ubiquitous he would appear with dramatic suddenness before his devoted disciples, reining in his handsome, snorting horse to deliver himself of the striking phrases expected of men of destiny. 'If I myself give the order to retreat, kill me with your bayonets,' he told a group of soldiers. And they did not doubt that he meant it.[1]

'Let the troops be first reminded of the word of God,' he commanded the priests, 'and then I will impart to them the word of the Czar.' And the priests became as ubiquitous as he was himself. As the men and women toiled to improve the town's defences, they were sprinkled with holy water and encouraged by Gregorian chants. The bastions were blessed and the spades and pickaxes were touched with holy relics. And all day long and for much of the night the priests walked on from trench to trench and gun to gun, singing and praying and holding high their crosses and images, their gonfalons and ikons, proclaiming that God was on the side of Holy Russia.[2]

The garrison had need of Him. Prince Mentschikoff, after his defeat on the Alma, had led his army into Sebastopol only to lead it out again. He had done, as General Burgoyne said, 'exactly what was right'. He had ensured that his field army would not be cut off from its supplies and reinforcements already on their way from Kertch and Odessa, and he had placed it in a position where it could hover unseen on the flank of the allies like a hawk in the fog, lay siege to the besiegers and attack them at their weakest points. But although Mentschikoff had done what was right, he took no advantage of his opportunities. At Mackenzie's Farm, when the straggling allied armies had stumbled into his rearguard and given him a chance to make them fight in the worst possible conditions, he had continued his march and left open the way to Balaclava. And now several miles away from Sebastopol, he did not even take steps to find out where the allies were, let alone attack them. He 'seemed lost', one of his officers wrote and he was certainly no help at all to the garrison.[3]

'Of the Prince,' Admiral Korniloff wrote in his diary on 26 September, 'nothing is to be heard.' The next day went by and there was still no news of him, and 'the evening passed in gloomy thoughts about the future of Russia'.[4] Mentschikoff had left Sebastopol to be garrisoned by sixteen thousand men, three-quarters of whom were sailors, some of them armed only with boarding-pikes.[5] General Möller, in command of the land forces, had a single battalion of engineers; the rest of his men were ill-trained militia. Both he and Vice-Admiral Nachimoff, who had been left to share the command of the sailors with Korniloff, were despondent and unsure of themselves and relieved when the dynamic Korniloff seemed willing to take supreme command. They were relieved also that there was in Sebastopol a man who was not content to rely for its defence on rhetoric, faith and courage.

Lieutenant-Colonel Franz Eduard Ivanovitch Todleben was a man whose talents as a military engineer were close to genius. Born in the Baltic provinces of Russia, Todleben was in appearance, origin and temperament a Prussian. He was tall and broad-shouldered and had a commanding presence. His eyes were penetrating, his nose long and beaked, his large, well-brushed moustache followed in its downward curves a wide, determined mouth. He was only thirty-seven but already enjoyed a reputation as a revolutionary military thinker, refusing to accept the concept of a fortress as a static position. The defences of a fortress, as of an entrenched position, must, he thought, be made elastic and capable of constant alteration and modification as the exigencies of the siege demanded. It was an idea which, given time, he was determined to apply to Sebastopol.

He was given the opportunity of doing so almost too late. He had been introduced by Gortschakoff to Mentschikoff as a man who had given helpful advice at Silistria and would certainly be useful at Sebastopol. On arrival in the Crimea he had received Prince Mentschikoff's permission to study the defences of Sebastopol, but his report had been so unflattering to the Prince that Mentschikoff had suggested that he should leave. Todleben did not immediately do so, and within a few days the allies had landed and the danger that Mentschikoff had dismissed as chimerical was real and urgent. The young Colonel of Engineers was left to do in a few days the work of months.

Immediately he accepted the impossibility of making Sebastopol impregnable overnight. The sea defences on the east were already strong. Several earthworks and stone gun-emplacements effectively covered the entrances to the roadstead, and a line of ships had been sunk on Mentschikoff's orders across its mouth. This had brought tears of rage and humiliation to Admiral Korniloff's eyes, as it had made it impossible for the Black Sea Fleet to get out of the Man of War Harbour, but it had at least made it impossible for the allied navies to get in. A successful attack from the west could also be discounted owing to the length of the roadstead and the deep and narrow ravine at its end which could be raked by a murderous fire from the fleet and from a few land batteries on the crests of the ridges above the ravine. And so it was on the north side that Todleben had expected an assault after the retreat from the Alma. The immense Star Fort had accordingly been strengthened and improved and other defences had been built. Even so he believed, as Raglan had done, that an attack on the north could not have been successfully resisted.*
But now the allies had gone round to the other side of the town, and he could devote all his energy and talents to the defence of the south.

Owing to Prince Mentschikoff's stubborn insistence that the allies would never reach Sebastopol and that good money should not be spent on needless defences, there was much to do. And Todleben, riding on his immense black horse backwards and forwards, day and night, along his line of gun-emplacements saw that it was done. Leaving a mass of letters, orders and directions unanswered or un-opened on the desk in the room he shared with Korniloff, he went out siting guns, extending fields of fire, linking batteries, ensuring that each night, if not complete, the defences were as sound as they could

* Sir George MacMunn's suggestion in *The Crimea in Perspective* (1935) that the expression of this view in the book which Todleben edited may have been influenced by his wishing to make Sebastopol's defences appear weaker at the beginning of the campaign than in fact they were, and thus his own achievement the more remarkable, seems not only uncharitable but false.

be made until a new day and a few more hours' reprieve brought the opportunity of improving them.[6]

On 25 September when Korniloff, looking through the high windows of the Naval Library, saw the allied armies marching down into the valley of the Tchernaya and realised that the south of the town would soon be threatened, these defences were little more than walls and mounds of loose earth and rubble. But slowly the 'thing like a low park wall' which General Cathcart had spoken of with such disdain became an extended system of formidable strength four miles long. There were six main redoubts, arranged in a semicircle so that the guns in those nearest the town, at either end of the line, could support the guns in those more advanced in the centre.[7] Nearest the sea on the west was the Quarantine Bastion; next to this the Central Bastion; in the centre and sticking out like the blunted point of an arrow towards the allied armies, the Flagstaff Bastion and the Redan; behind and to the east of the Redan, the Malakoff; and farther to the east, the Little Redan. Heavy guns were trundled out of the town and placed in battery in these six redoubts and the smaller ones between them; sailors dragged up ships' guns from the harbour; women carried out wash-tubs and linen-baskets filled with round shot and ammunition; convicts were brought out of the prison and set to work with pickaxes and spades; and children, screaming with excitement, helped their parents throw up these gigantic sand-castles under the warm sun by day, and by the light of flaring torches by night.[8]

The days and nights passed and the assault expected each dawn did not come. On 28 September, Lieutenant Stetzenko came into the town from Prince Mentschikoff to 'enquire about the state of Sebastopol' and was told that the garrison must be reinforced. Two days later the Prince himself arrived, and the request for more men was repeated. Mentschikoff, although his field army had been reinforced by 10,000 men from Odessa, demurred. He had lost so many officers at the Alma, the enemy armies were very strong, he was just about to make a threatening movement against their right flank. Admiral Korniloff lost patience with him and wrote him a letter of remonstrance, a copy of which he intended should be seen by the Czar. Persuaded at last that further resistance might be damaging, Mentschikoff gave way. On 1 October fourteen battalions of Russian infantry entered Sebastopol. By the 9th, 28,000 Russian troops had moved in.[9]

At last Admiral Korniloff could feel secure. 'Notwithstanding the number of our enemies . . . on the south side of the bay,' he now confided to his diary, 'we have no fear of not repelling them. Unless', he added in touching humility, 'our God forsakes us; and in that case His holy Will be done. It is the duty of men to submit to Him in resignation as He is always just.'[10]

Todleben also felt more relieved. Each day his defences were securer than the day before. When it became obvious that the allies were settling down to a siege the garrison troops shook each other cheerfully by the hand as if they had won a great battle. 'Everyone in Sebastopol,' he said, 'rejoiced at the happy event.'

For three weeks the allies had remained silently on the plains to the south, their guns not firing, their fleet lying placidly at anchor. Only the cluster of thousands of tents gave evidence of the presence of large armies, and only the lines and mounds of broken earth suggested what those armies intended to do.

9

BOMBARDMENT

The defences were completely paralysed
Lieutenant-Colonel Franz Ivanovitch Todleben

I

'My own opinion,' General Airey had written to Lord Hardinge in
Whitehall at the beginning of October, 'is that we are here for the
winter.'

It was an opinion which was by now shared by most of the officers
in the army.

At first they had been struck by the unexpected charm of the undulating countryside south of Sebastopol. 'This is a most beautiful
country,' Cornet Fisher told his parents, 'just like England—the
houses are very nicely furnished, quite luxury.' The Russian inhabitants too, he thought, were very pleasant. They 'are', he wrote, 'a
remarkably nice-looking people, most polite in their salutations, and
seem to like us pretty well. They are mostly dressed in long white
blouses, trousers and caps, quite'—it seems to have been for him the
final compliment—'like Englishmen.' Indeed, after Bulgaria, the
Crimea was to everyone a welcome relief.

There were occasional showers, but the weather was still quite
warm and usually sunny. The health of the men had greatly improved
and by 9 October all of them were under canvas. Everywhere there
was fruit for the picking. Poultry could readily be bought by the
officers and stolen by the men. Water was plentiful and so were hay
and firewood. Midshipmen roamed happily about in the harbour
shooting geese and ducks. 'We get 1 pd. of biscuit and ¾ pds. of pork
or 1 pd. of fresh meat per day and a ¼ of a gill of rum,' Lieutenant
Richards told his aunt, 'not much you will say to live on, but we
manage by foraging to eke it out with cabbage, turnips, fowls,
pumpkins, water melons and grapes, the latter beautiful, and we find
have improved the health of the men wonderfully. We even capture
a hive of bees occasionally.' The ships in the harbour were well
supplied, and even if prices were high there was nothing else for the

men to spend their money on, and the goods were readily sold. Officers happily paid £2 17s. for a ham, 3s. for a pound of salt, 5s. a pound for soap, 1s. 3d. each for candles, 1s. a loaf for fresh bread, 10s. a bottle for sherry and 1s. an ounce for tobacco.[1]

On the gentle sea breezes the strains of lively music came across from the French lines, and from the Turkish camps a 'sort of uncouth music with pipes, not altogether destitute of harmony'. The soft green turf was covered with blue crocuses. It was, in fact, compared with what the army had come from, 'quite a garden of Eden'.[2]

The British headquarters were established in a 'kind of country villa with large farm buildings'. The main house, white-washed, one-storied and with a roof of red tiles, faced on to a yard in which the officers of the staff pitched their tents. The yard was enclosed at its far end by a low stone wall and on either side by cottages and sheds, now used as offices and stables, built of mud and stone. It was surrounded by six acres of vineyard. Lord Raglan in his 'little country-house' shared his soldiers' enthusiasm for the pleasantness of his surroundings.[3]

But as the days of early autumn passed and the campaign seemed to have reached a standstill, the mood of the army changed. On their arrival at Balaclava, they had had no doubt that Sebastopol would soon be taken after having been blown to bits by siege-guns. '48 hours will reduce it to ruins,' an officer in the Royal Fusiliers cheerfully told his father. But after a week the siege-guns were nowhere near to being in position, and yet every day there seemed to be new guns firing from Sebastopol, doing little damage admittedly, but giving proof of what they could do when the allied trenches approached closer to them. Digging these trenches, parallels and zigzag approaches was in itself a hated task and had not even begun until 9 October. The ground was hard and stony under the turf, and at the end of each day the distance covered seemed absurdly small. And all the time there were those 'damned Rooskies', 'plainly visible through the glass.' 'They are working like bees', the correspondent of *The Times* reported. 'Women and children are carrying up earth baskets, and already the White Tower on the right of our lines is blocked up with a double line of earthworks pierced for guns'.

The frustrating slowness, working on the men like an irritant, was not the only cause of their ill-temper and complaints. Within a few days the lovely countryside, prolific with fruit and vegetables, had been picked bare as if by a swarm of locusts. And the army returned to its unrelieved diet of salt meat and biscuits, the very thought of which was enough to make a man with diarrhoea or dysentery feel sick.[4] Cholera spread again. In the hospitals in Balaclava twenty-five men a day were reported to be dying at the end of the first week, with 'only a little opium and rum to give them'.[5] Balaclava itself had already become a stinking, congested shambles with ships packed tightly in the harbour like leaves in a blocked drain. Piles of stores, boxes, sacks, bundles of hay, lay in muddled heaps on the quayside, and rubbish and refuse floated and stagnated in the water. Over-worked commissariat officers picked their way through the muddle with bundles of forms and requisitions, invoices and inventories, doing their frantic best to bring order to the chaos; badgered at every corner by enraged regimental officers, who hated and despised them for trying to carry out their duty according to the cumbersome regulations of the Service and who accused them of all manner of dishonesty and neglect. 'That most infernal Commissariat,' Lieutenant Richards said, had converted a few derelict houses 'into what they call stores. . . . When anything is applied for you find Mr. Commissary Jones, Smith or Robinson smoking a cigar (which most likely has been sent out for the army but which he has bagged), who tells you that really he is very sorry he believes that the article is somewhere in one of the stores, but where he has not the slightest idea, and at present he has no time to look for it.'

Even on the plateau above, the mess and muddle and smells in some of the camps were appalling. The streams of clear, fresh water had been trodden to mud, and it was no longer possible to wash in most of them. And as it was getting colder now, the men had little inclination to take their clothes off anyway. Some men indeed ex-cused themselves from doing so by saying that their uniforms would not stand up to the strain. Bleached by the sun, shrunk by the rain, rubbed by equipment, used as bedclothes, torn by brambles, the clothes of many of them, worn continuously for months on end, were certainly not likely to last much longer. 'My shirt is in rags,' a Guards officer told his father as early as 7 October, 'and shoes all worn out, but we are all alike.'[6]

Most soldiers, apart from those like Sir George Brown, to whom a loose button was an acutely painful sight, could happily put up with a ragged, threadbare uniform in summer. But now when the cold autumn winds reached through the flapping rents, sound vests and jackets and greatcoats were enviously admired. Particularly so as all the firewood on the plateau had been collected and consumed as quickly as the fruit and vegetables. 'A very cold night,' Colonel Bell briefly noted in his diary on 9 October, 'and a colder morning. No fuel but the green brushwood.'

In their growing discontent the soldiers looked around anxiously for scapegoats, wondering what on earth the generals were up to.

II

Persuaded by the French and by his own engineers to abandon his idea of an immediate assault before the heavy artillery was landed, Lord Raglan had then decided that the siege-guns should be got as near as possible to the town without spending time in laboriously digging approaches. In order to do this, however, several infantry battalions would have to be advanced in the open to provide support for the engineers. Even if this were done at night, and only the minimum cover were provided for the guns, the undertaking could be a hazardous one. General Burgoyne agreed, nevertheless, that the hazards of waiting for the construction of siege-works might well prove more dangerous. Apart from anything else, the lack of transport in the engineers' department was acute. Indeed, the engineers' total transport comprised less than fifty country carts, and as this was so the conduct of a full-scale siege might well prove impossible.[7]

Lord Raglan's alternative plan of pushing forward siege-guns with infantry support was put to a council of the divisional commanders. In a letter marked 'Most Confidential', the Duke of Newcastle was told that they had unanimously opposed it. Sir George Brown came out particularly strongly against it, not hiding his dislike of a plan supported by Burgoyne, a mere engineer. The suggestion was dropped.[8]

Meanwhile the landing of the heavy guns and siege equipment was proving an operation of extreme difficulty. The pass which led up on to the plateau was steep and narrow. There were not enough animals, too few experienced men. The sailors who cheerfully carried up their naval guns and ammunition had to get up at half-past four in the morning and worked till half-past seven at night. The eighteen-pounder guns were dragged up on travelling carriages lent by the artillery, the others were lashed to drag-ropes and tugged up the hill, fifty sailors to a gun, with the smallest man in the crew sitting on top of it singing a cheerful song or playing a fiddle or whistle. The soldiers, neither so well fed nor so fit, watched them with a reluctant admiration as they themselves struggled up, cursing and grumbling, with loads which they succeeded in making look twice as heavy as they were.[9]

And then on 8 October General Burgoyne 'astonished' Lord Raglan by telling him that 'he saw insuperable difficulties in carrying on his engineer works within breaching distance'. Owing to the rocky nature of the ground below the top few inches of soil, all the British could hope to do was to support the French, on whose front the ground was not so hard, by long-distance bombardment.

Lord Raglan immediately went to tell Canrobert this and to assure him that even so the British would, of course, join in the assault which was to be made as soon as the French cannonade had proved effective. Canrobert was generous and understanding, and the two generals parted on the best of terms.[10]

During the following night, relays of French working-parties of 1,600 men each, digging energetically from dark till dawn in a north-east wind which muffled the clank of their spades and pickaxes, threw up an immense work on a ridge of land, which they called Mont Rodolphe, less than a thousand yards from the Central Bastion. It was an impressive achievement. And they held on to Mont Rodolphe and daily improved its defences, despite the concentrated efforts of the Russian gunners to dislodge them by day, and the attacks of Russian patrols and raiding-parties which tried to drive them off by night.[11]

The British could offer nothing to compare with the French batteries on Mont Rodolphe. Their own works on Green Hill and the Worontzoff Heights, begun on 10 October and later to be known as the Left and Right Attacks, were almost half as far away again; while the two sunken batteries containing the new elliptically bored Lancaster guns were much farther away still. The Russians, indeed, concentrated their fire on the French, believing the British were as yet too far off to constitute a really dangerous threat.[12]

A fortnight had gone by now, and little progress of any value had been made. 'They call it a siege,' an officer wrote home in despair. 'It's more like garden digging. We shan't get anywhere like this.'[13] Then there were other delays. The wooden gun-platforms, which had seemed to be excellent when tried out on soft flat ground at Woolwich, were useless on these hard, uneven slopes. The roofs of several houses on the plateau were stripped of their timbers to make new ones. The Russians burned the rest of the houses down before the engineers could get to them. And so another week went by; and it was not until the night of 16 October that the allies were ready to begin the tremendous cannonade which they believed would lay open Sebastopol to their assaulting armies. But by then yet another of those clashes of personalities for which the campaign was already notorious had overshadowed the hope of success.

III

Rear-Admiral Sir Edmund Lyons had gone to sea for the first time at the age of eight. His features strongly reminded men—and those who were irritated by his noble attitudes maliciously but truthfully claimed that they also strongly reminded himself—of the features of Lord Nelson. He had, as *The Times* said, 'the same complexion, the same profusion of grey, inclining to white hair, the same eager and half-melancholy look'. And it was upon Lord Nelson that he had endeavoured to model his character and career. He was brave, confident, ambitious and energetic. He did not trouble to hide the fact that he considered his superior officer, Admiral Dundas, none of these things. It was a view which both the army and navy shared. 'Everybody,' wrote Captain Ross-Lewin of the 30th, 'wants Sir E. Lyons to get command of the Fleet.' 'Were it not for Sir Edmund,' Kingscote thought, 'I am sure we could not get on. Admiral Dundas thinks he had a near escape from a shot coming through his cabin when he himself was on deck. Did you ever? He ought to be flogged. If he can make a mess of a thing he does it.'[14]

Lyons was nearly sixty-five, Dundas not yet sixty. And although both came from those good, rather poor middle-class families which then supplied the Royal Navy with most of its senior officers, Lyons was the widower of a not very successful novelist, whereas Dundas had inherited from his first wife a life interest in very large estates in Berkshire and Wales and was now married to the daughter of the Earl of Ducie. He was extremely conscious of his social superiority as well as of his naval importance as Commander-in-Chief in the Mediterranean. On board his flagship, General Canrobert noted with envious surprise, he had all his home comforts, including cows and 'housemades'.[15]

Although, of course, he never expressed it publicly, Lord Raglan shared the general opinion of Dundas as obstructive, difficult and excessively cautious. He and Lyons, on the other hand, had become close personal friends and were often together at the British headquarters. Admiral Dundas felt an understandable resentment that the views of the sometimes scarcely less than mutinous officer commanding his inshore squadron should be so much respected by Lord Raglan when his own views as Commander-in-Chief were not even asked for. He never himself visited Lord Raglan, who, in turn, never went aboard his flagship.[16] This curious and difficult relationship was not only known in London but even encouraged there. The Cabinet as a whole, it is true, were not aware of the extent of Lyons's dislike and contempt for Dundas; but the Duke of Newcastle was, and told Lord Raglan that, in any open breach between Lyons and Raglan on the one hand and Dundas on the other, Lyons would have the support of the Government.[17]

The undercurrent of hostility between the three men was likely to make the co-operation of the navy in the coming bombardment unnecessarily difficult to arrange. In the first place Dundas and Lyons did not agree on what part the fleet could effectively play. Dundas had in mind a feint on the north side of Sebastopol and a bombardment of the north shore batteries. Lyons favoured the more daring project of a general attack on the sea forts and on the ships at anchor in the roadstead and harbour.

Unlike Admiral Hamelin, the French naval commander, who was under General Canrobert's orders, Dundas enjoyed an independent command, and it was evidently in fear that his co-operation might be refused altogether that Lord Raglan wrote him a letter on 13 October in which he emphasised the 'great importance' he attached to the 'active co-operation of the combined fleets, upon the day (fast approaching) on which the French and English armies open their fire, and commence their attack upon Sevastopol'. Time was most precious, Lord Raglan wrote, 'and we have not much left to capture the place which we have been called upon by the united voice of the Queen, the Government and the country, to take possession of. . . . Not to disappoint these universal expectations, the combined efforts of all branches of the naval and military services are necessary, and none, I am sure, will be withheld.'[18]

Admiral Dundas accepted this polite but stiff and formal letter with good grace. He replied to it immediately in similar vein.

Britannia, off Sevastopol, 14th October, 1854

MY DEAR LORD RAGLAN,

Colonel Steele has just arrived with your Lordship's letter of yesterday's date, and you may depend upon my using every exertion with my French colleagues to aid you in your object . . . .

I will consult with Admiral Hamelin as to your joint operations, and will thank your Lordship to let me know the time when you intend to attack.

I do not wish to detain Colonel Steele, and therefore leave it to him to explain what has passed between us.

Yours faithfully,

JNO. D. DUNDAS.[19]

The following day a conference was held on board the French ship *Mogador*. It was agreed that the allied navies would carry out the plan suggested by Lyons, and that the army commanders could decide whether the limited amount of ammunition could be used at the time the siege-guns opened their bombardment, at the time of the assault, or half at one time and half at the other. Raglan and Canrobert, hoping that a sudden and simultaneous cannonade from both the fleet and the army would throw the Sebastopol garrison into confusion, replied in a joint letter to the effect that they preferred a cannonade at half-past six in the morning, when the army's bombardment was due to begin.[20]

But at whatever time the cannonade began, the fleets, in adopting the plan of bombarding the hard stone sea forts and the ships of the Black Sea Fleet behind their protective line of sunken craft at the roadstead's mouth, were committing themselves to an extremely dangerous enterprise.

IV

On 17 October everything went wrong from the beginning. It had been intended that at half-past six in the morning the signal for the start of the sudden and colossal bombardment would be given by the firing of three shells from the French batteries. Unfortunately, as dawn broke the Russian gunners in Sebastopol saw that the banks of the earthworks of Mont Rodolphe had been cut in several places to form embrasures, and without waiting to be fired on they opened fire themselves. The psychological advantage of an abrupt and instantaneous fire from all the allied batteries was lost, and the guns came into use one after the other with disappointing lack of co-ordination.[21]

In the naval battery the sailors used their guns as if they were still on board ship, firing thunderous and instantaneous broadsides instead of the staggered shots which the engineers considered would be more effective and less wasteful of ammunition. Their loss in life was heavy, for they could not resist the temptation of poking their heads over the earthworks after each discharge to see what had happened. 'They would persist in jumping on top of the batteries to see the effect of their shots,' Timothy Gowing noticed. 'They were shot down as soon as they got up, for the enemy's sharpshooters were ever on the alert.'

Within a few minutes, however, the smoke was so thick that scarcely anything could be seen, and the guns were fired blindly down the slopes. The noise was tremendous. Henry Dixon of the 7th, trying to write a letter, decided that the row was 'too great to write a line'. Dr. Skelton, also trying to write a letter with his forage cap for a desk and with the 'roar of the cannon thundering near' him, soon gave up. Several days later his ears were still ringing. All over the plateau men had to shout to make themselves heard.

Out at sea, however, where officers had expected the noise of the cannonade to be even greater, there was no firing at all. The naval plans had been completely altered. At half-past ten the previous evening Admiral Dundas on board the *Britannia* had received a message from Admiral Hamelin, who told him that he did not intend, after all, to open fire before about half-past ten the following morning 'as his shot would not last long and, if expended early, the enemy might think that he was beaten off'. Dundas considered this 'reason a fair one' and sent Lyons a note to say that he intended to arrange for the British fleet to comply with it.[22]

And then at seven o'clock the following morning when the land bombardment had already begun, Admiral Hamelin himself came on board the *Britannia* and told Dundas that, on instructions from Canrobert, the whole plan was to be altered again. It had previously been agreed that the ships should be allowed the freedom of manoeuvring while delivering their broadsides; now they were to be anchored in line. And, moreover, anchored in line at a preposterously long distance from the forts.

Even the cautious Dundas baulked at this. He refused to agree. Very well, then, replied Hamelin, the French navy would have to act alone. Realising, as he noted in his diary later on that day, that the French Admiral meant what he said, Dundas gave way.[23]

But it was not until well on into the afternoon that the fleets were in position. After having been under fire for half an hour from the sea forts, the French ships delivered the first broadside from over six hundred guns. Hamelin's flagship in the centre of the line was only a little less than a mile from the nearest sea fort, the ships at the end of the line considerably more. Apart from being too far away, they were engaged in an almost impossible task. The ships were nearly all of wood, the forts were of that hard limestone known as the 'stone of the steppes'. And although the French guns outnumbered those in the forts with which they were engaged almost five to one, the damage done to the forts was negligible. Very few guns were dismounted, and only fifty Russian troops were killed or wounded.[24]

The Royal Navy fared worse. The cannonade from over five hundred starboard guns was tremendous. 'From the experience of fifty years,' Dundas later reported to Lord Raglan, 'I can assert that so powerful a cannonade . . . has never taken place on the ocean.'[25] But it was also a disastrous failure.

Dundas, despite a circular order issued to all captains the previous evening, instructing them to keep their ships out of danger, had apparently decided that some show of spirit must be made and signalled to the inshore squadron, 'Proceed and attack batteries.'

Lyons's fine screw-ship, the *Agamemnon*, led the way with the *Sanspareil* and the *London*, to within half a mile of the coast. Sailing ships lashed to smaller steamers followed.

A furious fire was maintained for more than three hours. The *Agamemnon* was hit in several places and was soon in difficulties. The *Sanspareil* and the *London* had to change position after receiving heavy damage. The *Bellerophon*, commanded by Lord George Paulet, was set on fire on coming to the help of the *Agamemnon* and was towed out of action. The sailing-ships *Arethusa* and *Albion* were so badly holed that they had eventually to go to Constantinople for refitting. The *Rodney* went aground. At half-past five Dundas gave the signal to haul off. Enormous quantities of ammunition had been wasted on the scarcely damaged forts. Over three hundred British sailors had been killed or wounded.[26]

V

Meanwhile, despite the failure of the navies to make any impression on the sea forts, the position in Sebastopol was becoming perilous. The bombardment from the land batteries on the crests to the south of the town was ceaseless. Steadily worn down by exploding shells, round shot and rockets the hastily constructed gun emplacements were beginning to crumble. There had been no time to make fascines, and the embrasures, revetted with planks, stones and sandbags, were constantly falling in. Many lives were lost as the gunners heroically tried to repair them under the never-ending fire. The whole semi-circular line of defences was covered in smoke, so that it was impossible to see across the plateau where the allied infantry were waiting. Every few minutes there would be a shout of alarm as a soldier thought he saw through the dense whiteness the dark shapes of assaulting troops with bayonets. Russian columns, drawn up to withstand the expected attack, were showered with flying earth and sometimes rent as a cannon-ball shot over the ramparts and flew into the ranks.[27]

Admiral Korniloff, magnificent in his last hours, galloped from post to post encouraging his sailors and the troops. He had about him the air of martyrdom. 'A slight smile played on his lips,' one of his staff wrote. 'His eyes—those wonderful, intelligent and piercing eyes— shone brighter than usual. His cheeks were flushed. He carried his head high. His thin and slightly bent form had become erect. He seemed to grow in size.'[28]

He seemed also to be taking unnecessary risks. Officers pleaded with him not to expose himself so carelessly on the ramparts. In the Central Bastion, Captain Ilynsky told him that he 'would take care to carry out his duty so that the presence of the Admiral would be unnecessary'. Korniloff answered, 'And if you are to do your duty, why do you wish to prevent me from doing mine? My duty is to see all.'[29] He was determined to do so. He climbed on top of the banquette to watch the effect of the Russian fire on the allied batteries, and as he stood there he was spattered with flying soil, splinters and sprays of blood. Admiral Nachimoff was with him, morose and fatalistic, blood streaming down his face from a head wound, wearing his full-dress admiral's uniform with its heavy gilt epaulettes, expecting to die amidst the ruins.[30]

Korniloff left the Central Bastion to go back to his house to eat a late breakfast. While there, Admiral Istomine, in command of the Malakoff, sent a message entreating him not to visit it. He immediately decided to do so. Calling first at the Flagstaff Bastion and then at the Redan, he arrived at the Malakoff some time after eleven o'clock. After a few minutes a round shot shattered his left thigh. 'Defend Sebastopol!' he murmured to an A.D.C. and lost consciousness. He recovered sufficiently to receive his final sacrament and prayed to God 'to bless Russia and the Emperor', to 'save Sebastopol and the fleet', and then he died.[31]

There was no one to take his place. The command of the land forces passed to General Möller; the command of the sailors to Admiral Nachimoff. Colonel Todleben was still there to guide them, but he was, after all, only an adviser with no recognised authority and the rather suspect manners and appearance of a foreigner; while Prince Mentschikoff, who might have taken supreme command, had left the town after a hurried visit and was now presumably back with his field army.

By the middle of the afternoon the bombardment, after a few hours' abatement, had reached a fresh violence, and a new and inspiring leader was a real necessity. The defences, particularly in the vicinity of the Malakoff and the Redan, were crumbling; the infantry columns had fallen back for shelter after nearly nine hours' heroically patient waiting. Soon after three o'clock a shell exploded in a powder-magazine in a salient of the Redan, killing over a hundred men on the spot, shattering the gun-carriages and overthrowing the guns. 'The defences of that part of the line,' so the Russians admitted, 'were completely paralysed.'[32] An assault was now considered a virtual certainty. And once again they felt it could not have been resisted. But it was not made.

VI

The British were ready for the assault, but the French were not.

The part of the line near the Redan, which the Russians now considered defenceless, was opposite the British batteries. Opposite the French, however, the guns in the Flagstaff Bastion were still intact. A supreme commander would perhaps have poured assaulting troops of both armies through the open breach. But there was no supreme commander, and Lord Raglan, haunted by the weakness of that 'delicate Alliance', refused to tax its waning strength by attacking without Canrobert.

From the first the French had been discouraged by the numbers of guns which had concentrated their fire on them rather than upon the British batteries, which were farther away from Sebastopol.[33] For four hours, shells from nearly a hundred heavy guns had been exploding all around them on Mont Rodolphe; the round shot had been bounding across the grass in remorseless waves like 'black battalions'; the earth around their feet was 'drenched in blood'.[34] At half-past ten a French magazine had blown up with such force that a mile away the ground shuddered as if rocked by an earthquake. A column of flame shot up into the air like a red waterspout, and when the dense smoke lifted the blackened corpses of more than fifty French soldiers lay around their overturned guns. A few seconds later a second shell had blown up an ammunition dump.[35]

General Hugh Rose, the senior English liaison officer at French headquarters, had ridden over to tell Lord Raglan that the explosions had completely destroyed the confidence of the remaining French gunners and that General Canrobert doubted if their cannonade could be resumed until the next day, and perhaps not until the day after that. From then on the British continued their bombardment alone.[36]

Lord Raglan still hoped that the French might recover. Out of range of the Russian guns, several of his infantry battalions detailed for the first wave of the assault were awaiting their orders; engineers had been ordered to act as guides and to form scaling-ladder parties; horses of field-artillery units stood hooked-in. For the whole of the rest of that day the air was thick with smoke and battered by the constant roar of guns. But it was all to no purpose. At dusk the bombardment ceased, and the hot guns cooled.[37]

All night long the Russians worked to repair the breach in their defences and to bring up new supplies of ammunition. By dawn the Redan looked even stronger than it had before the bombardment began.

The British guns opened up again, and again by nightfall the Redan was in ruins. But the French batteries were silent all day, and no assault was made. On the third day the French, having repaired their works and established new batteries, began firing again. By the early afternoon, however, after two explosions and several hours of fiercely returned fire the batteries once more gave up the struggle. For over a week the bombardment continued. The town became 'a perfect hell', one of the Russians inside it wrote afterwards. 'The frightful din, smoke, groans and cries of the wounded as they were carried from the batteries rendered the place the most horrible it is possible to conceive.' But at sunset each day the fire was abandoned, and during the night the Russians not only rebuilt their defences but improved them.[38]

'We are *promised* an assault', Captain Shakespear wrote to his brother, underlining the word heavily, 'whenever we open fire.' But no assault was ordered. And without it the bombardment was point-less. During the first day over a thousand Russians had been killed; on the second about 550; on the third a few more than 500; on subsequent days, owing to improved defences and deep traverses dug with extraordinary skill and energy and owing also to a slackening fire from the dispirited allied gunners, an average of only 250.[39]

'I have never', *The Times* correspondent heard Lord Cardigan say to his friend Hubert de Burgh, who had recently come out to watch the siege in Cardigan's yacht, the *Dryad*, 'I have never in my life seen a siege conducted on such principles.' It was a general and well-justified complaint.

Officers had been talking of a siege lasting eight hours or at the most three days. Now they discussed not how soon they might take the town, but how on earth they would manage to re-embark if they didn't take it.[40] In the naval brigade officers who had accepted bets that Sebastopol would fall within twenty-four hours collected their winnings, and offered the same odds against it falling within a month.[41]

VII

It was a sadly dispiriting time. The weather was getting colder every day. 'It is really too cold to write,' Lord George Paget told his wife, 'one can hardly hold one's pen and it is so irksome to write with thick gloves on. We don't seem to get on, and are quite in the dark about everything. Every day we hear that on the next the attack will commence.'

The infantry were kept hard at work improving the forward trenches, making new approaches to the batteries, carrying up ammunition to the guns. 'When the hell will we attack and get out of here, sir?' a soldier asked an artillery officer, who sadly shrugged his shoulders.[42] Every night covering parties crawled forward into pits beyond the batteries. 'It was,' as Timothy Gowing described it, 'killing work lying down for hours in the cold mud, returning to camp at daylight, wearing out with cold, sleepy and hungry—many a poor fellow suffering with ague or fever—to find nothing but a cold, bleak, muddy tent, without fire, to rest their weary bones in; and often not even a piece of mouldy biscuit to eat—nothing served out yet. But at ten, as soon as we reached camp, the orderly would call out: "Is Sergeant Gowing in?" "Yes, what's up?" "You're for fatigue at once." Off to Balaclava, perhaps to bring up supplies in the shape of salt beef, salt pork, biscuit, blankets, shot or shell. Return at night completely done up; down you go in the mud for a few hours rest—that is if there was not an alarm.'

There frequently was an alarm. Sometimes there was good cause for one, as the Russians were becoming experts at sudden, terrifying raids with the bayonet on unsuspecting posts, but more often the alarms were given by nervous officers or sentries frightened by the wind or by animals rustling in the grass. 'About once every day and night,' a cavalry officer reported disdainfully, 'a fellow gallops in with a report that the Russians are advancing in numbers. . . . Every fool at the outposts, who fancies he hears something, has only to make a row and there we all are, generals and all.'[43]

The sailors treated these alarms with fine contempt. 'Retire!' an officer shouted one night to the soldiers of an unarmed digging-party, who immediately scattered, leaving their wooden canteens of rum and water in the trenches. When the expected attack did not materialise, the soldiers returned to find their empty canteens heaped in a pile in the trenches and a group of sailors lying dead drunk against them.[44]

In the atmosphere of frustration and fear, tempers were easily frayed and quickly lost. Friendships were strained. Rivalries became vendettas; dislike changed into hate and disrespect into contempt. Men blamed their officers, their officers blamed the generals, and the generals blamed each other.

General Cathcart, angry with Lord Raglan for not taking him into his confidence or seeking his advice, became more and more difficult and unmanageable. On 4 October he had written him a bitter letter complaining that Sir George Brown and General Airey were constantly consulted whereas he, although he was to take over the army in the event of the Commander-in-Chief's death, never was. Brown and Airey, he considered, were in the habit of issuing orders in Lord Raglan's name and behind his back. 'My duty to my sovereign,' the letter ended, 'demands that I should request an interview at the time most convenient to you, without delay at your headquarters.'[45] The interview was granted, but even then the position remained as before. Cathcart could have got into Sebastopol, he often maintained, and it was Raglan's fault and Burgoyne's that he had not been allowed to try.[46] 'We hear that Cathcart is very angry,' Paget told his wife, 'at the way things are going on and at his never being consulted.' A captain in the 46th, however, was not surprised at his never being consulted. He would, in fact, have been surprised if Lord Raglan had consulted any of his generals. 'I declare,' he told his aunt, 'that I would as soon ask the advice of one of your little girls.'[47]

General England, for instance, another officer wrote, was a 'terrible fool'. 'It is quite disgusting to serve under him. He never knows his own mind and it takes him an age to get his Division into position.' Sir George Brown continued to live up to his 'reputation of being the greatest brute possible'. General Burgoyne was 'a shocking old Dolt'. The Duke of Cambridge, usually so genial, was now strangely reserved. He had never properly recovered from the shock of the Alma, and his gout was getting worse. And Lord Cardigan, the newly styled 'Noble Yachtsman', and Lord Lucan, the 'Tyrant', were, of course, 'again hard at it' and hated by almost the entire army.[48] Feeling was particularly bitter against Lord Cardigan, who with Lord Raglan's permission now dined and slept on board his yacht every night. He was certainly unwell and had only recently recovered from a bad attack of diarrhoea. He looked pale and washed out, one of his colonels thought, and apart from this it was perhaps as well that he should be kept away from Lord Lucan as much as possible. With this in mind Lord Raglan ordered two regiments of the Light Brigade to form a separate camp under Lord Cardigan away from the rest of the cavalry division. It was, as Paget said, absurd that the dispositions of the cavalry should be regulated by the necessity of keeping 'two spoilt children' apart. But the need to do so seemed now to be stronger than ever. On 7 October a cavalry picket on the far right of the army's position had spotted a large Russian force. The cavalry divison formed up and rode over to investigate. The Russians seemed to be inviting a charge, but Lord 'Look-on' lived up to his name. Cardigan was on board ship, but when he heard what had happened he was almost beside himself with rage and disgust. The officers of his own regiment, the 11th Hussars, might at least have been expected to charge without orders, but they were nothing but 'a damned set of old women'. But, after all, what could you expect with Lord Lucan commanding them? He was nothing but a 'cautious ass'.[49]

The trouble was, of course, that Cardigan in his turn was a 'dangerous ass'. There was, indeed, an officer in the 4th Light Dragoons decided, little to choose between them. Cardigan, he wrote, 'has as much brains as my boot. He is only to be equalled in want of intellect by his relative the Earl of Lucan. Without mincing matters two such fools could hardly be picked out of the British Army.'[50]

Up till now Lord Raglan had escaped the general calumny. Captain Jocelyn, writing home on 12 October, had said that he seemed 'as cool and contented as possible, and I think he knows what he is about, and that the army have great confidence in him'. Ten days later, when the bombardment had raged to no effect and only Lord Raglan's staff understood the anxiety which he felt and the position into which the French command was putting him, opinion had altered. 'I do not know,' an exasperated artillery officer exclaimed, expressing a growing discontent, 'which is the greatest ass, Raglan or Burgoyne.'[51]

The French were not the only cause of Lord Raglan's anxiety. The Ministers of the Government at home were in a mood of wild and aggravating optimism. At the beginning of September Charles Greville reported them as being 'not at all satisfied with Raglan, whom they think old-fashioned and pedantic.'[52] Now they praised him with enthusiasm. One of them, who before the battle of the Alma had urged that Lord Raglan ought to be examined by a Court of Enquiry, now stood up in the House of Commons and suggested to cheers that he should be honoured by the Garter. The Duke of Newcastle wrote to tell him that he and his brave army would now 'be able to pass a merry Christmas, and be able to enjoy the comfortable reflection that in the coming year' they would return home to a 'grateful country, full of honours'. 'The boldness with which the masterly flank movement was designed is only equalled,' he assured him in another letter, 'by the decision with which it was executed. Her Majesty attributes the success of this striking military exploit to the consummate judgment displayed by your Lordship in directing the remarkable night march of the army.'

Lord Hardinge told him that 'nothing can exceed the universal admiration of all of us, for the judgement, ability and nerve shown by you in all your operations. The flank movement by your left, bringing your Army and siege guns down to a safe harbour at Balaclava and at a short distance from Sebastopol and in communication with the Navy, is a masterpiece . . . the greatest operation of modern times.' The Government, in fact, could see 'no cause for apprehension'. The difficulties would 'eventually only prove to Europe that the walls of Sebastopol were not more impregnable than the heights of the Alma'.[53]

On 23 October Lord Raglan replied to these excited commendations and expressions of confidence. He enclosed a letter from Mr. Charles Cattley, one of his interpreters, who had been British consul at Kertch and knew the Crimean peninsula well. Mr. Cattley had warned what a bad Crimean winter could be like. 'Bleak winds, heavy rains, sleet, snow and bitter cold' might all be expected. And once in every few years there came a fortnight or so of 'Russian cold', and when Mr. Cattley used that phrase he meant a cold so intense that 'if a man touches metal with an uncovered hand the skin adheres'. It was a prophetic warning and it was not heeded. 'Before concluding,' Lord Raglan ended his letter, 'I may be permitted to say a word with regard to this army. It requires, and should not be denied, repose. Although the marches have not been heavy, fatigue has pressed heavily upon the troops. The very act of finding water and of getting wood has been a daily unceasing exertion, and the climate has told upon them: and, independently of cholera, sickness has prevailed to a great extent. . . . Cholera, alas! is still lingering in the army.'

The great need, he had emphasised, was for more troops. He was finding it impossible to carry out the siege operations effectively, while at the same time guarding his exposed flank and his base at Balaclava.[54]

VIII

Balaclava was, in fact, protected by little more than a token force of Turks, Marines and Highlanders. They were disposed on the plain above the harbour in a semicircular line to the north and east of the village of Kadiköi. In front of them was the cavalry camp, and beyond the cavalry, over the hills which enclosed the plain on every side, were the infantry divisions spread out on the ridges and spurs looking down upon Sebastopol.

The distance from Balaclava to Sebastopol is about seven miles. The road between the two places was a mere track for about three miles up from Balaclava until it joined the Worontzoff Road. This was a relatively good road running south-east out of Sebastopol, through the infantry camps, down and across the Plain of Balaclava and then on down again to the Tchernaya River, which it crossed by a bridge two miles below the village of Tchorgoun (see map, p. 134).

It crossed the Plain of Balaclava from left to right on a narrow ridge of land known to the army as the Causeway Heights. The low ground beyond this ridge and the Fedioukine Hills, which enclosed the plain on its northern side, was called the North Valley; while the ground on the near side of the ridge was known as the South Valley. These two valleys, divided by the Causeway Heights and shut in at each end by sharply rising hills, were soon to be the scene of two of the most spectacular charges in military history.

The Causeway Heights, carrying the Worontzoff Road across the Plain of Balaclava, were not only vital to the defence of Balaclava and the rear and flank of the army's position, but also to its line of communication. For to lose the Heights would mean to lose the one good road across the Plain leading to the camps and siege works overlooking Sebastopol. Lord Raglan had realised the importance of this road and had constructed six redoubts along the Heights to protect it from attack. In each of the redoubts was a twelve-pounder naval gun manned by Turkish troops. Lord Raglan's opinion of the Turks had somewhat altered since he had read the reports of the battle of Giurgevo, and General Cannon, who had fought with them there, assured him that although they were not always reliable in the open they could be trusted behind a defensive work.[55] So Lord Raglan left his own troops to concentrate on the siege and accepted General Cannon's advice. He took the precaution, however, of sending a few Royal Artillery N.C.O.s on detachment to the redoubts in case the Turks felt in need of help and encouragement when the time of danger came.

These Turks, and some others assisting the Marines and the 93rd Highlanders around Balaclava and Kadiköi, had been recently put under the command of Sir Colin Campbell. Formerly, Lord Lucan had been in charge of the defence of the army's base, but Lord Raglan had decided a more capable man was required and recalled Sir Colin from the command of the Highland Brigade. Although the latter had the reputation of living in an almost constant state of worry when not actually fighting, he thought his position tenable and assured Lord Raglan that he considered he would be able to hold his 'own against anything that may come against us in daylight'.

He was soon to be put to the test. For several days reports had been coming in that a large Russian army was collecting around the village of Tchorgoun about five miles to the east of Balaclava beyond the Tchernaya River. By 24 October this army was said to number twenty-five thousand men, under General Liprandi, one of Russia's most talented generals. That evening a Turkish spy came to Campbell's headquarters and said that the Russian force was about to fall on

Balaclava.* Campbell and Lucan examined him and decided to send a report to Lord Raglan. The report, in the form of a letter from Sir Colin to Lord Raglan, was carried up to the Headquarters by Lord Bingham, the Earl of Lucan's son and A.D.C., who handed it to General Airey, as the Commander-in-Chief was in conference with General Canrobert. Airey read the letter and decided to break in upon their conversation. So many similar reports had reached Lord Raglan during the past few days that he cannot, perhaps, be blamed for not paying particular attention to this one. The army was getting worn out by constant alerts and false alarms. General Cathcart was still cross because he had marched his division down into the plain a day or two previously only to find the report which had precipitated the movement a false one and had had to march back up the hill again. Lord Bingham was sent back down to the plain with the acknowledgment—'Very well.' No further action was taken.

It was a cold night. Before dawn a wind came up, and the men huddled together in their tents as the wet canvas flapped against the ropes. The engineers in the forward trenches could hear the sounds of Russian bands playing loudly in the villages down by the river.

* The British headquarters, following the lead of Lord Raglan's known prejudice, did not like making use of spies. The Russians, more realistically, had no such old-fashioned scruples. Enemy officers wearing British uniforms were on several occasions discovered inspecting the French trenches; and men in French uniforms frequently wandered through the British lines and then scampered back into Sebastopol. One day a friendly-looking man wearing civilian clothes walked into a gun battery and said he was a surgeon. He asked several questions in a Yorkshire accent and then inquired the best way to the forward trenches. He was seen a little later running headlong for Sebastopol (Wood letters). British intelligence, on the other hand, was mainly confined to the conflicting and unreliable information of Russian deserters (nearly all Poles) and to the often misleading reports of Turkish spies such as the one now at Campbell's headquarters (R.C.P., M.M. 201, Charles Cattley's file).

10

THE BATTLE OF BALACLAVA

There my Lord! There is your enemy! There are your guns!
Captain L. E. Nolan, 8th Hussars

I

An hour before dawn on 25 October the cavalry turned out as usual and waited in their lines while Lord Lucan with two staff officers trotted off across the plain towards the Causeway Heights. As they passed the Light Brigade camp Lord George Paget joined them.

It was beginning to get light as the four officers approached the most easterly of the six redoubts, and through the early morning mist one of them saw two flags flying.

'Hello,' he said, 'what does that mean?'

'Surely that's the signal that the enemy is advancing?'

'Are you sure?'

As they looked and hesitated, one of the guns in the redoubt suddenly opened fire and settled the question for them. Almost immediately the fire was returned, and a round shot came hurtling towards Lord George Paget. 'Aha,' said his jovial orderly in high good-humour, 'it went right between your horse's legs.'[1]

It was now about six o'clock.

There were about five hundred Turks in the redoubt and they had three twelve-pounder guns. The Russians advancing on them outnumbered them twenty to one and had ten times as many guns. The Turks could not hope to hold their ground for long, but for the moment they remained where they were. As the fire of the Russians' thirty guns increased, the Turks, despite appalling losses, still held to their redoubt; but then the Russian infantry charged with the bayonet, and at last they fell back, leaving 170 corpses behind them. They had given their allies an hour and a half's respite in which to bring up reinforcements. But it was not enough.

As soon as Lord Raglan heard of the Russian attack he had ordered the 1st and 4th Divisions to come down on to the plain from the Sapouné Ridge. Neither the Duke of Cambridge nor Sir George

Cathcart was a fast mover. It was over half an hour before the Guards and Highlanders of the 1st Division began their difficult march down the steep slopes. The 4th Division was a great deal slower, for Sir George Cathcart was in a particularly difficult mood. The staff officer who galloped breathlessly up to his tent with the Commander-in-Chief's orders afterwards reported the following remarkable conversation:

'Lord Raglan requests you, Sir George, to move your division immediately to the assistance of the Turks.'

Cathcart replied with predictable asperity.

'Quite impossible, sir,' he snapped, 'for the 4th Division to move.'

'My orders were very positive. And the Russians are advancing on Balaclava.'

'I can't help that, sir. It is impossible for my division to move, as the greater portion of the men have only just come from the trenches. The best thing you can do, sir, is to sit down and have some breakfast.'

'No, thank you, sir. My orders are to request that you will move your division immediately to the assistance of Sir Colin Campbell. I feel sure every moment is of consequence. Sir Colin Campbell has only the 93rd Highlanders with him. I saw the Turks in full flight.'

'Well, sir, if you will not sit down and have breakfast, you may as well go back to Lord Raglan and tell him that I cannot move my division.'

The staff officer saluted and left the tent. He mounted his horse and rode away. But he had only ridden a few yards when he decided that he could not return to Lord Raglan with this mutinous message. He turned his horse round, rode back to Sir George's tent and said with commendable determination that he had received an order to come for the 4th Division and that he would not leave until it was ready to move off.

'Very well, sir,' Cathcart said, giving way at last. 'I will consult with my staff officers, and see if anything can be done.' [2]

Several minutes later the bugles sounded throughout the camp, and the 4th Division unhurriedly marched down towards Balaclava.

Already the situation was desperate. It would be nearly two hours before the infantry could get down on to the plain. Lord Lucan, blaming Lord Raglan for not having paid attention to the spy's

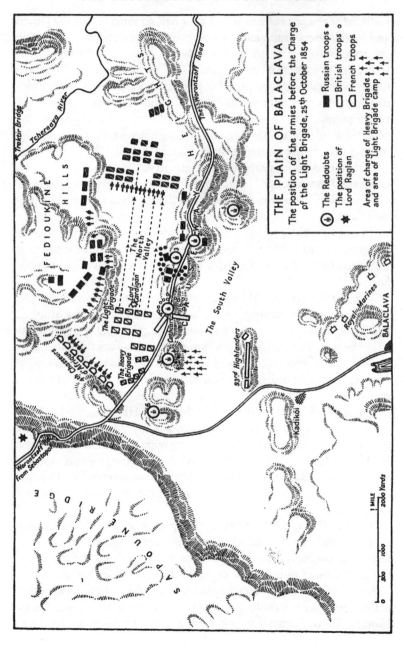

THE PLAIN OF BALACLAVA

The position of the armies before the Charge
of the Light Brigade, 25th October 1854

⊕ The Redoubts   Russian troops ■
✹ The position of   British troops □
   Lord Raglan   French troops
↑↑↑
Area of charge of Heavy Brigade
and area of Light Brigade camp

report of the night before, was unhappily manoeuvring his division in an unsuccessful attempt to prevent or delay the Russian advance and, to the fury of his officers, was steadily falling back before it. Lord Cardigan had not yet come up from his yacht.

The Turks, seeing the terrifyingly superior numbers of the Russian troops and dismayed by the fate of their unsupported fellow-countrymen in the forward redoubt, had now understandably lost their nerve and were flying headlong for Balaclava 'like a swarm of bees', shouting 'Ship! Ship! Johnny! Ship!'³ They dashed past the camp of the 93rd Highlanders, the last line of defence above Balaclava, stopping on their way to pick up anything which looked inviting, especially empty bottles, for which they appeared to 'have a great appreciation'.⁴ Several of them, as they stopped to pick up their loot, were beaten savagely over the back by the fierce wife of a soldier, who upbraided them angrily for their cowardice and for trampling over her washing laid out to dry in the sun.⁵ 'The currs never stopped till they got into Balaclava,' Captain Shakespear told his brother. 'Our sailors kicked their *seats* of *disgrace*. I shook my fist in their Colonel's face and scowled at him. Curr! I really believe the scoundrel tried to fancy I was complimenting him.'

Four out of the six redoubts were occupied by the Russians, who were now swarming in ever-increasing numbers across the Causeway Heights and down the Worontzoff Road. Beyond the Heights several squadrons of their cavalry trotted unopposed up the North Valley; on the south side another cavalry force advanced on Lord Lucan's division, which was still falling back on to the Highlanders. On Sir Colin Campbell's advice Lord Lucan withdrew his cavalry to the side of the plain, where they would be out of the line of the Highlanders' fire and where they could attack the Russians in flank.

'Remember, there is no retreat from here, men,' Sir Colin called in his rich Scottish accent as he rode in front of the Highlanders, now joined by about a hundred invalids and fifty men who had been on fatigue duty in Balaclava under two officers of the Guards. 'Remember, there is no retreat. You must die where you stand.'⁶

'Aye! Aye! Sir Colin,' one of his men replied. 'We'll do that.'⁷

They were lying down. But as the Russian horsemen got closer to them, they stood up and seemed on the point of charging when Sir

Colin turned in his saddle and shouted at them, angry and reproachful, '93rd! 93rd! Damn all that eagerness!'[8]

Then suddenly that curious and alarming silence which men had noticed before the battle of the Alma again fell upon the field. 'The silence is oppressive,' *The Times* correspondent noted, 'one can hear the champing of bits, and the clink of sabres in the valley below. The Russians on their left draw breath for a moment and then in one grand line dash at the Highlanders. The ground flies beneath their horses' feet; gathering speed at every stride, they dash on towards that thin red streak topped with a line of steel.'

Prevented by Campbell from charging, the Highlanders fired their rifles instead. No Russian rider fell from his saddle, but a few were wounded, and the leading squadron immediately wheeled to the left.

'Shadwell!' said Sir Colin to his A.D.C. in a tone of surprised admiration, 'that man understands his business.'[9]

Showing that he too understood his, Campbell reorganised his line so that the left of it faced the new direction of the Russian advance. Again the Russian wheeled to the left and again the line of the Highlanders changed its shape. Their determined stand and well-conducted movements apparently alarmed the Russian commander, for he ordered his men to retire. As they did so Campbell's guns opened up on them, and round shot was sent flying across the plain into their retreating backs. The Highlanders threw their bonnets in the air, cheering excitedly.

II

The larger force of Russian cavalry, however, was still advancing across their front in the North Valley.

The Highlanders could not, of course, see these other Russian horsemen, as the Causeway Heights hid them from view. And the Russians in their turn could see neither the Highlanders nor a force of six squadrons of English cavalry advancing towards them on the opposite side of the Heights.

The English force formed part of the Heavy Brigade under General Scarlett, which Lord Raglan had ordered up to the help of the Turks in the redoubts farther along the Heights. The order had been given to Lord Lucan by one of Lord Raglan's A.D.C.s some time previously, when, if immediately executed, it might have given the Turks the confidence they had so completely lost. But now the Turks were gone and the Heavy Brigade was advancing unsupported towards the middle of the Russian spearhead.

General Sir James Scarlett was fifty-five. Despite the rather ferociously warlike aspect of his brick-red face and white moustaches, which led men to believe he had fought in numerous Eastern campaigns, this was his first battle. Unlike Lucan and Cardigan, however, who strongly deprecated such a demeaning attitude, he had welcomed the support of two experienced 'Indian' officers, Colonel Beatson and Lieutenant Alexander Elliot, and had appointed them both his A.D.C.s. Lieutenant Elliot, indeed, who had had to leave India on account of ill-health and had accordingly never obtained promotion at home in a regiment which did not care for 'Indians', was the constant companion and adviser of his General and was now his saviour.

Glancing up to the crest of the high ridge of the Causeway Heights on his left, he saw a row of lance-tips jiggling against the sky. He pointed them out to Scarlett, who could not at first believe they belonged to Russian lancers.

In any event he would, no doubt, have difficulty in seeing them, as he suffered from that disability which might well have been considered an occupational disease of British generals. He was extremely shortsighted. In a moment, however, a line of Russian helmets came into view and he immediately ordered his squadrons into line to face up the slope of the Heights.

The Russian lancers, prevented from continuing their leisurely advance up the North Valley by the fire of a British gun from the Sapouné Ridge in front of them, had decided to cross the Causeway Heights and were as surprised to find the English below them as Scarlett was to find them above him.

At this moment Lord Lucan, warned by Lord Raglan of the Russian cavalry's approach, galloped, breathless and agitated, on to the scene. He found some squadrons of the Heavy Brigade trotting still farther down the South Valley so as to avoid a vineyard at the bottom of the Heights and thus have a clear run for their charge. Lord Lucan, misinterpreting their movement, known in military handbooks as 'taking ground to the right', and thinking that they were still advancing towards the redoubts across the Russian cavalry's front, told them to wheel into line. Then he rode on to Scarlett and told him to charge; which, of course, Scarlett was preparing to do.

The Russians, now over the crest of the ridge, began to move down its south slope. But at sight of the Scots Greys calmly dressing their lines, as if on parade, they halted.

Lord Lucan, almost beside himself with impatience, ordered his trumpeter to sound the charge. The trumpeter did so several times. No one paid him the least attention. The meticulous dressing of the ranks continued.

The Russians still sat motionless in their saddles half-way down the slope, wearing their enormous yellowish-grey overcoats, watching the parade-ground movements in the valley below. There were three thousand of them and less than six hundred of their enemies. They looked completely confident. The English cavalry had never charged them yet and they could hardly be expected to now.

In contrast to the dense, sombre ranks of the Russian horsemen, the British cavalry in their gay scarlet uniforms appeared, to the spectators on the hills to the west, absurdly frail.

The Scots Greys in their top-heavy bearskins, the Dragoon Guards and Inniskilling Dragoons in their heavy, embossed helmets, seemed to be playing at war. Their officers presented their backs to the enemy, as they conscientiously arranged their men in neat ranks.

Well in front of the first line General Scarlett sat stolidly with Lieutenant Elliot. He wore a blue coat over his uniform and the same helmet as his men. Elliot wore the cocked-hat of a staff officer. He had turned out that morning in a forage cap, explaining to General Scarlett that Orders now permitted it. 'Damn the order', Scarlett had said. 'My staff shall be properly dressed.' Elliot had gone back to his tent and found the chin strap of his cocked-hat loose. He had begun to sew on a button when Scarlett called him out. He left the strap and stuffed a big silk handkerchief in the hat to make it tighter.[10] It was to save his life.

At last the horses were arranged to everyone's satisfaction, and General Scarlett turned in his saddle and said to his trumpeter, 'Sound the charge!'

As the notes sounded Scarlett galloped off. The Scots Greys behind him had some difficulty in picking their way through the pegs, ropes and still standing tents of the Light Brigade camp and were soon left well behind. Elliot pointed this out to Scarlett, but the General would not wait. Looking over his shoulder, he shouted 'Come on!', waved his sword in the air and galloped with magnificent concentration at the still halted Russian ranks, as a blind Don Quixote might have galloped at a windmill. And the Russians looked back, 'as if fascinated, unable to move'.[11]

Standing in the way of Scarlett and Elliot was a single Russian horseman. Scarlett rushed past him, as if he did not see him, while Elliot ran the man through with his sword and twisted his body completely round in his saddle as he pulled it out. And then the two officers, the pale young lieutenant and the red-faced general, disappeared into the grey mass of the Russian troops.

The Scots Greys followed them with a 'low eager, fierce moan', the Inniskillings with a cheer; and soon to the spectators on the hillside it seemed that these two regiments which had led the charge had been swallowed up in the grey sea of Russian troops.

So closely were the men packed that there could be no displays of fine swordsmanship. The best that they could do was to hack about them frantically as if using an axe. This suited Scarlett well enough, as he was not much of a swordsman anyway. His helmet was stove in and he was slightly wounded five times, but he kept on swinging his sword about him as his horse, like the other horses, bent his head down to avoid the swinging blades. Elliot was less fortunate. Wearing so conspicuous a hat he was the object of many furious attacks. His horse kicking out with his back legs saved him from being cut down from the back, but he received in all fourteen sabre-cuts before he slumped unconscious in his saddle. His cocked-hat was cut through and through. The silk handkerchief, however, saved his head from being cut open.

Around him the fight continued. The men grunted and cursed as their swords bent and bounced on the heavy grey coats so thick and unyielding that they might have been made of india-rubber. Some of them, however, possessed sharp Wilkinson swords which, if used with skill, could not only cut through the thick cloth but divide an exposed skull down to the chin.* The Russians made 'zizzling noises' between

* The troopers had some difficulty in exchanging blows with the Russians. They had been rigidly trained in their sword exercises and were unprepared for the enemy's less orthodox approach. According to their training each cut had to be followed by a guard. 'How came you to get this ugly cut?' a surgeon asked a man with a deep wound in the top of his

clenched teeth. Spectators up on the hills heard the sounds as 'the continuous roar and roll of the sea', and as they watched through their telescopes they saw British troopers push their way right through the Russian column and then turn round to hack their way back again.[12]

Scarcely more than five minutes had passed since the charge had begun, but already the Russians were wavering. The other squadrons of the Heavy Brigade now charged into the struggling mass. Then a few troops of the Light Brigade who had stolen away from their regiments charged in too, like uncontrollable schoolboys joining a pillow-fight, and finally two butchers dashed forward in their shirt-sleeves, swinging swords as if they were meat-cleavers.[13]

Soon the Russians were noticeably backing away, then breaking, then retreating. Eight minutes after Scarlett had ordered the charge they were galloping away over the Worontzoff Road at the top of the Causeway Heights. At the sight of the Russians retreating, the watchers on the hillside threw their hats in the air and burst into cheers while the soldiers below, whose determined charge and frantic courage had brought about their astonishing victory, watched their enemies disappear over the crest of the heights, their sword-arms hanging tired and loose at their sides, their hands and uniforms spattered with blood, tears rolling down their cheeks.[14]

As the dead and wounded were dragged away to the tents behind them, an A.D.C. from Lord Raglan cantered up to General Scarlett and handed him a simple message—'Well done, Scarlett.' The General turned away quickly, as if to hide his emotion, and he crumpled up the piece of paper and put it in his pocket.[15]

Lord Cardigan was less generous. 'Damn those Heavies,' he said. 'They have the laugh of us this day.'

He could, of course, have attacked the Russians in flank while the Heavy Brigade was still hacking at them with such ferocious energy. And he could also have pursued them, which the disorganised Heavy Brigade were quite incapable of doing. But throughout the short battle, and now while the Russians were getting away, the Light Brigade sat motionless five hundred yards higher up the valley.

A French major supposed that the Light Brigade were prevented from joining the fight by the rules of '*le boxe*'. The British officers

---

scalp. 'Well, I had just cut five' [a body cut], the man replied indignantly. 'And the damned fool never guarded at all but hit me over the head' (Wood letters).

themselves were wild with impatience. One of them, a young officer, only a captain but through the death of more senior officers in temporary command of his regiment, the 17th Lancers, went up to Lord Cardigan and said:

'My Lord, are you not going to charge the flying enemy?'

'No,' said Cardigan. 'We have orders to remain here.'

'But, my Lord, it is our positive duty to follow up this advantage.'

'No,' Cardigan said again. 'We must remain here.'

'Do, my Lord,' Captain Morris pleaded in agonised impatience. 'Do allow me to charge them with the 17th. Sir, my Lord, they are in disorder.'

'No, no, sir.' Cardigan's 'hoarse, sharp' words were clearly heard by a trooper some way behind him.[16]

Cardigan was as angry as anyone that the Light Brigade were held back. For this, of course, he blamed Lord Lucan, whose orders, he considered, did not permit him to move. Lucan, on the other hand, afterwards maintained that his parting orders to Cardigan made it quite clear that the Light Brigade had permission to take advantage of so obvious an opportunity. In any event, he decided, spreading the blame farther, it was Lord Raglan's fault that they had not moved, not his. 'They had been placed in position by Lord Raglan,' he wrote. 'They were altogether out of my reach . . . to me they were unavailable.'

Lord Raglan watched this further evidence of the 'wretched' handling of the cavalry with dismay. He felt he must make the most of the opportunity presented to him by the Heavy Brigade's success, but he had so few troops available. The Duke of Cambridge was not yet down on to the plain. Sir George Cathcart had at last arrived, but he was carrying out his orders 'to advance immediately and recapture the redoubts' with exasperating slowness. His division marched past the ground on which the Heavy Brigade had fought, towards the empty works, and occupied the nearest two of them which were empty. But then it halted. Lord Raglan watched as the leading regiments deployed across the plain and a few skirmishers went hesitantly forward. Cathcart gave the order to the artillery to open fire on the remaining redoubts occupied by Russian infantry. The range was much too great. Cathcart seemed to share the illusion of most of the other generals, as one artillery officer angrily noted, that 'artillery are good for any distance'. It was pointed out that there was no sense in firing nine-pounders from such a long way off. But no effort was made to provide infantry cover for getting them any closer.[17]

The minutes passed. Cathcart seemed immobile. The Duke of Cambridge was advancing steadily now, but was still too far away to be called into action. The Highlanders could not be taken away from the last defensive line and pushed against the redoubts unsupported. Lord Raglan decided to use the cavalry again.

He sent down an order to Lucan, 'Cavalry to advance and take advantage of any opportunity to recover the Heights. They will be supported by the infantry, which have been ordered to advance on two fronts.'

Lucan received the order but for three-quarters of an hour he did not move. Afterwards he said that he took the order to mean he should only advance when the infantry came up to support him, and he could not see any infantry ready to do so.

Lord Raglan looked down with growing impatience at the cavalry, moving position slightly but making no effort to attack. His face for once had lost its look of composed tranquillity. Time and again, *The Times* correspondent noticed, he raised his glass to his eye and lowered it again with a gesture of frustration. He knew he could not delay much longer. Instinctively he felt that a second cavalry attack would be successful. He did not pretend to be a great soldier, but he had a great soldier's insight and perception when judging the mood of his men. He sensed the atmosphere of a battle. And he knew now that the cavalry were ready to attack and that the morale of the enemy had been badly damaged. They would retreat from the redoubts, he felt confident, when the cavalry thundered across the Heights towards them.[18]

But Lucan still did not move. And then as the army waited, teams of Russian artillery horses came into sight trailing lassoo tackle over the ground behind them. 'By jove,' a staff officer said, 'they're going to take away the guns.'[19]

In desperation Lord Raglan called to Airey to write Lucan a categoric order. Airey scribbled a few words in pencil on a scrap of flimsy paper supported on his sabretache. He read them out to Lord Raglan, who dictated a few more. The final order read: 'Lord Raglan wishes the cavalry to advance rapidly to the front—follow the enemy and try to prevent the enemy carrying away the guns. Troop Horse Artillery may accompany. French cavalry is on your left. Immediate. Airey."

As General Airey's A.D.C. galloped off with the order, Lord Raglan called after him, 'Tell Lord Lucan the cavalry is to attack immediately.'[20]

III

General Airey's A.D.C., Captain Lewis Edward Nolan, was a remarkable young man. His Irish father was in the British Consular service, his mother was Italian. He was extremely intelligent, good-looking and excitable. He had written books on cavalry tactics and was considered by his fellow-officers as something of a prig. 'He writes books,' Lord George Paget said with some distaste, 'and was a great man in his own estimation and had already been talking very loud against the cavalry.' His contempt for both Lucan and Cardigan, but particularly Lucan, was violently and frequently expressed. He was, however, a superbly skilful horseman and it was because of this that Lord Raglan had chosen him rather than a more respectful officer to take the order to Lord Lucan six hundred feet below. A.D.C.s with previous orders had taken their horses carefully down, picking their way cautiously. Nolan went diving down the hill by the straightest and quickest route.

He galloped up to Lord Lucan and handed him the order. Lucan read it slowly with that infuriating care which drove more patient men than Nolan to scarcely controllable irritation. He read it, in fact, as he himself later confessed, 'with much consideration—perhaps consternation would be the better word—at once seeing its impracticability for any useful purpose whatever'. He urged 'the uselessness of such an attack and the danger attending it'.

'Lord Raglan's orders are,' Captain Nolan said, already mad with anger, 'that the cavalry should attack immediately.'

'Attack, sir! Attack what? What guns, sir? Where and what to do?'

'There, my Lord!' Nolan flung out his arm in a gesture more of rage than of indication. 'There is your enemy! There are your guns!'[21]

And leaving Lord Lucan as muddled as before, he trotted away to ask Captain Morris if he might charge with the 17th Lancers.

The trouble was that Lord Lucan had no idea what he was intended to do. He could not, on the plain, see nearly as far as Lord Raglan could on the hills above him. He could not see any redoubts. And he could not see any guns being carried away. Since the battle had begun he had taken no steps to find out what was happening beyond the mounds and hillocks and ridges which cut off his view of the ground that had fallen into the hands of the enemy. The only guns in sight were at the far end of the North Valley, where a mass of Russian cavalry was also stationed. Those must presumably be the ones Lord Raglan meant. Certainly Nolan's impertinent and flamboyant gesture had seemed to point at them. His mind now made up, Lord Lucan trotted over to Cardigan and passed on the Commander-in-Chief's order. Coldly polite, Lord Cardigan dropped his sword in salute.

'Certainly, sir,' he said in his loud but husky voice. 'But allow me to point out to you that the Russians have a battery in the valley in our front, and batteries and riflemen on each flank.'

'I know it,' replied Lucan. 'But Lord Raglan will have it. We have no choice but to obey.'[22]

Cardigan saluted again, turned his horse, murmuring loudly to himself as he did so, 'Well, here goes the last of the Brudenells!', and he rode up to Lord George Paget. On the way he passed some men of the 8th Hussars who were smoking pipes. Their colonel angrily told them to put them out as they were 'disgracing his regiment by smoking in the presence of the enemy'. Paget himself was smoking a 'remarkably good' cigar and was embarrassed by Colonel Shewell's comment and then annoyed with Cardigan, who, after telling him to take command of the second line, added, 'and I expect your best support—*mind, your best support*', repeating the last sentence 'more than once'.

'Of course, my Lord. You shall have my best support,' Paget replied, obviously nettled. He decided to keep his cigar.[23]

Cardigan galloped back to the front of the brigade and drew it up in two lines. The 13th Light Dragoons were placed on the right of the front line, the 17th Lancers in the centre, the 11th Hussars on the left but slightly behind the regiments to the right of them. The 4th

Light Dragoons and the 8th Hussars formed the second line. At the last moment Lucan, without consulting Cardigan, told Colonel Douglas to withdraw the 11th Hussars, Cardigan's regiment, from the first line and to take up a position in support of it.

Cardigan himself rode forward to sit for a moment quite still and bolt upright in his saddle well in front not only of the first line but also of his staff. The spectators on the hills above excitedly leaned forward to watch what Camille Rousset afterwards referred to with cruel aptness as 'ce terrible et sanglant steeple-chase'. They could see quite clearly the two white legs of Cardigan's chestnut charger.[24]

They had, indeed, a magnificent view. They were on the Sapouné Ridge, which at this point overlooks the valley from its eastern end and falls down to the plain in a succession of grass-covered steps. On these steps those with no duties to perform sat in comfort and safety to watch the battle. Below them stretched the long and narrow North Valley; on their right the Causeway Heights; on their left the Fedioukine Hills. In front of them at the end of the valley, and facing the Light Brigade immediately below them, were the squadrons of Russian cavalry which had retreated over the Causeway Heights from the Heavy Brigade. Twelve guns had been unlimbered in front of them; three fresh squadrons of Lancers stood on each of their flanks; along the Fedioukine Heights were four additional squadrons of cavalry, eight battalions of infantry and fourteen guns. Opposite them, across the valley on the Causeway Heights, were the eleven battalions that had stormed upon the Turks and were now being gently prodded by Cathcart, and with them were a further thirty-two guns. Only a madman, as Lucan afterwards said, would expect men to charge into that open, mile-long jaw.

'The Brigade will advance,' Lord Cardigan said in a strangely quiet voice.[25]

IV

Lord Raglan and his staff did not immediately realise that anything had gone wrong. The direction of the advance was perhaps a little inclined to the left but not yet alarmingly so, and soon no doubt when the pace quickened the Light Brigade would swing to the right on to the Causeway Heights. This undoubtedly was what the Russians were expecting, for as the cavalry came slowly but determinedly towards them they withdrew from all but one of the captured redoubts and formed up in squares near the crest of the ridge. Here was Sir George Cathcart's opportunity, and some of his staff anxiously waited for him to take quick advantage of it. His division was still halted in the position it had taken up an hour or so previously, but he refused to move it, even though the redoubts he had been ordered to recapture were now no longer occupied. A staff officer urged him to advance. He said no, his mind was quite made up on the matter, and he would write to Lord Raglan.[26]

For the first fifty yards the Light Brigade advanced at a steady trot. The guns were silent. Lord Cardigan in his splendid blue and cherry-coloured uniform with its pelisse of gold-trimmed fur swinging gently on his stiffly thin shoulders looked, as Lord Raglan afterwards said of him, as brave and proud as a lion. He never glanced over his shoulder, but kept his eyes on the guns in his front.

Suddenly the beautiful precision and symmetry of the advancing line was broken. Inexcusably galloping in front of the commander came that 'impertinent devil' Nolan. He was waving his sword above his head and shouting for all he was worth. He turned round in his saddle and seemed to be trying to warn the infuriated Lord Cardigan and the first line of his men that they were going the wrong way. But no one heard what words he was shouting, for now the Russians had opened fire and his voice was drowned by the boom and crash of their guns. A splinter from one of the first shells fired flew into Nolan's heart. The hand that had been so frantically waving his sword remained rigidly above his head, and his knees, as if even in death they could not forget the habits of a lifetime, still gripped the flanks of his horse. The horse turned round and, as his rider's sword slipped from the still raised hand, he galloped furiously back with his terrifying burden, which suddenly gave forth a cry so inhuman and piercingly grotesque that one who heard it described it as 'the shriek of a corpse'.[27]

The pace began to quicken, and there could be no doubt now that most of these seven hundred horsemen were riding to their death. From three sides the round shot flew into the ranks and the shells burst between them, opening gaps which closed with so calm and unhurried a determination that men and women watched from the safety of the hills with tears streaming down their cheeks, and General Bosquet murmured, unconsciously delivering himself of a protest against such courage which was to be remembered for ever, '*C'est magnifique, mais ce n'est pas la guerre.*' 'The tears ran down my cheeks,' General Buller's A.D.C. wrote, 'and the din of musketry pouring in their murderous fire on the brave gallant fellows rang in my ears.' '*Pauvre garçon!*' said an old French general standing at his side, trying to comfort him, patting him on the shoulder. '*Je suis vieux, j'ai vu des batailles, mais ceci est trop.*'[28]

Cardigan was still in front. An excited officer of the 17th Lancers rode up alongside him, and Cardigan held out his sword across his breast. 'Steady! Steady! the 17th Lancers,' Cardigan shouted above the roar of the guns.

Behind him could be heard the fragmented shouts of squadron commanders—'Close to your centre!' 'Do look to your dressing on the left!' 'Keep back, Johnson, back!' But more frequently than any other order—'Close in! Close in! Close in to the centre!' For men and horses were falling now in appalling numbers, and with every fifty yards the charging lines became narrower, more ragged, split and uneven, more confused. Wounded men stumbled back through the muddle of bleeding horses and their dead and dying friends. Terrified riderless horses thundered out of the smoke.

Seeing the Light Cavalry massacred in front of him, Lord Lucan turned to Lord William Paulet and said to him, 'They have sacrificed the Light Brigade, they shall not have the Heavy, if I can help it.' And he ordered the halt to be sounded, withdrawing the brigade to a position where he might be able to prevent the light cavalry being pursued on its return. Wounded in his leg, he had shown complete indifference under fire and earned the grudging admission of one of his most violent critics that 'Yes, he is brave, damn him.' It took courage of another sort to withdraw the Heavy Brigade at such a time and give his enemies further opportunity to misunderstand his reason for doing so.[29]

The Light Brigade was almost on the guns now. The officers had lost control of their men, who rushed on furiously, forcing Cardigan to increase his pace. Still so angry with Nolan that the only other thing he could think of was what it would be like to be cut in half by a cannon-ball, he picked out the smoke-filled space between the red flashes of two guns and rode straight for it. He was less than a hundred yards from the guns when all twelve of them simultaneously exploded in his face, rocking the earth and filling the air with thick smoke and flying metal. The Russian gunners had fired their last salvo before crawling under the guns. Cardigan was almost blown off his horse, but steadied himself and charged on into the battery at a speed, so he calculated with careful concern for accuracy, of seventeen miles an hour.

Only fifty men of the front line remained alive to follow him. But in they rushed, slashing at several brave Russian gunners who had not dived after their comrades under the guns but were pulling at the wheels in their efforts to drag them away. About eighty yards behind the guns were ranged the unmoving ranks of Russian cavalry. Cardigan looked at them with distaste. They all appeared to be gnashing their teeth. He took this to be a sign of greed at the sight of the rich fur and gold lace of his uniform. But other men had noticed before these 'numberless cages of teeth' in the pale, wide faces, and it was believed to signify not greed, nor even ferocity, but annoyance and impatience due to a thwarted wish to charge.[30]

As Cardigan looked at them disdainfully, one of their officers, Prince Radzivill, looked back and remembered having met him at a party in London. He ordered some Cossacks to capture him alive. The Cossacks came forward, encircled him, and prodded him with their lances, cutting his leg. Cardigan glared scornfully at their wretched-looking nags, keeping his sword at the slope, as he considered it 'no part of a general's duty to fight the enemy among private soldiers', and then galloped away. He left his private soldiers to continue the fight while he trotted back up the valley to lodge a complaint about the infamous conduct of Captain Nolan.

Behind him the struggle continued unabated. Officers and men hacked at the Russian gunners, who hunched their heads between their shoulders as they tried to drag off their guns; while beyond the guns Captain Morris with what remained of the 17th Lancers charged at a mass of Russian cavalry and drove them back in disorder. He pursued them for some way until an enormous number of Cossacks forced his men back again.

Another body of Cossacks rode down on the men still fighting in the battery. Colonel Mayow, the Brigade Major, led the men out and drove the Russians off, as Lord George Paget galloped up and charged into the battery with the second line. The 4th Light Dragoons fell upon the gunners with a frightening savagery and massacred them with the ferocious excitement of Samurai. One British officer, maddened by the smell and sight of blood, clawed frenziedly at them with his bare hands, another swung his word in the air screaming hysterically.[31]

When all the Russian gunners were dead, the Dragoons charged on towards the cavalry beyond. But as they galloped through the still thick smoke, they ran into the 11th Hussars retreating before a vastly superior force of Russian lancers.

'Halt, boys!' Lord George shouted. 'Halt front. If you don't halt front, my boys, we're done.'

And so the two regiments, numbering between them less than forty men, stood at bay to face the advancing enemy. Suddenly a man shouted, 'They are attacking us, my Lord, in our rear.' It was true. Their retreat was cut off.

Lord George turned to Major Low. 'We are in a desperate scrape. What the devil shall we do? Where is Lord Cardigan?'

But Lord Cardigan had trotted away, and there was only one thing that could be done.

'You must go about,' he called to the men, 'and do the best you can.'

The men rode hard and straight up the valley at the Russian lancers formed up across their line of retreat as fast as their 'poor tired horses would carry' them.[32] The Russian lancers backed away as if they were preparing to fall on the flank of the retreating horsemen when they galloped past. But they did not do so. Restrained perhaps by that curiously indecisive leadership which was becoming a feature of Russian cavalry tactics, the lancers allowed Lord George's men to graze past them, half-heartedly pushing at them with their lances. Or perhaps it was that they were moved to compassion by the sight of these tattered remains of the most splendid-looking cavalry in the world.

For the men of the Light Brigade presented a pitiable sight. Their gorgeous uniforms were torn and smeared with blood, their horses as damp and bedraggled as water-rats. And they were the fortunate ones. Others went past on foot, alone or in pairs or dragging loved horses limping and bleeding to death behind them.

The ground was 'strewn with the dead and dying'. Horses in every position of agony struggled to get up, then floundered back again on their mutilated riders.

Even now the guns still fired at them. But only from the Causeway Heights. On the Fedioukine Hills the Russian artillery had been driven from their positions by a spectacular charge of the 4th Chasseurs d'Afrique, who had shown what brave horsemen can do when well directed and skilfully led.[33]

The leader of the Light Brigade was already home. He, at least, felt clear of blame for the unskilful manner in which the brigade had been directed. 'It is a mad-brained trick,' he said to a group of survivors. 'But it is no fault of mine.'[34]

He rode up to Lord Raglan to offer the same excuse.

'What did you mean, sir?' Raglan asked him, more angry than his staff had ever seen him before, shaking his head from side to side, the stump of his arm jumping convulsively in its empty sleeve. 'What do you mean by attacking a battery in front, contrary to all the usages of warfare and the customs of the service?'

'My Lord,' Cardigan said, confident of his blamelessness, 'I hope you will not blame me, for I received the order to attack from my superior officer in front of the troops.'[35]

It was, after all, a soldier's complete indemnification. Lord Cardigan rode back to his yacht with a clear conscience. And when his anger had cooled Lord Raglan had to admit that the brigade commander was not to blame. He had 'acted throughout', he wrote in a letter typical of many generous comments on Cardigan's part in the disaster, 'with the greatest steadiness and gallantry, as well as perseverance'.[36]

With Lucan, Lord Raglan was not so forgiving. Soon after his conversation with Cardigan, who had naturally put the entire blame on his brother-in-law, Raglan said to Lucan sadly, 'You have lost the Light Brigade.'

Lucan vehemently denied it. He had, he said, merely carried out an order given to him both in writing and verbally by an A.D.C. from Headquarters.

Lord Raglan, according to Lucan, now made a curious reply.

'Lord Lucan,' he said, 'you were a lieutenant-general and should, therefore, have exercised your discretion and, not approving the charge, should not have caused it to be made.'

Whether or not Lord Raglan made this remark—and although there is no other account of the conversation than Lucan's he might well in anger and worry have done so—he never afterwards suggested that a divisional commander should exercise discretion with regard to so emphatic an order. Cardigan was not to be blamed for obeying an order. Lucan could not be blamed because he also had obeyed one.

What Lord Raglan might have said, and what afterwards he did say, was that Lucan had misinterpreted the order; had taken no steps to find out the dispositions of the Russian army, which would have made the order quite clear to him; had not asked for the assistance of the French cavalry which the order had told him were on his left; had not made proper use of the horse artillery.

All this was, of course, true and undeniable. But Lucan was not entirely to blame. The order had been handed to him by a young officer who hated and despised him, who had answered his request for its elucidation by a disdainful and misleading gesture and, if Lord Burghersh was to be believed, a purposely misleading gesture. And the order itself was not as clear as it should have been.

Well aware that he had a case, Lord Lucan was determined to make the most of it. As Lord Cardigan contentedly drank a bottle of champagne aboard his yacht with Hubert de Burgh, Lord Lucan sat in his uncomfortable tent sharing with a sort of masochistic pride the hardships of his division. 'I do not,' he wrote, in that characteristic hand, at once outlandishly large and contemptuously illegible, 'I do not intend to bear the smallest particle of responsibility. I gave the order to charge under what I considered a most imperious necessity, and I will not bear one particle of the blame.'[37]

Lord Raglan, with that innate kindness he showed even to those he could not like, tried to shield him from much of the blame that people at home were bound to try to put upon him.

In his despatch to the Government the Commander-in-Chief emphasised the glory and heroism of the charge, 'the brilliancy of the attack, and the gallantry, order and discipline which distinguished it'. The fact that Lord Lucan had committed what he confessed in a private letter to the Duke of Newcastle as being 'a fatal mistake', he did not mention. He suggested only that there had been 'some misconception of the order to advance' and that Lord Lucan had 'fancied he had no discretion to exercise' but 'was bound to attack at all haz-ards'.[38] Lord Raglan wanted to leave it at that. A mistake had been made. He considered Lucan was responsible, but he did not intend to carry the matter any further. Lucan, on the other hand, was deter-mined to vindicate himself. In his heated interview with Lord Raglan he had hinted how far he was prepared to go in doing so. General Airey went to see Lucan to try and pacify him, to induce him to give up his intention of 'airing the matter publicly', which could only do the Army harm. Lord Lucan would not be dissuaded. He did nothing, however, until Lord Raglan's despatch was published. Airey had assured him that it would not put the blame on him. But when he saw the despatch he was furious. It could not be said actually to blame him, but it did not exculpate him either; and complete exculpation was what he was determined to have. He wrote a letter to the Duke of Newcastle and in accordance with Army Regulations sent it to the Commander-in-Chief for onward transmission. Once again Airey went to Lucan to dissuade him from sending a letter to the Govern-ment which 'would not lead to his advantage to the slightest degree'. Lucan insisted and Lord Raglan sent it.[39] When he received it, the Duke of Newcastle said that he was 'very sorry for the unfortunate course taken by Lord Lucan'. He had already seen the letter, as Lucan had sent a copy to London to be published in case Lord Raglan did not send on the original. He felt that Lord Lucan could not now re-main in charge of the Cavalry Division. A fortnight later he was recalled. The Earl of Cardigan had already gone home at his own request.

The dissensions of the senior officers, of course, meant nothing to the troops. 'The Light Brigade,' a sergeant in the 7th bluntly wrote on the evening of the charge, 'is but a clump of men.' A fellow-sergeant of the 11th Hussars went up to him and said, 'Ah, my old Fusilier, I told you a week ago we should have something to talk about before long.'

'But,' the Fusilier replied, 'has there not been some mistake?'

'It cannot be helped now—we have tried to do our part. It will all come out some day.'[40]

Around them other survivors of the charge had their wounds dressed or were carried down to the ships. Few of those who had returned had not been wounded, but many wounds were mercifully

slight, for the Russians' swords were blunt as pokers. One of the men
wounded that morning had fifteen sword-cuts on his badly bruised
head, none of which was more than skin-deep.

Under flags of truce the dead and wounded were brought back
from the now silent valley, while patrols trotted slowly across the
space separating the two armies. Horses streaming with blood and
unable to get to their feet bit at the short grass with froth-covered
teeth. And every now and then men winced at the sharp, melancholy
sound of the farriers' pistols. Nearly five hundred horses were lost.[41]

V

Of the 673 men who had charged down the valley less than two
hundred had returned. The Russians, as well as the allies, were deeply
moved by such heroism. General Liprandi could not at first believe
that the English cavalry had not all been drunk. 'You are noble fellows,' he told a group of prisoners, 'and I am sincerely sorry for
you.'[42]

The allies had need of sympathy. The engagement could not,
whatever feats of courage had been displayed, be considered a victory.
Balaclava admittedly had not been taken, but the Russian armies now
straddled the Causeway Heights. And the road, which ran along the
top of them and which might have saved the army from some of the
horrors of the coming winter, was lost.

11

THE BEGINNING OF WINTER

*I will not conceal from your grace that I should be more satisfied
if I could have occupied the position in considerably greater strength*
Lord Raglan

I

In the worsening weather the siege continued. The heavy guns fired
relentlessly at Sebastopol; but as day followed day the town seemed as
formidable and strong as ever, and some thought stronger. 'Unless we
want Sebastopol to become the strongest place in the world,' Cornet
Fisher wrote home, 'we had better leave it, for the more we besiege it
the stronger it gets.' Cracks in the defences would appear at nightfall,
only to be filled by morning. Rockets were fired at the dockyard
buildings in an attempt to fire the town, but when the smoke cleared
the people who could be seen flying up the streets, soon returned to
put out any fires that might have started. They rarely did start. Doors
and window-frames had been removed. Even the inflammable roofs
of some buildings had been taken off and replaced with metal sheets.
Sebastopol might have been made of asbestos. 'A storm,' Captain
Shakespear wrote, giving a common opinion, 'is our last chance.'

But many officers already doubted that the army was now strong
or confident enough to storm the town. Four days after the battle of
Balaclava an infantry sergeant told his parents how miserable and depressed the men were. Describing a spell of duty in the trenches, he
wrote:

We had a rough 24 hours of it. It rained nearly the whole time. The
enemy kept pitching shells into us nearly all night and it took all our time
to dodge their Whistling Dicks [the large Russian shells that flew through
the air with a curious whirring noise]. We were standing nearly up to
our knees in mud and water, like a lot of drowned rats, nearly all night;
the cold, bleak wind cutting through our thin clothing (that now is getting very thin and full of holes, and nothing to mend it with). This is
ten times worse than all the fighting . . . . We have not one ounce too
much to eat . . . . We are nearly worked to death night and day. We

cannot move without sinking nearly to our ankles in mud. The tents we have to sleep in are full of holes,* and there is nothing but mud to lie down in . . . . I suppose we shall have leather medals for this one day— I mean those who have the good fortune to escape the shot and shell of the enemy and the pestilence that surrounds us.[1]

The following day the commanding officer of the Royal Regiment confessed that he had not had his clothes off for forty-six days and nights, except occasionally to wash. 'The poor men were all in filthy rags,' he wrote. 'Russian knapsacks were cut up and bound round their legs, their feet were swollen, and many were without shoes. They converted old Russian coats into sandles, and wore them day and night, wet or dry.'[2] Their red coats were almost black, another officer wrote, 'and all the foolish lace tattered and torn'. When an auction of the belongings of dead officers was held on 1 November the prices given for clothing were 'fabulous. An old forage cap fetched 5l. 5s. 0d.; an old pair of warm gloves 1l. 7s. 0d.; a couple of cotton night caps 1l. 1s. 0d.'. At another auction a pair of old gloves fetched 35s., two small pots of cocoa 24s. each and a lot comprising a pot of pomatum and 'a little tooth powder' 36s. Hussar jackets, however, gorgeous but useless, worth £40 when new, sold for less than £2 6s.[3]

Both officers and men had money. And they had little else. Despite their sad condition, however, the men had not yet lost their admiration for their commander. At the sight of his erect figure they would rush towards him waving and cheering. Acutely embarrassed by such displays of feeling he would go to absurd lengths to avoid them, making long detours round working-parties with an enormous scarf round his ears and mouth. He even rode away from men who ran towards him wanting to give him a cheer and hoping to get in return a few words of encouragement or praise.

Even Sir George Brown, heartily disliked in the Light Division and quite unconcerned by his unpopularity, once told him that he really ought to show himself more to the men.

'What good will it do?' Lord Raglan asked him.

'Oh! It will cheer the men up. Why, sir, numbers of my men don't even know your name.'

'But they don't know *your* name, George!'

* They had been made for the army in Spain in 1811 or 1812, according to Captain Ross-Lewin of the 30th, and certainly 'let the rain through like a sieve'.

'Every man in the Light Division knows my name.'

'I'll bet you a pound the first man we ask does not.'

'Done.'

They rode to the Light Division camp, where Lord Raglan won his bet. All the soldier could say to Sir George was, 'You're the general, sir.' But even that was more than many other soldiers knew about the 'kind-looking gent' in the civilian coat.[4]

This abhorrence of any form of homage, this almost obsessional dislike of popular enthusiasm or strong and open emotion, this avoidance of all contact with the more excitable or demonstrative of his men, was both ungracious and inadvertently unkind. More important, it was open to misrepresentations that were shortly to be widely accepted in the army. Lord Raglan was soon considered too proud to acknowledge the cheers of the men; he would not take the trouble to go out amongst them; he avoided them because he was too lordly to talk to them; he did not know how they were suffering; he did not care. The indifference was the most generally voiced complaint, and it is not difficult to understand how the accusation arose. Two days after the battle of Balaclava Lord Raglan rode through the camp of the 4th Dragoons. The men, their colonel told his wife, rushed out 'to cheer him in their shirt-sleeves. But he did not say anything. How I longed for him to do so as I walked by his horse's head. One little word. "Well, my boys, you have done well"; or something of the sort, would have cheered us all up, but then it would have entailed on him more cheers.' These the colonel knew would have been painfully 'distasteful to him; more's the pity, though one cannot but admire such a nature'.[5] Admirable or not, it was the main cause of a rising feeling against him. It was a mistake which modern generals have learned not to make.

Apart, of course, from an innate aversion to obvious emotion, Lord Raglan behind the calm exterior was desperately worried.

'What we want at this moment,' he wrote to the Duke of Newcastle on 28 October, 'are troops of the best quality. 10,000 men would make us comfortable. As it is the divisions employed in the trenches are overworked and, of necessity, scattered over a too extensive frontier.' A few days later, on 3 November, he wrote again: 'I will not conceal from your grace that I should be more satisfied if I could have occupied the position in considerably greater strength.'

The extracts from these two letters demonstrate what has been interpreted, with some justification, as another weakness in Lord Raglan's capacity as Commander-in-Chief. In addition to his hatred of ostentation and showmanship, he had a profound distrust of emphasis in both speech and writing. His letters and despatches are often full of understatements which a heavily attacked and almost panic-stricken Government found no difficulty later in presenting to Parliament and the country as deliberate deceptions. His reasons for this studied underestimate of his needs and difficulties, however, unlike his refusal to accept the noisy affection of his men, were based on something more than personal prejudice and the susceptibilities of an essentially reticent temperament. After the war was over his Quartermaster-General explained them to a Board of Inquiry in a speech of wonderful fluency. General Airey's arguments were a determined and uncompromising vindication of the man he loved, who, he felt, had been so unpardonably wronged; but they contained beneath the panegyric a true interpretation of Lord Raglan's motives. In times of stress, Airey said, the Commander-in-Chief

> ceased to be equal with other men . . . . Men went to him anxious and perturbed. They came away firm. By a like happy ascendancy he sheltered the home authorities from the dangers of undue apprehension. He knew that their fears would rapidly spread panic in England, and that panic in England would be injurious to the efficiency of the forces. Yet he did not conceal—he carefully denoted—the wants of the Army, and it is singular that he should find words to do so effectually without creating alarm . . . .
>
> It is possible that—by one unaccustomed to military affairs—the true import and consequence of the facts thus conveyed would have been more completely understood if the narrative had been given in that form of lamentation which can be appropriately adopted by civilians when labouring under heavy trials. But it was not well that that should be, and perhaps too, it may be confessed that against such a way of writing and speaking, Lord Raglan had a soldier's prejudice.[6]

He knew as well, from his own experience at the Horse Guards, how soon even private letters and secret despatches became public property. Compelled to describe an unfortunate engagement or to outline a future plan, he would send home the information by the longest route, so that by the time it reached London dismay at bad news would be lessened by the knowledge that the situation had had time to improve, and conversations about his proposals and intentions could not be damaging, because by the time the indiscreet talk had been reported by telegraph to St. Petersburg the future plans had already been put into operation.

Taking such extravagant care to keep his military secrets from the enemy, Lord Raglan was understandably annoyed that the newspapers took no trouble to do the same. The attacks which the newspapers—and in particular, and far more bitterly, *The Times*—were soon to launch upon Lord Raglan and his staff had not yet begun to assume their later malevolence. It is indicative, indeed, of the type of man Lord Raglan was that while these cruel, personal attacks should have been considered unworthy of response—still less of censorship—the printed revelations of the army's strength and dispositions drove him as near as he ever got to fury.

For weeks *The Times* had been printing information which Lord Raglan felt could not fail to be of use to the Russians when it reached Sebastopol.* And it was at this time that he had proof that his fears were justified. On 23 October *The Times* in an article describing the condition and dispositions of the army—the number of its guns, the location of various regiments, and its dearth of round shot, gabions and fascines—gave also the exact position of a powder-mill which some time later was the object of a heavy cannonade. Here was the evidence, as he told the Duke of Newcastle, that this sort of detailed information 'must be invaluable to the Russians. I am quite satisfied,' he continued, 'that the object of the writer is simply to satisfy the anxiety and, I may say, the curiosity of the public, and to do what he considers his duty by his employers, and that it has never occurred to him that he is serving more essentially the cause of the Russians.' The innocence of his intention did not, however, diminish the evil he inflicted; and something must 'be done to check so pernicious a system at once'.[7]

Lord Raglan went as far as he considered advisable by instructing Mr. Romaine, the Deputy Judge Advocate, to call a meeting of newspaper correspondents and press upon them the 'inconvenience of their writings and the need for greater prudence in future'.[8] The real check on these disclosures, he thought, should come from the Govern-

---

* *The Times* reached Sebastopol, in fact, so General Simpson told Lord Panmure, before it got to Balaclava.

ment; and he suggested to the Duke that he ought to write to the editors of the newspapers concerned. The Duke ultimately did so, but the letters he wrote were cautious and diffident. In his letter to Delane, the editor of *The Times*, he said that he was convinced it was very far from the war correspondent's 'wish to do anything but what is patriotic and useful, but his pen runs away with him sometimes'.[9] Delane replied that he would in future confine all his 'correspondents exclusively to their version of past events', but his paper still printed the details its readers had learned to expect.[10] It was apparent that the Government held back from more forceful action for fear that an imposition of censorship might be interpreted as a determination to hide from the public its responsibility and guilt. Indeed, as the weeks passed, members of the Government seemed content to leave *The Times* undisturbed and free to print what it liked as long as its main criticisms were directed against the army commander and his staff and not against themselves. And so the evil which Lord Raglan had condemned continued as before. Repeated complaints to the Duke of Newcastle were apparently ignored. He did not complain, as Lord Clarendon the Foreign Secretary complained, that *The Times* declined 'to throw a veil over our shortcomings'.[11] There was no reason why *The Times* should not print criticisms it knew to be true, but he complained bitterly when it printed military secrets. And then, after reading what he took to be some particularly ill-advised disclosures, Lord Raglan sent the Duke a letter of scathing indignation. 'I pass over,' he told him,

> the faults which the writer finds with everything and everybody, however calculated his strictures may be to excite discontent and encourage indiscipline; but I ask you to consider whether the paid agent of the Emperor of Russia could better serve his master than does the correspondent of the paper that has the largest circulation in Europe . . . . I am very doubtful whether a British army can long be maintained in presence of a powerful enemy, that enemy having at his command through the English press and from London to his Headquarters by telegraph, every detail that can be required of the numbers, condition and equipment of his opponent's force.[12]

But it was no good. *The Times* and other newspapers continued until the end of the war, despite the protestations of Lord Raglan and both his successors,[13] to publish facts and figures which undoubtedly provided the enemy with both comfort and guidance. 'The enemy at least', Lord Raglan sadly commented, 'need spend nothing under the head of Secret Service.'[14] It was an ironic observation which the enemy endorsed. 'We have no need of spies,' the Czar was reported as saying, quoting one of his generals, 'we have *The Times*.' The paper itself confessed that it had 'gone to the verge of prudence'.[15] Its correspondent's claim that his articles were out of date before the Russians got them, and that when the war was over Prince Gortschakoff told him that he had learned nothing from them that he had not known already, were excuses which were not entirely convincing. Certainly they would not have convinced the angry officers of the Royal Fusiliers. 'That blackguard Mr. Russell of *The Times* ought to be hung,' one of them wrote.

> The Russians left off shooting at our camp entirely but Mr. Russell must needs go put in his paper that the balls had reached us. We saw it in *The Times* a fortnight ago and at the moment I saw it I said that as soon as the Russians heard it we should be shot at again, and sure enough the night before last just as we were at dinner they commenced their evening's performance. Russell takes precious care to live about a mile out of range.[16]

A more reasonable excuse was that Russell was after all only the correspondent of the paper. 'I am writing for *The Times*,' he said himself with a kind of apology. 'And it is for the editor on the spot to decide what ought to be made public and what ought to be suppressed.'[17]

The editor, however, suppressed very little; and what particularly distressed Lord Raglan at this time was *The Times*'s insistence on the weakness of the British army and its virtually undefended eastern flank. 'This infernal *Times*,' Lord Burghersh angrily complained, 'is inviting the Russians to attack us at our weakest point.'

The Russians, of course, had no need to be told where the allies were weakest. The 2nd Division, facing eastwards on a long front beyond the Plain of Balaclava, was pitifully inadequate to defend so extended a position. The Plain itself, now that the Causeway Heights were lost, was even more vulnerable than before. Wherever the attack came along those miles of the British right flank, it would perhaps take more strength than the army had left to repulse it.

On the very day after the battle of Balaclava, while General Liprandi still threatened Balaclava, Colonel Federoff led a force of nearly five thousand men on the British right farther north.[18] The Russians advanced unseen until Captain Hibbert of the Royal Fusiliers caught sight of them in his glass and sent a message to his colonel. By the time the message had reached the divisional commander the outlying pickets of the 49th, having put up a hard fight, were retreating.

General De Lacy Evans watched the men falling back through the scrub, ignoring suggestions that he should support them. His main force was collected on a ridge of rising ground above the retreating pickets, and he decided to wait for the enemy there. But the Russian attack was not pressed. Colonel Federoff took his men away in the face of a heavy artillery fire.

When Lord Raglan rode up, his horse's mouth white with foam, the short engagement was over. The Russians had learned what they wanted to know. No one doubted that one day soon they would come back; and that when they did there would be many more than five thousand of them.

II

That evening Lord Raglan received from the Duke of Newcastle a letter which gave him some slight relief from the worries that seemed to beset him on every side. The Government, he read, had decided that Sir George Cathcart should relinquish his 'dormant commission' to succeed to the command of the army in the event of Lord Raglan's death. This decision had been taken, the Duke said, because it was felt that Sir George Brown's energy in preparing for the expedition to the Crimea and his gallant conduct at the Alma made it obvious that, despite other considerations, his seniority should now be allowed to exercise its prerogative. Lord Raglan welcomed the decision. It was, he told the Duke, 'an immense relief to me. . . . Now, all is right'. He had, he confessed, hated being the unwilling keeper of a secret shared only by himself, Cathcart and the Duke of Cambridge. It had made his 'usual intimate relations with Brown . . . a great deal less comfortable than before'. He disabused the Government, however, of the idea that Brown would succeed to the command. He was senior to Cathcart, but Sir John Burgoyne, as Raglan reminded Newcastle, was senior to Brown and, although an engineer, he was quite capable of assuming command, and should in fact do so.[19]

Cathcart professed himself delighted at the Government's decision. He had kept the commission in his breast-pocket in a waterproof bag and told his A.D.C. how relieved he was when he took it out and returned it to Lord Raglan. He had not at all liked the 'arrangement . . . and had only consented to receiving the document at the earnest entreaty of the Queen'.[20] But he did not live long in his newly found relief. Ten days after receiving the news that his commission was cancelled, 'the most gratifying' news that he 'could possibly receive', he was shot in the chest at Inkerman.

LORD RAGLAN

THE BATTLE OF THE ALMA
20 September 1854

THE CHARGE OF THE LIGHT BRIGADE
20 October 1854

THE GUARDS ATTACK AT INKERMAN
5 November 1854

A BURIAL PARTY AT BALACLAVA

THE TRANSPORT OF THE LIGHT DIVISION

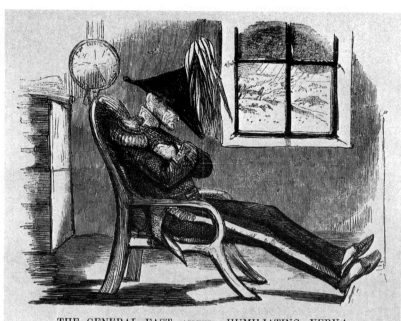

THE GENERAL FAST (ASLEEP). HUMILIATING—VERY!

THE QUEEN VISITING THE IMBECILES OF THE CRIMEA.

AT THE CAMP OF THE 4TH DRAGOON GUARDS
Spring 1855

BALACLAVA HARBOUR
Spring 1855

A COUNCIL OF WAR
Lord Raglan, Omar Pasha and General Pélissier

12

INKERMAN

In God's name, fix bayonets and charge!
Captain the Hon. Henry Clifford, Rifle Brigade

I

As daylight faded on the evening of Saturday 4 November General Pennefather rode up to the crest of a hill which commanded a distant view across the Tchernaya valley. For several days past he had been concerned by signs of increasing activity around the strangely shaped ruins of a town which had once stood on the hills beyond the valley. A dreary drizzle of rain had been falling all afternoon, and it was difficult to distinguish the shapes which moved across the lens of his field-glass. But there was no doubt that enormous numbers of Russian troops were collected on the rocky heights which rose up sharply on the other side of the river below him. Smoke rose above the castellated walls and crumbling towers; and through the arches and openings cut into the flat face of the rock he could see fires burning. Horsemen trotted constantly along the hillside tracks; and on the road leading down into Sebastopol he caught sight of a small yellow object which 'attracted and detained his attention'.[1] It was, in fact, the carriage of the Grand Dukes Nicholas and Michael, who had come to watch their father's army win its promised victory.

Concerned by the appearance of growing urgency across the river, Pennefather sent two officers, Captain Carmichael and Major Grant, down into the valley to see if they could discover anything of the enemy's intentions. After a careful watch the two officers reported that the Russian army appeared, for the moment anyway, to be static. A new force of cavalry, which had not previously been noticed, patrolled the banks of the river, and large flocks of sheep were driven into pastures near the Inkerman ruins. But no threatening movements were being made.

Darkness fell and the rain came gloomily down. The night was unusually quiet. The only sounds were the constant patter of the rain on the canvas tents and, in the distance, the creak of wheels turning on the soft wet ground. At four o'clock in the morning the church

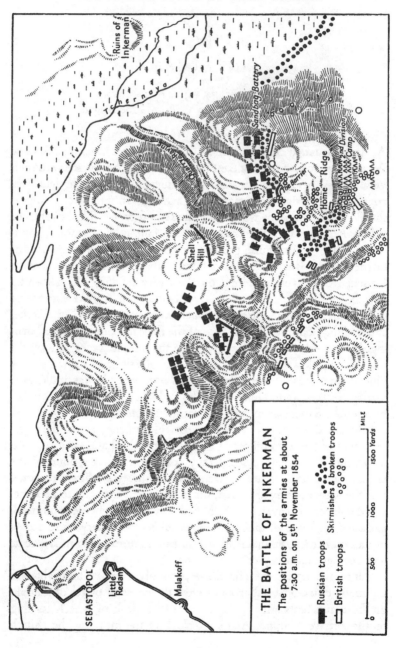

THE BATTLE OF INKERMAN

The positions of the armies at about
7.30 a.m. on 5th November 1854

■ Russian troops   ●●● Skirmishers & broken troops
□ British troops   ○○○ooo

500   1000   1500 Yards   MILE

bells of Sebastopol clanged in dreary unison to summon the garrison to Mass.[2]

A little before dawn Captain Ewart, an officer of General Airey's staff, rode through the early morning mist to collect the reports of the divisions at the front. At each headquarters he was told there was nothing to report. The 2nd Division, on his arrival, had been dismissed from their dawn stand-to, and the men were already going out as usual to collect wood and bring water for the camp.

General Codrington watched the relief of the forward pickets and the men, who had been on duty all night, coming back quietly to their tents. Then through the mist, now closing down more densely over the ground, he heard the sound of rifle-fire. At first it was spasmodic as if an outpost had panicked in the fog, but soon it became intense and was taken up all along the line. Codrington stopped the night pickets returning and ordered his brigade under arms. Captain Ewart, making his way back to Army Headquarters with his divisional reports, reined in his horse, wheeled round and galloped back to find out what the firing was. As he approached the 2nd Division's camp he was stopped by Sir George Brown, who ordered him to ride for all he was worth to Lord Raglan and tell him that the army was under attack.

II

Lord Raglan received the news with characteristic calm. At seven o'clock he was in his saddle riding hard through the fog towards the noise of the guns. He knew that on the outcome of this battle would depend the fate of the army. He knew too that even if it were won, a heavy and costly engagement would inevitably mean that the army must spend the winter in Russia. He had taken great chances to avoid this. He had concentrated all his available forces on the siege and capture of Sebastopol. The French had at last been persuaded of the advisability of an assault, and an appointment with Canrobert had been arranged for that very evening to discuss the details of an attack on the town provisionally fixed to take place on 7 November. But now, two days before, it was he who was being attacked. He had gambled and had lost.

Every since he had reached Balaclava nearly two months before,

Lord Raglan had decided that his small army was not strong enough both to lay determined siege to Sebastopol and adequately to defend itself. In attempting to save the army from a winter campaign, which it was hopelessly ill-equipped to maintain, he had withdrawn only the 2nd Division and the Guards Brigade of the 1st Division from the front line of the siege-works. These nine regiments were all he had felt able to spare for the defences of the army's flank. They were in a position of extreme vulnerability, and Lord Raglan knew it. Two days previously he had written that in the event of an attack 'it is probable the enemy will move upon the 2nd Division'.[3] They were not entrenched in a defensive position, the divisional commanders believing that so extensive and uneven a line could best be defended by troops operating in the open, making use of natural cover and fighting a delaying action until reinforcements could be brought across from the trenches and siege-works in front of Sebastopol.

The main part of this small defensive force was encamped on spurs of what became known as Inkerman ridge, looking down upon the Tchernaya. The undulating top of the ridge and the slopes running down to the river in the valley below it were densely covered with scrubby brushwood and thick bushes growing in tufts to a height of about four feet. The river itself ran through green and tranquil meadows, which were in startling contrast to the sheer walls of rock that rose beyond it, slab upon grey slab, to the ruins of Inkerman and the headquarters of the Russian field army.

The very sight of these massive precipices was alarming. 'For some reason,' an officer wrote, 'they made us feel how weak we were.'[4] The position would not have been so precarious if Canrobert had been willing to help. On more than one occasion Lord Raglan had asked him for French troops to assist in the defence of this exposed flank, but the French general had said that none of his men could be spared until new drafts arrived. The French force at this time, in fact, numbered over 40,000 men, the British only 24,800 including the naval brigade. And although 5,000 Turks were assigned to the French Army and 6,000 to the British, Lord Raglan believed that they had completely lost heart since the battle of Balaclava and refused to make any use of them, openly maintaining that they would be more trouble than they were worth.

The Russian army was more than half as great again as the combined forces of the allies. Since the beginning of October Russian troops had been pouring into Sebastopol, and on 5 November Mentschikoff's total forces numbered some 120,000 men.[5] For weeks it had been known that these troops would soon be used for a full-scale attack on the besieging armies. British officers had even had letters from relatives at home telling them that friends in Russia had warned them of it. A coded letter from Prince Mentschikoff to the Governor of Warsaw for onward transmission to the Czar had fallen into the hands of the British Ambassador and given him notice of Russian hopes and intentions. And then at five o'clock in the afternoon of 4 November printed orders to the Russian army were issued in Sebastopol. But the allies had no spies in the town, and when the next morning sounds of firing and the whistle of shells were heard in the British camps, and dark grey figures were seen moving down the valley through the drifting fog, no one was sure what the Russians intended to do.

In fact the Russian plan was direct and uncomplicated, and on a bright winter's morning might have been divined. The main attack under General Dannenberg was to be made upon the 2nd Division and the Guards on Inkerman Ridge. To keep the French out of the battle two diversionary movements were to be made. On the French left a Russian force was to make a sortie out of Sebastopol and prevent Canrobert from bringing his troops across the allied front in the direction of the real attack; while Prince Gortschakoff was to move down the Tchernaya valley towards Balaclava to stop Bosquet's division from leaving the Sapouné Hills overlooking the Plain of Balaclava. The Sebastopol garrison was to make sallies on the allied trenches and siege-works whenever an opportunity offered, thus adding to the confusion and keeping the weak flank unsupported.[6]

Greatly helped by the fog, which in parts of the field was so thick that soldiers could not see men standing two yards away from them, the Russian preliminary feints were at first successful.

Worried by what he could see of Prince Gortschakoff's troops moving down the valley below him, General Bosquet hesitated when the Duke of Cambridge asked him to come up to support the Guards Brigade, which the Duke had taken forward to the threatened edges of the Inkerman Ridge. 'On verra,' he said and for an hour he stayed where he was, anxiously watching Gortschakoff's men through the occasionally lifting fog and wondering what to make of the conflicting reports which came in from his outposts. At about seven o'clock, however, he decided that Gortschakoff's threat was not a serious one and moved north with part of his division as the Duke of Cambridge had asked him to do. On the way he met Sir George Brown and Cathcart and immediately offered them his help. The offer was declined with firm bluntness.

'Our reserves,' said Brown as if to be offered French help was an insult to the British army, 'are sufficient to take care of all eventualities.'[7]

Bosquet was asked to take his men and artillery to a position from which he could watch the British rear. He remained there inactive for almost two hours until called up by Lord Raglan. On his own responsibility, however, he sent General Bourbaki with the 7th Léger and the 6th de Ligne to the help of the confident English.[8]

On the Sebastopol front the Russians had a similar success. Canrobert seems to have decided, about the same time that Bosquet did, that the main attack was being made on the British right and by eight o'clock had given orders for some of his battalions to march across the front of the town to the help of their allies.[9] They were, unfortunately, extremely slow in moving. And at half-past nine, when a large Russian force sallied out of Sebastopol, other battalions, which had been ordered to hold themselves in readiness to move to the help of the British as occasion demanded, were thrown by Prince Napoleon against this new threat in a successful effort to repulse it. Encouraged, however, by the Russians' withdrawal, the French pursued them too far, charging up to the walls of the town, where they came under a savage and destructive fire. It was half-past eleven before Prince Napoleon had extricated his men and was able to march them off to Inkerman. He arrived too late to take any part in the battle.

III

The British troops facing the main attack were being slowly driven in. In the hollows and ravines between the 2nd Division's camp and the sharp slopes falling down to the valley, pickets and outposts fought isolated battles with Russian units of immensely greater strength, seeing only their own fights, knowing nothing of what was happening elsewhere, desperately holding their ground until by sheer weight of numbers they were forced back towards their camp.

Captain Elton of the 55th, sent down to the front to support the pickets, found to his 'horror that only about 15 muskets out of the company would go off and out of those fifteen only about six men would follow' him to the front. 'However,' he told his father in a letter two days later,

> there was nothing to be done but push to the front and I soon joined the advanced picket which I found in much the same state with regard to the arms as my own. We retired gradually before them as they were coming on in masses of columns supported with a very powerful artillery, and soon had more desperate work almost hand to hand in thick brushwood with the guns playing on us in a most fearful way, and ours answering them over our heads, while we were firing musketry into each other at 15 and 20 paces distant, now and then charging and driving them back with the bayonet and then being driven back by superior numbers again.[10]

General De Lacy Evans, the divisional commander, would have allowed his pickets to fall back unsupported, relying on his artillery to shatter the advancing columns as he had done when Colonel Federoff had attacked him the day after the battle of Balaclava. But Evans was ill and although he got up from his sick berth aboard a ship in the harbour when he heard his division was threatened, he allowed General Pennefather, his senior brigadier, to conduct the battle in his own way. And Pennefather believed his outlying pickets should be constantly reinforced and supported. Knowing that the kidney-shaped mound known as the Home Ridge, in front of the division's camp, was his last line of defence, he pushed forward all the troops he could spare down into the fog to delay for as long as possible the bitter, savage hand-to-hand fighting he felt must soon take place on the higher ground where he stood.

Lord Raglan, like Evans, allowed General Pennefather a free hand. He ordered up more troops and as many guns as could be spared, but when they arrived it was left to Pennefather to decide how to use them.

When, for instance, the Connaught Rangers came up from the Light Division they were sent down through the dense brushwood to help the 2nd Division's scattered pickets 'dispute every inch of the ground'. The brushwood was so thick that they had to open out in skirmishing order and disappear singly into the fog, each man losing himself in the damp, impenetrable whiteness, calling constantly to his neighbours to reassure himself that he was not walking alone into the fire of the enemy. The shells and round shot hissed and whistled over the soldiers' heads, the artillery on both sides firing blindly into the bewildering air.

Captain Browne of the Rangers almost walked into an officer of the 2nd Division. He asked him what was going on.

'Oh, you'll soon find out,' the officer told him. 'There are six thousand men on the brow of the hill.'[11]

A few minutes later the slender line of Rangers was cut in two by a strong Russian column which pushed through its centre. The right of the line was rolled back by the Russians, but the men on the left fired at the looming figures and then charged at them with their bayonets. The excited Irishmen chased down into the glen shouting and cheering, firing wildly at the ghost-like shapes, until they came on to another and larger column moving slowly but menacingly forward. Withdrawn by the notes of a bugle they fell back and stumbled into an artillery battery which was eagerly advancing against the enemy, already having penetrated the leading line of Russian skirmishers. Realising now how far forward he had brought them, Colonel Wood in command of the gunners quickly ordered them to fire case as the Rangers retreated past them. But before they could obey, the Russians came out of the fog only ten yards away from the leading three guns. There was no chance now either of firing or of getting the guns away. The artillerymen threw themselves ferociously at the Russians in an attempt to save their guns from capture. Hacking at them with swords, swinging furiously at them with rammers, sponge staves and even bare fists, they succeeded for a minute or two in holding them back. But the rolling weight of the Russians bore them down. The guns were captured and the inexorable advance continued.

More regiments were now coming up to the help of the 2nd Division and pushed past the tents of the camp and into the unseen declivities beyond them. In the shallow dip to the left of the camp four companies of the 77th led by the immensely tall Colonel Egerton went bravely down into the fog, which lay so thick here that when a line of moving shapes appeared on the brow of a hill less than fifteen yards away it was impossible to see at first what they were. General Buller was with this regiment of his brigade and could not believe that the figures so close to him were enemy troops. 'It was a moment or two,' his A.D.C. remembered, 'before I could make General Buller believe that they were Russians. "In God's name," I said, "fix bayonets and charge!" He gave the order and in another moment we were hand-to-hand with them.'[12]

The fight, like so many others that morning, was bitterly ferocious and somehow unreal. The whine of bullets, the damp whistle of shells, the screams of agony and rage, even the constant, raucous shouting which those who fought at Inkerman afterwards remembered more clearly than anything, were muffled by the thick and suffocating air. Hands and arms appeared to move with the frustrating sluggishness of sloths. Dark shapes heaved out of the whiteness with the suddenness of apparitions or melted away into it silently, like bodies slowly sinking in a mist-bound sea. Men looked like bushes, bushes like men. On both sides they were wearing overcoats, and it was almost impossible to tell who were friends and who enemies. It was like fighting in a nightmare. Only the fear was real, and the pain.

The usually dense and compact power of the Russian columns was broken up by the straggling brushwood, and the men had to fight singly or in clumps. Many of them had been sent out that morning with extra rations of vodka and brandy and some of them were drunk, but their fear had not been dulled. Finding themselves alone, no longer a part of the encouraging and comforting mass in which they had been trained to fight, they began to lose their nerve. They hid in the bushes or lay down where they were, pretending to be dead. Sensing their fear, the English soldiers rushed at them like wolves, jabbing furiously with their bayonets at the long grey coats or swinging their rifles round by the barrels to bring the heavy stock down with a sickly, satisfying thud against the white, strangely expressionless faces.

As the men of the 77th knocked and hacked their way through the isolated groups of Russian troops, and trampled over the dead and those who pretended to be dead, they came out of the dense patch of fog and saw more Russians on the rising ground in front of them. These solid, stationary columns of troops had not yet been touched, but, seeing the enemy soldiers jumping out of the wall of fog below them, they broke and ran. The 77th rushed off in pursuit, with the 'resurrection boys', as they were afterwards derisively called, getting to their feet and hurrying along behind and beside them. These resurrected Russians were far too numerous for the 77th to take prisoner, and they seemed tacitly to have accepted the fact that, provided they did not interfere with the chase of the column flying in front of them, they would be allowed to escape.[13] After pursuing the enemy for almost half a mile, however, the 77th were halted on the slopes of Shell Hill, a high, pear-shaped ridge on the crest of which the Russians had established several guns in battery. The men of the 77th lay down there, panting, under a heavy fire from the guns above them.

Soon the fire lifted, and as it did so hundreds of men ran past them in the fog, now swirling across the slopes of the hill like steam. Mistaking the hurrying figures for British infantry advancing, the 77th shouted at them a few encouraging insults. But they were Russians, whose heavy columns had been overthrown by case shot hurled against them from the batteries on Home Ridge, retreating out of range.

Farther away on the right the Russians were also retiring. Here some companies of the 41st and the 30th had charged with the bayonet when their rifles, piled all night in the damp mist with uncovered muzzles, had failed to fire. And so on this part of the front also, thousands of the dispirited enemy were retreating before the determined charges of a few hundred men. What had seemed impossible an hour before was now a reality. The Russians were being thrown back all along that narrow front on which they had hoped to roll back the allies into the sea.

It was half-past seven in the morning.

IV

Lord Raglan rode along the crest of the ridge to the north of the 2nd Division's camp trying to piece together into a coherent whole the contradictory reports which came to him. The fog was still thick and he could see nothing. Only the muffled noises of battle told him that the crisis of the first assault had passed.

But it could not be long, he believed, before a new attack was made in even greater force. The only doubt was when it would come. The doubt was soon resolved. At about a quarter to eight news came to him that General Adams, commanding the 1st Brigade of the 2nd Division, was being heavily pressed on a spur of land about half a mile north of where he stood.

Adams had with him rather less than seven hundred men, mainly of the 41st and the 49th. A tall, commanding figure on an immense horse, he rode up and down his lines as the Russian columns came on, were repulsed and came on again. He could not hope to hold back the enemy unaided much longer. Already he was being slowly outflanked and forced to give ground. And then as a fresh column lumbered towards him out of the fog, his brigade major galloped up to say that the Guards were on their way towards him and would soon be there. He lifted his hat in the air and cheered, shouting to his men that the Guards were coming. Four young officers of the 41st sprang out of the ranks at his words and waving their men on with their swords dashed at the massive Russian column. They charged it alone and all four of them were killed. Their men refused to follow them in such heroics. 'All right,' one of them said, 'so the bloody Guards are coming. Let them do some fighting for a change.'[14]

The fact was that the Guards were widely supposed to be incapable of it. At the Alma, where they had been unjustifiably suspected of cowardice, their reputation had been severely damaged. 'A report is rife which I hope will *not* spread,' an officer in the Royal Fusiliers told his father, 'that the Guards cut it.'[15] A captain in the Grenadiers confirmed it. 'We did not think much of it,' he wrote, giving a fairer account of the retreat of the Scots Guards than some officers of line regiments had done, 'as they had to sustain very heavy fire, but when one reads of their remarkable gallantry in the papers, it is right that the public should have a true version of the case—which is that they retired, causing our men, who were in line on their right, to cry out "Shame!", saying at the same time they wished the Queen could see the favourites now.'[16]

The Scots Fusilier Guards came up to the help of General Adams, determined to retrieve their honour. They were led by Colonel Walker. On their right were the Grenadier Guards commanded by Colonel Reynardson. Both General Bentinck, the brigade commander, and the Duke of Cambridge were with them. They marched along the top of the spur under heavy fire.

Towards the eastern edge of the spur was a half-built semicircular wall about ten feet high with two deep embrasures where it had been intended to place two guns. Although of no importance in itself hundreds of men were to die in ferocious fights for possession of it. It was known as the Sandbag Battery, but Bosquet, who later saw the piles of bodies sprawled in the grotesque postures of death all round it, called it more dramatically but with terrible accuracy, 'l'abattoir'.[17]

Already the ground there was covered with dead and wounded men. When the Guards came up the defenders had just been driven off, and it was temporarily occupied by the enemy. After unsuccessfully trying to get their wet rifles to fire the Grenadiers charged with the bayonet, and once more the Russians were tumbled out of the battery and down the steep slopes of the hill beyond it. Ordered to occupy the ground on the Grenadiers' left, Colonel Walker took the Scots Fusilier Guards in the indicated direction when he saw two new Russian columns marching steadily up the slopes of the hill towards him. Quickly he changed his line of march to meet this fresh threat. His men were just about to open fire when the Duke of Cambridge rode up and in a thunderous voice demanded, 'Where the devil are you going to, sir? Form on the left of the Grenadiers!'[18]

The Duke, as he had shown at the Alma, was not at his best in an emergency. His usually cheerful and friendly expression was replaced by an aspect of distracted fury. Disdaining to point out the reason for his change of direction, Colonel Walker recalled his men and took them where the Duke of Cambridge had ordered them to go. By this time, however, General Bentinck had also seen the Russian columns approaching, and he sent Colonel Walker back again. Once more Walker recalled his men and in doing so his already hoarse voice failed him altogether, and General Bentinck had to do his shouting for him.

Now at last in position the Scots Guards were ready to show how misjudged they had been at the Alma. They fired a volley into the dense columns now less than fifty yards from the brow of the hill and then charged down the slope with a kind of bitter fury. Seeing the angry-looking Scotsmen in their vast bearskins rushing through the brushwood at them, the Russians fell back. The Guards threw themselves after them until a frantic A.D.C. sent by the Duke of Cambridge ordered Colonel Walker to bring them to the top of the hill again.

On reaching it Colonel Walker was horrified to see that the Grenadiers had evacuated the Sandbag Battery, having rightly decided that it was a worthless possession, as after they had captured it they were in a hopelessly inadequate position to defend it, impotent behind its high, restricting walls. They had sensibly occupied more commanding ground above it, leaving it open for the Russians to pour into it once more, loudly cheering in triumph. This was too much for Colonel Walker. Leading his men on foot, for his horse had just been shot under him, he charged back into it, and yet again the Russians were driven out of it at bayonet point.[19]

On both sides of the high, curved wall the bodies of the dead and dying now strewed the ground like slaughtered animals, in some places three deep. General Adams, Bentinck and Walker were all wounded. The confusion in the battery was appalling; the screams of the wounded and the rattle of fire unceasing. The fog was slowly lifting, but the air was filled with smoke and it was still impossible to see more than forty yards. As the Scots Guards watched uncertainly behind the temporary safety of the sandbags, some wandering about amongst the bodies as if in a daze, others crowding round the embrasures or peering round the edges of the wall, a larger Russian force than any that had so far assaulted the battery swarmed up the slope towards it. Even through the smoke and the sickly-sweet scent of death, it was possible to smell 'distinctly, that peculiar, strong, leather-like smell' always perceptible in the close presence of Russian troops.[20] The dark, lumbering shapes of the early dawn had now become the more familiar, clearer figures of the Alma. It was possible even to see their features again, the flat, broad, white, young faces with the high cheek-bones under the shaven heads and 'muffin caps'. And here and there a brighter, keener face than those hundreds of others so dazed and blank and alarmingly alike, sometimes one looking, as Colonel Dalrymple White noticed with surprise, 'just like an Eton boy'.

They came up over the brow of the hill, and over the top of the battery wall. 'I scrambled up the barbette of the battery,' one of their officers wrote, 'and saw by the red coats that we were engaged with Englishmen. They had tall black caps. What they were for I did not know.'[21] All around him his men were firing their muskets into the milling crowd below. Colonel Francis Seymour, who had taken over from Colonel Walker, did not share his predecessor's feeling for the honour of the position and took his men away before they were all killed where they stood. The Russians jumped down on to the still or squirming bodies that the Scots Guards left behind them, cheering excitedly 'like lunatics'.[22]

Now it was the turn of the Grenadiers to feel outraged by the Russians' shouts of victory. Although they had run out of ammunition and for several minutes had been hurling stones and rocks at the Russians in their front, when they saw the Coldstream Guards marching up to their assistance, regimental pride overcame their discretion. Led by Colonel Henry Percy and Colonel Charles Lindsay they rushed back into the battery, thrusting and jabbing and slashing with their swords and bayonets as if they too had all gone mad.

On several more occasions that morning the Sandbag Battery was lost and won again. Russians were driven down the slopes by the British soldiers only to swarm back up again and once more to be pushed and kicked and slashed away. Afraid of losing their almost hysterical men in the brushwood, the officers shouted and cursed as they ordered them back to the colours, refusing them the pleasure of chasing their enemies down the hill. But Colonel Townshend Wilson of the Coldstream, shout and swear as he did, could not get his men back and was carried down after them, right to the bottom of the valley, where General Kiriakoff, 'frantically waving his Cossack whip', cracked it at the men as he shouted at them to turn round and face their enemy.[23]

At a time when every man counted, the wild pursuit of the Guards was dangerous. For the brigade, magnificent in its courage, was visibly shrinking. There were few of General Adams' original men of the 41st and the 49th left. The Duke of Cambridge, who had galloped off for reinforcements to stem the tide, had been given five hundred men of the 20th, the 95th and the Rifle Brigade by Pennefather; but had been met by stern refusals from Sir George Cathcart and the colonels of Bosquet's two battalions, the 7th Léger and the 6th de Ligne, which had just arrived but which could not be moved, they said, without 'higher authority'.[24] Unless more men came soon the Russian swould surely break through.

The only men at this time available were four hundred of the 46th and 68th Regiments. They were the only troops of the 4th Division which still remained under Sir George Cathcart's orders. On arriving at the camp of the 2nd Division Cathcart had asked General Penne-father where the men he had brought with him were required. 'Everywhere,' Pennefather had replied. And taking him at his word Cathcart had split his division up and sent individual companies and battalions off in any direction where they seemed most needed. With the four hundred men he had left, he decided the best thing to do would be to go down into the valley and attack the troops he saw immediately below him.

No one agreed with him. The Duke of Cambridge wanted him to support the Guards, Pennefather also urged the necessity of closing the wide and undefended gap between the Guards and his own division. Lord Raglan, who had been watching the Guards fighting so courage-ously at the Sandbag Battery and knew that they must either be sup-ported or withdrawn, decided to support them. He sent Airey to Cathcart with the necessary order. Cathcart was extremely annoyed. Here was yet another example of his advice and opinion being con-sidered worthless. If he suggested one thing, Lord Raglan was sure to order another. He argued with Airey. Whose order exactly was it any-way? 'Move to the left,' Airey said coldly, refusing to discuss it. He spoke in that curt, dismissive, emphatic way that the most argumenta-tive men accepted as ending all further altercation. 'Support the Brigade of Guards. Do not descend or leave the plateau. . . . Those are Lord Raglan's orders.'[25]

Cathcart wheeled his horse round. He was damned if he was going to be ordered about like this. He had a good pack, he told Captain Hardinge, Lord Hardinge's son who was acting as Airey's A.D.C., and did 'not want to be cautioned'. Despite his obvious annoyance, however, he spoke quite good-humouredly, Hardinge thought. He had, perhaps, decided already to do what he wanted to do, whatever Lord Raglan's orders were. Certainly a few moments later he gave the order to attack, and the four hundred men of the 46th and the Durham Light Infantry went charging down into the valley.

The fog had cleared now, and as they had taken off their greatcoats their red tunics were a good target against the brown and green of the slope.[26] They were soon under a heavy artillery fire, but they came on so determinedly that the enemy below began to waver. Encouraged, they increased their pace, and General Cathcart trotted proudly after them. Suddenly from the high ground behind him he heard the crackle of small-arms fire, and several of his men fell to the ground shot in the back. He thought at first the Guards had made a terrible mistake, but when the smoke cleared he saw, through his telescope, not immediately trusting the evidence of his shortsighted eyes, that a battalion of Russian troops was lining the brow of the hill behind him. They were standing on the ground that Lord Raglan had ordered him to occupy, and the open gap between the Guards and the 2nd Division was thus penetrated by the enemy.

There was nothing to be done, Cathcart immediately decided, except turn round and charge back up the hill again. Sending an officer of his staff to recall the men still rushing down the slope, he called together about fifty men of the 20th who had seen their comrades of the 4th Division charging the enemy and had run across to help them. With these fifty men formed roughly into line, Cathcart and his staff once more attacked the enemy. The slope at this point was particularly steep and the going rough. By the time the men reached the brow of the hill, where the Russians outnumbered them almost fifteen to one, they were exhausted and panting for breath. Nearly all of them were killed by the close and concentrated fire with which the enemy were able to receive them. But a few of them clambered to the top of the slope and one or two of them succeeded, with frantic energy and a useless courage painful to remember, in cutting their way through to the back of the dense mass of Russian infantry lining the summit.[27]

Cathcart, himself now only a few yards from the enemy, saw the last of his men disappear behind the packed front rank. He turned to one of his staff officers, Major Maitland, who was riding by his side. 'I fear,' he said with sublime self-control, 'we are in a mess.'

A moment later he fell from his horse, shot through the heart.[28]

V

Around the Sandbag Battery the battle went on amidst the carnage with a growing despair and reluctance. On both sides now men followed their officers with obvious unwillingness and sometimes refused to do so. In the swirling fog the confusion was appalling. Once as the enemy infantry poured up towards the battery a volley of musket-balls thudded into their backs from another column farther down the slope, who mistook them for British troops advancing.[29]

Russian officers, waving their swords, would jump through the front rank of a wavering column, making phrenetic gestures in their efforts to induce their men to carry through a charge which had come to an uncertain halt. Sometimes a single officer would rush forward cheering and, followed by only three or four men, would clamber to the top of the battery wall and throw himself down the other side to an agonised death on the bayonet-points below.

British officers too, accepting the impossibility of fighting success-fully behind so constricting a wall, would jump with shouts of encouragement through the embrasures, only to find themselves alone on the far side. Hearing some men sulkily complaining that if only an officer would lead them out of the battery they would follow him, Sir Charles Russell, a young and unusually short officer of the Grenadiers, shouted 'Follow me, my lads', and leaped through the left embrasure firing his revolver. Only one man followed him.

Captain Burnaby was even less successful. Jumping to the top of the parapet and down to the other side, he ran a few paces towards the enemy until, realising that no one at all was going to join him, he was forced to go back again. By this time another attack was being made upon the battery, and soon after Captain Burnaby got back to his men a Russian soldier appeared on the walls above them. Burnaby ran the man through with his sword and, shouting 'We *must* charge', once again leaped to the top of the parapet. This time he was followed by six or seven men, who ran after their captain into a whole battalion of Russian troops. Encouraged by the sight of Burnaby killing with one slash of his sword the immense officer who led them, other Grenadiers came out of the battery to join in the fight. Sir Charles Russell came out again and two officers of the Scots Fusilier Guards with several more men behind them.[30]

Now that they were out in the open again, confidence began to return. One Guardsman, flamboyantly adjusting his sights to 300 yards, said that he had decided to shoot nothing less than a general; another, although badly wounded in the mouth, killed four men and having bayoneted a fifth was jumping on his head when his sergeant sharply reprimanded him for kicking a man that was down.[31] More and more men came out of the battery and ran into the now ferocious fight on the slopes beyond it. Slowly the Russians were pushed back down the hill. Ignoring the Duke of Cambridge's urgent shouts of command to come back to the high ground, the excited men advanced into the valley, driving the Russians before them, trampling over those who threw themselves to the ground and shouted 'Christos!' for mercy, and leaving His Royal Highness on the plateau with less than a hundred men. Within minutes the Russian column which had moved across the high ground to cut off Cathcart had got behind him also.

The Duke of Cambridge was surrounded by the enemy.

At first no one appeared to realise it. When he and the few men with him came under fire, Captain Higginson of the Grenadiers said 'Hullo! Hullo! Our own people are firing at us.' But Captain Peel of H.M.S. *Diamond*, who chanced at that moment to come by on a pony, quietly pointed out to Higginson that the fire came from the enemy.[32]

Not possessed with Cathcart's blind courage, the Duke of Cambridge did not order his few men to charge the Russians behind him, but decided to extricate them as best he could. Inclining to his left and riding fast he managed to scrape past them, escaping with an arm grazed by a musket-ball and having his charger shot under him. Most of the men with him succeeded in running past too, although on his right a group of Coldstream Guardsmen, led by a warlike surgeon of the 20th, lost half their number trying to charge through the outstretched flank of the obstructing Russian force.

Down in the valley behind him, the other remnants of the Guards Brigade had now realised their mistake in chasing the enemy so far. Completely disorganised in the brushwood, there seemed no hope of re-forming to charge back up the hill at the Russians now lining the summit. Lord Henry Percy decided that they must climb back by sheep-tracks which he saw meandering up the slope and outflanking the enemy's present position. Other officers, not under his command, followed his example and took their men up once more by other sheep-tracks to the heights. When they arrived on the plateau they were not only exhausted; not only weak with hunger, for, like almost the entire army they had eaten nothing for about fifteen hours; but they were also out of ammunition. Finding a staff officer there, Lord Henry asked him where they might get some more.

' 'Pon honour,' the staff officer replied, as if at a party in London he had been mistaken for a footman, 'don't know.'[33]

VI

The Grenadiers' temporary loss of their ammunition was, however, a minor misfortune compared with the catastrophe that had befallen the Duke of Cambridge. He had lost practically the whole of the Guards Brigade, and was 'driven almost to distraction' as minute followed minute and he could not find where they had got to.

'The Guards, sir,' a young officer cheerfully reassured him with infuriating nonchalance, 'will be sure to turn up.'[34]

Almost as he spoke he saw coming towards him out of the mist, which was once more beginning to fall thickly over the ground, a straggling group of soldiers mostly in bearskins but some others wearing the less distinctive caps of the line. Carried high above their heads were two drooping standards. The Colours of the Grenadiers at least were safe again.

They had almost been captured. When most of the Guards Brigade, and the other soldiers of the line still fighting with them at the Sandbag Battery, had charged down into the valley, the few men left with the Duke of Cambridge had included the Grenadier carrying the Colours. The corded staves had been raised high in the air to serve as a rallying point and the sight of the English soldiers converging on their flags had, of course, attracted the attention of the Russians, who advanced to capture them singing a tuneless hymn.

The dangerous predicament of these surrounded men was noticed by the redoubtable Captain Burnaby, who, followed by only about twenty men, had scrambled out of the valley straight back to the Sandbag Battery instead of taking the roundabout route that the other Guards officers had done.

'Get close together,' shouted Burnaby, 'and charge!'

'I thought it perfectly useless,' a Guardman with him afterwards wrote, 'so few of us trying to resist such a tremendous lot; but for all that I did so.'[35]

The little group of tired men rushed at the mass of troops threatening the Regimental Colours. Nearly all of them were killed. Those few that cut their way through the column to its other side turned back to see the Russians bayoneting both dead and wounded as they lay on the ground.

The advance of the Russians on the Colours, however, had taken them across the front of one of those two French battalions which previously had refused to move for want of higher authority. General Bourbaki now gave it that authority, and it attacked the Russian column in flank with such force that it immediately retreated.

By the help of this sudden French attack, the British stragglers were able to continue their withdrawal to the higher ground to the west.

Two thousand, six hundred men had been engaged on the spur of land around the Sandbag Battery and over a thousand were left there dead or wounded. By their heroic, savage resistance the weak gap in the defences had been kept closed, and now the French were there to keep it so. But it was not yet half-past eight. The fog had come down again, and on the Home Ridge, where the attack had been made on the 2nd Division almost two hours before, it was being pressed harder than ever.

VII

The men had still not eaten and were tired as well as hungry. The 30th, under Colonel Mauleverer, had been in action all morning charging and withdrawing, retaking ground and retreating from it, and had at last been pushed back beyond the crest of the Home Ridge, where some of them were so exhausted that they straight away fell asleep. Roused a few minutes later by shouts of 'Up! 30th! Up!' they scrambled to their feet once more, their bayonets red and still wet with blood, and rushed at the Russians, who had quietly advanced to within a few yards of the ridge.[36]

On every side now the Russians were forcing in ever closer to the artillery on the Home Ridge. General Pennefather, hidden by the smoke and fog, could be heard constantly shouting and swearing, pushing a few companies forward to halt a Russian attack at one point, only to find a more serious threat elsewhere. The Rifle Brigade under Colonel Horsford, the 63rd, the 49th and the 21st all repulsed attacks made by numbers of the enemy far exceeding their own. To the right of the ridge a particularly strong attack was made by two of the Russians' five Iäkoutsk battalions and was thrown back by the

57th and some companies of the 20th, brought up by Lord Raglan and sent roaring down the slope filling the air with their terrifying, unearthly war-cry known as the 'Minden Yell'.[37]

But slowly the overwhelming superiority of the Russian numbers and the dogged persistence of their troops began to tell. There were at this time 17,000 of them on the Inkerman Ridge with nearly a hundred guns in battery. And so far only 1,600 French had crossed to the help of the 3,300 British and their forty-eight guns.

Soon after half-past eight, on the left of the Home Ridge, a swarm of Russian infantry, many of them bareheaded, ran up the slope to the three guns in battery there, 'howling', one of the artillerymen said, 'like mad dogs and drunk as usual'.[38] The gunners fought wildly to defend their guns. Sergeant-Major Henry in command of the left-hand one refused to leave it, receiving twelve bayonet wounds, some of them as he lay on the ground still struggling and slashing at the trampling feet of the enemy, until he fainted through loss of blood. But after a few moments of brave resistance the gunners were driven back, and the enemy were left in possession of the guns, which they tried to spike with pieces of wood. Within three minutes, however, sixty Zouaves, who had wandered over from their trenches to join in the fight, drove them off the ridge in a brilliant, unauthorised charge.

In the centre of the ridge, also, the Russians broke through some men of the 55th who had mistaken them for other companies of their own regiment retiring. More and more Russians came through the broken centre of the ridge. It was a moment of acute danger. For behind the 55th there were no supports. The 7th Léger was approaching, but it was still some distance away and it was marching forward with obvious reluctance. At the foot of the ridge it halted altogether. The men were advancing in line and hated it. A British staff officer rode over towards them and angrily upbraided them in excellent French, asking if they could possibly be of the same nation that had so nobly fought against us in the Peninsula. Stung by his remarks the French sulkily moved on again. But the fire was heavier now; the musket-balls whirred through the smoke; and after a few paces, refusing to move any farther without artillery support, the regiment stopped again, then broke, then retreated down the hillside.[39]

The fog, which a few minutes before had been thick all over the plateau, now lifted in this part of it; and Lord Raglan, sitting with his staff close to the advancing Russians on the reverse slope of the ridge, could see quite clearly the French retreating. He was, for the first time that day, seen to be angry. He uttered 'an exclamation of astonishment and annoyance' and sent an A.D.C. to Colonel Warren of the 55th, who was re-forming his men a little way below him to his left.[40] Colonel Warren had only about a hundred men left under his command, but Lord Raglan had great faith in him and in his regiment, and ordered him to attack.

'The shot, shell and bullets were coming about us like hail,' one of his officers wrote, 'and I certainly thought my time was come.' But he felt sure that if he could get his men close enough they would make 'three or four times their number run like hares', for the Russians 'could not stand the bayonet'. He led the remains of his company up the hill, with the other men of his regiment in a cheering pack around him, 'hoping for the best'.[41]

The Russian artillery had not ceased firing when their infantry had broken over the centre of the ridge, and the round shot still flew relentlessly over the crest, cutting lanes in the growing mass of troops on top of it. With this fire directed at their backs and the charging bayonets in front of them the Russian column began to break up and then to fall back. As the men of the 55th reclaimed their ground, the 77th also came on to the ridge, supported by the 7th Léger advancing now in column and its confidence thus restored. So the defences which a few minutes before had seemed irreparably shattered were patched up once more.

But until the French came up, the thin line could not expect to hold. Including the 7th Léger there were less than fifteen hundred men on the Home Ridge now, and the last of the scattered pickets were falling back towards it, their ammunition finished, many of their friends lying dead in the scrub behind them. And all the while the heavy Russian artillery thundered in the batteries established on Shell Hill, the enemy gunners having judged the range so finely that the round shot skimmed the crest of the ridge three-quarters of a mile away from them and flew down the other side only two or three feet above the ground. The shells too dived through the sky with the uncanny accuracy of hawks. The British 9-pounders were far too light to reply to the heavy guns above them—'mere playthings' by comparison, an artillery officer angrily commented.[42]

Lord Raglan and his staff were, of course, under as heavy fire as anyone on the ridge. The round shot whistled past them and the shells exploded amongst them, but in the calm, unruffled presence of the Commander-in-Chief no one dared show that he was afraid. An A.D.C. begged him to choose a less dangerous position. 'Yes,' he said with a politeness which in the circumstances was almost absurd. 'They do seem to be firing at us a little, but I think I get a better view here than in most places.'[43] A little later a sergeant of the 7th had occasion to walk past Lord Raglan. As he drew himself up to salute, a round shot knocked his forage cap off. The sergeant picked it up carefully, dusted it on his knee, put it back on his head and completed his salute with solemn determination.

'A near thing that, my man,' Lord Raglan said, smiling at him.

'Yes, my Lord,' the man replied, 'but a miss is as good as a mile.'[44]

There were other scenes less diverting. A shell flew into the stomach of Colonel Somerset's horse and exploded there, showering the officers standing near with blood and entrails. A moment later a round shot tore off General Strangways' leg as he was talking to Lord Raglan. Strangways was a fine old man, gentle, brave and polite. The men of the Royal Artillery whom he commanded loved him with a devotion which other generals might well have envied. Lord Raglan, who had fought with him at Waterloo, confessed afterwards that the tears filled his eyes as his old friend bent down to look at his leg hanging by a shred of flesh and a bit of cloth, his long silver hair falling over his forehead. 'Will someone,' Strangways asked, polite and gentle even now, his face perfectly controlled, 'will someone be kind enough to lift me off my horse?' Two hours later he was dead.[45]

Almost at the very time that he was wounded, the gunners on the Home Ridge increased their rate of fire as though in a valedictory salute. Pouring up from the Quarry Ravine in front of them, like the slow, inexorable roll of volcanic lava, was the main force of a new attack. Lying down on the ridge between the guns, the few British troops awaited the assault. Joined now by the 7th Léger on the right of the 57th and a group of about sixty Zouave volunteers, the British soldiers watched the advancing columns, for the moment holding their fire.

As soon as they felt sure of being able to use what remained of their ammunition to the best advantage, the British riflemen opened fire.

The Russians, who had been advancing steadily against the guns, seemed now to waver. But then they steadied themselves and came on again as determinedly as before. The ground between them and the defenders of the ridge slowly narrowed. Shells blew gaps in the dense ranks; round shot tore rents in them; men in the front were shot by rifle bullets, fell and were trampled on; but the great grey lumbering mass still came forward.

Lord Raglan, for the first time during the campaign, believed that the Russians would be sure to break through. He turned in his saddle to Canrobert, who had recently joined him on the ridge.

'*Nous sommes—nous sommes,*' he said, hesitating for the appropriate word. '*Vous avez un mot d'argot qui exprime bien ce que je veux dire.*'

'*Nous sommes foutus,*' said Canrobert. '*J'espère que non, milord.*'[46]

The French troops of the 7th Léger who had been firing with expert precision began to think the advancing columns could not be stopped. Some of them, when the Russians had reached the bottom of the ridge, crawled away despite the furious shouts of their officers. Soon others began to look as if they were ready to follow their example. Officers walked bravely between the lines of faltering men, encouraging them, swearing at them, striking, with the flat of their swords, those who had got to their feet to run away. Behind them British staff officers shouted at them in atrocious French. Despairing of all other means of holding them, a French officer hoisted a cap on his uplifted sword and, joined by an English officer and two soldiers, ran straight down the slope through a storm of musket-balls at the enemy now less than thirty yards away.

'*Avancez les tambours!*' a voice called out behind them; and so, recalled to their heroic past, the 7th Léger rallied at last as their drummers and buglers ran out to the front and the Russians brought down their bayonets for the final charge.[47]

The enemy columns had just begun their charge when Colonel Daubeney of the 55th, with scarcely more than thirty men, threw himself into their right flank. The Russian ranks were so densely packed that as soon as he had forced his way into them he was quite unable to move his arms, and coming face to face with a Russian officer who was similarly pinioned the two men smiled at each other in friendly acknowledgment of a shared predicament. Behind the Colonel, however, a colour-sergeant of enormous strength was pushing and hacking a path for himself and for anyone who could get close enough behind him. Laying about him with the butt-end of his rifle, smashing his fist into any face he could reach and kicking the shins and ankles in his path, he forced his way through the Russian column from one side to the other. Making use of the clear space which his sergeant had opened up for him, Colonel Daubeney also came through with about half the men who had charged with him.[48] The damage done to the Russian formation was negligible, but the psychological effect was immediate. The men in front, believing that those behind them were under heavy pressure, hesitated in their charge and then halted it altogether.

Pennefather saw his opportunity. At his shouted command the French and British soldiers on the ridge leapt forward and dashed cheering down the slope. The Russians once more fell back. As they retreated towards the Quarry Ravine the infantry covering their flanks were also thrown back; the men on their right by a magnificent charge of the 21st and the 63rd, those on the left by well-directed blasts of artillery fire.

But the allied forces available on the plateau were still far too weak to permit of this temporary advantage being followed up, and soon the Russians were pressing forward again. To the right of the Quarry Ravine the French 6th de Ligne and the 7th Léger, which had gone well forward to support it, were falling back before several Russian battalions pushing remorselessly towards the Home Ridge. To the left of the French, Colonel Haines of the 21st, who had taken over from Colonel Ainslie, mortally wounded in his regiment's recent charge, was also withdrawing towards the head of the Quarry Ravine. Here General Goldie, since Cathcart's death in command of the 4th Division, was doing his best to hold back the Russian troops constantly appearing over the edge of the Ravine. The troops with him were a mixture of several regiments muddled together in the thick brushwood on either side of a loose stone wall built at the head of the Quarry Ravine by the 2nd Division to protect its advanced picket and to block a track which led out of the ravine and into the plain at this point. The wall was known as the Barrier, and there, as at the Sandbag Battery, a few brave men fought with ferocious determination to hold back the forceful advance of vastly greater numbers.

General Goldie sent back Major Ramsey Stuart with an urgent

message to Pennefather. 'If we don't get support,' Goldie told him, 'we shall be cut to pieces.'[49] It was no less than the truth. But Penne-father had no troops to spare, and when Major Stuart returned he had been able to collect less than two hundred men, whom he had found in the 2nd Division camp or wandering about lost on the plateau. They were thrown into the fight, and for a few minutes longer the Russians were held back. General Goldie was killed. Major Rooper took over from him and was then badly wounded. Colonel Haines, who had just returned to the Barrier with a company of the 77th which he induced Pennefather to give him, now assumed the command there; and by a display of astonishing courage, energy and skill was able to beat back every attack until the pressure on his heroic but diminishing troops was relieved by a new force which was to alter the aspect of the battle.

VIII

It was now almost two hours since Lord Raglan had ordered up two 18-pounder guns from the siege-park. The A.D.C. to whom the Commander-in-Chief had entrusted the order had delivered it to the wrong officer. Instead of taking it direct to Colonel Gambier at the siege-park, he gave it to Colonel Fitzmayer, commanding the field batteries on the Home Ridge. Fitzmayer, naturally considering it madness to leave his already threatened position to go back to the siege-park, where there was a perfectly competent officer already, answered the A.D.C.'s request with a single word, shouting above the roar of his guns: 'Impossible!'[50]

The reply was taken back to Lord Raglan, who politely expressed his dislike of so categoric an expression and sent the A.D.C. to the siege-park, where he should have gone in the first place.

Fortunately the two 18-pounder siege-guns were prepared for field service, Colonel Gambier having anticipated the order and got his men into harness as he had no draught-animals. The great iron guns each weighed more than two tons, and the gunners were already ex-hausted by their struggles to drag them over the uneven ground when it was discovered that they were pulling them in the wrong direction. By the time they got into position it was after half-past nine. Colonel Gambier, wounded by a round shot on the way up, had handed over to Colonel Collingwood Dickson, who lost no time in opening fire. Within minutes the range was found and the 18-pound balls were crashing into the enemy batteries on Shell Hill. A furious return-fire was provoked. Round shot came hurtling back, smashing and bouncing through the brushwood; the fragments of countless shells hissed in the smoke. Within a quarter of an hour nearly twenty of Dickson's fifty men had been killed or wounded. But encouraged by the presence of the Commander-in-Chief, who had got off his horse to stand with them, sharing their danger, the gunners maintained their fire with wonderful accuracy and calm determination.

Every shot found its target on Shell Hill. Sharply outlined against the sky in the now clear light, splinters and the shattered wheels of guns, showers of earth and the wreckage of wagons could be seen shooting up above the low, drifting clouds of smoke. An ammunition tumbril exploded with a satisfying roar. And as the minutes passed it seemed that these two heavy guns were slowly gaining a mastery over the enemy's numerous batteries, which all that morning had been firing unchecked at the allied infantry on the plateau below. More British gunners were killed, but others came to take their place and the guns themselves never fell into silence. The return-fire slackened; the Russian batteries moved from the exposed positions on the forward slopes of the hill to others more protected, but the siege-guns found them out, being laid by an officer with minutely calculated judgment each time they fired. As the enemy's artillery fire quietened the French also were able to get six heavy guns in battery and then another six. And so when at last Bosquet arrived with reinforcements and moved to the support of the French troops operating to the right of the Quarry Ravine, he was able to do so in relative security.

IX

Indeed the scene on Inkerman Ridge amazed the French general. Not only was the enemy's artillery fire nothing like as heavy as he had been told it was, but the British army seemed to have disappeared. 'Ah, I knew it!' he had said when Colonel Steele handed him Lord Raglan's request for help, thus overruling the proud rejection he had met with earlier from Sir George Brown and Cathcart. He had expected nothing like this.[51]

He passed several of those groups of men which could be seen all over the plateau, walking back to the camp for fresh supplies of ammunition. Away to the right he could see a tall officer in a red coat and a bearskin wandering about amongst a group of other men in their '*bonnets de poil*' lying down in the brushwood. Staff officers trotted about on apparently indeterminate errands. There were no indications that the ground was being defended to the last ditch. In fact whole sectors of it did not seem to be defended at all.[52]

Despite this alarming impression he moved across the front of the British position without consulting either Pennefather or Raglan. Frantically urged by an excited staff officer, who waved his naked sword in the air in emphatic gestures of dismay, to come to the help of the two French battalions engaged to the right of the Quarry Ravine, he took his men quickly over towards them.[53]

There were at present only 450 of them, comprising four companies of Chasseurs à pied led by a cheerful, short, and enormously fat French captain, who, to the delighted laughter of the English soldiers, marched in front of his men with his cap held aloft on the point of his sword. But soon the Chasseurs were followed by more troops—a battalion of Algerians marching to the rhythm of drums, a battalion of Zouaves led by a pretty *vivandière*, a regiment of French cavalry and lastly the two hundred survivors of the British Light Cavalry Brigade, commanded by Lord George Paget.

Apart from the supporting cavalry, there were 3,000 men in all with twenty-four guns, and the British staff hoped that Bosquet would soon be using them to drive the enemy off the field of battle.

Bosquet, however, was already having reason to regret that he had not consulted his allies. Having seen no sign of their expected infantry battalions in his march across the plateau, he supposed they must be along the right bank of the Quarry Ravine. His troops were accordinly sent a long way down the spur between the Ravine and the Sandbag Battery where they were halted in an extended line facing west, and there took up a position not only of quite exceptional danger but of utter uselessness.

They were well behind the enemy lines, in easy range of several Russian batteries. Their left was unsupported, their right overhanging a vertiginous cliff which dropped sharply to the river two hundred feet below. There were no enemy infantry in front of them.

Riding beyond the left of his prolonged and precarious line in order to discover the exact dispositions of the English infantry he expected to find there, Bosquet came upon a bare and deserted hollow. He went up to the edge of the ravine and looked down to see a column of Russian infantry marching up the steep slope to the very point where he sat in his saddle.[54]

An A.D.C. was sent back immediately for the artillery. Two guns came up quickly and were unlimbered and placed in battery; but before they had time to open fire the Russians were upon them. One of the guns was captured and taken down the slope.[55] Bosquet himself, with his escort and pennon-bearer, was not molested. An A.D.C. thought this was because the Russians were so excited to have captured a gun that they wanted to get it away quickly; Bosquet, on the other hand, thought that they were too simple to consider themselves entitled to show disrespect to a general, even an enemy one. Certainly they looked at him as if they would rather salute than capture him.[56] But as the captors of the gun went back down the slope, other enemy infantrymen came up and spread over the spur along the left of the French line. At the same time more infantry columns came up from ground below the Sandbag Battery to threaten the Zouaves in the rear.[57]

The French were surrounded, and if pressed back northwards along the spur would be forced to fight with their backs to a sheer precipice down which there could be no retreat. But the Russians were as slow to recognise their opportunity as the French were quick to react to their danger. Before the enemy understood that more than three thousand allied troops were at their mercy, the French had sprung back out of the trap and were scattering across the plateau towards the safety of their guns.

The French batteries, however, were now under heavy fire from Russian guns on high ground out of range of the allied 18-pounders. 'Nous sommes massacrés,' the officer in command of them said to Colonel Dickson. 'Eh bien!' he added with that kind of cheerful resignation which the English soldier so greatly admires. 'Ça c'est la guerre.' Nevertheless he withdrew his guns.[58]

Canrobert waiting anxiously for the Russians to pursue his retreating infantry, and, already having lost heart with the suddenness of a peculiarly volatile nature, called up the cavalry and prepared to lead them in person in an act of final, heroic self-immolation. But a shell burst in front of the Chasseurs d'Afrique, and soon the cavalry were in retreat also.

'*Mon officier*,' a French staff officer urgently called to Colonel Dickson, 'save your guns! All is lost!'[59]

Minutes passed and inexplicably the Russians did not pursue the French. Slowly confidence returned. Three new French battalions came up under General d'Autemarre, and Bosquet determined to make amends for his recent brief discomfiture. Leaving the three fresh battalions on the plateau, he sent his Algerians and Zouaves diving down into the gorge by the Sandbag Battery to attack the Russian column which had just been threatening his rear. 'Prove yourselves, children of fire', Bosquet shouted after them in Arabic as the Algerians rushed past him.[60] They flew across the ground screaming in excitement, and, joined by a knot of Coldstream Guardsmen, they flung themselves at the startled Russians, viciously stabbing scores of them with their exquisitely sharp bayonets, and after several minutes of desperate fighting they chased the survivors down into the valley and out of the field of battle. 'They are panthers', said Bosquet excitedly. 'They are panthers bounding into the bush.'[61]

X

It was a moment of triumph for the French army. Lord Raglan, offering Bosquet his left hand in congratulation, delighted the young French general by saying that he wished he had several hands to shake with him. '*Au nom de l'Angleterre*,' Lord Raglan said, '*je vous remercie.*'[62] Canrobert, almost in despair a few minutes before, was now also refreshingly encouraged. He had been wounded by a shell splinter in his arm, and this also—for it was not a deep wound—had apparently restored his confidence. He had shared the dangers of his triumphant men. Already he had one of his arms in a sling because of a wound received at the Alma, now he had both.[63]

Hoping to get Canrobert's agreement to a general exploitation of this particular success, Lord Raglan sent Somerset Calthorpe to Pennefather for a report while the French general was still with him. Pennefather told Calthorpe that the opportunity was too good to miss and if he were reinforced he had no doubt he could 'lick them to the

Devil'.[64] The message was conveyed to Lord Raglan, who translated Pennefather's characteristic remark into literal French for Canrobert's benefit.

'What a brave fellow!' said Canrobert enthusiastically. 'What a brave man! What a good general!'[65]

But when Pennefather himself came up to Lord Raglan and mentioned the sorry state of his own division, although reinforced by the 4th, Canrobert's enthusiasm vanished. He had in hand about seven or eight thousand troops. He would not agree, however, to use them offensively.

'*Mais, ma foi, milord,*' he said in some exasperation at one point during the discussion, '*qu'est que je puis faire? Les Russes, ils sont partout. Ils sont là, là et là.*'[66]

And so the French army remained in a state of suspense, ready to spring but held back from doing so. The British army was, however, saved from a similar inactivity by one of those sudden, unauthorised displays of initiative and heroism for which the battle of Inkerman will always be famous.

Still fighting at the Barrier, Colonel Haines was now joined by a friend of his, Colonel Lord West of the 21st, who had come over from a quieter sector farther west. Lord West went up to Lieutenant Acton of the 77th and said to him: 'I see several of your men here. Get them together.' Then he told him to join two other companies which were some little way farther off and, pointing to one of the batteries on Shell Hill, added the brief and startling order: 'Attack that battery.'

Acton went off immediately to the two companies indicated. 'If you'll attack the battery on either of its flanks,' he told the officers in charge of them, 'I'll do so in front.'

The two officers were not so ready to accept Lord West's hazardous instructions as Lieutenant Acton, and flatly refused to co-operate with him.

'If you won't join me,' Acton said, 'I'll obey my orders and attack alone with the 77th.'

He ordered his men forward, but they did not move.

'Very well, then,' he said in desperation, 'I'll go myself.' And he began to walk up the hill.

He had only gone a few yards when one of his men, a private, ran out calling, 'Sir, I'll stand by you.' Then a man from one of the other companies ran out, and soon, ashamed of their reluctance, Acton's whole company rushed after him.

The fifty or sixty men dashed up the slope as the guns in the battery roared down at them. Behind them Colonel Dickson sent his 18-pound shots whistling over their heads. The two flank companies, refusing to let the 77th go on alone any longer, joined in the charge. And the Russians, afraid of losing their guns, hastily limbered up and took them off. Acton's men dashed over the crest of the hill and into the deserted battery followed by several other men, mainly of the 49th, collected together by an enterprising staff officer and pushed forward to hold the ground so bravely won.[67]

XI

It was one o'clock.

Whether it was this last heroic attack, coming so soon after the brilliant charge of the Zouaves and Algerians, which persuaded the Russian Commander that his stolid, numerous, well-trained but unimaginative troops were not able to withstand these constant onslaughts of a disorderly, fragmented but courageously determined enemy; whether it was that he believed his opponents were able to throw fresh troops into the attack; or whether it was true, as he afterwards maintained, that he was persuaded by the 'murderous fire of the enemy's artillery',[68] to retreat into Sebastopol, no one afterwards knew. But the Russian commander did retreat, and left the whole of Inkerman Ridge in the hands of the allies, who, on Canrobert's insistence, refrained from pursuing them. The battle was over. Not for more than half a century was Europe to be the scene of another one so bloody, so fierce and yet, in the end, so sadly inconclusive.

13

AFTERMATH AND STORM

Everything went whiz bang in less time than I have taken to tell you
Paymaster Henry Dixon, Royal Fusiliers

I

An officer of the 46th who landed at Balaclava to join his regiment on
11 November, found the army 'in deep gloom'.[1] Once again it was being proved, as Captain Shakespear wrote home with bitter scorn, that
it was '*necessary* for England to lose her army first *at all times* before
she settled down to do things well'.

Of the army's best men, 2,573 had been killed or wounded at Inkerman. The Russians had lost, Lord Raglan thought, as many as 20,000
men,[2] but they, as Captain Biddulph sadly commented, 'could well
afford them'. Sebastopol still stood as it had always stood—as some
began to think it always would stand—strong, immutable, scarcely
scarred.* The British troops had been told that the people in the town
were suffering as much as they were themselves, but all the prisoners
looked 'fat and healthy' enough.[3] Sometimes, though, when the wind
blew from the north, the smell was 'pretty frightful.'[4]

Three days after the battle the dead were still being buried. The
allies proposed to Mentschikoff that he should send burial-parties out
to help them inter the Russian dead, but the Prince replied that it was
customary for this work to be done by those left in possession of the
battlefield. Four thousand Russian soldiers were thereupon shovelled
by allied troops into communal graves. The work was done with scant
ceremony. The Turks, making use of an empty limekiln, dragged a
hundred bodies to it by the heels and pitched them in.[5]

Many of the corpses still maintained, pathetic and grotesque, the
once natural attitudes of life. Hands were raised to ward off blows,
fingers clutched musket-stocks; mouths were open, teeth bared and
neck muscles tense. Men killed instantaneously when in the midst of
some strenuous effort were found with turf and soil clenched between

---

* When Florence Nightingale came out it still looked so. It was like 'a fairy palace', she
told her parents. 'So beautiful, so unscathed, so gorgeous' (Verney Papers, 10/5/55).

their teeth, surprising those who buried them with the knowledge that 'biting the dust' is not always a fanciful phrase.

The faces of some of the allied dead were marred by distorting grimaces of rage and terror and hate, for the Russians had bayoneted the wounded as they had done after the Alma.*[6] Under a flag of truce a formal complaint was sent to Prince Mentschikoff, who replied to the accusation of barbarity by denying that the complaint was generally justified. Particular cases were due to the 'outraged piety of an eminently religious people . . . who had been filled with horror' when they learned that French troops had pillaged a Russian church near Quarantine Bay.[7]

The Russian troops had certainly been instilled with the belief that the allies were monsters. The wounded scowled and muttered at the men who came to carry them back to the makeshift hospitals, and glared out 'from the bushes', *The Times* correspondent wrote, 'with the ferocity of wild beasts'. They had been told that if they fell into the hands of the enemy they would have their ears cut off at least. Holding out their hands in reluctant supplication, they cried for water and when given it turned away to drink, as if ashamed to have become indebted to such evil men.[8]

As late as 7 November they were still being discovered 'scattered about in the bush'. When lifted up on to mules, lent to the British army by the French, they rent the air as their wounds opened afresh with 'life's last shriek of agony . . . their legs and arms and mutilated bodies only hanging together'.

'Did you ever hear anything so terrible as the screams of those poor fellows?' General Pennefather asked. 'I am going away to get out of the hearing of such misery. They are all about my tent here, lying day and night on the wet ground, starving and dying and screaming in agony.'[9]

---

* Lieutenant McDonald of the 95th lived to give evidence of this. When wounded he ordered his men to leave him behind and prop him up against a bush. A party of advancing Russians saw him and fired at him. Some balls hit him. The Russians then came up to him and stabbed him with their bayonets. He felt no pain, only the coldness of the steel. He managed to get up on one leg and lunged at the soldiers with his fist, but they continued to bayonet him and knocked him down to the ground, where he received several more stab wounds and was stunned by the butts of their muskets. Roused by an English voice saying, 'The poor fellow's done for,' he could not find the energy to deny it. Suddenly he felt himself being lifted into the air and then dropped heavily to the ground, which seemed to the English soldier the best way of discovering whether or not he were dead. At last he managed to speak. (*Proceedings of a Court of Enquiry held at the Camp Before Sebastopol, 9/11/1854.*)

There seemed to be no end to them. 'The whole side of the country was covered with wounded. Fatigue-parties from every corps were out all day collecting them', and carrying them 'groaning, yelling, agonised and dying', to the hospital enclosures, where most of them died under the surgeon's knife. 'The dead being then removed, fresh patients were brought in to fill their places.'[10]

The hospitals were too inadequate, the surgeons too few to cope with the British wounded, let alone these thousands of the enemy. Even before the battle the numbers of sick, daily increasing now that the weather had finally broken, had strained the limited resources of the Medical Department of the army to the point of collapse. If the men 'reported themselves sick', Timothy Gowing complained with understandable exaggeration, 'the medical chests were empty'.

In the midst of this suffering the morale of the army declined to new and depressing depths. 'Everyone', Doctor Robinson noted in his journal the day after the battle, 'seems much disheartened at the gloomy state of affairs.' 'Night after night,' Corporal Spurling of the 63rd told his sister,

> down to the trenches up in the morning get your rations go and cut wood fetch water cook your food salt Beef and pork with Ship Biscuit in fact nothing else but Ship Rations only no pea soup or in fact anything but Beef and Biscuit and sometimes a short supply of that. We get two glasses of rum daily and coffee sugar and rice when it can be provided. Mind you we have to roast the coffee and pound it ourselves. I have not put a razor to my face since 12 Aug last and I could pass very well for a Jew. We use no blacking no nothing all is required is men and muskets. I wish to God this was over.

The discouragement was almost universal. General Buller, given temporary command of the 4th Division, was voicing an opinion quite common amongst the general officers when he swore 'everything present and future is most damnable, that the Anglo-French Army is in a very nasty position, and that nothing can be more dismal for the future'.[11] De Lacy Evans advised Lord Raglan to abandon the siege and evacuate the Crimea altogether. Many officers openly talked of sending in their papers and going home, and some had already done so. On 11 November Lord George Paget gave up command of the 4th Light Dragoons and sailed home to his young and beautiful wife, whom he had married only a few days before coming out. And few blamed him.* 'We are heartily sick,' Lieutenant Richards told his mother, 'of this humbug they call a siege.'

Accusations and recriminations were hurled backwards and forwards with the thoughtless indiscrimination which comes from anger and despair. What could you expect of an army with such generals and such a staff? Sir John Burgoyne was a 'nincompoop'; the Duke of Cambridge—so distraught at having made such a fool of himself at Inkerman—was going off his head; Sir Colin Campbell was getting 'very fidgety'; so was Sir George Brown, who was in addition 'the biggest fool in the army'; General Bentinck was 'the biggest fool ever'; as for Lord Raglan's staff they were lazy idiots who 'had a *very late* breakfast the *morning* of *Inkerman*'.[12]

So soon after the battle it was natural that most complaints should centre upon the generals' conduct of it.

In the first place it was disgraceful that the army should have been surprised on Inkerman Ridge and that no defences, except a half-finished two-gun battery and a few picket walls, should have been built. 'The necessity of throwing up, at any rate, a breastwork was pointed out by every officer in the Army, but Sir John Burgoyne would not hear of it.'[13] The disgrace was the more inexcusable because Colonel Federoff's attack on the 2nd Division on 26 October should surely, the accusers thought, have given the generals warning of where the main attack was intended. But on the contrary, an artillery officer wrote, 'Lord Raglan was much pleased and thought like an old ass as he is (mind this is now the opinion of the whole army) that after this dressing they would not attack again. . . . His sapient Lordship said, "Pooh, pooh, they have had such a dressing they will not come again. . . ." The Engineers, however, advised his strengthening it by heavy guns and some earthworks, but he being in his second childhood said, "Nonsense, they will not dare to come again".'

And now Raglan was to be made a field-marshal. Some officers doubted that he had ever turned up for the battle at all. Others, more generously, could not see how anyone could have directed a battle in all that fog, but even if he could have seen what was going on he

* 'We hear Lord George Paget was greatly snubbed at home for leaving this place,' wrote Major Walker-Heneage. 'Everyone here thought him a most sensible man for leaving when he was tired of it, but the English people are such fools.'

198

would probably have been content to 'sit and watch as usual'. 'The Queen ought to break his baton over his head.'[14]

So the attacks went on, contradictory, unreasonable; sometimes malicious, always understandable. For these young and bitter officers, whose vehement accusations were soon to give the newspapers valuable evidence in support of their assault upon the whole Army system, could know nothing beyond their own experiences. Their Commander-in-Chief's difficulties with the French, his anxiety to avoid the now inevitable winter campaign and the calculated risks he had taken in his efforts to do so, the disobeyed and misinterpreted orders, were all largely unknown to them. They thought of him beside his fire in his comfortable farmhouse, surrounded by servants and his incompetent aristocratic staff, an old man dreaming of the Duke and their shared and glorious past. They painted a portrait of a haughty muddler, inconsiderate, foolish, misinformed and doting, which was accepted by many as no more than a justified caricature, and by some as a true likeness. It was an image which the public at home were soon taught to recognise.

II

During these early days of November, when the tension and fury of Inkerman relapsed into this mood of despair and bitterness, when the weather worsened and the noise of the siege-guns slackened and often fell into silence, the war had still to be suffered and endured.

'Men in the trenches twenty-four hours at a time,' Colonel Bell wrote in his diary on 13 November, 'soaked to the skin. No change when they come up to their miserable tents, hardly a twig to get to boil their bit of salt pork. Short of rations too for want of transport. Everything cheerless.'

The next day, as if Nature wanted to join forces with man in dragging the army into further misery, there was a new disaster.

The previous night had been cold and wet. But the rain, falling with dreary insistence since dark, had stopped a little before five o'clock, and Paymaster Dixon standing outside his tent thought he had never seen so wonderful a morning. 'Warm and starlight and the moon shining beautifully—soon afterwards the sun rose amid a bank of red, blood red clouds.' Half an hour later it was raining more heavily than ever. By six o'clock the sound of the downpour and its 'heavy beating on the earth had become gradually swallowed up by the noise of the rushing of the wind and by the flapping of the tents'.[15] Then suddenly 'everything went whiz bang in less time than I have taken to tell you'. Tents leapt into the air and went flying over the plateau, looking like bits of paper; stones were lifted from the ground and crashed into any obstacles in their path, cutting men's faces, tearing into the sailing canvas, smashing bottles, ringing against cans. 'Great barrels could be seen bounding along like cricket balls.' Heavy waggons were thrown headlong through the camps, dragging bullocks after them 'as if they were mere kittens'. Hospital marquees collapsed, their poles torn out of the ground, and the sick were tossed in their muddy blankets helplessly across the ground. Men huddled behind walls, in holes in the ground, tied themselves together, clawing at the greasy, slippery earth as they tried to resist the force of the hurricane. In Balaclava trees were uprooted and flung across the streets of the town. Part of the roof of Lord Raglan's farmhouse, looking curiously white against the black background of the sky, was torn off and flew away in the stream of smoke from his chimney.

Occasionally there were scenes of grotesque humour. Dr. Robinson, weak from a recent severe attack of diarrhoea, had gone to bed in his underpants, as his uniform trousers were so caked and hard with mud, and he had been carried on his servant's back to another tent when his own had been blown down. Soon that tent too was blown away, and Robinson was hurtled across the ground with the wind buffetting at his back, his billowing blanket outspread around him like the wings of a giant bat. His servant eventually caught him and dumped him, too numb to protest, in a pool of ice-cold mud behind a wall. Midshipman Wood of the Naval Brigade, also weak from diarrhoea, tried to crawl on his hands and knees towards the protection of a low stone wall surrounding some powder-boxes. But he was blown well past it and had to be dragged back by a lieutenant and two sailors, who scrambled towards him holding hands. When all four of them had got back to the wall, they lay down beneath it, making bets on the length of flight of the articles, including two drums, that bumped and rattled past them.[16]

General Buller's tent-pole broke, and he went 'floundering about like a rabbit in a net'. He was so cross and miserable and sulky he '*would* go and sit in the open under a small mud bank, built to protect his horses'. His A.D.C. could not even get him to move to an old ruined house close by. Other senior officers felt equally indignant. Sir George Brown behaved as if the hurricane were a personal affront; and General Estcourt, 'his mien for once disturbed', clung for dear life to one of the shrouds of his marquee, while Captain Chetwode tore past him, in his underpants and shirt, after his cap, which turned out, when eventually he caught it, to be his sergeant's.[17]

The correspondent of *The Times*, the guest of a surgeon who was so proud of his well-pitched tent he felt sure it would stand up to anything, warned his confident host that the end of their home was near.

'Get up, Doctor. The tent is coming down!' he shouted above the roar of the wind.

The doctor got calmly out of bed, looked at the pole blandly—it was sharply bent and he insisted that that was the secret of its strength —shook it, and said, 'Why, man, it's all right; that pole will stand for ever.'

He got back into bed again, burrowing under the tumulus of his bedclothes, and as soon as he was still again the pole and tent crashed down upon him.[18]

But if it was possible to laugh at the absurdity of man in misfortune on the hurricane-swept plateau, down in the harbour and on the raging sea outside it the struggle to survive was terrible and grim. Mrs. Duberly, on board the *Star of the South*, looked out at a harbour seething with foam. 'The spray, dashing over the cliffs many hundred feet, fell back like heavy rain into the harbour.' Even holding on with both hands she could scarcely keep her footing. The sternwork of the ship was being ground away by the huge sides of the *Medway*, rocking and creaking against it in the packed and heaving harbour. Smaller ships, driven against the rocks, broke up and sank in a few minutes. She watched the little clipper *Wild Wave* rolling helplessly in the roaring breakers, and three cabin-boys left on its lurching decks trying to clutch at a rope which some other members of the crew on the rocks above threw down to them. Two of the boys were washed overboard; the third caught the rope and leapt ashore just as the ship fell down on a tumbling wave and disappeared in a scattered mass of splinters, broken masts, bales of cargo, hay and boxes. The *Progress* and the *Wanderer*, the *Kenilworth* and the *Resolute*, the *Rip Van Winkle*, the

Marquis and the *Mary Anne*, borne dizzily along towards the shore in the scudding waters, cracked open on the sharp reefs and rocks in a whirl of planks and spars, and sent down into the grey, foam-lashed sea hundreds of tons of gunpowder, millions of cartridges, thousands of pounds' worth of stores.[19]

In the outer anchorage the *Prince*, a fine screw-ship with a crew of 150, had lost her two sheet-anchors and was riding on a stream-anchor only. Her captain had 'foolishly cut away her masts', and when they had fallen overboard they had got entangled with the screw. She was driven broadside on upon the rocks and smashed up in the moment of impact. Less than ten of her crew got ashore. Her full cargo of supplies, including forty thousand greatcoats, boots for almost the entire army, and 'everything that was most wanted', was lost.[20]

The *Restitution* lost two of her anchors and was saved only by the skilful handling of her captain, who, having got rid of his upper guns, kept her riding the storm. The Duke of Cambridge was aboard her, recuperating from the nervous shock of Inkerman, and according to the gaily malicious Cornet Fisher was 'most undignified, and held the Steward's hand, bewailing his fate, saying "Oh! Is it come to this? Oh! Oh! We shall be lost."'

All morning the torrent raged and the rain flew down through the howling wind, and then at two o'clock the force of it slackened. Men got up from their hiding-places, covered in mud, their eyes streaming from the cold of the sleet, and looked 'at each other in a sort of despair, shivering in wet rags'.[21] The mud-covered ground was littered with the damp, sprawling canvas of the tents, broken lengths of rope, smashed boxes, torn blankets, furniture, pots, pans and, against the windward side of the walls and protecting banks, muddled piles of unrecognisable and mud-splashed debris. The dead lay around the collapsed and tattered hospital tents and under the waterlogged canvas; horses blown from their picket-ropes walked amidst the chaos and nibbled at the wet and sprawling bales of hay.

At five o'clock it became much colder; the 'hail and rain changed to a heavy snow'. Captain Campbell, on his way back to the camp of the 46th from the forward trenches where his men had spent the last twenty-four hours in thick, sticky mud nearly a foot deep, began to have great doubts whether he would ever be able to get them back. He had had to leave seven of them behind, two of them unconscious, under the care of the officer in command of the relief. The rest took four hours to march back to camp with the snow and wind in their faces all the way. When they reached it they found the hospital tents blown down, the sick and dying—nearly a third of the regiment were in hospital—lying on the freezing mud under the falling snow. The other men, shivering, apathetic and miserable, sheltered themselves as best they could under the wet canvas. Loose horses wandered about in all directions.

As night began to fall the men scraped the mud and snow from their tents and tried to pitch them again; their movements were slow, their fingers numb with cold.*

The commanding officer of the 1st Regiment remembered:

A ration of green raw coffee berry was served out, a mockery in the midst of all this misery. Nothing to roast coffee, nothing to grind it, no fire, no sugar; and unless it was meant that we eat it as horses do barley, I don't see what use the men could make of it, except that they have just done, pitched it into the mud! How patient those men of mine; how admirably they behave. In silence they bear with all privations; away they go . . . ankle deep in mud, and wet to the skin, down to the trenches. Thus is the British soldier most to be admired. This is discipline; here he is in all his glory.

In the yard of Lord Raglan's farmhouse men crammed into every available shed like herrings in a barrel. The barn which the Commander-in-Chief's escort used as a stable was crowded with silent figures, huddled against the walls and crouching on the floor, looking gloomily out at the snowflakes drifting past the doorway and through the holes in the shingle roof. There were sick from the hospital marquee, Turks smoking their foul pipes, Frenchmen, hussars of the escort, horses kicking and biting in savage ill-temper, all cold, miserable, wet and hungry. In the middle of the night one of the most tremendous cannonades that they had ever heard woke those few of them who had been able to sleep. Through the chinks in the roof

---

* Many of them subsequently copied the French and surrounded their tents with palisades or walls of snow to break the force of the wind, or dug holes to pitch their tents in. A few summoned the energy to copy the Turks (it was, Somerset Calthorpe thought, 'the only thing which these gentry' did well) and moved into underground trenches, walled with stones and covered with anything—even skeletons—which would support a roof of mud.

and the cracks in the wall they could see the flashes of the roaring cannon.[22]

The Russians were making an attack on the French forward trenches. The French, with the reckless fury of exasperation, counter-attacked with such force that they drove the Russians back beyond their own earthworks and spiked some of their guns.

The fighting had started again.

14

CHAOS

*Something must really be done to place the supply of the army upon a
more satisfactory footing*
Lord Raglan

I

'The rains have swelled into torrents,' Colonel Bell noted in his diary
on 23 November, 'streaming down the valleys like highland floods,
country inundated, roads or rather mud tracks impassable. Men
worked to death, rations curtailed. Men from the trenches this morning going down again to-night in this dreadful weather wet to the
skin. Don't see how they can survive.'

The siege by now was 'only nominal'. A few shots were fired each
day. But the constant rain had made it almost impossible to get the
ammunition up from Balaclava. 'The oxen and horses for transport',
General Buller's A.D.C. wrote home on 27 November, 'are either
dead or too weak to work. In every direction they are to be seen dead
or dying in the mud and our men, working more like beasts of burden than Christians, are floundering about up to their knees in mud.
Three horses in each cavalry regiment die on an average every night
of cold and hunger. . . . They have eaten each other's tails off. . . . I
saw a horse to-day eating a piece of canvas covered with mud.'[1]

It was not only the horses that were dying. 'It is reported that several
men died from the cold' the night after the hurricane, Captain Godfrey wrote in his journal, 'and numbers could not leave their trenches
without parties being sent from camp to assist them. . . . Everything
looks very bad.' The men 'were dying by wholesale,' Timothy Gowing said, 'for want of shelter, clothing and food. . . . The whole camp
was one vast sheet of mud, the trenches in many places knee deep;
men died at their posts from sheer exhaustion. . . . The army was put
upon half rations—half a pound of mouldy biscuit and half a pound of
salt junk [beef or pork]; coffee was served out, but in its raw state;
with no means of roasting it. No wood or firing was to be had, except
a few roots that were dug up'. Men would come staggering into the

camp from the trenches, soaked to the skin and ravenously hungry and be given their mouldy biscuit and salt junk 'so hard that one almost wanted a good hatchet to break it. The scenes were heart-rending.'

The Commissariat, he maintained, 'had completely broken down'. It was distressingly true. The track leading down to the stores at Bala-clava was only distinguishable now by the 'dead horses, mules and bullocks, in every stage of decomposition', which lined its route. To get up from Balaclava to the camp of the 2nd Division and back, Captain Clifford discovered, was a full day's hard work. The men, dragging foot after foot in the heavy, cloying mud, exhausted by the weight of the stores and ammunition on their backs, helped by the few remaining emaciated animals, could only hope to carry up just as much as the army needed to survive. The rations, which previously had filled *The Times*'s correspondent with enthusiasm as being 'excel-lent and ample', were by the end of the month severely cut, sometimes to a quarter.

In Balaclava itself the chaos was utter and appalling. Admiral Boxer, then in charge of the transport arrangements at Constantinople, was quite incapable of reducing the muddle. Captain Shipley, in hos-pital there recovering from a wound received at the Alma, told his mother that he understood there was no 'Head at Balaclava. There is, however,' he continued, 'a Head here, but such a *thing*. It is called Admiral Boxer, and they say he has never done anything properly in his life.' Ships arrived without notice in the congested harbour at Balaclava, and no one was quite sure what was in them. Sometimes they went all the way back across the Black Sea to Constantinople without being unloaded, and when they arrived there Boxer sent them back again. He seemed not to know how many ships he had available or even where they could refuel. He said no transport was available when ships were lying idle in his own docks. He kept no records.[2] 'As regards Admiral Boxer,' wrote Lord Raglan in exaspera-tion, 'I am powerless. No man can make him a man of arrangement.'

For days, for weeks on end, ships lay outside Balaclava waiting to come in and unload. And when they did so their crews, although well used to Eastern harbours, were appalled. Since the storm the ghastly pale-green waters were like a stagnant cesspool into which all imagin-able refuse had been thrown. Dead men with white and swollen heads, dead camels, 'dead horses, dead mules, dead oxen, dead cats, dead dogs, the filth of an army with its hospitals', floated amidst the wreckage of spars, boxes, bales of hay, biscuits, smashed cases of medicines and surgical instruments, the decomposed offal and butchered carcasses of sheep thrown overboard by ship cooks.

On the quayside the muddle was grotesque. Heaps of charcoal were piled on top of split sacks from which the flour poured out in damp lumps; bales of clothing were used as stepping-stones through the mud; broken boxes, rotting meat, cases of ammunition, thousands of tent-pegs, bits of wooden huts, were dumped together higgledy-piggledy in stores or in the streets. Men sat smoking on powder-barrels. The stench was nauseating. Rats and pariah dogs scampered everywhere. Turkish soldiers, ill and starving, fell down and died in the street. 'I never saw people die,' Mrs. Duberly said, 'with such a dreary perseverance.' The hovels of the little town which they used as hospitals were crowded to the doors—or rather to the pieces of mud-covered rotting canvas hung across the doorways—through which the muffled sounds of weak groans came out from the fetid darkness inside to be ignored by the passers-by, inured to pain as to squalor and death. Inside these fearful hospitals the Turks died 'like flies', and all day long silent bearers could be seen coming out of them on their way to the burial-grounds, where gravediggers, gaunt and listless, scratched at the surface of the mud to scoop out a hollow for the daily consignment of dead. Around them limbs and bones and partially buried carcasses protruded from their shallow graves.[3]

Into this nightmarish town officers and men came down to entreat and bully, threaten and plead with the commissariat officials, who, despite the vertiginous muddle into which they had been plunged, tried to deal with each request according to the regulations of the Service and the system in which they had been meticulously trained.

A typical exchange of argument and counter-argument has been preserved.

The Medical Officer of the *Charity*, an iron screw-steamer docked in Balaclava for the reception of the sick, went on shore to see the commissariat official in charge of the issue of stoves.

'Three of my men,' he told him, 'died last night from choleraic symptoms, brought on in their present state from the extreme cold of the ship; and I fear more will follow them from the same cause.'

'Oh! You must make your requisition in due form; send it up to H.Q. and get it signed properly.'

'But my men may die meantime.'

'I can't help that. I must have the requisition.'

'Another night will certainly kill my men.'

'I really can do nothing. I must have a requisition properly signed before I can give one of these stoves away.'

'For God's sake, then *lend* me some. I'll be responsible for their safety.'

'I really can do nothing of the kind.'[4]

And sincerely he believed that he could not. He was in an impossible situation. If he gave this doctor what he wanted, who could say what other doctors would come demanding a similar issue? He had a limited number of stoves in store. There might have been more in the holds of the ships; but the ships came in with their cargoes in a hopeless mess, and no one seemed to have much idea what was in them. It could take two days to unload the crates on top of the stoves, which might have been stored away in the bottom of the hold. And what was he to do with all the stuff on top of them? There was nowhere to put it. And, anyway, it did not come under his particular department.

It was not altogether stupidity that made men reason like this, although the newspapers said it was; it was not altogether indifference, although the regimental officers said it was; it was not altogether, as the commissariat officers themselves insisted it was, the necessity of compliance with rigid regulations. It was that the whole system of supply had collapsed in the presence of an emergency that no one had foreseen or provided for. And it would take not days or months, but years to revolutionise that system and make it work in an army that had been violently awakened from a dream of past glory into a modern world where heroism was not enough.

In the meantime, however, men were dying and something must be done.

II

'Something must really be done,' Lord Raglan told Mr. Commissary-General Filder in a memorandum of unusual severity on 13 December, 'to place the supply of the army upon a more satisfactory footing or the worst consequences may follow. I receive complaints almost daily of some impediment being thrown in the way of issues.' He cited the report of an officer going down to Balaclava to collect some vegetables for his regiment and being told that the department's regulations would not permit an issue of a quantity of less than two tons.* 'I hope,' Lord Raglan continued, 'that this is not true. If true the answer is pure nonsense and nothing else and I must desire to know what Commissariat Officer authorised such an answer to be made . . . I cannot help feeling that there is not infrequently a flippancy in the answers given, without consideration to the fact that it is the duty of all to unite in facilitating the issue of supplies and in providing for the maintenance and comfort of the troops.'[5]

Almost daily he received complaints, and daily in an unending stream orders, letters, memoranda, despatches, commendations, reprimands, instructions, flowed from his pen. He took the trouble to write to the parents of all officers who had died. He even designed an ambulance-cart which he hoped might take the place of the few new ones which had just arrived from England, but which were found to be impossibly heavy and cumbersome. Every document that came to Headquarters he read himself; every document that went out he checked himself, and most of them he wrote himself. Details that could have been, and should have been, dealt with by others he attended to personally. He would never allow anyone to touch his papers, but spread them out all over his bed, on his writing-table and on the floor of his room, where he could get at them easily with his one hand. He got up at six o'clock, wrote by candle-light until breakfast at eight. After breakfast he would interview the Quartermaster-General, the Adjutant-General, the Chief Engineer, the officer in command of the artillery, the Commissary-General and the Inspector-General of Hospitals, and discuss with them their morning reports. Then he returned to his desk and wrote again until luncheon at one o'clock or two. In the afternoon he saw the divisional generals and any other officers who wanted to see him. These interviews over, he would go out on his rounds sometimes alone, at others accompanied by two A.D.C.s and a mounted orderly, returning after dark to write in his

* Major Foley de St. Georges, General Rose's rich and amusing Anglo-French A.D.C., was not deterred by a similar regulation. He went down to Balaclava to buy a few nails. Nails, he was told, were only issued by the ton. Very well, he said, he would have a ton, and paid for them. (BAPST, II, 239.)

room until dinner at eight o'clock. After dinner, which was often merely an opportunity to hold a conference with the French, he would finish any outstanding business with his staff and then go back once more to his room, where he worked at his papers, silent and alone. No one knew how long he stayed up, writing at the table by his bed. But it was always till past midnight, and sometimes the candle was not blown out till an hour or two before dawn. And even when he had gone to bed his voice could be heard talking to Airey through the wooden partition which divided their rooms. Only on Sundays, when he regularly attended divine service, read his Bible and received Holy Communion in his room, was there an alteration in the strict pattern of his days.[6]

Every aspect of the army's business came to his notice, and every detail of suffering affected him deeply. He heard one day that the wife of a corporal in the 23rd Regiment had given birth to a baby girl in a hole in the ground. He sent out his doctor to see her with some hot food from his kitchen. The following day he went to see her himself. It was a day so cold that officers writing letters in their tents found that the ink froze in little pellets on their nibs. A howling wind sent flakes of hard snow into Lord Raglan's face as he rode along. When he arrived at the Light Division's camp, his A.D.C. asked where the woman was and when he found her he knelt in the snow at the flap of her little dog-tent and talked to her and her husband. He gave her some warm clothes and food, and the next day he sent her a rubber sleeping-bag lined with flannel that someone had sent him from England.[7]

No one was more aware than he of the army's danger, its suffering and its needs. But when afterwards he was to take the blame for its destruction, only those close to him knew how desperately hard he had worked to save it.

Long before the army sailed for the Crimea he had asked for more land transport and had been refused. On the day of its arrival there he had told Airey to make an urgent request for baled hay. As early as 8 August he had told the Duke of Newcastle that he entertained grave doubts as to the possibility of wintering in Russia with the army's limited means of supply and subsistence. On 12 October he had instructed Filder to lay in a stock of fuel at Scutari. To the Government's gaily voiced confidence he had always been careful to reply with cautious restraint. But when, before the battle of Balaclava, he had sent on to London Mr. Cattley's warning of the occasional appalling severity of a Crimean winter, the Duke of Newcastle replied that he must have been 'greatly misinformed' and sent out a book which showed that the Crimean climate was 'one of the mildest and finest in the world'. In no doubt what the results of the battle of Inkerman would be, he sent an officer on 7 November to the southern shores of the Black Sea to buy timber for huts for the whole army, those promised by the Government not having arrived. Ships were also sent for planking to Sinope, Samsoon and Trebizond.

On the same day he sent a minute to William Filder telling him that the army would winter in the Crimea and asking him to provision accordingly.[8] A few days after receiving it, Mr. Filder wrote to Sir Charles Trevelyan at the Treasury and put his finger on the two difficulties which were proving insuperable.

> I am full of apprehension as to our power of keeping this Army supplied during the coming winter . . . . In this crowded little harbour only a proportion of our vessels can be admitted at a time . . . . With all the siege and other stores which are being disembarked, we can do little more than land sufficient supplies to keep pace with the daily consumption of the troops; and to add to our difficulties, the road from the harbour to the camp, not being a made one, is impassable after heavy rains; our obstacle in these respects will increase as the winter comes. We shall have many more stores to convey than we have hitherto had—fuel, for instance. In short, I am full of anxiety and dread on the subject.[9]

This letter was written on 13 November. The following day the hurricane swept across the harbour, and Mr. Filder's anxiety and difficulties were fearfully increased. Of hay alone he lost twenty days' supply.[10]

Lord Raglan was quick to act. 'I earnestly recommend,' he wrote to the Duke of Newcastle the morning after the storm, 'that not a moment should be lost in replacing the ammunition. The Commissariat losses are very heavy, and lead Mr. Filder to apprehend that we may be very shortly deficient in supplies of ammunition and forage. . . . Fresh rifle ammunition should be sent in the fleetest vessel without a moment's delay.'[11]

The following day he and Airey went down to Balaclava to see for themselves the damage that the hurricane had caused. They were appalled. They ordered all the wreckage to be collected and made into hospital huts for the sick; the hides of all slaughtered animals to be preserved for roof coverings; the despatch of vessels for charcoal and for timber for huts.[12] The next morning Lord Raglan wrote again to the Duke of Newcastle. 'You cannot send us,' he told him, 'too many supplies *of all kinds.*'[13]

On the 18th he sent Major Wetherall to Constantinople with a long list of articles he was to buy. Mr. Filder was authorised to buy hay and straw from any place he could on the shores of the Black Sea, as the supplies ordered two months previously from England had not yet arrived.

As for the road, both Lord Raglan and Airey had realised that without it many of these supplies would be useless. Burgoyne had been asked to report on the numbers of men who would be required for its construction. It would take a thousand men two months, he said. And even if the men could be found, there were insufficient tools and those available were of the poorest quality. An officer of the Quartermaster-General's Department was accordingly sent to Constantinople to buy more.[14] But the problem of manpower remained.

'It was not in my power at any time since the troops ascended this ridge,' Lord Raglan explained to the Duke of Newcastle, 'worked as they have been from the first, to employ them in building a road.'[15] There were three thousand sick and wounded in the Crimean hospitals, eight thousand more in Turkey. On some mornings when the returns were added up the men supposed to be capable of bearing arms numbered less than these eleven thousand sick. And although returned as fit for duty the men were in reality often barely able to stand up. Their spells of duty in the mud-filled trenches lasted for sixteen and even sometimes twenty-four hours at a stretch. Never less than five and sometimes as many as six nights a week were spent there.[16]

An attempt was made to employ the Turks on road construction, on collecting stones for metalling and on digging drains, but, underfed to the point of starvation, they could scarcely lift their spades. They died in hundreds. Hired labour was also used, but the workmen died more quickly than the Turks did.[17]

Appeals were made to the French. But they had, they said, too many troubles of their own. Lord Raglan pressed them, he told the

Duke of Newcastle, 'as far as was politick'. They could not be persuaded. And 'the advantage of keeping on good terms with them' was 'too obvious to require discussion'.[18] He pressed them more urgently than his despatches implied, but Canrobert was immovable.[19]

The road could not be made. Carts had to be abandoned more or less completely, while pack-animals became increasingly difficult to feed. 'Our horses are dying fast,' Lord Raglan wrote. 'But until we are sure that we can feed them I would not recommend any addition here.'[20] And so thousands of tons of supplies rotted in the Balaclava stores and in the holds of the ships, while men struggled up through the mud, past the rotting corpses of animals, the broken carts, the dead and dying Turks, carrying on their backs the bare means of keeping alive. And every day the sick in the hospital tents were packed and squeezed closer together to make room for the new arrivals, pale, dirty and shivering, who could carry on no longer with their duties outside.

The Medical Department of the army, like the Commissariat, had completely broken down under the strain of work for which it was quite unprepared and for which its system was outrageously inadequate to cope. An immense amount of Lord Raglan's time was spent in vain attempts to improve its organisation and efficiency and in visiting the sick, for whom he confessed to feeling a deep and personal responsibility.

Constantly obstructed in his efforts by Dr. Hall, Inspector-General of Hospitals, who refused to agree that anything serious had gone wrong in his Department, he had occasion at least once a week, and sometimes on several consecutive days, to complain of some particular case of negligence or stupidity.

Dr. John Hall, soon to be created K.C.B. ('Knight of the Crimean Burial Grounds, I suppose,' commented Florence Nightingale with justified acidity), was a bitter, influential, hard and self-satisfied man who had felt himself entitled to a more important post than that of head of the medical staff of the Expeditionary Army. Lord Raglan could neither like nor respect him, and soon after the army came to Balaclava he was sent back to Scutari to report on the base hospitals there. Miss Nightingale had not yet arrived, and they were, as she subsequently discovered, 'destitute and filthy'. Dr. Hall reported them as having been put 'on a very creditable footing'. Nothing, he said, was lacking.[21]

He came back to the Crimea and gave further evidence of his incapacity.

The transport *Avon* had lain in Balaclava harbour for the reception of the sick since 19 November. A fortnight later the ship was full. The men lay on the bare decks covered only by their greatcoats or a blanket, under the care of a single young surgeon. Their suffering was terrible; the condition of the ship unutterably foul. An officer went on board to see one of his men and, angry and horrified, rushed immediately to Lord Raglan.

It was past midnight when he got there. Lord Raglan sent for Dr. Hall and asked him for an immediate explanation, and soon after gave instructions for an inquiry to be held. 'It is absolutely necessary,' Lord Raglan told Mr. Romaine of the Advocate General's Department, 'that I should do all in my power to arouse the Medical Department to a sense of duty.'[22]

Dr. Lawson, the principal Medical Officer at Balaclava, was held to be responsible and was dismissed. But Dr. Hall, himself rebuked by Lord Raglan in a General Order published on 15 December, replied to this interference with his Department by appointing Lawson Senior Medical Officer at the Barrack Hospital in Scutari.

In another General Order, when given further evidence of neglect and incapacity, Lord Raglan wrote:

The Commander of the Forces is sorry to have to animadvert very strongly upon the conduct of the medical department, in an instance which came under his observation yesterday. The sick went down from the camp to Balaclava under the charge of a medical officer of the division to which they respectively belonged; but on their arrival there it was found that no preparations had been made for their reception. The Commander of the Forces is aware that Deputy Inspector-General of Hospitals Doctor Dumbreck gave the necessary order verbally to the staff medical officer at Balaclava, but that officer neglected to inform his superior and the consequence was that the sick, many of them in a very suffering state, remained in the streets for several hours, exposed to the very inclement weather. The name of the officer who was guilty of this gross neglect is known to the Commander of the Forces. He will not now publish it, but he warns him to be careful in future, and to be cautious how he again exposes himself to censure. Doctor Dumbreck will, in future, give his orders *in writing*, addressed to the responsible officer. When a convoy of sick is sent from the camp either to the hospitals, or to be placed on board ship, it is henceforth to be accompanied not only by a medical officer, but likewise by the D.A.Q.M.G. of the Division, who will precede it to the place of deposit, and take such steps as may ensure the due reception and care of the men confided to his charge.

But it was like patching up a dam, Lord Raglan told an A.D.C.; as soon as one leak was repaired another would appear. Orders, advice, new rules, suggestions of improved methods, poured from Head-quarters to all the departments of the army. As constituted, however, they were beyond redemption. Too many of their officers were unchangeable and obstinate, too much of their organisation was incapable of improvement without that wholesale reform which was certain to come, but which would come too late to help those men now suffering from the want of it. What could you do, Lord Raglan asked in exasperation, with an official of the Commissariat Department who objected to the Commander-in-Chief's order that the form of requisition for a new greatcoat—a 'most elaborate' document with two schedules attached and twenty-four blanks to be filled up in duplicate —should be simplified? What could you do with a man who objected to this alteration on the grounds that it would lead to great abuse because, as everyone in the Department knew, regulations 'did not authorise the issue of regimental overcoats more frequently than once in three years'?[23]

'If Lord Raglan had the genius of the Duke of Wellington,' exclaimed Captain Campbell in understanding sympathy, 'he would find it a hard matter to make things work in this army!' He might have gone down and 'raised hell in Balaclava', but what good would that have done? Balaclava was run by 'a gang of raving lunatics'.

III

Disastrous as the muddle was in the Crimea, in London it was a great deal worse. In the bewildering labyrinth of offices through which requisitions passed on their way to someone who could give them his attention, the chaos was stupefying. A list of urgent requirements might, for instance, pass through as many as eight different departments before it was even known whether or not the items needed could be supplied from stock. If they could not be supplied from stock there were long discussions and conversations, unrecorded arguments between contractors and officials, until a satisfactory price and date of delivery had been agreed. Everyone was satisfied, all commissions were paid and mouths silenced; and then weeks and perhaps months later goods of disgraceful inferiority were supplied.[24]

But whether the stores were already in stock or not, there might be other delays. The Admiralty were often unable to provide a ship to carry them in. It seems scarcely credible that the greatest seafaring nation in the world, owning half the total number of merchant-vessels and the largest Navy, should have been unable to find ships immediately for such an urgent purpose. But General Airey found that it was so. Though he worked conscientiously at his carefully calculated requisitions and did 'more than two other men could', his 'unceasing energy and indefatigable exertions' might well have been more usefully employed in the trenches.[25]

On 28 November 1854 he sent a requisition to England for 3,000 tents, 100 hospital marquees and several other items, including 6,000 nosebags and various quantities of spades, shovels and pickaxes. On 4 April 1855 this requisition was still the subject of lengthy correspondence in Whitehall.

The Secretary to the Board of Ordnance carefully explained to the Under-Secretary of State for War:

> The Contractors for tents were unable to furnish them in sufficient numbers to meet the pressing wants of the service . . . The demand for tents previous to the war being very limited, and not having sufficient skilled labour in the market to meet the additional heavy demands consequent upon the war. 1,000 circular tents were shipped for the Crimea in the *William Becket* on the 28th March, that vessel having been appointed by the Admiralty upon an application from this department, dated 13th January. . . . 1,000 circular tents are still due, and for the conveyance of them application was made by this Department on the 2nd Instant.[26]

On 23 April, the Under-Secretary was advised in another letter, a ship had still 'not yet been allotted' by the Admiralty.

In his evidence before the Chelsea Board, General Airey mentioned several other instances of similar delay. The requisition for 2,000 tons of hay on 13 September 1854 was finally complied with eight months later, when most of the horses were dead. In four private letters and three official despatches Lord Raglan was obliged to call the Government's attention to its non-compliance with this requisition. A floating steam bakery requested on 8 November was sent at the end of the following May. Most important, the organisation of a Regular Transport Brigade, suggested by Lord Raglan in June 1854, was eventually agreed to in a despatch from the Duke of Newcastle dated 20 January 1855, in which it was implied that the idea of its formation originated with the Government.

'Seeing that such obstructions could occur in London, the greatest commercial market in the world,' General Airey said with justified indignation, 'the Board will, I am sure, estimate rightly the difficulties of those who were suddenly called upon to provide for a winter campaign amid the snow and clay' of the Crimea.

Despite the 'unceasing exertions' of Raglan and Airey and of General Estcourt, the Adjutant-General, the attacks against them, and indeed against the whole of the Headquarters' staff, mounted and increased in venom. Someone must be to blame for the army's terrible suffering. What better target could there be than the man in command of it and his 'frightful staff'?

'Lord Raglan,' wrote Cornet Fisher on 17 November 'is in great discredit with the Army.' General Canrobert, he added, enjoyed a higher reputation in the British Army than any of its own generals, as he was the only one who had 'not made a fool of himself'.

'Every man knows Canrobert,' Captain Shakespear said, confirming this view. 'There is not a soldier French or English that does not know him. . . . He looks over everything himself and is always on the *qui vive*. . . . The British soldiers run out and cheer him, another man no one knows.'

Lord Raglan was, of course, to blame for this. Not only did he ride about the camps as inconspicuously as possible, never with more than three companions, but often after dark and always in a concealing, big-sleeved cloak which Lady Westmorland had sent him from Vienna. Men who had seen the Commander-in-Chief and even spoken to him were frequently under the impression that they had talked with a civilian visitor. Mrs. Freemantle asked her cousin, a young officer invalided home from the Crimea, if all the talk in the newspapers about Lord Raglan not being 'sufficiently amongst the Troops' was justified. He said there was certainly a lot of talk in the army too 'as well as in the newspapers', and that he was speaking to an officer one day who said he did not even know what Lord Raglan looked like.

> 'I never saw him,' said the officer. So I said to him, 'Well there he is, going into the hospital.' 'What,' said the officer, 'that Lord Raglan? Why, I have seen him constantly, but I never dreamed that was Lord Raglan.' The fact was Lord Raglan walked or rode about with perhaps no one with him or perhaps one A.D.C. and those who did not know him personally never guessed, and if told would not often believe, that that unattended man was their commander.[27]

Canrobert, on the other hand, although less flamboyant than St. Arnaud, was always accompanied by six or eight staff officers, one or two Spahi orderlies and an escort of twenty hussars preceded by a *porte-drapeau* bearing the French flag.[28] At sight of him soldiers of both armies were turned out to salute and cheer. And this was what Lord Raglan took pains to avoid. But his officers cannot be blamed for believing that he never visited them and for telling their families and friends that he did not do so.

Their complaints at first did little harm. Soon, however, the rumbles of accusation were reinforced by the publication of an indictment which carried almost the weight of an official pronouncement.

On 25 November the correspondent of *The Times* began his despatch in the following words:

> It is now pouring rain—the skies are black as ink—the wind is howling over the staggering tents—the trenches are turned into dykes—in the tents the water is sometimes a foot deep—our men have not either warm or waterproof clothing—they are out for twelve hours at a time in the trenches—they are plunged into the inevitable miseries of a winter campaign—and not a soul seems to care for their comfort or even for their lives.

The attack had begun.

15

THE PRIVATE WAR

I have at last opened fire on Lord Raglan and the General Staff
John Delane

I

William Howard Russell, the principal war correspondent of *The Times*, a big, cheerful, black-bearded, thirty-five-year-old Irishman with an excellent appetite and a taste for brandy, had been with the Expeditionary Army since the beginning of the war. He had earned a reputation as an extremely amusing *raconteur* and drinking-companion whose ludicrously woeful accounts of his misfortunes were enlivened by an extravagant imagination and a rich Irish brogue. Always sure of a warm welcome in the tents of junior officers, he had a great talent for making them talk unreservedly about their sufferings and prejudices. For, unlike most men of bluff and garrulous geniality, he was a good listener. He was also a good writer; and his despatches, sharp, clear and evocative, sometimes funny, often moving, always vivid, were eagerly awaited and avidly read by almost the entire literate population of London.

There were, of course, men who disliked and distrusted him, who were irritated by his unflagging *bonhomie*, who found his reckless sarcasm in occasional ill-taste, who resented his consistently rude remarks about the generals and the staff and refused to talk to him. 'If you tell Mrs. Dixon,' an officer in the 7th told his father, 'that Mr. Russell, the correspondent of *The Times* out here is *an Irishman, she* will probably know how much to take as truth.'[1] Captain Clifford was more explicit:

> He is a vulgar low Irishman, an Apostate Catholic (but that is neither here nor there), but he has the gift of the gab, uses his pen as well as his tongue, sings a good song, drinks anyone's brandy and water, and smokes as many cigars as foolish young officers will let him, and he is looked upon by most in camp as a Jolly Good Fellow. He is just the sort of chap to get information, particularly out of youngsters. And I assure you, more than one 'Nob' has thought best to give him a shake of the

hand rather than a cold shoulder *en passant*, for [he] is rather an awkward gentleman to be on bad terms with. Of course, he is no great favourite *chez nous*.²

His aversion to most of those generals who did not give him a shake of the hand, and to Lord Raglan in particular, was unconcealed. He was, in the first place, conscious of a grudge against them. For although John Delane, his editor in London, had assured him that Lord Hardinge had made arrangements for him to travel with the Guards, when he arrived at Southampton no one seemed prepared to receive him and he had to make his own way out to Malta. From there he was able to move on to Gallipoli only with the help of a man in the dockyard who was persuaded to find him a berth in a transport. At Gallipoli he was given neither quarters nor rations, and when he asked the army to supply him with transport he was refused. 'I run a good chance of starving,' he told Delane, 'if the Army takes the field. . . . I have no tent nor can I get one without an order; and even if I had one I doubt very much whether Sir George Brown would allow me to pitch it within the camp. All my efforts to get a horse have been unsuccessful. . . . I am living in a pigsty.'³

A month later Russell heard that Delane had received confirmation from the Horse Guards that he was to be allowed to draw rations and live with the army. By then, however, his condemnation of the entire structure of the army's administration had made his relationship with its senior officers an extremely strained one. Although no names were yet mentioned he had attacked, by implication, the Army Medical Department for 'the continued want of comforts for the sick'; Sir George Brown for 'the arrangements, or rather non-arrangements, for the reception of our troops at Gallipoli'; the Quartermaster-General for the siting of the camps, and the Adjutant General for the drunkenness which continued 'to be the great evil of the Allied army'. The management of the army was 'infamous'. The contrast with the French a 'painful' one.⁴ Most of his strictures were well merited; but he cannot have been greatly surprised when, having bought a tent and had it pitched within the Light Division's lines, it was taken down and laid flat outside the camp, allegedly because it did not comply with regulation standards but really because it belonged to the 'ruffianly' correspondent of 'that infernal *Times*'.

Russell went to see Lord Raglan, but an A.D.C. informed him

that the Commander-in-Chief was much too busy to see him. It was a rebuff which Russell was always to remember. 'I have just been informed on good authority', he told Delane, 'that Lord Raglan has determined not to recognise the Press in any way. . . . The promises made in London have not been carried out here.'*5

In their efforts to protect him from what they took to be the prying attentions of an ill-bred journalist Lord Raglan's A.D.C.s did him irreparable harm. Such high-handed treatment of the representative of the most influential newspaper in the world would be unthinkable in a modern army, but the power of the Press was as yet unappreciated. The Duke of Wellington had once spoken of the newspapers as 'just a damned nuisance', and Lord Raglan had no cause yet to consider them anything worse. Certainly he made no efforts either to get rid of their correspondents or to censor what they said. Unless they were guilty—as indeed they often were—of providing the enemy with secret information, he ignored them. 'The only way to diminish their importance,' he advised the Duke of Newcastle, 'is not to notice their reports.'6

If he had not ignored them, if in particular he had not ignored Russell, much of the abuse with which they were to blacken his name would not have been written. Russell could base his letters and despatches only upon what he saw and upon what men and officers— and they were mainly junior officers—told him. If he had been able to see Lord Raglan and his staff at work, if he had been told the details of each case of apparent negligence, of the appalling slowness and muddle in London, of the incorrigibility of the existing departmental system, he would have been able to correct much of the misinformation by which his observations were coloured. But the Press was denied even the most tenuous contact with the Headquarters staff. And so Mr. Russell never even so much as spoke to the man for whose death, so

* Russell was not the only correspondent to receive a cold shoulder at the British headquarters. 'Somehow or other,' Somerset Calthorpe wrote, 'I don't know how it is but the reporters of the English journals have made themselves very unpopular. They appear to try and find fault whenever they can, and throw as much blame and contempt on the English authorities as if their object was to bring the British army into disrepute with our allies. Altogether they seem to write in a bad spirit, and in a manner calculated to occasion much discontent and grumbling. . . . A few days ago two reporters of newspapers went to Headquarters and asked for an order for tents and animals to carry their luggage, rations for themselves and their servants etc., etc.; and when told that no provision could be made for them, appeared to think they were very hardly used.' (Letters from Headquarters, I, 37–40.)

Delane later told him, he was 'universally admitted' to have been responsible.

'Universally admitted' or not, however, Delane should himself have taken the larger share of Russell's responsibility. Up till the beginning of December Russell's criticisms of Lord Raglan had been confined to private letters. But these were distributed by Delane to members of the Cabinet.[7] In one of them, written on 8 November, Russell had been particularly vindictive. He granted that the Commander-in-Chief was brave and a 'polished gentleman', but at Inkerman he had been a 'mere cool and callous spectator'. 'I am convinced,' he said, 'that Lord Raglan is utterly incompetent to lead an army through any arduous task. . . . The most serious disadvantage under which he labours is that he does not go among the troops. He does not visit the camps, he does not cheer them, and his person is in consequence almost unknown to them. . . . I am sure of my facts.'[8] In another letter Russell told Delane that Raglan had 'not been down to Balaclava for a month, has never visited a hospital, and never goes among the men'.[9]

With Russell's private letters as their authority the leader-writers were set to work. The attacks on the Army became less general and more personal. On 23 December *The Times* told its readers that 'the noblest army ever sent from these shores has been sacrificed to the grossest mismanagement. Incompetency, lethargy, aristocratic hauteur, official indifference, favour, routine, perverseness, and stupidity reign, revel and riot in the Camp before Sebastopol. . . . We say it with extreme reluctance, no one sees or hears anything of the Commander-in-Chief.'

A week later *The Times* returned to the attack. A leader-writer declared:

> There are people who think it a less happy consummation of affairs that the Commander-in-Chief and his staff should survive alone on the heights of Sebastopol, decorated, ennobled, duly named in despatch after despatch, and ready to return home to enjoy pensions and honours amid the bones of fifty thousand British soldiers, than that the equanimity of office and the good-humour of society should be disturbed by a single recall or a new appointment over the heads now in command.

A few days later Delane wrote to Russell. 'Probably before this reaches you,' he said, 'you will have heard that I have at last opened fire on Lord Raglan and the General Staff. According to all accounts their incapacity has been most gross and it is to that and the supineness of the General that the terrible losses we have undergone are principally to be attributed.' [10]

Once having opened fire, he maintained the bombardment and increased its fury. The attacks on privilege and the aristocratic rule of the Army became more and more frequent; week by week the circulation of the paper rose; disgruntled officers, confident of publication, were encouraged to write bitter and scurrilous letters; everyone felt obliged to read *The Times*, for everywhere it was discussed. It spoke of the soldiers dying in the mud and then of 'their aristocratic general, and their equally aristocratic staff' viewing the 'scene of wreck and destruction with gentlemanlike tranquillity. Indeed,' it added, 'until stung into something like activity by the reflections of the Press, the person on whom the highest responsibility for this situation devolves had hardly condescended even to make himself superficially acquainted with its horrors. The aristocracy are trifling with the safety of the Army in the Crimea.' [11] Five days later it suggested that Lord Raglan, whiling 'away his time in ease and tranquillity among the relics of his army', would soon return home with his well-born staff and 'their horses, their plate, and their china, the German cook and several tons' weight of official returns, all in excellent order, and the announcement that, the last British soldier being dead, they had left our position to the care of their gallant allies.' [12]

The letters published were no less sardonic than these articles. Everyone was 'grumbling and growling', according to 'a letter received by a gentleman from his son, an officer in the —— Regiment' and published on 2 January. Everything was 'grossly mismanaged. . . . Everyone leaves everything for the others to do and consequently nothing is done. Lord Raglan has not been seen for three weeks and the report is that he has gone to Malta for the winter. In fact he has succeeded in giving general dissatisfaction.'

'A Field officer mentioned for distinguished conduct' had a letter published the following day. 'Lord Raglan,' he said, '(if Lord Raglan be really here and not in London) is never seen. Whether he knows anything of how things are going on I do not know. . . . And yet he has been made a Field-Marshal. The blood of his officers and men has done it for him and not his own abilities.'

'A Guards Officer' was quoted as having written: 'Lord Raglan is fast getting into bad odour with the whole army for his total carelessness of everything; there will be a great outcry against him before long. . . . There have been sixty or seventy in the English army buried daily—all Lord Raglan's fault in not seeing that clothing and shelter were provided for them, which was in his means, but he does not care.'

Other officers accused Lord Raglan of being hoodwinked by his staff, who let him see nothing and persuaded him that everything was going well, to make 'things pleasant to him'.[13]

'One can hardly believe,' Somerset Calthorpe wrote home indignantly when printed copies of these letters 'purporting to be written by officers' reached the Crimea, 'one can hardly believe in their really being the productions of English gentlemen'. When the one from the 'Guards Officer' was read, he and Lord Raglan's other A.D.C.s tried to find out who was responsible for it. The Guards officers were well known as the 'biggest grumblers', but this was 'really too much'. They got friends in the Brigade to ask every officer in the Guards whether he had written it. Each one denied it.[14]

Lady Westmorland, indeed, had no doubt that most of these letters were 'manufactured in London'.[15] And there were others, including Nigel Kingscote, who agreed with her. Many more, while apparently not doubting their authenticity, felt that their authors had been both cruel and unforgivably disloyal.

An old officer of the 43rd, writing to his cousin at Oakham, spoke of the 'villainous letters in *The Times* newspaper'.

If ever a generous or a kind-hearted man—yes, a soldier's friend, was to be found, that man's name is 'Raglan'—not only a brave soldier but his moral character stands *nulli secundus*. I speak not only from my heart that loves [him] but from my long servitude under that glorious soldier and man . . . who will arise from the disgusting abuse of newspaper correspondents, *if possible*, higher in renown, greater in worth, richer in honours, and fuller of usefulness to his sovereign and *I trust* his admiring country. Forgive me in writing so fully of such a man as Lord Raglan but my old soldier's blood boils up with indignation at *The Times* and other abusive papers.[16]

'Some of the letters written by officers are too bad,' Henry Clifford thought; 'it is a great shame to publish them. . . . If every young gentleman who writes home and abuses Lord Raglan and this and that and finds fault with everything and everybody, did his *duty* and looked well after his men *on* or *off* duty, much of the mismanagement would not have existed. . . . It makes me furious to see Regimental officers crying out "stinking fish" when they have helped to make it so.'[17]

Much of the anger of these regimental officers undoubtedly sprang from the quiet, unemphatic tone of Lord Raglan's despatches and his adherence to the Duke of Wellington's practice of rarely mentioning the names of officers other than those of generals and their staffs. Letters frequently begin with this complaint and then go on to fulminate against '*hauteur*', 'indifference' and the insensitivity of an aristocratic field-marshal who did not 'concern himself with the sufferings of ordinary men'. 'The army here is a good deal disgusted at the slight notice Lord Raglan took of the sanguinary battle of Inkerman', said Captain Campbell of the 46th. 'Like the Duke,' complained a captain in the artillery, 'Lord Raglan mentions every arm but the artillery. This has caused *very great* dissatisfaction amongst us. It is really *too* bad.'[18] The Guards, also, considered themselves to have been poorly treated; and a colonel of the Grenadiers thought it his duty to make a formal complaint to Lord Raglan.[19]

But if the Commander-in-Chief might reasonably be blamed for following an outdated custom in the compilation of despatches, other accusations which were made against him are not so readily understandable. For some officers he became, it seems, an ogre who was responsible for their every disappointment and misery, for the slowness of their promotion, their difficulty in getting permission to sell out, even the delays of the Postmaster in despatching and delivering letters. Cornet Fisher told his parents that he supposed, not having heard from them lately, that his Lordship was using their letters to light his fires with! A fortnight later, when his own letter missed the mail, the reason was that 'the monster, Raglan, wishes to get his own start of the other letters which might state that his right division got no food for two days and meat for three'.

Captain Duberly of the 8th Hussars wrote to a friend, whose husband was a Member of Parliament, to tell her that when after the storm Commissary-General Filder had gone to Lord Raglan to tell him that he could not now undertake to provision the whole army and suggested that the cavalry should go to Scutari for the winter, 'Lord Raglan's answer was, "Let the men eat their tent poles, not a man or horse shall leave until Sebastopol is taken."'

Articles based upon letters such as these were now almost daily appearing in The Times, the Daily News, the Morning Herald and other London and provincial papers. Lord Raglan, ignoring their personal spite and misinformed backbiting, took them as symptomatic of a deeper discontent, straws in the wind of an artificial storm. 'The attacks upon the officers of the Army,' he told the Queen in a long reply to a letter from her in which she had spoken of her grief at the 'infamous Articles in the Press',[20]

which have so lately filled the columns of the newspapers have been written not alone with the design of injuring them in the estimation of Your Majesty and that of the Public but likewise with the object of changing the constitution of the service, wresting the command of it from Your Majesty whom it is the pride of all ranks to serve and obey, and placing it under the more immediate control of Parliament. Lord Raglan was more than a quarter of a century immediately connected with the administration of the Army. During that period there were several occasions in which the country was convulsed by political excitement and the services of the troops were required. In all that time, the steadiness, loyalty and discipline displayed by them were most remarkable and there was in no instance the smallest demonstration of party feeling, although they were officered by gentlemen professing every shade of politics.

He spoke—for he was nothing if not conservative in all military matters—of the 'excellence of the present system' and took the 'liberty of expressing his earnest hope that no change will be introduced which shall have the effect of discouraging the Gentlemen of the Country from entering into a profession in which they have hitherto served with honour and fidelity and with advantage to the crown.'[21]

This letter immediately evoked a predictable and heartfelt response. By what right, the Queen was later to demand in exasperated anger, did The Times try her officers?[22] She now professed herself in entire agreement 'as to the object of the infamous attacks against the Army which have disgraced our newspapers'. The authority of the Queen over the Army was 'one of the Queen's dearest prerogatives'. She was 'fully impressed with the importance of upholding the position of the Army . . . and of not allowing Parliament to usurp that authority'.[23]

Lord Raglan thanked the Queen for receiving 'with indulgence his observations'. He was 'more and more convinced of the truth of his remarks'. It was 'curious that General Canrobert has more than once in conversation alluded to what he supposes to be the design of the Press and expressed his earnest hope' that the English Army would not become a democratic one. The French Army was essentially democratic. The evils resulting from it were, in Canrobert's opinion, 'excessive, notwithstanding that every exertion is made to diminish them by selecting for promotion those who have not risen from the ranks'.*[24]

Lord Raglan's heartfelt conservatism, so clearly displayed in his correspondence with the Queen, was something which most officers of the Army shared. And if he was right in thinking that the real purpose of the newspapers' attack was to change the constitution of the Army and indeed, as Charles Greville was not the only man to think, the 'whole system of Government',[25] his officers would have been horrified to know that their uncensored letters, written in haste and anger and despair and sent by indignant relatives to newspapers, often without their knowledge or consent, were being used for such a purpose. Several intelligent officers, although not accepting Lord Raglan's theory of a widespread national plot, did realise that many of the more vindictive letters were being published for reasons other than those altruistic and public-spirited ones which the newspaper proprietors and editors professed. They realised too that when an army meets disaster its commander is the obvious target for blame and abuse; and that, in this case as in others, the man pushed forward as a sin-offering is only the epitome and incarnation of a general sense of guilt.

'I see,' Captain Elton wrote home, 'that The Times is letting into Lord Raglan pretty heavily. . . . I think people in general are beginning to get so indignant at the want of management that they must find some outlet for their wrath and put it all upon him while a great deal is due to parties much nearer home.'[26]

Officers like Elton knew, as Lord Stratford said, 'that every whale

---

* In the British Army, however, men from the ranks were at this time being commissioned. Officers were falling sick in greater proportion than the men, and leaders had to be found. Four sergeants of the 55th were granted emergency commissions. From the Army List it seems that they lost them on returning home.

must have a Jonah when the sea runs high'. But they could think of others than Lord Raglan more deserving of sacrifice. 'The real fault,' Major Jocelyn thought, 'lay with the Home Government more than anyone else.' 'I believe it is not Lord Raglan's fault,' another officer said. But 'there ought to be a terrible example made of that old Traitor Aberdeen. . . . I would not give him much for his skin if we got him out here. . . . I am sure they would eat him up alive without salt.'[27] 'The Government,' Colonel Bell thought, 'recognised themselves as responsible for all our trials and difficulties. But were too anxious to keep straight with the public and the press.'

Certainly somewhere a scapegoat had to be found.

But members of the Government were determined that they, at least, should not play the part.

II

'I am pained, *so humiliated*, so furious,' the Countess of Westmorland wrote from Vienna to a friend on 31 January, 'at the part my country is playing. . . . Amongst all the Ministers who have spoken in Parliament, anxious to justify themselves personally and collectively, there is not one who has had the courage to undertake the defence of Lord Raglan. They are too afraid of offending their masters, the newspapers! You see I am very exasperated.'[28]

It was largely true. Since the beginning of December the Government had been under constant attack in both Houses. Anyone connected with the administration of the Army, which indeed as Prince Albert said could not be defended, was insulted and ridiculed not only by Parliament but also by the Press. 'Things have gone mad here,' the Prince wrote to the Dowager Duchess of Coburg. 'The political world is quite crazy. The Press, which for its own ends exaggerates the sufferings of our troops, has made the nation quite furious. It is bent upon punishing all and sundry, and cannot find the right person, because he does not exist.'[29]

Lord Raglan's name and those of his staff, particularly Airey's and Estcourt's, had been frequently mentioned in terms of the severest stricture and often of abuse. Occasionally they were defended by the newspapers, but almost never in Parliament. The inescapable impression was that Ministers were content to accept their ruin, provided they themselves were left in peace. 'The opinion about Raglan appears to be rapidly gaining ground', Charles Greville wrote in his diary on 31 January. 'And the Ministers have arrived at the same conclusion. . . . Still they can do nothing, for he has done nothing and omitted nothing so flagrantly as to call for or justify his recall.'

Refusing to defend himself, disdaining to answer the most outlandish charges, assuring the Duke of Newcastle that they were merely symptoms of the Englishman's passion for grumbling, Lord Raglan appeared to his staff as calm and unruffled as ever. Lord Burghersh, who saw him every day, told Lady Westmorland that the attacks in Parliament left the Commander-in-Chief as unmoved as did those of the Press and of his own anonymous officers.[30] He never referred to them. But in letters to his wife he could not but show how profoundly unhappy he was. She saw, she told her sister, that he was 'blessé au coeur'. And her sister knew 'what he must suffer with a heart so tender and sensitive as his'.[31]

He felt, he confessed, an overwhelming sense of loneliness and desertion. Even the Queen, whose friendly and grateful letters had previously meant so much to him, now seemed more distant, worried and reserved.

When sending home the letters he had had from her, and from Lord Aberdeen and the Duke of Newcastle, about his nomination to be a field-marshal, he had told his daughters how 'most gracious she had been', and how 'very kind' everyone at home was about his receiving a distinction of which he felt 'entre nous quite unworthy'.* 'The Queen's letter is most gracious,' he said, 'It is impossible to be more so, and Lord Aberdeen's expression towards me and my services are most flattering but far beyond what I could expect in a man with so cold an exterior, tho' I believe with a warm heart. I have every confidence in the Duke of Newcastle's attachment to me.'[32]

But now everything had changed. The Queen's letters were still polite and gracious, but there was, he could not help feeling, an undertone of accusation. Writing from Windsor on New Year's Day

---

* According to Nigel Kingscote Lord Raglan was very conscious of not having been able to do much at Inkerman. He said he had 'done nothing to deserve' the promotion and was 'rather disgusted than otherwise at it'. (Raglan Private Papers D(1)223.)

1855, she briefly acknowledged his previous letter and returned 'her best thanks for it'. And then without further preliminaries she went straight to the apparent purpose of her letter.

> The sad privations of the Army, the bad weather and the constant sickness are causes of the *deepest* concern and anxiety to the Queen and the Prince. The braver her noble Troops are and the more patiently they bear all their trials and sufferings the more *miserable* we feel at their long continuance.
>
> The Queen *trusts* that Lord Raglan will be *very* strict in seeing that *no unnecessary* privations are incurred by any negligence of those whose duty it is to watch over their wants. The Queen heard that their coffee was given them green instead of its being roasted and several other things of the kind. It has distressed the Queen as she feels so conscious that they should be made as comfortable as circumstances can admit of. The Queen earnestly trusts that the larger amount of warm clothing has not only reached Balaclava but has been distributed and that Lord Raglan has been successful in procuring the means of hutting for the men. Lord Raglan cannot think how much we suffer for the Army and how painfully anxious we are to know that their privations are *decreasing*...[33]

Lord Raglan replied immediately and at length. Each point was carefully dealt with. Without pained excuses or extravagant promises he did his best to set the Queen's mind at rest. Everything that could possibly be done was being done. He could, he said,

> with truth assure your Majesty that his whole time and all his thoughts are occupied in endeavouring to provide for the various wants of your Majesty's troops. It has not been in his power to lighten the burden of their duties. . . . Much having been said, as Lord Raglan has been given to understand, in private letters, of the inefficiency of the staff, he considers it to be due to your Majesty, and a simple act of justice to those individuals, to assure your Majesty that he has every reason to be satisfied with their exertions, their indefatigable zeal, and undeviating close attention to their duties.

He told her that roast coffee had been ordered from the Treasury three months before, but had not yet arrived. In the meantime the captain of the *Sanspareil* had got his engineers to make machines for roasting the green coffee which had been sent instead, but they had so far not produced as much as the army required.[34] The Treasury was not blamed. Indeed, only when he knew every fact did Lord Raglan blame anyone.

It was then with unusual indignation that he answered the more specific charges that the Duke of Newcastle was now making.

Until the end of 1854 the Duke as the Government's spokesman had sympathised with Lord Raglan in his difficulties, telling him how unfairly and ungenerously he had been 'attacked by the ruffianly *Times*'. But now the tide was turning. *The Times*'s attack was widening. The Government too was being implicated by being shown to be a part of 'that huge imposture our military system' and an abettor of the army's 'lamentable failure', which had brought the country to the 'verge of ruin' and the 'eve of a great national disaster'. 'I shall, of course, be the first victim of popular vengeance,' the Duke complained to Raglan. 'And the papers, assisted by the Tory and Radical parties united, have pretty well settled my fate already.'[35]

The tone of the Duke's private letters changed. They were now full of accusations; the compliments and sympathy were no longer expressed. They spoke of 'want of system and organisation', 'neglect of duty', 'indifference to the army's fate', 'unawareness of the Government's dilemma', 'carelessness amongst the higher departments'. They mentioned many of the complaints which Members of Parliament and private people were constantly forcing upon his attention. Palmerston had asked about a letter which he had seen, accusing the Commander-in-Chief of not arriving on the scene of the battle of Inkerman until it was almost over. Someone else wanted to know how it came about that the Headquarters Staff were living like fighting-cocks while the army was starving. Why were sick men employed in bringing up flotsam from the harbour for Lord Raglan's fires? An officer's wife demanded an explanation for her husband's 'want of change of linen'.[36]

Lord Raglan replied with calm self-control, ignoring altogether the most outrageous and absurd imputations. Then the Duke of Newcastle wrote with at first vague and finally categoric charges against Generals Airey and Estcourt and other less senior officers of the staff, whom it was suggested might well be dismissed.[37] Lord Raglan flew to their defence with a vehemence almost shocking in a man who had scarcely even troubled to correct misrepresentations against himself.

He 'positively and distinctly' denied the accuracy of the Government's 'severe observations'.

It is with the deepest concern that I observe that upon the authority of private letters, you condemn Generals Airey and Estcourt, and the staff generally, and this without reference to me, or the expression of a desire to have my opinion of their qualifications or imputed deficiencies. I have been conversant with public business nearly half a century, and I have never known an instance of such condemnation before. The officers above named are perfectly efficient. I am witness to their daily labours, their constant toil, and I can with truth say that they merit the tribute of my warmest approbation. . . . Am I, or are the writers of private letters, in the better position to pronounce upon their merits? . . .

It is impossible for me to deprive them of their appointments without, so far as I know, any ground whatever.

You must pardon me for adding that I can only regard your adoption of the imputation against these officers as a reflection on myself, and an indication that you consider me incapable of judging of departmental officers, the chief of whom receive their orders from me.

I find that the attack upon the Staff generally has been so indiscriminate as to extend to my personal Staff, who are accused of aristocratic hauteur, incivility and God knows what besides. This, indeed, is a matter of surprise, more particularly as it has been frequently mentioned to me by officers of the highest rank and consideration that the general opinion was quite the other way. They are all perfect gentlemen, extremely intelligent, zealous beyond everything, and most courteous to all. . . . There is not one of them who is not ready at the slightest hint from me to undertake any duty at all hours of day or night.[38]

After receipt of this surprisingly heated defence the Government decided not to press for the immediate dismissal of Airey and Estcourt. Something must be done, however, the Duke of Newcastle suggested in his next letter, to satisfy the public and the Opposition in their clamour for a victim. Would Lord Raglan agree to Airey's being transferred to a command in the field? 'I deem it necessary,' Lord Raglan replied as soon as he received this letter, 'not to lose another moment in saying that, if he be removed from the appointment of Quartermaster-General, a very great injury would be inflicted on the service and on myself personally. I should have the greatest difficulty in getting on without him. I consider his services invaluable.'[39]

But the Government had decided that in Airey they had a man who would ideally fit the role of scapegoat, and they used every means they could to persuade Lord Raglan to get rid of him. The senior officers of the army, Lord Raglan was assured, did not like Airey. While Cathcart, his most vociferous critic, was dead, Sir George Brown was said to dislike him almost as much.[40] And neither Lord Cardigan nor Lord Lucan, for once in agreement and talking their heads off in London, had any good to say of him. De Lacy Evans, although less openly condemnatory, could not get on with him, and in his letters to Delane, who was an old friend of his, did not trouble to hide the fact. Extremely intelligent and hardworking, highly impatient and often brusque to the point of insolence, Airey refused to suffer fools gladly and had accordingly, in an army with more than a fair share of them, made many enemies. He was to discover how ruinous, in times of failure, this could be.

'This very day,' the Duke of Newcastle in pursuit of his quarry, wrote on 1 January, 1855, 'an angry relative of an officer dying from sickness said to be brought on by avoidable causes, asked me how a Quartermaster-General was likely to attend to his important duties who found time to write long private letters to at least half a dozen fine ladies in London.'

Lord Raglan answered:

I can, of course, give no reply, to the charge of an officer dying from avoidable causes: but I can say this, that the Quartermaster-General can have nothing to do with these causes. He has not the charge of sick officers. General Airey pleads guilty to having written to Miss Hardinge who was in great anxiety about her brother, then confined by illness to this house, and to Lady Raglan to let her know how I was; and these are the only ladies he has written to except to his wife.

I really cannot understand any gentleman venturing to intrude upon you such an insinuation. . . .

I can arrive at no other conclusion than that I no longer enjoy your confidence. This, which is strongly impressed upon my mind, I regard as a heavy misfortune, and as calculated to increase the difficulties and add very seriously to the anxieties of my present position, the only alleviation to which has been the countenance and support which you have hitherto invariably manifested towards me. My duty, however, to the Queen will induce me to persevere in doing my best to carry on the service to the utmost of my ability, apart from all personal considerations.[41]

Throughout the weeks of early winter the correspondence continued. Required to waste hours of his time in answering the Government's constant questions and complaints, Lord Raglan, already more than fully occupied with every aspect of the army's business, worked harder and longer even than before. Some mornings he came into breakfast looking as though he had not been to bed at all.[42]

Despite the strain of overwork, however, he managed to stand up to it, Nigel Kingscote thought, 'marvellously well, though his mind at all events must have very great wear and tear. Did you ever see such villainous articles and letters as that abominable *Times* publishes,' he asked indignantly. 'Why they have made such a run against the staff I cannot for the life of me conceive, and no one hits the right nail on the head, and which has been the whole cause of our misfortune, namely the want of transport. . . . I have no patience with the Government, and least with the Duke of Newcastle.'[43]

Nor, understandably, had Lord Raglan's family at home. In a letter of touching pathos Charlotte Somerset told a friend:

> We do indeed go through a great deal just now. And the only thing that keeps up our spirits is the comfort that God in His mercy preserves dear Papa in such good health and gives him strength to bear up against all the anxieties and cares he has to undergo, and under *all* circumstances to preserve his calmness and equanimity of manner, and what is all the more wonderful, I am told he is never out of humour. He works all day and half the night, and rides about a great deal; sometimes, even in the coldest weather, he is on horseback six hours at a time. . . . Kitty and I amuse ourselves by reading old Annual Registers. The debate after Talavera in 1810 in both Houses is so like what is going on now that it is quite curious. But there is this difference, *then* the Government supported the Commander-in-Chief, now it is content to see him abused and vilified without interfering. . . .
>
> Poor Richard feels it a great deal, but I sometimes think it is better for him to be away, as he avoids the numerous impertinences and absurd stories which people take pleasure in coming and telling us. . . . I live in hope that *truth* will prevail at last.[44]

16

NIGHTMARE

The poor men are certainly suffering more than human nature can stand
Captain the Hon. Henry Clifford

I

A few days before Christmas Captain Clifford sat in his tent wishing
that Charles Dickens, whose new book he was reading, could have
come out to Russia and written a sequel, *Hard Times in the Crimea*.

Through the partly open flap he could see a party of men from the
4th Division going to fetch water. The night had been stormy and the
snow was melting. 'Poor fellows!' he thought. 'They have no doubt
been up all night wet through in the trenches or on picquet. There is
little about them to tell their profession.' The corporal, an Irishman,
has his head cast down and is 'trying to get shelter in the cape of
his greatcoat, or rather what remains of it. . . . He has parted with
any superfluous flesh. . . . His forage cap without chin-strap or top-
knot is pulled over his ears and his shaggy hair, moustache and beard,
left to themselves since he landed in the Crimea, are left for use and
warmth, not ornament.'

There was only one 'spark' of scarlet cloth in the whole party.
Trousers were patched with the clothes of dead Russians. One man
was lucky enough to have a pair of Russian knee-length boots,
through which his big toe stuck. The legs of the others were bound up
with old sacks, raw hide and sheepskins.[1]

It was not an exceptional spectacle. No two men in any regiment
dressed alike. Officers were asked to wear their swords as there was
'now no other way of telling them from the men';[2] or, for that matter,
of telling that they were soldiers at all. One day a major in the Light
Division was standing outside a shanty he had built, wearing amongst
other improbable garments a pair of French uniform trousers and a
fez. A Zouave officer passed by and mistook him for a *cantinier*.
'*Allo,*' the Frenchman said, '*As-tu de l'absinthe?*' By chance the officer,
who had lived in France for many years and spoke French perfectly,
had a bottle. He poured out a glass for the Zouave and then another,

then several more. *'Combien?'* he was asked at last. *'Mais rien,'* he said. *'Pas de blague!'* the Zouave said almost threateningly; *'on ne donne pas de l'absinthe pour rien.'* The English major then confessed his identity.[3]

The British officers wore beards so long, Lieutenant Richards told his sister, that you could scarcely recognise even their faces. His own was a foot long, he said. 'In fact I look very much like an owl looking out of an ivy bush. I intend to turn all the hair to good account, if I return, in the bed stuffing business.'

Some of the officers had hay-bands bound round their legs, others had

> long stockings outside their rags or trousers; some had garters made from old knapsacks; others had leggings made from sheepskins, bullocks' hides, horse hides—anything to keep out the extreme cold. . . . Our men's coats were nothing but rags tacked together. As for head dress some had mess tin covers that could be pulled down well over the ears; others had coverings for the head made out of old blankets four or five times doubled. . . . Some of their beards and moustaches were almost two inches long, and sometimes these were so frozen that they could not open their mouths until they could get a fire to thaw them.[4]

And fires were now luxuries rarely to be had. Every tree, every bush, had vanished from the plateau, and every root had been dug from the frozen ground—even the vine roots, hard as ebony. There was 'not a twig to be seen now as thick as any one's finger; all cut away and burned up'.[5] Even the patches of brushwood left in the outlying valleys had been fired by the Russians.[6] Sometimes men would struggle up from the harbour with a few bits of wreckage or a bag of charcoal and huddle round a fire in their tents, where several of them died from the fumes.

But few men had the energy to collect fuel, and most of those that had the energy had not got the time. For regiments were dangerously short of men.* One day in the middle of January the 63rd Regiment was reduced to a strength of twenty.[7] And it was not an extraordinary

---

* There were reports early in January that foreign mercenaries were coming out. The army was appalled. 'Broken and overworked as officers and men are, this proposal has filled us all with the greatest indignation and disgust . . .' Captain Clifford wrote. 'Germans to fight for us! Why Germans? Why not Red Indians?' 'We have just heard of the Foreigners' Bill,' another officer wrote, 'I would not advise them to send any of their 2/- murderers here. The men would kick them out of the camp.'

case. 'The army,' as Lord Raglan told the Duke of Newcastle, 'is suffering very much,' and it needed 'all the men that could be sent'. The Guards left home '2,500 strong and reinforcements amounting to 1,500 had joined them; but by the end of 1854 they could only muster about 900 men fit for duty'.[8] Two months later, Colonel Jocelyn wrote home, 'the Brigade of Guards has almost ceased to exist'. He had attended a funeral of fellow-officers after Inkerman and had watched 'twelve young fellows all buried in a row', and sickness since had taken so many more that when at the beginning of February Lord Rokeby came out to replace the Duke of Cambridge, who had gone home ill and on the verge of a nervous breakdown, the Brigade was 'a pitiable sight'. Lord Rokeby called the Guards officers together to read them letters from the Queen, but the sight of so few and such haggard faces was too much for him, and he burst into tears. [9]

The reinforcements who were now arriving in response to Lord Raglan's repeated requests fell sick within a few days of their landing and died 'like rotten sheep'.[10] When writing home on 13 December to the Duke of Newcastle, Raglan said that he wished he could say that the men were tolerably healthy, but the reverse was the case. The 46th had lost 102 men; the 9th had less than three hundred men under arms, and the sickness had 'told dreadfully on the newcomers'.

Three days before, the commanding officer of the 1st had looked at his young, red-cheeked reinforcements and wondered, 'Where will they be in a month? Forty of the last batch died in three weeks.' He decided to keep them out of the trenches for a week to 'acclimatise them in a small way'.[11] Colonel Tomline said that his recruits, 'young boys from the Depot, came and knelt down at my feet praying me to send them home'.[12] It would not have greatly mattered if he had been able to do so, for they were not much use. They had been given the briefest possible training and had 'no more idea of a Minié rifle than a theodolite'.[13] Would they be able to fight, Captain Clifford wondered, as he looked at their anxious, simple faces and thought that he was answered when, a few days later, he heard one of them shouting, 'Run, boys, run. The Rooshians are a-coming.'

There were, perhaps fortunately, not many of them. Recruiting, given a boost by the stirring tales of Inkerman, was now not going very well in England. The early enthusiasm for the war had died. *The Times*, indeed, on 25 January wiped its hands of the war under the existing management. If the Government and the House of Commons 'choose to sell themselves to the Aristocracy, and through the Aristocracy to their enemies', it was their own affair. But *The Times*, repeating the metaphor, wiped its hands of the national suicide and had 'no choice left but to protest against the further prosecution of an enterprise which leads to nothing but ruin and disgrace'.

Men were not encouraged to join an army which according to the newspapers was grossly mismanaged and dying on its feet, and which —and this was particularly discouraging—was so badly fed.

It was, of course, only too painfully true.

Queen's Regulations provided that each soldier should receive 1½ lb. of leaven bread or 1 lb. of biscuit and 1 lb. of fresh or salt meat a day. For this his pay was stopped 3½d. Anything else he needed he was expected to buy. Lord Raglan recognised that this system was unworkable in Turkey and the Crimea and had ordered that, for the stoppage of a further penny, each soldier should receive an ounce of coffee and 1¼ ounces of sugar. Later on he ordered that two ounces of rice or barley should be added to the daily ration, an extra half-pound of meat and a free issue of a quarter of a pint of spirits.[14] But transport difficulties had made it impossible to get these rations up to the men. For three or four days at a time they sometimes had nothing to eat but biscuit.[15] The fresh meat that came up perhaps once in ten days was 'seldom eatable'.[16] On Christmas Day Colonel Bell's men got no rations at all. 'I kicked up a dust', he noted in his diary. 'At the close of the day the Commissary did serve out a small portion of fresh meat. Too late! no fires, or means of cooking!'

The men, in any event, had little appetite and often when the full rations did come they were too exhausted to collect them. They were more concerned in getting their coffee and rum than anything else; and they went to great trouble with their green coffee-berries, using cannon-balls and shell-cases to grind them with, and anything they could lay their hands on to cook with.* When only four bags of fuel were served out to the three thousand men of the 3rd Division's 1st Brigade, on 31 December, they were issued with one pound of coal each. A few days later they were using old broken boots instead.

---

* The coffee was sent out raw as it is not so much affected by damp when green as it is when roasted.

'Well, my lads,' said their brigadier, 'this is a sort of fuel I never saw tried before.'

'Oh! indeed, sir, they burn very well. If only we had more of them and they were a bit drier.'[17]

An officer of the 46th saw his men cutting up their dried meat into little strips and using that as fuel to cook their coffee with.[18] Men pilfered bits of gabions and even pick and shovel handles and chopped them up before they could be recognised.[19]

By the beginning of the second week of February scurvy was more or less prevalent in all regiments, and the men's teeth, loosened in their soft and spongy gums, could not eat their biscuit until it had been soaked in water. Scurvy also made salt meat taste revolting, and it was impossible to boil out the salt as nearly all the camp kettles had been thrown away before the army reached the Alma, and the mess-tins did not hold enough water. Ten weeks before three steamers had come into the harbour loaded with vegetables. But much of the cargo was already rotten on arrival, and there was no means of getting the remainder up to the camps. Three thousand pounds' worth of vegetables were thrown overboard. On another occasion a commissariat officer refused to accept a cargo of fresh vegetables as he 'had no power to purchase' them.[20] On 19 December 20,000 lb. of lime-juice arrived in the harbour, but it was not until Lord Raglan called for a return of goods in store that anyone in authority seemed aware of their arrival. On 29 January he ordered that lime-juice should form part of the soldiers' ration. But even this presented difficulties of transportation.

For the problem of supply had still not been solved, and now could not be solved. A day of biting, almost arctic cold would be followed by one of torrential rain; for days and nights on end the snow would fall through an icy wind, and then perhaps—and often suddenly—there would be a fine, quite pleasant day and then the rains would fall again. Men going down to Balaclava with hard, thick snow underfoot would return the following day up to their knees in slush and mud. Seeing the snow-covered slopes one day in early January, Colonel Bell suggested to a scornful commissariat officer that the country-carts should be turned into sledges, but a few days later, on either wheels or runners, the carts would have sunk into a bog of slush. In any case there was scarcely a single animal left strong enough to draw them.

What remained of the cavalry had been put to transport duty. The horses of the Royal Horse Artillery, whose officers were extremely proud of them and tended them devotedly, were handed over to the Commissariat. But weeks of under-nourishment had told upon them, and they were pitifully weak. 'My teams,' Captain Shakespear sadly told his mother, 'would disgrace a pedlar.' Fresh pack-horses sent over from Constantinople had arrived on 2 December but by 5 January they could be seen dying every day.

The track from Balaclava was, by the end of January, a 'positive charnel house'.[21] Horse after horse had sunk down into the mud and quietly died. As soon as the British soldiers in charge of a dead horse and cart thus stranded had gone off for help, a group of enterprising Zouaves or starving Turks was as likely as not to fall upon the abandoned cargo and carry it off. When the soldiers returned everything had gone, including most of the cart. Lying in the snow or mud were a few splinters of wood, the rims of the wheels, and the skinless carcasses of the horses from which the hides and huge hunks of meat had been cut.[22]

But despite their known depredations, for which indeed many of the British troops openly admired them, the French were becoming as respected as once they were despised. 'Our only stand-by is the French,' Captain Campbell thought. 'They are still an army.' He wondered what Lord Raglan thought when he contrasted his own men with theirs.

There was, of course, much sickness in the French army too, but their organisation for dealing with it was, compared with the British, exemplary.* At Kamiesch, Captain Robert Portal noticed, 'they have erected long huts and made quite a village. . . . The wounded are carefully laid on beds in rows, then come the sick and so on; everything clean and nice; the man's name and complaint on a piece of paper over his bed, as if he was in a barrack hospital. Then they have huts in which all the medicines are arranged and everything got at, at a moment's notice. Then again, close to the hospital huts, are large cooking huts where soup is constantly made.'

Both sick and those on duty were kept warm in the 'most comfort-

* Kinglake gives a horrifying picture of naked French corpses being tipped out of carts at dead of night. Certainly great efforts were made to conceal the sufferings of the army from the French public. A rigid censorship was enforced. But these sufferings were undoubtedly far less than those which the British endured. Despite a surprisingly high rate of scurvy the health of the army remained relatively good. (*Rapport au Conseil de Santé des Armées.*)

able looking sheepskins'. They were well fed on good bread, peas and beans, rice, dandelions, coffee, sugar and 'bellyfulls of warm soup'.[23] Their transport system was so well run that on Boxing Day they were able to lend the British army five hundred of their horses. And although their front line was much more frequently assaulted by raiding parties from Sebastopol than the British line was, on 27 December several hundred men were ordered to Balaclava to help in carrying up shot and provisions from the harbour. During the next few days more French troops came to the help of the British. They might have done more, Lord Raglan thought, but even a few hundred men were 'very welcome'.[24]

An artillery officer, who had previously not 'reckoned much to them', now thought the French 'splendid fellows. Opinions had entirely changed'.[25] They were, another officer considered, 'a very civil lot'.[26] Their camps were filthy, but British soldiers were always sure of a welcome there, and an evening in a French canteen where brandy and wine were served by pretty *vivandières* was the greatest pleasure that life could then afford.* The Zouaves, who in spite of the filth around them always looked as smart and clean as if they had just left Paris, were admired above all.[27] Their cheerful ruthlessness and zest for living and fighting were undimmed. When Lord Rokeby's patent water-closet was stolen one night the whole British army was delighted. No one doubted that the Zouaves had taken it, perhaps to make soup in.[28] For they, like all French soldiers—and unlike most English ones—were expert cooks, making delicious dishes from the most unpromising-looking rations—from tortoises, and even from rats, which they would politely ask permission to catch in Balaclava and take back to their camps impaled on long sticks.[29]

Their other allies, however, were held by the British in savage contempt. Ever since their behaviour at the battle of Balaclava, they had been maligned and despised. Everyone had a 'blow or a kick for the poor fellows, and nothing but brutal hard language'. The evil-tempered Cornet Fisher went so far as to buy a whip so that he could 'beat every one across the head'. 'I have ridden over one or two already, to teach them not to run away,' he heartlessly confessed. 'And

* The French, of course, made the most of the Englishman's full pockets. Five francs, Lieutenant Stacpoole complained to his brother, was the price charged 'for the very worst *vin ordinaire* that you could get for six sous in Paris'. Brown bread baked daily in the French army's ovens was 5s. a small loaf.

have caught every Turk who came near me and flung him into the most muddy place I could see. . . . How I hate them. The Russians are angels compared to these dogs.'

Captain Clifford, a devout Catholic and a much more charitable man, described the Turks as 'broken-hearted, despised, neglected, ill-treated, miserable men'. Because of the sickness in the British regiments they had been tried out in the trenches, but 'a small boy with a spoon would have been a match for any of them'.[30] They had become 'great thieves, driven to it by want' and were severely punished for it. One Turk, caught stealing a pair of gloves, received 'twenty-five lashes before the eyes of the English officer he stole the gloves from, twenty-five more before the Pasha commanding the Turkish troops, twenty-five before the colonel of his regiment, and twenty-five more before the men'.[31]

In the British army, too, floggings were becoming distressingly frequent, and many men were deserting to the enemy in consequence of them. Between fifteen and twenty men deserted in the first fortnight of January, most of them after having received corporal punishment. Lord Raglan was known to disapprove of flogging, but Queen's Regulations allowed commanding officers a free hand, and many of them felt that they could not otherwise prevent their men's increasing indolence and insubordination. Drunkenness too was on the increase and in some regiments was punished with fifty lashes of the cat.[32]

In Balaclava almost every house was now a shop or store. Small boards announced that 'some Jew, Greek or Maltese rascal supplied spirits, groceries, beer etc.'[33] And men who came down to the harbour on some errand for their regiments usually managed to take back a few bottles of coarse and fiery spirits in their pockets. There was little else for the men to spend their money on, and 2s. was cheerfully given for a bottle of porter and five times as much for brandy.[34] In the 55th Regiment alone, of the seventeen men who were treated for brain disorders during the campaign all but a few were believed to have brought on their madness by excessive drinking, and, of the four of these who died, three were suffering from delirium tremens.[35] 'I must be honest and say plainly,' wrote Sergeant Gowing of the 7th, 'that a vast deal of the sickness was brought on by the men themselves by excessive drinking.'

But few officers found it in their hearts to blame their men for trying to escape from the miseries of their existence by getting drunk when they could. 'The poor men are certainly suffering more than human nature can stand,' Captain Clifford wrote on 19 January. 'They are dying off fast every day. . . . We have fifty-five men frost-bitten in the division. I saw one poor creature brought, frost-bitten in the feet, from the trenches, and when his stockings were taken off, his toe-nails and part of his flesh came off too. One man was found dead in his tent this morning frozen to death.'

Three days earlier, Colonel Bell had found five of his 'poor men dead and frozen' in a single tent. Continuing his rounds he had called 'at the regimental hospital tent and asked "What rations do the sick get here?" (Knowing very well all about it). "Salt pork and green coffee berry, sir."' He returned to his tent and wrote out 'an official report of all this frightful scene and barbarous mockery'.

Other commanding officers, accepting the uselessness of written complaints, tried to keep their regiments fed and clothed by the sheer force and violence of their characters. Colonel Yea, for instance, feared and disliked by his men as he was, afterwards earned their respect for the merciless way he bullied and cursed and swore until he got what he wanted and often a good deal more than his regiment's share;[36] while others, gentler and less unscrupulous, got tired of so much red tape in Balaclava, of being 'pitch forked from one officer to another' and went home to their camps in disgust.[37]

It was not enough, of course, to bully the quartermasters, the commissaries, the clerks and storekeepers in Balaclava, for the goods once released had to be carried up to the camps. You had, Colonel Yea decided, in times like these to bully your own men too. Coming across a sad and listless-looking sergeant one cold January day, he asked him sharply where he had been. 'When the poor fellow said that he was returning to the cemetery and that he had just interred two men, the Colonel roared out: "Then where are the blankets, sir? Go back and get them and parade them before me when washed!"'[38]

Grudgingly his men had to admit that their Colonel was right. It was not a time for squeamishness or pity. If the sergeant had not been made to unwrap the corpses from their blankets, the Turks would have looted the graves. The Turks, indeed, stripped their own dead naked before burying them. And when the rains came and the corpses were washed out of their shallow graves, they were covered only in mud.

Through sheer necessity the most fastidious of the British troops began to acquire the Turks' indifference. When Midshipman Wood's boots gave out he gave a sailor ten shillings to find another pair in the Russian graves on Inkerman Ridge. Many other officers and men followed his example, and held on to the boots they found there, even when new ones arrived from England; for the new boots were not only of such shamefully bad quality that 'the soles dropped off after a week's wear', but many of them were also so small that 'women could scarcely have got them on'.[39] 'They are far too small,' Lord Raglan told the Duke of Newcastle in an exasperated letter, 'and *extremely* ill made.'[40] So ill-made, in fact, were some pairs issued to the 55th Regiment that on 1 February when, after a day or two of bitter cold, the weather became suddenly mild again, turning the plateau once more into 'one vast black dreary wilderness of mud', they sank into the thick and sticky slime, and the strain put upon them when they were lifted out again sucked their soles off. The men threw the rest of their boots away and marched on to the front in their stockings.[41]

For some of them it was their fifth night running in the trenches.

Over long periods the men in many regiments had about three hours' sleep in twenty-four. So exhausted were they that punishments for sleeping on duty could no longer be enforced. Captain Campbell of the 46th noticed, as most fighting soldiers do, that when a man becomes excessively tired he can sleep through practically anything. He slept himself, half immersed in mud, through the noise of cannon-balls and Minié bullets hissing and whining over his head and even crashing and thudding into the parapet immediately above him. The challenge of a sentry, however, would make him spring to his feet, 'like an electric shock'.

But sometimes even the sentry could not keep awake and slipped down into the mud. One night a major and twenty-seven men of the 50th Regiment were bayoneted in their deep, uncaring sleep.

Such a death was, for many, a welcome release from an existence which they felt no longer able to endure. Indeed, the sight of death and the smell of death were so familiar as to be scarcely noticed. Burial-parties walked through the camps, two men carrying a stretcher, two more with pick-axe and spade, and the sentries did not even look at them.[42] The grisly cavalcades of dying men strapped to mules, borrowed from the well-equipped medical department of the

French army, struggled through the slush to the hospitals at Balaclava in a never-ending procession. Russell one day passed such a file of mules jogging silently along and noticed that all the gaunt and ragged riders were close to death; their eyes were closed and only the thin streams of breath drifting into the cold air from their open mouths showed that they were alive. One man, strapped rigidly to his mule and swaying stiffly from side to side, like an effigy in a religious procession, was already a corpse. His eyes, wide open, stared in front of him; his teeth were set on his protruding tongue. A soldier, passing up the slope, saw this ghastly cadaver and, nodding towards it, remarked unconcernedly to his companion, 'Well, there's one poor fellow out of pain anyway.'[43]

The familiarity of such horror and suffering had given to the army's existence the awful probability of a nightmare. Nothing was startling any more. Life was like this now. The whole ghastly scene was at once unreal and acceptable.

Vultures and ravens swooped over the camps 'with their ominous croak-croak',[44] a man sat down in the snow and with calm deliberation blew his brains out,[45] another slowly took his boot off to put a bullet through his foot;[46] down the hill from the 1st Regiment's camp a woman, one of ten or twelve 'who stuck to the Regiment throughout the winter', sat on her husband's grave. She was always there, shivering in the cold.[47] Another woman lay on the wet ground suffering from fever. On 24 February she had been there twelve days with a few bits of food by her side in the mud. 'She having failed to make herself popular among the women during her health, was left by them when she was sick; and not one soul had offered to assist the poor helpless half delirious creature, except her husband and a former mate of his when he was a sailor.'[48]

Over the whole plain, down in the ravines and along the crests above them, the carcasses of animals lay unburied and putrefying. Everywhere miserable, exhausted men could be seen digging graves, to the distant accompaniment of French bands playing with remorseless gaiety. But for every grave dug there were two corpses to fill it. Skeletons gnawed by dogs and picked clean by birds stuck out of the snow and mud like wrecked and broken hulks. Here and there a scattered line of graves showed where the men of a picket had run for camp and had been shot and buried where they fell.[49]

And in the air, cloying and constant, was the smell of the battle-ground, a smell of ordure and putrefaction and gun-smoke, curiously sweet and horribly distinctive, which those who have known it can never forget.

With this tainted air always in their lungs, with the weather changing from extreme cold to mild humidity, the men, badly fed and tired out, found it difficult to get well again once they fell ill, and many of them never did. Dr. Blake, surgeon of the 55th, kept a medical history of his regiment, whose average strength in 1854–5 was 818. He treated 640 men for fever including typhus, and of these 57 died; there were 368 cases of respiratory diseases including pneumonia and tuberculosis and 17 deaths; 1,256 cases of infections of the bowels and stomach including diarrhoea and dysentery and 76 deaths; 91 cases of cholera with 47 deaths; 6 deaths from frostbite, 3 from scurvy, 4 from diseases of the brain and 21 from 'unknown causes'. These figures were for the whole campaign in the Crimea down to the end of 1855, but the great majority of them referred to the months of December, January and February. He also treated 9 men for heart diseases, 290 for boils and ulcers, 90 for venereal diseases, 98 for diseases of the eyes and 41 (the greatest number of which were after Lord Raglan's death) for lacerations received in flogging. He treated a total of 3,025 cases of sickness as compared with 564 men treated for wounds; and his regiment was one of those most heavily engaged at Inkerman.

He treated them too in conditions of the most disgraceful squalor. 'The hospital accommodation through the greater part of the winter,' he wrote, 'was so limited that it was necessary to fill the few tents' allotted to him for his patients 'literally as full as they could hold'. There were 'no *medicines*, no medical comforts, no bedding. . . . It was not uncommon for the only ration procurable for the sick to consist of rice and powdered biscuit boiled into a kind of soup.' Yet Dr. Blake was a conscientious, hard-working, enterprising surgeon whose hospital was considered one of the best-run in the Crimea.

Another surgeon, who landed at the 'confused aggregation of wrecked houses, huts, stores, stables, tents, mud and dirt and slush' that was Balaclava on 2 February, found his regimental hospital in a 'fearful state'. Men were crammed side by side in small bell-tents, their heads towards the pole, on the bare ground and wrapped only in their threadbare greatcoats. An unqualified dispenser acted as surgeon; and this was not considered any great disadvantage as almost the only drug not in short supply was calomel, which was used for practically every purpose including the killing of maggots in the undressed wounds and sores.[50]

'It is an extraordinary thing,' an officer of the 18th told his mother with a surprise that others may not have felt, 'that numbers of Doctors are going mad out here.'[51]

The sick who were sent down to the hospital at Balaclava could expect little more comfort or care there than in the regimental hospitals. For appalling as the base hospitals at Scutari were, the Balaclava hospitals were worse.

Elizabeth Davis, a tough, bossy, masculine Welsh nurse, with the face and manner of a gruffly sympathetic sergeant-major, had quarrelled with Miss Nightingale at Scutari and had come to the General Hospital at Balaclava with ten other volunteers. She has described the terrible conditions she found there. Warned of what to expect by Miss Nightingale, who had not wanted any nurses to go to so filthy and inefficient a place, where the orderlies were undisciplined and the rooms crammed to suffocation with the sick,[52] she discovered conditions were even worse than she had imagined.

'I shall never forget the sights as long as I live,' she wrote. Told by the superintendent of her party, a Sister of the Sellonites, not to speak to the patients, she could not resist asking the first man she attended how he was. The Superintendent

scolded me for doing so, and repeated her order that I should not speak to them.

I began to open some of their wounds. The first that I touched was a case of frost bite. The toes of both the man's feet fell off with the bandages.

The hand of another fell off at the wrist. It was a fortnight, or from that to six weeks, since the wounds of many of those men had been looked at and dressed. . . . One soldier had been wounded at Alma. . . . His wound had not been dressed for five weeks, and I took at least a quart of maggots from it. From many of the other patients I removed them in handfuls.

There were no beds; the men lay on boards with their greatcoats for pillows. 'The sick and the wounded were alike neglected, unclean, and covered with vermin.' There were only two surgeons in attendance.

Two days after the nurses' arrival Lord Raglan came to see how they were getting on. He felt a particular responsibility for them as he had asked for them against the wishes of the Medical Department, who hated the idea of females in their hospital; and Miss Nightingale had only consented to send them because she did not want to disoblige a man for whom she felt a great respect.[53]

Miss Davis was delighted when he came in and she recognised him as a man she had often seen in London. She had been a maid with a family who had a house near Lord Raglan's, and he had frequently trotted past her in the early mornings when she was cleaning the steps. 'He never passed,' she remembered, 'without giving me a pleasant look and a civil word, such as "Cold morning" or "Fine morning" and once I heard him say to his groom, "That woman's always up."'

He recognised her too, and before he spoke to anyone else went up to her and said, 'I know you. Didn't you live in Stanhope Street?'

'Yes, my Lord.'

'Then you know me?'

'Yes, my Lord.'

'The best woman I ever saw for getting up in the morning.'

Then he spoke to the other nurses and said he already saw an improvement. He told them he was trying to organise a hospital nearer the front, as it distressed him so to see the men carried down to Balaclava. He was a frequent visitor, Miss Davis said, and visited the sick in that hospital alone three times a week.[54]

He spoke to them with an intimate friendliness and sympathy, a lack of restraint which he found impossible when confronted by them healthy and *en masse*, an engrossed attention that they felt was quite sincere.

He always behaved so. One day on his way to the headquarters of the 3rd Division he had visited the 1st Regiment, and had stopped to admire the ring of cannon-balls and the mud-scraper outside the tent of the colonel who thought that he had 'never known a kinder heart, nor a more brave, cool decided, gallant soldier. He could not say an unkind word to anyone. . . . A better heart never breathed.'[55]

Three weeks later Midshipman Wood delivered a letter at Headquarters for General Burgoyne. Breathlessly he told his mother:

In I stalked into a large room filled with Lord Raglan's staff at Luncheon and I looked about me and saw at one end of the table all by themselves two old gentlemen so I thought to myself one must be Sir John. When I got up to them one said, 'Well, young Gentleman. Have you just walked up here?' so I said yes. Ain't you tired? Not very sir. Well are you hungry? Tolerably. Sit down and have some luncheon. Looking then at the old gentleman I saw it was Lord Raglan who I had not seen before close to. Seeing some ham at the other end of the table I was getting up to cut it (they don't allow servants in there) Lord Raglan said 'Sit still, sir. Captain Markham (I think it was) bring this young gentleman some ham and what he requires. . . . After luncheon time he talked to me and I parted from this old gentleman thinking him a regular old Brick.[56]

It was becoming a frequently voiced opinion. Officers preparing to meet Lord Raglan for the first time expected to encounter a cold, haughty, pompous old man, and found one 'more like a Parish priest than a general, he was so tender and gentle. They never spoke badly of him again.'[57]

The private soldiers and N.C.O.s rarely had done so. 'Lord Raglan has done everything for our comfort that lay in his power,' a sergeant wrote home on 19 January. 'It is very easy for gentlemen sitting by the fire in a nice comfortable room to find fault.'[58] As far as Corporal Hector Macpherson's 'humble opinion' was concerned, it was 'the highest of injustice to fasten the blame on Old Rag'.[59] 'He is a very feeling Gentleman,' a private soldier told his family in Cornwall on 12 February. 'He has done all he could to Comfort the Army. . . . He cannot avoid bad Weather. . . . I got my Fingers touched with the Frost' he added, as if to say that some would have blamed his Lordship for it. 'They all right again.'[60]

Most letters, indeed, from private soldiers speak well of Lord Raglan. But there are comparatively few of them. Many soldiers could not write. Nor could they read. And the pitiless injustice of the attacks on Lord Raglan came as a surprise and a shock to those who had not already heard them.

A reporter for the *Liverpool Mercury*, who had gone down to the docks to interview some wounded soldiers as they disembarked, gave evidence of this. 'They were horrified,' he said, when told and shown what was said at home of their commander. 'There never was a better general,' one of them insisted, provoked into an extravagant defence. 'And right well every man in the army knows it.' 'Why, sir,' another one said, 'I fought under Lord Gough and Lord Hardinge; they were looked upon as splendid fellows; but there never was a general better liked by his soldiers than Lord Raglan.' 'A braver man never breathed,' a corporal in the Grenadiers put in. 'Why, the men thought he was far too much among the bullets.'[61]

On another occasion a rifleman's 'lips quivered and the tears were in his eyes' when a remark was made to him concerning all that had been said in England against Lord Raglan, and he answered, 'The *soldiers* did not think so.'[62]

But whatever the soldiers thought, those 'gentlemen sitting by the fire at home' had not finished with him yet.

17

THE ARISTOCRATIC STAFF

We must at the next cabinet seriously consider the question as to
removing Airey, Estcourt and Filder
Lord Palmerston

I

Well after midnight on 29 January 1855 the House of Commons
divided on a heatedly debated motion 'that a Select Committee be
appointed to inquire into the condition of our Army before Sebastopol, and into the conduct of those Departments of the Government
whose duty it has been to minister to the wants of that Army'.[1]

The resolution had been moved by Mr. John Arthur Roebuck,
Q.C., Member for Sheffield and a Radical whose forceful speech and
aggressive sincerity were both admired and feared. The vehemence
and enthusiasm of his speeches were emphasised by a nervousness of
delivery and a paralytic disorder which obliged him frequently to
pause for breath, and on this occasion to falter and almost to collapse.
He was the friend of John Stuart Mill, and a devoted admirer of
Bentham and of Hume. With such sympathies he might have been
expected to arouse a deep distrust in the House, and amongst many
Members he did, in fact, do so. But he was for the moment the voice
of the people.

Sydney Herbert had, of course, in replying for the Government,
voted against his motion; so had Gladstone, who regarded it as 'useless
and mischievous'; Palmerston spoke of 'vulgar clamour', but none of
them—nor anyone else—said anything worth while in support of the
army. Sydney Herbert, indeed, as Secretary-at-War the main Government spokesman in the Commons, clearly implied that the whole
responsibility for the Crimean calamity lay with that 'collection of
regiments which called itself the British Army and not with the
Government'. 'When you come to the staff,' he said, 'can you expect
men who have not only never seen an army in the field but have never
seen two regiments brigaded together, to exhibit an acquaintance with
the organisation of an army?'[2]

The House was not impressed by this determined effort to shuffle the whole of the blame on the Army. Mr. Roebuck's motion was carried by a two-thirds majority. The next day Lord Aberdeen resigned. The Government had fallen with 'such a whack', as Gladstone put it, that 'they could hear their heads thump as they struck the ground.'[3]

Although he was over seventy, Palmerston was the obvious choice as Lord Aberdeen's successor. But the Queen, who did not like him, who considered his unpunctuality and his patronising, not to say domineering manners, a conscious affront to her dignity, was determined not to have the rude old man she called 'Pilgerstein' as her Prime Minister if she could help it. She sent for Lord Derby, but he refused to take office. She even sent for Lord John Russell, whose resignation from the Government as soon as he had heard of Roebuck's motion had recently filled her with 'indignation and disgust'. Russell accepted, but he could not find sufficient support. And the Queen was obliged to send for 'Pilgerstein'.

He was deaf and short-sighted, he dyed his hair and had 'false teeth which would fall out if he did not hesitate and halt so much in his speech'.[4] But he still had much life and vigour and sound sense in him. And he knew a good deal about the Army. He had been Secretary-at-War when he was twenty-four and he had worked hard and well in this appointment for nearly twenty years, earning the dislike of George IV, of practically all his colleagues and of everyone connected with the Horse Guards. 'It is quite extraordinary,' Mrs. Arbuthnot said, 'how he was detested.'[5]

He had had frequent clashes with the Duke of Wellington, and held most generals in some contempt. He had seen 'a good deal of Raglan' and thought him 'not much of a hand at forming opinions or inventing plans'.[6] His views on what was wrong with the Army were decided and acute. He appointed as War Minister a man who shared them.

Lord Panmure, thick-skinned, impulsive, energetic, direct, boorish and shrewd, had also been Secretary-at-War and had been pressing for a unified control of the Army since 1850. In reply to a memorandum sent him by the Prince Consort he set out his sensible opinions on the difficulties which the present administration of the Army raised.

The lamentable results which have attended our present expedition are solely to be attributed to the want of proper control by a single Minister of every department of the Army. . . . I concur in His Royal Highness's remarks that our Army is a 'mere aggregate of battalions'—each of these perfect in itself and admirably formed, governed and drilled, but only pieces in the entire structure of an Army as the wheels, etc., are in the mechanism of a clock. The regimental system is nearly as perfect as it can be. The system by which an army should be provisioned, moved, brought to action . . . is non-existent. . . . We have no means of making general officers or of forming an efficient staff. . . . It is owing to our *regimental* system and the intrinsic worth of our officers that we have succeeded in the little wars in which we have been engaged from time to time. For great operations we are inadequate, as the result has proved.

Panmure and Palmerston were determined to show the country what a determined Administration could do to remedy the worst defects of the Army system, even though, apart from themselves, all its principal members had been in the previous Government.*

Already the Colonial Office had been made a separate Ministry. Now the post of Secretary-at-War was abolished, and Panmure as Secretary-for-War was given considerably greater powers. He had been in office less than a week when, at a Cabinet meeting held on 12 February, he showed how energetic he would be in using them.

He suggested to the meeting that a Chief-of-Staff should immediately be appointed to the Crimean army to 'convey Lord Raglan's orders to the Staff, and through them to the army, and see these orders quickly and implicitly obeyed.' The Chief-of-Staff was also to act as a sort of Inspector-General 'to enquire into the manner in which the Staff Officers perform their duties and to report fully thereon'. The Cabinet immediately agreed to the appointment. Other 'measures taken to establish a better order of things in the Crimea' were noted down by Palmerston. Officers were to be sent out to inquire into the Commissariat and the army's sanitary arrangements. Civilian doctors were to be temporarily enlisted in the Medical Department. A Sea-Transport Board was to be formed; a Corps of Scavengers procured in Constantinople; and a Land Transport Corps was to be organised.

The more important of the measures suggested had already been taken by the Duke of Newcastle, but as Panmure confessed to Lord Raglan he had not yet had time to acquaint himself sufficiently with the details of former correspondence.

* Gladstone, however, disagreed with Palmerston over the scope and regulation of the committee formed in consequence of Roebuck's motion. He resigned after a fortnight with those Peelites who had consented to join the Government.

As an impatient man he preferred to make a clean start rather than to improve and modify the arrangements begun by others. He made up his mind that something should be done and he did it. Not on account of his big, shaggy head alone was he known as 'The Bison'. He decided that Raglan needed firm treatment and that, whatever the Chief-of-Staff reported of the officers at his headquarters, they must be changed. On the day of the Cabinet meeting he wrote a private letter to Lord Raglan and told him so.

> I am sorry to be obliged to send you a despatch embodying my views of the grievances in the camp, their cause and their remedy, or rather my strong advice that you should try and get a more energetic and efficient officer than Airey seems to be. The public are roused and the House of Commons has already sacrificed two victims to their disappointment in the persons of Lord Aberdeen and the Duke of Newcastle. . . . I know well the chivalrous feeling that will induce you to protect your subordinates, but I hope you will not push this too far. . . . Your staff must be changed, as the least that will satisfy the public, and that radically.[7]

The despatch which accompanied this letter was a great deal more severe, and in parts defamatory. 'I cannot find,' it began, 'that your Lordship has been in the habit of keeping Her Majesty's Government acquainted in a clear and succinct manner with the operations in which you are engaged. . . . Your notices of the conditions of the Army are brief and unsatisfactory.'

Lord Raglan was peremptorily asked for an explanation of the misery of the army, told to submit fortnightly returns in a new form drawn up by the Prince Consort, informed that a Chief-of-Staff would be coming out to report on the staff and their capabilities and to list the names of those officers unfit for the positions which they occupied. Finally he was advised that Generals Airey and Estcourt should be given new posts immediately. 'It would appear,' the despatch continued, 'that your visits to the camp were few and far between, and your staff seem to know as little as yourself of the condition of your gallant men.'[8]

Few commanders-in-chief can ever have received so curt and so unjust a despatch. Lord Raglan replied to it with unwonted warmth and a deep sense of injury.

> I have visited the camps as frequently as the constant business in which I am engaged . . . will permit; and though I have made no note of these

visits, I find one of my *aides-de-camp* who keeps a journal, and who frequently, though not always, attends me has accompanied me above forty times in the last two months. A ride is not taken for pleasure on this ridge and in this weather.

Your Lordship has not hesitated to apply to me the charge that I know nothing of the condition of the Army, and that the Staff is equally ignorant of it. I do not deserve this reproach and I have to request you to be so good as to name the person who has uttered the slander.

In my despatches of January 30th I have fully stated my opinion of Major-General Airey. I adhere to that opinion, and in expressing my sense of his services I deem it to be due to state that they were continued when he was suffering under severe illness; an illness which he caught in the execution of his duty on a wet and tempestuous night.

Your Lordship is doubtless in a position to dispense with the services of this or any other staff officer but you will permit me to observe that I cannot in fairness be called upon to withdraw my confidence from, or alter my opinion of, officers whom I hold in the highest estimation. . . .

The duties of General Estcourt are less intricate, and do not bring him quite so constantly under my notice, but he merits the expression of my approbation. . . .

He ended on a note of sad and unaccustomed *amour-propre*:

My Lord, I have passed a life of honour. I have served the crown for above fifty years; I have for the greater portion of that time been connected with the business of the Army. I have served under the greatest man of the age more than half of my life; have enjoyed his confidence, and have, I am proud to say, been regarded by him as a man of truth and some judgement as to the qualification of officers; and yet, having been placed in the most difficult position in which an officer was ever called upon to serve, and having successfully carried out most difficult operations, with the entire approbation of the Queen, which is now my only solace, I am charged with every species of neglect.[9]

The most cruel humiliation, although fortunately he never knew it, was that the Queen now also was persuaded that the cries of condemnation were in large part justified. Her early exhilarating enthusiasm, replaced by a worried and somehow accusatory sympathy, had now given way to reproach. 'The Court exceedingly alarmed and annoyed at Raglan's failures,' Charles Greville had noted in his diary on 14 January.

Lord Panmure had sent the Queen a copy of his censorious despatch.

She expressed herself as 'much pleased with it'. 'Painful as it must be to have to write or receive it,' she wrote to Panmure, 'the truth of everything stated there is undeniable.'[10]

At the end of the week the Queen wrote again to return the 'Morning State of the Army in the Crimea' which Panmure had sent her, and to agree with him in expressing 'astonishment at the meagre and unsatisfactory reports from Lord Raglan which contain next to nothing'.[11] This reluctance of Lord Raglan's to use expressions of either enthusiasm or alarm, and his reliance on the bare figures of the 'Morning States' to give the Government the information it required, were a source of real anxiety to the Queen. In time her patience, 'indeed she might say *nerves*', began to be 'most painfully tried' by it.[12] She was, like Prince Albert, passionately interested in the Army, and liked to be given the fullest information about it. Lord Panmure, so he told Raglan in confidence, had never known 'anybody so entirely taken up with military affairs'.[13] 'Whenever any instructions of any importance are sent to Lord Raglan,' she told Panmure, 'the Queen would wish to see them, if possible *before* they are sent.'[14] She did not, as her husband did, want to advise and to instruct but she did want, as she put it herself, to be '*told everything*'.*

Lord Panmure aggravated her irritation by pointing out to her, when sending on Lord Raglan's communications, their lack of descriptive detail. On 27 February he sent on the 'only despatch which has arrived from Lord Raglan by this mail. There is no private letter, nor is the usual Morning State up to the latest date forwarded in any shape, at which Lord Panmure feels some surprise'.[15]

But for Lord Panmure, Lord Raglan's worst offence was his refusal to agree to the dismissal of any officers of his staff. Old General Burgoyne had been ordered home without reference to the Com-

---

* Her main concern at this time, as perhaps was proper for a Queen, was for the quick distribution of medals. Her correspondence with Lord Panmure is full of this. From 28 February until 18 May, when she awarded them herself, she mentions them in almost every letter. 'The Queen said to her wounded Guards when she saw them, she hoped that they would soon have their medals' (28/2/1855). 'When will the medals be ready?' (5/3/1855); 'The Queen has since thought that the value of the medals would be greatly enhanced if *she* were *personally* to deliver' them (22/3/1855); 'How are the medals getting on?' (1/4/1855); 'The Queen wished to know whether it would be possible for her to distribute the medals *any day* next week?' (14/5/1855). In the Crimea they were thought of with less enthusiasm. 'Half a crown and a pennyworth of ugly ribbon,' commented Colonel Sterling. There were to be three clasps, the troops were told, one for Alma, one for Balaclava and one for Inkerman. 'What shall we get for Sebastopol?' a private in the 7th asked. 'Why, a star, of course.' 'Huh! A crack on the head more likely.'

mander-in-Chief, but he was after all only an independent adviser and his recall was not enough. 'I must do something to satisfy the House of Commons', Panmure insisted.[16] He told him 'seriously to consider' whether the continuance of Filder, Airey and Estcourt in their appointments was 'the best arrangement' he could make.[17] He hoped he would 'give way to the current of public opinion'.[18]

Lord Raglan would not give way. Nor would the Government. Palmerston indeed was so insistent that even Panmure was induced to comment that he listened 'too much to the people'.[19]

When Lord Raglan's categoric refusals to surrender to public opinion were received in London, Lord Panmure felt inclined to let the matter rest until the newly appointed Chief-of-Staff made his report, but the Prime Minister continued to urge the replacement of Airey, Estcourt and Filder as the least that would satisfy the House. 'We must at the next Cabinet,' he told Panmure, 'seriously consider the question as to removing Airey, Estcourt and Filder. My conviction is that they are all three unfit for their respective situations. . . .' If anything went wrong 'all the world will throw the blame, and justly, upon the Government. If we remove these men and put others in their place we shall at least have done our best.'

If Airey and Estcourt 'were replaced', he repeated a fortnight later, 'we should be able to make a good defence in Parliament. . . . But I for one cannot undertake to stand up in my place and defend an inactivity which would leave our Army . . . the victim of that knot of incapables who in the last eight months have been the direct cause of the disability and death of thousands.' 'These changes are desired in order to prevent our men from becoming victims to incompetence and incapacity,' he told Panmure in another letter. 'Raglan will never of his own accord make any change; he is a creature of habit, and is himself wanting in that energy which would be required for the making of changes. . . . We must cut the knot for him. . . . He is too sensible a man not to acquiesce if the matter is properly and civilly explained to him.'[20]

Other members of the Cabinet agreed with Palmerston that the knot should be cut, and that, as Raglan's consent was withheld, Airey —if not Estcourt—should be dismissed without it. But then, quite suddenly and unexpectedly, the clamour died down. 'You shall hear no more from me as to your Staff,' Lord Panmure assured Lord Raglan. 'I have told my colleagues that I acquiesce in your reasons for not submitting to a change, and that I will press it no further.'[21]

II

Lieutenant-General James Simpson, appointed Chief-of-Staff to the British Army, had arrived in the Crimea. He was a friendly, sensible, tactful man who soon overcame the resentment his appointment had caused. He had fought for a short time in the Peninsular War as a subaltern in the Guards and had been severely wounded at Waterloo. His experience and his stiff military bearing, softened by a sympathetic way of talking in a gentle Scots accent, helped to dispel the suspicion that he was a spy for the politicians. He had, he confessed, come out with that 'considerable prejudice' shared by everyone at home. But he had, as Admiral Houston-Stewart told his old friend Lord Panmure, plenty of 'good sense'. 'I like,' the Admiral continued with nautical enthusiasm, 'the cut of his jib *much*—fine soldierly appearance, who gives you the idea of mild yet firm decision. I believe he will tell you that things are not nearly as bad as he expected.'[22] Houston-Stewart was right. Soon after his arrival General Simpson sent home an emphatic report.

I consider Lord Raglan [he wrote unequivocally] the most abused man I ever heard of! . . . How he gets through all that he does is wonderful. . . . His correspondence is far beyond what any man can get through, and he likes to do it himself. It is grievous to see, in the midst of every serious operation at present demanding constant attention, a huge bag of letters, *twice* a-week per mail, laid on his table, demanding the utmost care in their perusal, quite sufficient to occupy entirely the mind of any man who has nothing else to think of.

The Staff here at Headquarters have, I am convinced, been very much vilified. They are a very good set of fellows—civil and obliging to every-one who comes. I am speaking of the *personal* staff, who have no responsi-bilities further than being generally useful. Nor have I any fault to find with Airey and Estcourt. . . . I see no staff officer objectionable in my opinion. There is not one of them incompetent. . . . You will see my views very different from those printed in our newspapers; but I judge from my own observation, and I hope with impartiality. . . . I must say I never served with an Army where a higher feeling and sense of duty exists than I remark in the General Staff Officers of this Army. It pervades all ranks, except among the low and grovelling correspondents of *The Times*.[23]

It was a determined exculpation. But the views it so definitely expressed were not so surprising as they would have been two months before. Since the middle of February the news from the Crimea had been steadily improving.

The appalling weather had ended. There were still days of biting cold, but the torrential rains had stopped. The huts which had arrived at Balaclava at the beginning of January had now sprung up all over the plain. The track up from the harbour was passable, and the supplies of warm clothing which had arrived in 'vast quantities' several weeks before had been taken up to the camps by a variety of animals—horses from Trebizond, mules from Spain, oxen, camels, dromedaries, even buffaloes, which, alarmingly hairless in parts, reminded Dr. Robinson of rare zoological specimens. Some regiments, indeed, had got so much clothing that the men were selling it for drink.[24]

On 13 February Lord Ellesmere's schooner *Erminia* docked at Balaclava bringing out the Hon. Algernon Egerton and Mr. Thomas Tower, the honorary agents for the Crimean War Fund, organised by *The Times*. And within a fortnight two other screw-steamers, chartered by the Fund, had arrived with a thousand tons of supplies. With reckless profusion the men were issued with 37,000 flannel shirts and jerseys, sheepskin coats, shoes, scarves, brushes, combs, beer, pepper, wine, toffee, pencils, Bibles. Hampers from Fortnum and Mason were dumped down in the huts of officers; and trunks, packed up in village halls, were bundled into the huts of the men. Out of the tissue-paper and sawdust came pots of honey, peppermint lozenges, arrowroot and ginger, messages of love and encouragement carefully written on scented paper, improbable-looking combinations and bits of knitting, handsome hassocks and velvet smoking-caps, knitted waistcoats, and woollen helmets which muffled the ears and filled the mouth with fluff. In short, 'enormous quantities of useless clothing', as Dr. Blake put it, 'fit only for a polar expedition' or a fancy-dress party. He was now 'living in luxury with the Crimean Fund in full work.'

Another doctor was amused to see his quartermaster at the stores in

Balaclava 'engaged in unpacking huge bales and boxes of warm clothing, socks, mufflers, goloshes, etc. of every description—the weather at the time being so warm as to cause him and his assistants to perspire copiously'. A week later, on the warmest day they had yet had, he himself was handed a 'kind of tweed paletot, lined with wool, apparently made (they were all alike) for a man of five feet nothing with arms proportionately short', two pairs of thick socks, two pairs of drawers, two vests and a comforter.[25] Somerset Calthorpe asked a sentry one night if he was comfortable. 'I should be, sir,' the sentry replied, 'if I hadn't got so many bloody clothes on.'

The food was almost as plentiful as the clothing. On 9 March Captain Campbell enjoyed a dinner of mutton broth, curried venison, plum pudding, cheese, a bottle of red Bordeaux, port and maraschino. Most officers fared as well; no soldiers went hungry. Apart from the supplies issued free by the Crimean Fund agents, other goods could be bought from them at extremely low prices. Sherry, for instance, could be had for 24s. a dozen bottles. By the end of the month several shops had been opened at Kadiköi, and most of the speculators in Balaclava went out of business.

There was even a tolerable restaurant in Kadiköi and, although it dealt 'chiefly in railway publications', a bookshop. Mrs. Seacole, a kind-hearted Jamaican mulatto, whose shack in Balaclava had throughout the winter supplied cups of tea to the sick waiting to be put on board ship for Scutari, now opened a much more imposing establishment.[26]

The whole area, in fact, took on more of the aspect of a garrison than a battle-ground.

Gangs of workmen—Croats, Albanians, Greeks, Montenegrins, Afghans, festooned with knives and daggers and reeking of garlic and onions—shouted and quarrelled as they laid the sleepers and track for a railway from Balaclava to the top of the col. The material had arrived at the beginning of February, and by the end of March the railway was in use. The sound of the wagons rattling over the tracks was nostalgic and comforting. Sometimes they were pulled up by horses, at others by a gang of seventy seamen, yoked in gun-harness and encouraged by the shouts and jeers of the passengers, who were frequently told 'if they didn't shut up they could bloody well get out and walk'.[27]

Balaclava itself seemed to be a different place from the shambles it had been in the winter. When Roger Fenton, the photographer, arrived there on 9 March he was surprised to find it so well organised. Although the work of clearing the harbour had only just begun, all the dead animals had been towed out to sea and sunk. The smell was still bad, but everything seemed 'in much better order than *The Times* led' him to expect. There were several stone landing-places, and new store-sheds were being built. The main street was paved with broken stones covered with sand.[28]

It was even possible now to find commissariat officials who would issue goods without too much delay or pettifogging objections. Indeed, they were almost cheerful.[29]

Most of the soldiers in the camps were certainly so. It was 'a comfort to go among' them. They were all 'cheerful to a degree—well fed and well clothed'.[30] 'It is no longer the camp of misery,' Captain Clifford wrote, 'and I could hardly believe my eyes to-day, all looked so happy, so contented, so lighthearted! . . . The poor men lay basking in the warm sun. . . . The French stood in wonder and asked if these clean, smart-looking soldiers could be the remnants of the English army.'[31]

They appeared almost to enjoy their turns of duty in the forward trenches, to which they went in high spirits now, as each man got a pint of beer from the Crimean Fund before he started. The bitter hatred of the enemy had now quite gone and had been replaced by an almost friendly rivalry. In some places the opposing trenches were less than a hundred yards apart, and the Russian and English sentries shouted good-natured insults to each other across the intervening space, and sometimes exchanged volleys of stones.[32] The Russians even came across without their muskets and indicated by gestures that they wanted lights for their pipes, and having lit them they would stay for a chat.

'*Inglis bono!*' a Russian would say.

'*Ruskie bono!*' an English soldier would reply.

'*Francis bono!*'

'*Bono*,' everyone agreed.

'*Oslem no bono!*'

'Oh? Ah! Yes, Turk *no bono!*'

The Russian then made a wry face and spat. And the Englishman pretended to run away. Then they all laughed, shook hands and wished each other goodnight.[33]

One day under a flag of truce an old Russian officer went bowing up to a group of about ten private soldiers to offer them snuff, which they accepted; and, being very strong, it made them sneeze uncontrollably. A Connaught Ranger, enjoying the sight, produced a bottle of rum and drank the officer's health, tapping him on the shoulder and saying loudly, '*Bono Russi! Bono Englisi!*'[34] 'The Russians like the English much,' another Russian officer said. 'We ought never to have gone to war with you. But it was the will of God.'[35]

One day in March Captain Clifford was in the forward trenches and could not help laughing at the 'absurd remarks' of the excited riflemen when one of them wounded a Russian 'We saw the poor devil limping off as well as he could', Clifford wrote. 'The men very properly did not fire at him but let him go away. The man who hit him said with a laugh as he re-loaded his rifle, "Bi-dad! And it's as good as rabbit shooting" . . . Every man was taking the greatest interest in what they called the "fine sport".'[36]

For off-duty hours there were other, less dangerous, sports. There were athletic meetings and dog hunts and centipede hunts; and, down in the Tchernaya valley, officers risked their lives shooting ducks while Russian guns fired occasional shots at them and French soldiers came along for the fun of keeping off the passing Cossack patrols.[37] It was 'a fine Country', Private Conn discovered, 'for hares and Partridges for the other night while making Century on the ridge of a Hill they were flocking about me in Thousands and they came so near that I killed five of them with the Butt of my firelock and almost every forageing party that is sent out brings a dozen or so of Hares with them'.[38]

At the beginning of March the first spring race-meeting was held. The Russians thought it was an impending attack or a large-scale reconnaissance and sent out their Cossacks; at sight of whom the race-goers scampered off the course.[39] Meetings were afterwards held in a hollow out of sight.

More reflective men could enjoy walks to the Monastery of St. George, where the former Commandant of Balaclava was allowed to live on parole with his 'half a dozen daughters almost all pretty' and where Captain Biddulph, who married one of these pretty girls, enjoyed the 'well conducted and even gorgeous' services of the monks, to whom he spoke in Latin.

It was a place of remarkable beauty. Wooded slopes fell down to a pebbled beach, and inland deep ravines veined with ridges of porphyry were filled with pebbles of jasper and bloodstone. Everywhere spring flowers were already shooting out of the turf. Men returned to their huts with bunches of primroses and violets, crocuses and wild peonies. And in the floor of their huts they planted vines, and outside them they planted flowers and vegetables and used empty salt-pork barrels as window-boxes.[40]

Lord Raglan, so Cornet Fisher said, joined in the general enthusiasm for horticulture. 'Our talented general,' he said with his agreeable if heavily ironic malice, 'is said to take great interest in the culture of the vines round his house, having them tended and watered carefully; who can accuse him of want of forethought after this? The old Duke never displayed so much providence, he evidently expects to be here in the autumn, which is gratifying indeed. . . . It would be a terrible blow to Lord Raglan if we took the place after all the trouble he has had with his vines.'

But, in fact, Lord Raglan had no time to trouble over his vines. Although most of the soldiers felt, when they were out of the trenches, as if they were enjoying a pleasant leave, he was working as hard as ever. Prodded by Palmerston and other members of the Government and indeed by 'every description of bore', Lord Panmure passed on the advice to the Commander-in-Chief with his accustomed tactlessness. 'I hope it is unnecessary', he had written in his very first letter, as if it were to a subaltern, 'for me to impress on you every vigilance on the part of your outposts, and should the weather prove coarse, the most frequent intercommunication between your main bodies and their advanced pickets.' He hoped Lord Raglan was turning his 'attention to supplies of water for the camp', and repeated the hope three times. The Sardinian army's camp should be moved. The assault should only be attempted if he was 'pretty certain of success'. The men ought to go bathing. What about a corps of shoemakers? Lord Raglan was told not to turn his eyes to Vienna, where from February to the beginning of June a weary and useless conference discussed the possibility of peace. This was 'for diplomats; our Generals must fight'. He was similarly instructed when the Czar died on 2 March not to 'build upon it as a means of shortening the war'. When Sebastopol was taken it ought to be 'thoroughly purged'. Lord Raglan ought to go up in a balloon to have a look at the town's 'inner defences and the obstacles', which he might have to encounter'.*41

'Sometimes', Lord Raglan told one of his nephews in a rare moment of exasperation, 'I think Lord Panmure believes I am either criminally negligent or a lunatic.'42

III

On some of these days of early spring it was difficult to believe, so Dr. Blake thought as he sat outside his hospital hut, that a war was being fought at all. You could hear the rattle of rifle- and musket-fire at the front and sudden explosions of activity at the batteries. Then the sounds would die away and all would be silent again.

With the rest that the men could now get, and the sunlight, the warm clothing for the cold nights and the occasionally still cold days, with the better food and the lime-juice and the beer, their health increasingly improved.

After the third week of February admissions to hospitals showed a marked decline, and deaths were far less. In January 3,168 men had died in hospital; in February 2,523, mostly in the first two weeks; in March there were 1,409 deaths; in April 582.

Being less crowded the hospitals could be better run. They were also now well supplied with instruments, medicine and special foods. By early May when Miss Nightingale came out on a tour of inspection they were excellent.

Miss Nightingale's party included Alexis Soyer, the *chef* of the Reform Club, who had gone to Scutari at his own expense—although with the Government's authority—to show the army authorities how to make the most of their rations. He was flamboyant, excitable and to the soldiers appeared rather absurd, but his ideas and suggestions were inspirational, and Miss Nightingale appreciated his sound sense and revolutionary inventiveness. He toured the Crimea with Miss

---

* A similarly original suggestion was made to General Simpson by Lord Dundonald a few weeks later. Dundonald thought he could smoke the Russians out of Sebastopol with the fumes of tar, sulphur and coke.

Nightingale and the soldiers ran forward to see and cheer the famous woman 'rather nice-looking, but not a bit pretty',[43] and the curious, enthusiastic man who was followed everywhere by his mulatto secretary. One of the regimental hospitals they visited was Dr. Blake's, who told his wife of the visit of this 'most incongruous party', one of whom 'he had long wished to see'.

> I was walking up and down the camp when we saw a lady and three gentlemen ride up to the hospital and an orderly came to say Miss Nightingale sent her compliments to know if I had any objection to her going over my Hospital. Of course, I had none so I joined the party which consisted of Dr. Sutherland (one of the Sanitary Commission), Soyer, and a *half-caste!!!* Miss Nightingale is a most pleasing person, *refined* and *delicate*, just fitted for the very trying position she fills. She was delighted with all she saw .... Soyer was in raptures with my kitchen, built by Sergeant Desmore (the Hospital Sergeant) and whilst Miss Nightingale and I were discussing matters of Hospital detail, Soyer rushed up and carried her off to see the establishment and his *delight* at the grate made of Turkoman gun barrels was beyond everything.[44]

Her reception at the two hospitals in Balaclava was not so friendly. These came directly under the supervision of Dr. Hall and were run on his strict, unimaginative lines. There was now no dearth of stores (Mrs. Davis, in fact, who was in charge of the cooking at the General Hospital, was wildly extravagant), but Miss Nightingale did not find them 'sweet and clean', as Nigel Kingscote insisted they were, but 'terribly seedy'; and certainly the nurses, compared with those under her discipline at Scutari, gave an 'immense amount of trouble'.[45]

Mrs. Davis, conscious that she was not alone in her antagonism, greeted her distinguished visitor with the rude comment that she would 'as soon have expected to see the Queen there' as herself. At the more recently erected hut hospital on the cliffs she was treated with similar disrespect by the staff, but she continued her inspection, making observations and criticisms, as if she were welcome. She was, however, not feeling well. The next day she fainted. Crimean fever was diagnosed, and she was taken back to the hut hospital from her ship, as men were at work clearing the harbour and the smell there was frightful.

For more than a fortnight she lay in her room, weak and delirious, covering sheets of paper with spidery writing, believing that her room was full of people shouting for supplies and that an engine was throbbing in her head.[46]

One day a man rode up to see her. He came alone and unannounced. He knocked on the door. A nurse rushed out, cross and startled, and severely reprimanded him for making such a noise. He asked if the hut was Miss Nightingale's. The nurse said that it was, but she pushed him back when he made as if to step inside. 'And pray who are you?' she asked him.

'Only a soldier, but I must see her. I have come a long way. My name is Raglan. She knows me very well.'

'Oh, Mrs. Roberts,' Miss Nightingale called out. 'It is Lord Raglan.'

Mrs. Roberts stood aside to let him in. He sat down on a stool by the sick woman's bedside, and they spoke together for a long time.[47]

When Lord Raglan got back to Headquarters, Nigel Kingscote noticed how tired and old and sad he looked. It was a passing expression which usually he took care to hide. Only those who knew him well understood how the strain of the past months was beginning to tell. It was not only that he was exhausted by the wearying months of worry and the loneliness of his responsibility; nor was it only that he felt deserted by everyone at home except his family. He was becoming, for the first time in his life, subject to fits of depression and melancholy which only his staff, and they not often, were permitted to see. Outside the Headquarters he seemed as strong and unruffled as ever. Sir John McNeil, who had a conversation with him in the middle of March, thought he looked cheerful, well and vigorous. 'He is,' he added, 'a great favourite with the men and much respected by the officers.'[48]

With the men, in fact, his popularity seemed to have grown during the winter months. Roger Fenton, who saw him in Balaclava on 9 March, said, 'The soldiers have nothing but good words to say about him; one of them told me that when the weather was at the worst he was constantly sitting amongst the men.'[49] He made efforts now to overcome his reluctance at showing himself to them and frequently endured the cheering which they were so anxious to give him. On 7 March when he inspected the 2nd Division, 'You never heard such a *roar*—the men throwing up their caps and rushing along cheering vociferously,' as he rode slowly back to his house, smiling and acknowledging their cheers. He had spoken 'so nicely' to them,

Colonel Wilbraham said, and had asked so many questions that 'there was scarcely a subject connected with the division' that he did not inquire about.[50]

As Sir John McNeil said, he was well respected now by the officers also. Even those who had written such biting letters so short a time before had, for the most part, changed their minds. 'It would now be a very great misfortune if Lord Raglan and General Airey were re-called', Captain Clifford thought. 'I see no one to replace our Com-mander-in-Chief . . . no one is more calculated to command respect and be beloved as he is.' It was generally agreed that the newspapers had gone too far. 'Never,' said Sir George Brown, 'was any poor man so unreasonably or unjustly assailed as he has been by those vile newspapers, or by those who are mean enough to act under their direction.'[51] 'The indignation at *The Times*,' a chaplain told his sister, 'is boundless. . . . In all companies it is the theme of conversa-tion.'[52] *The Times*, Captain Campbell thought, had 'overshot the mark' in its 'crusade against the aristocracy'.[53] As for the politicians, Colonel Maxwell of the 88th thought they were 'disgusting'. 'I would delight to see these paltry knaves,' he told his brother Sir William, 'exposed to the showers of shot and shell which never even raise the colour in our gallant commander's face. I would like to see the scurvy poltroons trying to hide their shivering frames.'[54]

In England too, as Panmure told General Simpson, the feeling against Raglan was subsiding.[55] And for this *The Times* itself was to a large extent responsible. It had changed its tack. It could take most of the credit for having roused the British people to an awareness of their responsibility and it had been the means of bringing about Florence Nightingale's cataclysmic decision to go out to Scutari. It could pride itself on having brought down the Government and for having organ-ised the War Fund, and for the fact that Mr. Roebuck's committee was sitting in Room 17 at the House of Commons asking the first few hundred of its twenty thousand questions. It had earned the right to rest on its laurels. Already by the end of February it was acknowledg-ing that the Commander-in-Chief was inspecting regularly. And later it agreed that Lord Raglan, who now went out to one of the divisions every day he could spare from his desk, might have had some excuse for not doing so before. 'Perhaps there is not a clerk in England,' Russell suggested, 'who has so much writing to get through, *ipsa manu*, as the Field-Marshal in command of the forces. I believe his Lordship is frequently up till two or three o'clock in the morning.'

But although *The Times* was prepared to make amends, Lord Raglan could not forget the injustice which it, and the Government, had done him. He told Sir George Brown that he did not allow the attacks to weigh on his mind. And he would not discuss them with his staff. In his letters to his wife and sister-in-law, however, he showed how deeply he had been wounded. To Lady Westmorland he wrote on 12 March:

> I can even now hardly comprehend the extent and violence of the abuse that has been heaped upon me. *The Times* took up the attack of the Crimea, the Ministers acted upon the same impulse, and both one and the other being unwilling to bear the blame, thrust it upon me, and have striven to make me responsible for the climate, the season, the want of tents, the sickness and labours of the troops and all the hardships of a winter's campaign. . . . From the time the tide turned against me, I received no expression of sympathy or assurance of support from [the Government] but long letters adopting all the charges in the papers and in private letters. . . . The Duke had his day of abuse, but he was not abandoned by the Ministry of the day; and all desired to uphold his character. Moreover he was a great man, to which I have no pretension, and he had in reality with his great superiority of mind and firmness no need of support. He could stand alone.[56]

A fortnight later he returned to the same rankling and distressing theme.

> Cholera, sickness, tempest, inclement weather were all laid, if not at my door, at those of the officers executing my orders. . . . Other officers in situations of responsibility have been blamed by the public, but there never was, I believe, an instance before, when a general was blamed by his employers for endeavouring to carry out their instructions and made answerable for the duty which in conformity therewith I was obliged to impose upon the troops. . . . All I can wish for is peace and release from an injustice which is hard to bear.

His unhappiness made him long for home. 'He is always thinking of you all,' General Airey told Charlotte, '*always*—and *longs* to be back and quiet. And no wonder! If any human being was ever shamefully treated he has been—He has two faults—he's too gentlemanlike and too goodnatured.'[57]

And his troubles were far from being over. The horrors of the winter were ended, and he was no longer publicly assailed. But victory seemed a long way off and sometimes unattainable.

For although the army was in good health again, it was, as General Simpson said, largely composed of troops 'very different from the splendid men who came out'. Thousands of those splendid men were dead, and the men who came to take their place might one day be good soldiers also; but for the moment too many of them, from a military point of view, were not much more use than 'miserable little boys', as Cornet Fisher disgustedly called them. 'I wish we had older men than those sent out,' Lord Raglan wrote home. 'Some of the drafts are little more than 16; and there is a boy with my guard who only enlisted nine weeks ago and though professing to be 16 looks about 14.'[58]

More and more he was compelled to rely on the French, whose large and well-equipped army was growing every day. But he relied on them with increasing reluctance; for the French command was being slowly reduced to a state of atrophy.

18

CANROBERT AND PÉLISSIER

The moment is come for getting out of the 45 in which you are
Napoleon III

I

The Emperor had decided to go to the Crimea himself to assume command of his army.

He had come to this decision some time before, and already in early February Marshal Vaillant, the French Minister of War, had given orders for the concentration near Constantinople of a large force of fresh troops which would, under the Emperor's leadership, complete the investment of Sebastopol by cutting its supply line to the north.[1]

Until the Emperor arrived nothing must be done to make this great object unattainable; and General Niel was sent out from Paris to see that the French command was kept in check until Napoleon came to win the war. General Niel landed at Kamiesch at the end of January and at once began to exercise a baleful influence.[2] At first not even Canrobert knew the real purpose of his mission. As '*le conseiller militaire de l'Empereur*' his views must obviously be respected, but the French Commander-in-Chief was not informed of his reasons for pressing them so persistently. Canrobert was put in an impossible situation. His own men blamed him for letting the siege operations drag their weary way on towards the middle of another year; the English blamed him for putting obstacles in the way of their every suggestion. Niel checked him each time he tried to overcome his already cautious temperament.

The Russians made the most of their opportunity. Since the middle of November they had had more than a hundred thousand troops in and around Sebastopol and nearly ten thousand workmen. The town's defences were now nearly as perfect as they could be made, and the besieged were beginning to take the initiative against the besiegers. Counter-parallels and rifle-pits were dug outside the main line of defences, and from these raiding-parties crept up at night to fall upon the allied trenches. Underground, in silent listening-galleries, Russian engineers pressed their ears to the yellow clay as the French burrowed noisily towards the Flagstaff Bastion, talking loudly as their earth-trucks rattled in the tunnels and told the enemy all they needed to know.

Todleben was an expert miner. He allowed the French almost to complete their subterranean passage and then stopped them with a camouflet.[3] The French then decided to blow the roof off part of their tunnel and so form a crater they could use as a forward trench; but as soon as the crater was formed, Russian troops ran out to occupy it.

The French now decided to switch the main line of their attack from the Flagstaff Bastion to the Malakoff, and Bosquet's division was moved over to the right of the allied line, taking over ground weakly held by the British, who were now wedged between the two wings of the French army opposite the Great Redan.[4] But again Todleben was ready for them, and in a single night three battalions threw up a new work on high ground towards the north-western end of Inkerman Ridge, which covered not only the new French batteries but also the ground which assaulting infantry would have to cross in an attack on the Malakoff.[5] The following night the French attacked the new redoubt, but were beaten back. And a few nights later Todleben built a second redoubt.[6]

At the beginning of March the French and British commanders met at a council of war. Among those who attended was General Niel. The meeting lasted several hours and decided nothing, the French insisting that even if the new Russian works could be captured they could not be held. The meeting was adjourned for two days. At the second meeting again nothing was decided and again it was adjourned.

The responsibility for the indecision did not entirely lie with the French. A firmer man than Lord Raglan, despite the growing weakness of the British army, might well have forced their hand. The criticism was well put by Admiral Houston-Stewart, who said that Lord Raglan allowed the French to do most of the talking 'although conscious, as he must have felt, of his own superiority'. Admiral Bruat more than once remarked to him 'after a conference, "Do you know Lord Raglan's own opinion or plan?" He gave none.'[7]

On 8 March a third meeting was held. The French now said that nothing further should be done until they had the assistance of Omar

Pasha, who three weeks before had heavily defeated a force which had attacked his army at Eupatoria. Lord Raglan gently disagreed, suggesting that further delay would be pointless and might be dangerous. But his views were not strongly expressed, so again nothing was decided. Two days later the Russians had twenty-two guns in their two new redoubts, and by 21 March a third work, straddling the Mamelon, a hillock commanding the approach to the Malakoff, was completed and armed with ten 24-pounders covered by twelve other guns behind them.[8]

The next night the Russians attacked the allied works in greater strength than ever before. Two minor sorties were made against the British, who were surprised and suffered severe losses in a short and fierce bayonet-fight. The main attacks were directed by 5,500 Russian troops against the French, who lost 600 killed and wounded before the attack was repulsed.[9]

After this it was decided that no attacks could be made on the Russian defences until they had been subjected to another heavy bombardment. General Niel voiced serious doubts as to the wisdom of the bombardment, which would, he warned, be a 'grave affair' and might bring on a general engagement.

Despite Niel's objections, however, in the mist and rain of the early morning of 9 April the bombardment began from more than five hundred allied guns.[10] It continued for more than a week. On the first day the Flagstaff Bastion was 'literally buried' by French guns 'under an enormous mass of hollow projectiles which inflicted upon it great damage and immense losses of men'. Also on the first day the new work on the Mamelon was brought to 'a state of ruin'. By the end of the second day the two redoubts on Inkerman Ridge had been demolished, and for once the Russians were unable to repair them in the night and drew up their infantry at dawn amongst the ruins to repel the expected assault. By 18 April the Flagstaff Bastion also was beyond immediate repair. Its artillery had been dismounted, its embrasures and merlons demolished and part of its salient had fallen in. 'We were,' Colonel Todleben wrote, 'continually expecting to see the enemy advance to the assault. . . . They had it completely in their power to take the Flagstaff Bastion and that would have carried with it the fall of Sebastopol.'

But it had already been agreed that no assault could be made. At a conference lasting four hours on 14 April the French insisted that an attack was impossible. Lord Raglan, whose own guns, despite the skill and bravery of Captain Oldershaw in one of the advanced batteries, had been unable to do any damage to the Redan, felt compelled to agree. Two days later, however, when an attack on the Inkerman Ridge works seemed certain to be successful, Canrobert was persuaded to attempt it. But that same day General Niel wrote to Marshal Vaillant in Paris. 'I am going to try to dissuade the commanders,' he told him, 'from making an attempt which would be as dangerous as it would be useless, and which I hope will be abandoned.'[11] On 19 April Canrobert went to see Lord Raglan and told him that he had changed his mind. The capture of these forts, he now said, 'would not be attended by any important advantage'.[12]

Lord Raglan had by now realised that Canrobert was being held back by something other than his own reluctance and uncertainty. It was then with both surprise and scepticism that he listened on the evening of 23 April to the French commander's suggestion that a determined assault on the town should be made at the end of the month after two and a half days of ceaseless bombardment. Lord Raglan immediately agreed. Canrobert, however, had already read out to him a passage from a letter he had received from the Emperor in which he had been instructed not to 'compromise' himself; and Raglan thought that on this occasion, when talking of the intended assault he 'did not seem comfortable'.[13]

Lord Raglan's doubt was justified. Two days after General Canrobert's visit, and the day before the intensive bombardment was due to begin, he received a visit from General Niel. Niel showed him a letter which said that French reserve troops for the new army at Constantinople would be embarked on 10 May and suggested that the proposed assault ought to be postponed. Lord Raglan noticed that the letter had left the Minister of Marine in Paris on 7 April and that it 'must have reached the Crimea during the previous week'. But now that he fully understood the reasons behind the French command's distaste for action he felt it useless to protest, and once more he was forced to comply with a decision which he 'deeply regretted'.[14] Acutely conscious that the French had every right now to consider him a junior partner, he was increasingly reluctant to press his views upon them. Although the health of his army was now 'hardly below what has hitherto been the usual standard of armies in the field',[15] his forces were pitifully inferior to the French both in size and equipment. It might once have been possible, political considerations apart, to have acted alone; now the army was manifestly incapable of doing so. It was aware, as Captain Biddulph put it, that it was 'playing second fiddle', and it did not like the part. It was disgruntled and bored.

'France will soon remain fighting alone', Bosquet said.[16] And it was close to the truth. 'French soldiers were much more interested in the war',[17] than the British, whose army was much weaker now as the Russians well knew. The enemy indeed had developed an awed respect for the French and found it far easier work in those less dangerous trenches facing the narrower British front.[18]

'I do not think I was ever so tired of anything in my life,'[19] said an English officer who had fought bravely throughout the campaign. The recruits were quite as disillusioned, 'evincing more desire to go home than to go into Sebastopol. You could hear them saying to the artillery when bringing up a gun from Balaclava "Oh! Take that old thing home again and bring up a load of praties; it'll be better for everyone", and such caustic remarks.'[20]

Jealous of the growing reputation of the French and hating the idea of their own comparative weakness, British troops once more began to think of the allies as 'all front and show off'. It was the greatest fun in the world, an artillery officer thought, to go to their race-meetings and laugh at them 'doing the Jockey. They are not any better fighters, all talk and bravado'. Bosquet and General Pélissier, now commanding the 1st Corps, were the only decent French generals. Canrobert's name ought to be changed to 'Robert Can't'.[21]

The irritation of the British with their allies was increased on 4 May by an event which, for Canrobert at least, was the final catastrophe.

II

The Russians had been aware for some time of the necessity of keeping closed the Straits of Kertch, the entrance to the Sea of Azof. Bad weather and adverse currents had prevented them from sinking ships across the straits, but powerful batteries had been erected on the Crimean shore of the straits.

On 29 April Canrobert agreed to Lord Raglan's suggestion that a raid should be made on Kertch to destroy the batteries and thus lay open the Sea of Azof and the north-eastern side of the Crimean peninsula to allied ships. On returning to his quarters, so Canrobert told Raglan, he was handed the report of a spy, who said that the Russian forces near Kertch numbered 27,000 men and not the 9,000 that had been supposed.[22] Twice the following day he wrote anxiously to the British Headquarters doubting the advisability of the raid and suggesting delay. Lord Raglan attempted to dispel his apprehensions in a well-argued reply.

The operation [he wrote in his excellent French] should not be undertaken unless immediately. The enemy is engaged on works which will bar the straits; and if he succeeds we shall have to give up all hope of occupying the Sea of Azoff which is an object to which both our Governments attach great importance. It might have been better if we had been able to spare more troops for the raid; but it is, I think, in quickness of action that we shall find our best chance of success. As we do not mean to establish ourselves permanently at Kertch but only by a *coup de main* to destroy the defences which prevent the passage of our ships, we may reasonably believe that 10,000 men will achieve this result. The enemy's numbers may be greater, but they are not concentrated; and to effect a concentration he would need more time than we should for our *coup de main*.[23]

Lord Raglan felt entitled to press his views more strongly than usual as he intended sending three thousand of his best men under Sir George Brown on the expedition. They were to comprise the Highland Brigade, seven hundred Royal Marines, some companies of the Rifle Brigade and his most experienced engineers. Canrobert, with profound misgivings, agreed to contribute rather more than seven thousand men, and in the late afternoon of 3 May the force embarked. Setting course for Odessa to mislead the enemy, the flotilla changed direction after dark for Kertch.

A few hours later Canrobert rode up to Lord Raglan's Headquarters in a state of 'high nervousness'. Lord Raglan greeted him with a tired smile as if he had been expecting him and knew what he was going to say.[24]

Only the week before a submarine cable laid between Varna and the Crimea had come into use, and the Emperor was already taking full advantage of what Colonel Sterling called this new 'engine for gossip'. Canrobert showed Lord Raglan a telegram he had just received from Paris instructing him to bring up the Reserve Army from Constantinople. He would be obliged to countermand the expedition immediately.

It was a little after ten o'clock. By one o'clock in the morning, when Canrobert left, he had been persuaded not to recall the troops 'upon the understanding that he relinquished his intention of doing so' at Lord Raglan's instance.[25] Hoping that for once he had been allowed to have his own way, Lord Raglan went to bed. At a quarter-past two a French A.D.C. burst into the Headquarters with a letter from Canrobert and another telegram from the Emperor.

The telegram made curious reading. 'The moment is come,' it said, 'for getting out of the 45 in which you are. It is absolutely essential to take the offensive 450.' Not even the French decoders at the telegraph office could fully understand the message, but the next sentence was unambiguous: 'As soon as the Corps of Reserve joins you, assemble all your forces and do not lose a day.'

Canrobert was placed, as he himself put it, under the 'absolute necessity' of ordering Admiral Bruat to return to Kamiesch. He had, in fact, already recalled the expedition when his A.D.C. broke in upon Lord Raglan.[26]

Even now Lord Raglan did not feel inclined to bring his own men back. He wrote to tell Admiral Lyons, who was in command of the fleet, what had happened and added that he was 'perfectly ready to support' Sir George Brown if he wanted to go on alone, and that he would hold himself responsible for any action which the commanders on the spot felt justified in taking.[27] Lord Raglan's letter was rushed out to the Admiral's flagship by fast despatch-boat. But neither Lyons nor Brown thought that they ought to carry out the attack without the French, and the whole force returned gloomily to harbour.

This fiasco was something which General Canrobert could never afterwards forget. Years later he confessed that it still weighed heavily on his mind as the culminating disaster of his anguished months of command. For some days he was close to losing his reason. He contemplated trying to get himself killed, and one day in full-dress uniform wearing his white plumed hat he walked across a plank towards a forward trench which was only used at night. For a few seconds he stood in full view of a company of Russian infantry until dragged down out of sight by his staff.[28] He tried to persuade General Pélissier to take over from him, but Pélissier reminded him that he could only assume command if Canrobert died or became seriously ill. At last he persuaded General Niel to support his application to resign. Accede to it, Niel advised Marshal Vaillant in a peremptory telegram, 'He is very tired. Answer by telegraph. General Pélissier is ready to take the command.'[29]

For some weeks Lord Raglan had been aware that Canrobert wanted to resign, and once he confessed to his staff that he hoped he would do so. 'Why Canrobert does not drive him mad I know not,' Kingscote exclaimed in a letter to Lord Raglan's son Richard. In fact, the two men, despite their constant differences, still got on wonderfully well. Raglan had always been perfectly understanding, Canrobert said later. He was one of the 'noblest characters' he 'ever knew, absolutely straight and his courtesy was exquisite'. Having spent all his previous active service fighting the French, he used sometimes in the early days of the campaign to speak of 'les Français' when he meant 'les Russes'. But 'he was always the first to laugh'. And Canrobert enjoyed the joke too. He always made amends for it, Canrobert said, by some complimentary remarks about the French army.[30]

On 19 May, to Canrobert's immense relief, General Aimable Jean-Jacques Pélissier became Commander-in-Chief of the French army. He was a very different man from his predecessor. Outspoken, determined, fierce in both aspect and manner, he was as reckless as Canrobert was cautious, as unafraid of sending men to death as he was of risking it himself. 'On ne peut pas faire des omelettes,' he was fond of quoting, 'sans casser des oeufs.' Short and stout with big black eyebrows and bristling hair and moustache, he looked more like the sergeant his father once was than the Commander-in-Chief of the French army that he had now become. He had a face, Roger Fenton said after photographing him, 'something like that of a wild boar'. And Nigel Kingscote thought that he was so fat and had so short a neck that he would 'go off like a ginger-beer bottle'. He found it impossible, indeed, with his fat little legs to stay on a horse and went careering about the camps in a trap.

General Niel might not have been so ready to let the pliable

Canrobert go, had the Emperor not now abandoned his intention of going to the Crimea himself. He had been forced to give up the idea, for no one with any influence supported it and he was strongly advised that it would be unwise to leave his own unsettled country for too long. On a State visit to England with the Empress Eugénie in the middle of the previous month this embarrassing topic was discussed in the Emperor's private rooms at Windsor Castle. Napoleon entertained a distinguished company. He had with him Marshal Vaillant and the French Ambassador when Prince Albert joined him with the Prime Minister, the Foreign Secretary, the British Ambassador in Paris, Lord Hardinge and Lord Panmure. And all of them, as Panmure said, 'seemed to arrive at one opinion as to the inexpediency of the Emperor's going' to the Crimea.[31] Two days later another discussion was held. This time it was at Buckingham Palace, and the Queen herself was present. But although she found the Emperor charming, 'a very *extraordinary* man with great qualities . . . wonderful *self-control*, great *calmness*, even *gentleness*' and a great '*power* of *fascination* . . . as *unlike a Frenchman* as possible, being much more *German* than French in character,'[32] she too gave him no real encouragement. A few days after his return to Paris he wrote to thank her for her kindness and to tell her that 'in view of the difficulties' which he found there, he was on the point of abandoning his plans. On the 28th as he was riding down the Champs-Elysées a man tried to assassinate him. By the beginning of May it was generally known that he was not going out.

His plan of operations, modified many times since its original inception, was, however, still to be considered. Although in detail extremely complicated, basically it was simple enough and, in its insistence on investment, sensible and valid. The allied armies should be split into three. The first army should remain where the allies now stood, to blockade Sebastopol and protect the bases in the south; the second army should advance round the town, attack the Russian field army on the high ground to the east of it and so complete its investment; while the third army was to land on the opposite shore of the Crimea from Sebastopol, advance across the peninsula towards Simpheropol, to cut Sebastopol's communications with the hinterland and then join the second army for a concerted assault on the town from the north.[33]

'All this,' as Lord Raglan said, 'would require immense preparations, vast supplies and abundance of means of transport.' He had
always himself believed that an advance across the Russian supply-
lines would be a desirable move. But he thought that the attack should
come from Eupatoria. The Emperor's plan envisaged the allied forces
being split up over a wide terrain in which they would find it extremely difficult to keep in touch with each other, and the enemy
therefore 'might fall in great force upon one body without the one
next it being able to render assistance'.[34] The plan, in any case, also
envisaged the splitting of the British army. And Lord Raglan could
not agree to this. It was too small, he insisted, and furthermore his
allies were unwilling to take over the vacated British trenches when
he led the proposed second army around Sebastopol to attack the
Russian field army.

Panmure bluntly called the whole scheme 'wild and impracticable'.
Pélissier, for his part, was determined to run the war his own way
without any help from the Emperor, whose schemes accordingly
came to nothing.

Pélissier's independence was, indeed, astonishing. The barrage of
telegrams, letters, orders and despatches with which Napoleon had
broken Canrobert's nerve had no effect on him at all. He merely put
the papers in his pocket, often, it was generally believed, without even
reading them. General Niel, who must have expected some difficulty
in dealing with the fiery little man, was horrified by his disrespect.
When Niel protested that the Emperor's plans must be carefully
considered, Pélissier lost his temper; telling him that if he went on
like that, he would be in serious trouble. '*Je vous ferai embarquer de
force*,' he shouted. '*Et puis, rappelez-vous que vous n'avez pas à com-
muniqués avec l'Empéreur, sans passer par mon intermédiaire.*'[35]

He took no trouble to hide the fact that he thought the Emperor's
opinions quite valueless and would have nothing to do with them. He
believed that once the Russian rifle-pits and counter-parallels had been
cleared and the defences brought down by a heavy bombardment the
allies could get into Sebastopol by a frontal assault without any fancy
ideas from Paris. He agreed with Lord Raglan that a diversion was
not in itself a bad idea, and that if it were to be made at all it should
come from Eupatoria. He also agreed with Lord Raglan that the
expedition to Kertch should never have been recalled. He agreed

with Lord Raglan about many things. He both liked him and respected him.[36] He even suggested, according to Sir Charles Wood, First Lord of the Admiralty, that Lord Raglan should have the chief command of all the allied armies.[37] Soon, indeed, he developed for the gentle, aristocratic Englishman, as unlike himself as any man could be, that devoted, almost passionate friendship to which rough and ruthless men are so peculiarly prone.

The two men decided between them to make a second raid on Kertch. It was led by Sir George Brown and it was entirely successful. The landing on 26 May was unopposed; the batteries were destroyed. Within four days of its passing through the Straits of Kertch into the Sea of Azof an Anglo-French squadron had sunk more than two hundred Russian supply-ships and the Russians themselves had scuttled almost as many. But when the main force moved on to Yenikali, leaving behind a few troops and sailors to guard Kertch and blow up its factories, an orgy of looting and violence began which even to-day its inhabitants still talk about with horror and disgust.

'Our attempts to prevent outrage and destruction,' Russell thought, 'were of the feeblest and most contemptible character.' He saw sailors carrying down to their ships that sort of useless loot which has always held for them a curious fascination. Enormous armchairs, feather beds, garish pictures of saints and of Jonah inside the whale, books in unknown languages and stuffed owls were pushed down on carts to the harbour, where officers gave the order for them to be tipped over into the sea. As usual the French succeeded in finding and taking away practically everything that was worth having.

The Turks, joined by Tartar bandits from the hinterland, not content with loot, roared through the streets, breaking into houses, smashing windows and furniture, raping women and cutting the heads off little children. By day the sky was filled with smoke, by night it was red with the fires of houses, stores, ships and factories. A fortnight later the pillaging at both Kertch and Yenikali was still going on. The beaches were crowded with homeless people waiting to be put aboard ships for Odessa and Yalta. Behind them the once handsome houses of Russian merchants which lined the quayside were blackened shells, and the Kertch Museum, which had contained one of the finest collections of Hellenistic art in the world, was ruined and its contents and glass cases smashed to splinters.[38]

It was a disgraceful episode, which Lord Raglan mentioned in a letter to his wife with shame and a sense of personal responsibility. The Turks, he thought, should never have gone. But neither his own men nor the French were blameless. Pélissier, however, regarded only the strategic importance of the expedition. 'We have,' he said, 'struck deep into the Russian resources. Their chief supply line is cut.'[39]

He was enjoying other successes too. On 23 May French troops attacked, captured and held a new line of Russian works outside the main defences. Two days later the Russian camp at Tchorgoun beyond the Tchernaya valley was destroyed by General Brunet with the help of Canrobert, now happily commanding Pélissier's old corps. These exploits, however, were merely designed to check indiscipline and boredom, and to give the troops practice in what was soon to be their real test, an assault on the Malakoff.

But to get to the Malakoff, the works on the Mamelon, which screened it, had to be taken first, as had the works on the edge of Inkerman Ridge which protected its flank. It was decided that the French should attack both these covering positions on the same night, while the British attacked the works in front of the Great Redan which were known as the Quarries. The bombardment which was to precede both attacks was to open on the morning of 6 June.

III

People at home awaited the news of an assault, which they felt sure would not now be long delayed, with a new confidence. Wanting to believe that all was right again with the Army, they were more inclined to agree with those who supported its present administration than with those who did not. 'Roebuck's committee is doing no harm,' Lord Panmure assured Raglan. 'Indeed a reaction is commencing here.'[40]

There were still a few men who wanted to dismiss various members of the staff. In May Lord Ellenborough had caused some concern to the Government by giving notice of a motion on 'the mismanagement of the war'. 'You have, I believe,' Lord Granville wrote to Palmerston, 'decided that Airey, Estcourt and Filder should be recalled. England is another who ought to be brought away.'[41] Palmerston was made nervous again. 'I clearly foresee,' he told Lord

Panmure, 'that unless you should be able to say that more efficient men . . . are appointed the debate will be as damaging to yourself and to the Government as the continuance of those men in their several places is detrimental to the welfare of the Army. . . . I have often urged these things upon you without effect; we shall now see what our opponents will make of them.'[42]

Palmerston need not have worried. The Government had 'a strong support from the Bishops', and 'all the military men' were opposed.[43] Lord Ellenborough's motion was heavily defeated.

The country was relieved. The weather was wonderful. The holiday season began. The horrors of the winter were almost forgotten. And the war, it was confidently asserted, would soon be won.

19

MALAKOFF AND REDAN

The fire was so tremendous, one could only put one's head down
and run on as fast as possible
Captain Hugh Hibbert, Royal Fusiliers

I

The visitors who came out to the Crimea in these days of early
summer found scenes reminiscent of a country fair. There were
regular race-meetings now, bathing- and picnic-parties on the shingly
beaches to the east of the harbour, fishing in the Tchernaya. At the
Zouave theatre outlandish farces were performed 'greatly to the
actors' own satisfaction', and all over the plateau regimental bands
played stirring military music and the gay tunes of Schubert and
Lanner.[1] British bandsmen too, with less heavy duties now amongst
the sick, cleaned their instruments and began once more their daily
practising. The best band, however, was that of the Sardinian army,
which played operatic arias to perfection. The Sardinian troops, sent
out by the astute Cavour with an eye looking forward to the days of
peace, added a new colour and excitement to the scene, with their
dark, handsome faces and their 'bandit-looking hats with large plumes
of black cocks' feathers in their sides'—the melodramatic headdress of
the Bersagliere.[2]

The beautiful Lady George Paget, who had come over from Constantinople with the Stratfords and their three daughters to join her
husband, recently returned to the Light Brigade, certainly found them
'ravishing'. And Della Marmora, their commander, returned her
compliment by getting his own private band to play for her night and
morning as she sat in the warm sunlight on board the *Caradoc*.[3]

For those who could not swim or sit in the shade, the heat was often
oppressive. The British soldiers still wore thick winter coats and
trousers, and Sir George Brown was in trouble again with the Light
Division for making them wear their stifling stocks and their collars
buttoned up around them. To escape the heat in the trenches, where
the baked white soil glared in the sunlight, men stretched canvas and

coats across spades and rifles to serve as sunshades. And out of sight of the enemy they stripped off their clothes and lay naked on the earth, picking the vermin out of their shirts as the sun shone down on their backs.[4]

II

The sun was shining brightly as usual when on the afternoon of 6 June Lord Raglan rode out from his house to watch the bombardment begin. There was a feeling of expectancy in the air. 'We knew that *this* time,' Mrs. Duberly said, 'the guns would not play an overture for another farce.'

Lord Raglan had invited Lady George, 'the belle of the Crimea' as Roger Fenton called her, to go with him. Men ran out of the camps in their shirt-sleeves to cheer him. Overcome with embarrassment he did his best to avoid them, turning his face round to talk to Lady George, trying to look as inconspicuous as anyone with so lovely a woman could hope to be. They watched the firing from a knoll, sitting among the rocks.[5] By six o'clock when they rode back to Headquarters the two redoubts on Inkerman Ridge, the works on the Mamelon and even the Malakoff itself were either wholly or partly in ruins.[6]

The next day at about half-past six in the evening a jet of rockets flew into the blood-red sky from high ground behind the French trenches, and the assault on the Mamelon began. 'It was as splendid as it was awful,' Captain Clifford thought, 'to see the brave Frenchmen rushing up under such a fire.' And when, ten minutes later, the tricolour fluttered from the parapet on top of the hill the tears ran down his cheeks.[7] But it was not to remain there long. A fierce counter-attack soon sent the French tumbling out of the works. With splendid determination, however, they attacked again, and within an hour, after the loss of more than five thousand men, French troops were in undisputed possession of the Russian entrenchments, and engineers were running forward to turn the works round to face the Malakoff.*[8]

---

* General Bosquet had foreseen the fearful losses. He had sat in his saddle next to Mrs. Duberly as the French infantry filed past. He turned to her with his eyes full of tears. She was also crying. 'Madame,' he said, 'à Paris on a toujours l'exposition, les bals, les fêtes, et dans une heure et demie la moitié de ces braves seront morts.'

The British attack on the works in front of the Redan was also successful. Of less importance to the Russian defenders, Lord Raglan believed they could be captured with far fewer men than the French had used. So, under covering fire from the newly captured positions on the Mamelon and from their own heavy guns, less than a thousand British troops went forward to assault the Quarries and the trenches linking them with neighbouring works. Before dark they had been captured, but all night long, as the men dug furiously to convert the works and join them with their own trenches, the Russians counter-attacked time and again. Dropping their spades to pick up their rifles, the men worked and fought for ten hours until many of them were on the edge of collapse. At dawn another attack came, and the British troops, so exhausted they could hardly stand up, appeared for a few moments incapable of action. 'It seemed,' an officer said, 'like the end of the world.' But then, encouraged to a final effort by the shouts of a few officers and sergeants, the men roused themselves once more to fight. And now for the last time, the Russians, despite the efforts of their officers to drag them forward by their collars and push them forward with their swords, once more fell back. Colonel Campbell of the 90th and young Captain Wolseley,* one of his bravest officers, were so exhausted that they both fell down among the dead.[9]

III

It was another encouraging victory. London was delighted. 'You cannot imagine', Lord Panmure had written after the news arrived of the successful expedition to Kertch, 'how pleased everyone is.' And now a cable came announcing this fresh advance. 'You spoil us,' Lord Panmure wrote again, 'by giving us a victory almost daily.'[10]

The Emperor was not so pleased. 'I admire the courage of the troops,' he told Pélissier coldly, 'but observe that a pitched battle disposing of the fate of the Crimea would not have cost more men.'[11]

Pélissier was now more determined than ever to justify himself. But in his obsessive determination, and in his fury with the increasingly irritating messages from the Emperor he made several serious errors of judgment.

* Field-Marshal Lord Wolseley afterwards remembered this night as the most exhausting of his long life.

The allied commanders had decided that the capture of the Mamelon and the Quarries should be followed not only by an assault on the Malakoff and the Redan, but also by an attack on the Flagstaff Bastion, which the Russians themselves most feared.[12] Against the advice of Lord Raglan, however, Pélissier decided to concentrate his attack on the Malakoff.[13] And against the advice of General Bosquet, who would have commanded the assaults, he decided to attack without sapping up close to its outer defences.

General Bosquet, already having quarrelled with Pélissier over his delay in handing over to him a plan of the Malakoff found in the pocket of a Russian officer, was replaced by the more tractable but inexperienced General d'Angely.[14]

At dawn on Sunday 17 June six hundred siege-guns in concert with the guns of the fleet once more opened up for what everyone hoped would be the last time.[15] All that day the fire was maintained. During the morning Pélissier came to Lord Raglan to tell him his plans for the following day. At dawn the next morning, he said, his guns would re-open their bombardment and continue it for two hours until at about half-past five the infantry would begin their assault by three attacks to be launched simultaneously at sight of a signal given by the explosion of a jet of bright rockets. Lord Raglan agreed to open his bombardment at the same time, but decided not to commit himself as to the exact time of his assault. The two commanders parted in friendly agreement.

But later that night Lord Raglan was told that Pélissier had changed his mind. Orders had been given for the French assault to take place without a preliminary bombardment at three o'clock the next morning.[16] No discussion was invited. The French decision, Lord Raglan was informed, was irrevocable.[17] It was too late to alter it now, and the British army was left to conform to the new French plan as best it could. Lord Raglan told Sir Harry Jones that he thought Pélissier was making a serious mistake. Nevertheless fresh orders were issued to the troops, and there was thereafter, as Somerset Calthorpe said, 'nothing but confusion and mismanagement'.

It was a beautiful warm midsummer night and the sky was brilliant with stars as the troops marched forward to their positions. The Russian defenders saw the movements and understood what they meant. Field-guns were dragged forward to the ramparts of the

Malakoff. And by two o'clock in the morning the forward defences of Sebastopol were crowded with infantry.[18]

Lord Raglan was riding with his staff to a mortar battery behind the Quarries, and Pélissier was riding with his accustomed difficulty to the high ground behind the Mamelon, when a shell thrown up by a French gun trailed light from its fuse and was mistaken by the general in command of the most right-hand of the three French attacks as the awaited signal. A minute or two later the roar of guns and sharp crackle of small-arms filled the air.[19]

In an effort to co-ordinate the three attacks Pélissier sent his rockets up earlier than he had intended, but his two other generals were not ready. By the time they moved forward to the assault they did so into an appalling fire. The French troops struggled bravely forward in the open, their ranks shattered by round-shot, canister, mitraille and the musket-balls and bullets of the infantry. They stumbled on through the dust and smoke and the hidden foot-mines. Some units on the left burst through the defences at the side of the Malakoff, now looking 'like a vast volcano', and fought the Russian infantry with bayonets in the streets and houses of the suburbs; but they were unsupported.[20]

As dawn broke Lord Raglan saw that the French attack had failed in terrible slaughter. Soldiers hesitantly holding their ground or tumbling back in confusion were being slaughtered by Russian guns.

He decided suddenly that he must encourage the French and order his own troops into the assault. He did so with extreme reluctance, but he considered it his duty. Indeed he felt, as he afterwards confessed, 'bound to' do so.[21] Sir George Brown and General Sir Harry Jones, the newly appointed Chief Engineer, both agreed with him.[22]

It was a fearful military error. There was no time to silence the enemy guns. The advance would be across a quarter of a mile of open ground. But he decided he could not stand by and watch the French troops die without trying to save them. He thought too that their leaders would try to attribute their failure to his own inactivity, and he knew that his own men would not blame him for his decision. They would go forward and they might succeed. Already men, although not under orders for the assault, were crowding the forward trenches determined not to be left behind.

The attack was to be directed against the Redan in two columns. General Sir John Campbell led the left attack with five hundred men of the 4th Division and a reserve of eight hundred under Colonel Lord West; Colonel Yea with a similar force from the Light Division led the right.

The drill had already been practised. A covering party of a hundred riflemen in extended order was to lead the way, followed by twelve engineers. Then were to come fifty soldiers carrying wool bags to fill the ditches; then sixty sailors and sixty soldiers with ladders and then the four hundred men of the storming party.

But General Campbell on the left was killed before he could get even a few yards beyond the parapet of the forward trench. Colonel Shadworth, the next senior officer, was killed soon after him. It seemed indeed a miracle that any man could survive in that torrent of fire. Guns which had previously been silent and which were believed to have been put out of action by the previous day's bombardment now opened up on the British troops. Lord West sent back a message to Sir George Brown that men were falling fast all round him, and that he must have more troops if he was to succeed in getting any farther.

On his right men were running with heads bent down as if against a storm. It was like rushing into a hurricane which had torn a whole arsenal into the air and thrown its contents into their faces. 'The fire was so tremendous,' wrote Captain Hibbert of the 7th, 'one could only put one's head down and run on as fast as possible.'[23] A few men did succeed in running across four hundred yards of open ground to the abattis in front of the Redan. They sheltered there in craters and folds in the ground, while the Russian infantry stood on the ramparts above them, shouting down at them, inviting them by shouts and gestures to come up, waving above their heads an enormous black flag.[24] Midshipman Wood, in command of a party of sailors carrying ladders, was one of the few officers to survive. Only recently recovered from a fever, and having lived for a week on tinned milk and rice, he felt weak and ill before the attack began. Now wounded in the thumb he saw his sailors, six to each ladder, falling to the ground on every side. Soon there was only one ladder still being carried forward, and he ran to help the two men struggling to get it to the abattis. The man at the back was shot, and the additional weight fell on to Wood's shoulder and nearly knocked him down. 'Come on, Bill,' the leading man called out, turning round to encourage his friend, but in the moment of recognising Wood he too was shot. Wood ran forward to the abattis, where a group of men had found some sort of shelter and were refusing to go on any farther. An officer picked a stick from the abattis and stood up to wave it above his head, shouting and cheering at the silent crouching men, until his body fell back riddled with bullets. As he fell a sergeant threatened to shoot the soldier next to him if he would not follow him to the Redan. 'Will you follow me?' he shouted hysterically at him. The man looked up at the hundreds of Russians, jeering and laughing above him and then back at the few men around him. 'No, I won't,' he said. The sergeant stood up to fire, but was struck down by a grapeshot before he could pull the trigger. And then some men of the Royal Fusiliers, 'under a perfect hell of fire', tried to get over the abattis or pull it down, but 'we might just as well', one of their sergeants wrote, 'have tried to pull down the moon'.[25]

Lieutenant A'Court Fisher of the Engineers, with the useless implements of his men scattered around him in the long rank grass and the upturned soil, ran back to find a senior officer who could give him further orders. He seemed to be temporarily cursed with the evil eye. He ran to Colonel Yea, who was shot through the chest as soon as he had asked him his question. Then he shouted to Captain Jesse, 'Well, Jesse, what's to be done?' Jesse too was shot before he could reply. Several other officers were approached by Fisher, and as soon as he had spoken to them they fell down dead at his feet. Despairing of finding an officer who could survive his questioning, and believing himself, in any event, the senior officer still alive, Fisher shouted out, 'Retire into the trenches the best way you can.'[26]

The men dashed back through the smoke with the Russian guns thundering behind them. Scrambling over dead bodies, tripping in holes concealed by the long grass, the men pushed past each other as they rushed for the safety of the trenches. With the screams of an officer, rolling about in the agonies of a stomach wound as he called out to God and his mother for protection, ringing in his ears Midshipman Wood was wounded again and fell down unconscious. He was roused by an Irish sergeant, who gently helped him to his feet and said, 'If you're going in, matey, you'd better go at once or you'll be bageneted.' Wood ran on and threw himself down into a shallow trench until he was unable to bear any longer the screams of other wounded men, whose shattered bodies were trampled on by men running for shelter farther back. He clambered out of the trench as it was swept by case-shot and made for a place where the parapet of the main forward trench had been worn down by the soldiers scrambling over it. He reached the parapet and tried to climb, but he slipped and fell and grabbed the butt of a rifle in front of him. The owner of the rifle turned round angrily, and shouted, 'What are you doing?' as a round shot smashed into his shoulders with a sickening thud. Wood struggled at last to the top of the parapet, where he hesitated a moment before jumping down for fear of jolting his wounded arm. 'Jump! Jump! You little devil!' a sergeant shouted. He jumped and again lost consciousness and was awakened this time by a surgeon who cheerfully assured him 'I'll have your arm off before ye know where ye are'.*[27]

Throughout the brief action Lord Raglan had been standing in the mortar battery behind the forward trench under heavy fire. Telling anyone whose duty did not compel him to watch the engagement to shelter behind the battery walls, he stood up himself to watch his appalling defeat. Men were hit all round him. Sir Harry Jones, standing next to him, was struck in the forehead and fell to the ground, his grey hairs matted with blood.[28] As he left the battery, guided through the trenches by Captain Wolseley, Lord Raglan went up to speak to an officer lying wounded on a stretcher. 'My poor young gentleman,' he said to him, 'I hope you are not badly hurt.' The officer 'in the rudest terms and most savage manner denounced him as responsible for every drop of blood shed that day'. Captain Wolseley 'would with pleasure' have run his sword through 'his unmanly carcass'.[29]

Slowly the roar of the guns died down to a rumble.

The British troops walked back to their lines, 'sullen and very quiet'.

The silence in the camps was oppressive and complete.[30]

---

* Evelyn Wood's arm, however, was saved. And despite his experiences he decided to transfer into the Army. He was awarded a V.C. during the Indian Mutiny and was promoted field-marshal after the Boer War.

IV

In the warm evening sunlight the stretcher-parties went out to bring back the already decomposing corpses. Looking at the worms and maggots so soon at work; at the blackened, swollen faces, some of which had burst; at the soldiers refusing to touch corpses of men who had belonged to regiments other than their own, Captain Clifford was violently sick. He stood for a moment by the great pit into which the reeking, colourfully dressed bodies were tumbled, and felt a profound disgust. 'This,' he supposed in a moment of bitter disillusion, 'was all part of the Honour and Glory.'[31]

20

THE DYING MAN

It was impossible not to love him
Florence Nightingale

I

On the day after the disaster an officer of the Coldstream Guards came to see the Commander-in-Chief. On his way out he went up to some members of the staff in the outer room. 'Do you not see the change in Lord Raglan,' he said to them. 'Good God! he is a dying man.'[1]

The change for some weeks now had been apparent. 'Lord Raglan came to see me to-day,' the officer in command of the telegraph office at the Monastery of St. George told his father on 4 June. 'I did not at first recognise him. He looks worn out. He was pleasant and kind—he always is. But he seemed quite done up.'[2]

When he returned to his headquarters on 18 June he was careful to maintain his usual appearance of calm and confidence. At dinner he even tried to cheer his neighbours up by telling them that all armies had their days of misfortune.[3] But he never recovered from the inner depression which the loss of fifteen hundred men had caused him. In a short letter to his wife he could not disguise his sorrow. It was as if this last catastrophe was the epitaph to all that had gone before.

On 23 June a violent thunderstorm broke from a suddenly overcast sky, and rain cascaded down in torrents on to the dry and dusty plateau, flooding the ravines. General Estcourt, who two days before had been taken ill with cholera, which was slowly spreading again through the army, died the following morning. It was a Sunday. Lord Raglan had been to see him the night before after visiting the front and the hospitals, although he himself was feeling ill, and was overcome by grief when he heard of his death. He dare not attend the funeral for fear of breaking down; but when it was over he went out alone to say a prayer by his grave.

The next day he was not well enough to come into dinner. His legs were cramped and he felt faint. Dr. Prendergast was called and prescribed pills of acetate of lead and opium.[4]

General Airey wrote that evening to Charlotte to tell her that if only her father would consent 'to lie quiet, on his back, and not write and do any business he will be quite right in a day—but he's a difficult patient'. The recent death of his sister, Airey continued, 'and then poor Estcourt and Captain Bocolls of the 10th Hussars has affected him deeply. He hates not being around to do his business—but in a day will be all right.'[5]

A few hours later, however, at two o'clock in the morning, he had a violent attack of diarrhoea and got back to his narrow camp-bed with difficulty. His voice was very weak. He slept exhaustedly for eight hours.

When he woke he said he felt much better, but Dr. Prendergast felt his pulse and found it very faint and his voice was little more than a whisper. He had no appetite. Soon he fell into another deep sleep. He awoke hiccupping at one o'clock in the afternoon. At three Lord Raglan's servant went to fetch the doctor again as his master had a bad stomach ache which was relieved by a cup of hot negus.[6]

An hour later Lord Raglan was seen to be dying. He himself would not believe it. Weak and tired as he was, he still clung to life.

General Airey went into the room and said, 'Sir, you are ill. Would you like to see someone?'

Lord Raglan softly but firmly answered, 'No.'

'You are very ill, Sir,' Airey persisted. 'Wouldn't you like to see someone?'

'No.'

Patiently Airey asked him the question again and this time, so softly that Airey could hardly hear the word, Lord Raglan said, 'Frank'.[7]

By the time Lord Burghersh arrived his uncle had lost consciousness. At six o'clock, however, he opened his eyes again and Dr. Prendergast asked Colonel Steele to tell him that he was dying.

When Steele went into the room, Lord Raglan remembered that he had himself been ill the day before and asked him how he was.

'All right, Sir,' said Steele. 'I hope you are not in pain.'

'Oh! no, my dear Steele. I shall soon be all right.'

'Alas, sir, I fear not.'

'Why?'

'The doctors have a very bad opinion of you, Sir, and have desired me to tell you so, and ask if you would like the Chaplain sent for.'

'They are quite mistaken, Steele. They are making a mistake altogether. Yesterday I was very bad, but now I am easy and comfortable. I do assure you they will find they are mistaken.'[8]

He spoke slowly and faintly but with an unmistakable determination. Half an hour later, however, when Nigel Kingscote came back to the bedside Lord Raglan did not recognise him. The Chaplain of the Forces was sent for, and while they waited for him in silence the people in the small room—the four A.D.C.s, Colonel Steele, General Airey and Lady George Paget—could all 'distinctly hear the breathing getting slower and slower, till at last a little noise in the throat warned them that all was over. And so it was.' Had it not been for the tracheal rattle, Steele said, 'the dropping to sleep of a tired child could not have been more composed or easy'.[9]

'Peace be to this house,' the Chaplain said, 'and all that dwell in it.'

Everyone in the room, as well as those waiting outside it, knelt down and prayed with him. When they stood up they looked at Lord Raglan's face, and instead of the expression of peace they had hoped to find there they saw the anxious, careworn features of a pale, tired, white-haired old man.[10]

In the morning the commanders-in-chief of the four allied armies came to the farmhouse with the admirals. General Canrobert came also, with Pélissier, to see for the last time the old Englishman he had grown to love. And when everyone else had gone, Pélissier went in again alone and 'for upwards of an hour' the harsh, fat, rude and ugly soldier, stood by the iron camp-bed and the green serge curtains 'crying like a child'.[11]

II

The army heard the news with the shock of unexpected grief and felt overcome by 'a dreadful gloom'.[12] It seemed to Mrs Duberly 'as though some pulse in this vast body' had 'ceased to beat'. 'The army is so quiet,' she wrote in her diary. 'Men speak in low voices words of regret.' Accustomed to meet death with resignation they 'looked at each other', Timothy Gowing remembered, 'as if they had heard of the loss of some near relative. We did not know, until he was taken from us, how deeply we loved him.' Even those who had criticised him in the past now admitted that he was 'universally regretted'.[13] He had 'passed away quietly', Captain Clifford told his father, 'without leaving a single enemy. Everyone who knew him loved and respected him.'

At about four o'clock on 3 July the generals and staffs of all the allied armies came to the British headquarters and waited in the afternoon sunshine outside the farmyard. They passed the time in the 'exchange of salutations and cheerful conversation'. Canrobert, hat in hand, was bowing and smiling; Bosquet looking rather bored; Omar Pasha chatting with General della Marmora. Pélissier remained 'aloof and awaited the commencement of the ceremony in silence and with downcast looks'.[14]

And then, at a quarter-past four, the carriage-wheels of a 9-pounder gun rattled out of the farmyard, and the crowds of chatting officers fell into sudden silence. The coffin, resting on the barrel of the gun, was draped with the Union Jack and a black cloak. On the flag was the plumed hat which its late owner rarely wore, and next to it his sword and a bunch of immortelles put there by Pélissier. The route to the sea was lined with double ranks of infantry, behind them were regimental bands, field batteries, troops of the Imperial Guard, and the French 1st Corps. Officers and men of every British regiment were there. The camps and trenches before Sebastopol were left dangerously bare; but, as if in mourning too, the Russian guns were silent.

To the roll of drums and the melancholy music of the *Dead March* the horses moved off and the gun-carriage rumbled forward on its way down to the sea at Kazatch. General Pélissier and General della Marmora rode on one side, General Simpson and Omar Pasha on the other. Behind them walked Lord Raglan's favourite horse, Miss Mary, saddled and riderless; and then the allied generals and their staffs, followed by thousands upon thousands of men, the greater part of their armies. It was, in fact, a procession which in his lifetime Lord Raglan would have been at pains to avoid.

At Kazatch the coffin was lifted aboard the launch of the English flagship, which moved off to the black-painted *Caradoc* as the guns of the artillery boomed across the water. The *Caradoc* steamed out of the bay with the signal 'Farewell' fluttering out at her mast-head.

III

At Scutari Florence Nightingale was told the news and was 'thunderstruck'. 'It was impossible not to love him,' she told her parents, 'I did. . . .' He had died, so the doctors in the camp had said, 'without sufficient physical reason. It was *not* cholera. The diarrhoea was slight but he was so *depressed* . . . the more by reason of his apparent equanimity which never failed. Peace be with him and with his hecatomb of twenty thousand men.' He was not a *very great* general, she thought, but he was a *very good* man.[15]

Indeed, only those outraged by the cruelty of the attacks made upon him claimed that he was both. He was not a great general; but he was something else. One of his soldiers described him in words which carried no hint of reproach, as a 'dear old Christian Gentleman', who had 'broken his heart'.[16] It was a fitting epitaph.

EPILOGUE

On 25 July 1855, the *Caradoc* sailed up the Bristol Channel. The next morning at six o'clock Lord Raglan's coffin was transferred to the steamer *Star* to a salute of guns and muffled bells. A little later the *Star* steamed slowly into dock followed by a double line of naval rowing-boats all painted black.

It was a short and simple ceremony. The Queen had wanted the disembarkation to take place at Portsmouth so that the Fleet, and as many units of the Army as could be assembled, should be able to pay the dead field-marshal the most impressive honours. But Lady Raglan asked that her husband should be brought back to Bristol with as little ceremony as possible. On 26 July he was buried at Badminton, privately and quietly as he would have wished.

In growing despondency the Crimean War dragged on. Cholera and drunkenness, courts-martial and floggings, increased in the allied camps. Even in Sebastopol the brief moments of elation after the victory of 18 June were followed by long days of despair. Admiral Nachimoff died on 13 July from wounds received three days before; Todleben was also wounded and left the town to convalesce in a villa on the Belbec. And when they had gone much of the spirit of resistance went with them. Behind the still strong defences many of Sebastopol's finest buildings were wholly or partly in ruins; and preparations were already being made for the evacuation of the town and a withdrawal to Perekop.

The French troops now considered their allies to be no longer of much use, and Pélissier a blunderer. The Emperor, of course, agreed with them and decided to dismiss Pélissier, who still firmly rejected his continued suggestions for operations in the field. The letter of dismissal had in fact already been sent when Marshal Vaillant and Pélissier's other supporters in Paris succeeded at the last moment in changing Napoleon's mind and intercepting the letter before it left on the mail-boat.

But if Napoleon had no doubt that General Niel would be a more effective commander, the Government in London had no idea who could replace Lord Raglan. For the time being General Simpson had been given temporary command and was hating it. 'I feel it very irksome and embarrassing to have to do with these Allies!' he told the

Government. 'No man can equal our lamented chief in that respect. I sincerely trust, my Lord, that a General of distinction will be sent immediately. . . . This is of vital consequence.'[1]

But what generals of distinction were there? There was talk that Lord Hardinge would succeed to the command. 'They seem to imagine Lord Hardinge will be sent,' Admiral Houston-Stewart wrote to Lord Panmure. 'I should think—I almost said I *hope*—not. . . . I doubt if Lord Raglan's loss will be as deeply appreciated in England just now as it is here. *Here* it seems to be thought almost *irreparable.*'[2]

But somehow the loss had to be made good, and General Simpson was clearly not the man to make it so. He was appalled by his responsibility and within a few weeks looked 'half a score years older'. On 8 September, however, he was still in command when in the cold, grey gloom of a windy morning he rode out in a black uniform to direct the army in its final assault.

Three weeks before, the French and Sardinians had heavily defeated the Russians at the battle of Tchernaya and the morale of the garrison in Sebastopol had sunk to new depths. The morale of the British troops was little better. It was common knowledge that the military opinions of General Simpson were of no interest to the French staff; and the British assaulting troops, sharing the French opinion, waited in the narrow forward trench in fear and silence. There were less than two thousand of them, and most of these were either raw recruits or old soldiers whose nerve had long since been shattered. It looked, officers said to each other, as if it was going to be another 18 June.[3]

A little before noon, when the Russian gunners were relieved, the roar of the allied artillery died down, and in a high wind which blew clouds of smoke and yellow dust in their faces the French troops leapt at the Malakoff. Within half an hour, after a savage struggle, the tricolour was flying from the top of the bastion. A moment later the British, encouraged by this splendid example, rushed at the Redan. Most of them succeeded in running across the two hundred yards of open ground and in reaching the foot of the work, but there the attack was halted. Officers could not get their men to go any farther. The supports came up and joined the assaulting troops, huddling behind the parapet. The Russian fire was now intense, and the men could not be moved. 'The plain truth is,' wrote Captain Campbell of the 46th, 'that from the moment they reached the parapet they showed the most arrant cowardice.' After a few minutes they decided they had had enough and flew back in panic to their lines.

It was a shameful and disastrous failure. About 2,500 men were lost. But the French, whose losses were nearly three times as great, held on to the Malakoff despite reverses elsewhere; and without the Malakoff, Prince Gortschakoff felt that he could not hold the town behind it. That night and the following morning, in a series of explosive roars that made the ground shudder as if shaken by an earthquake, the arsenals, barracks, magazines and docks of Sebastopol were blown into the air; and the allied armies moved down into the smoking ruins.

Although the Treaty of Paris was not signed until the end of the following March, the war was as good as over.

The post-mortems had already begun. The evidence of Roebuck's Committee was issued to the public in three lengthy reports. Then the report of the Hospital Commissioners was published, followed by that of the Sanitary Commissioners. Generally polite and unprovocative, they found much fault with the administrative system of the Army's various departments, but less with the officers whose duty it was to try and make that system work. But in February 1856 Sir John McNeil and Colonel Alexander Tulloch issued their report on the Commissariat, and the names of officers were mentioned, particularly those of Airey, Lucan and Cardigan, with disrespect. The Army flew to their defence and a Board of General Officers was directed to assemble at Chelsea Hospital to 'allow the officers adverted to in the report to have an opportunity of defending themselves'. They took the opportunity eagerly and they were all exonerated with more or less success. Airey, who had certainly been maligned by the Government and unjustly criticised by McNeil and Tulloch, was completely cleared of all blame. But in their openly expressed determination to exculpate the Army, the generals of the 'Whitewashing Board' increased its disrepute. The Board's published finding that the blame should be placed almost entirely upon the Government was considered disingenuous. Perhaps most of the blame did lie with the Government, but the Army system too was at fault. And intelligent officers who had fought in the Crimea knew that it was and the public knew it too.

Meetings of protest at the Chelsea Board Report were held in London and several other towns. For public-spirited English people knew that, whatever the generals said, the Army must be reformed. So, slowly, it was.

And so, in this respect, the war had not been in vain. It had cost the lives of more than twenty-one thousand British soldiers—and even this was less than a twelfth of the total number of dead—and had decided little internationally. The Danube was to be an international waterway and the Black Sea was to be neutral, but Sebastopol had to be returned to the enemy. Russia, which had seemed previously to dominate Central Europe, now had, for some years, less influence in European affairs; but not for many years. The Turkish Empire was propped up, but only temporarily. The alliance of England and France remained an uneasy one; and the problem of the Holy Places, which the war had supposedly been fought to settle, was not even mentioned in the treaty, which, in any case, fourteen years later the Czar repudiated.

The British Army, however, was improved and altered for ever. And the private soldier became for the first time in his career an object of respect rather than of resentment. 'I suppose one day,' Lord Raglan once wrote when a man had been flogged for stealing a blanket, 'the British soldier will be treated with humanity by his officers and his country. I hope so. He is, for all his faults, a noble creature.'

NOTES ON MILITARY TERMS

ROUND SHOT: The solid iron ball, which had been in use for centuries, was gradually being replaced by the explosive shell. It was still, however, an effective weapon. It came hurtling through the air or bouncing across the ground at great speed and could kill up to ten men standing in file. It was perhaps more effective at battering down masonry and against troops drawn up in mass than against isolated bodies of men, as it was possible for a quick-sighted soldier to jump out of its path when he saw it coming.

During the course of the war, gunners became adept at sighting their guns so that balls were made to ricochet round corners and jump over obstacles in their path.

SHELLS: The hollow interior of the spherical shell was filled with gunpowder poured in through a funnel and ignited by a time fuse—a wooden stopper with holes at regular intervals filled with clay. The powder inside the fuse burned at the rate of an inch every five seconds, so that by removing the clay filling in one of the holes in the stopper the flame could be timed to jump out of the stopper and burst the shell with some degree of accuracy. A fuse with all its holes filled exploded the shell half a minute after firing. A fuse with a filling pushed out was used by gunners for air bursts and when firing at close range.

GUNS: Complaints were constantly made by gunners that their guns were too light for use against the heavier Russian artillery. Guns firing 9-lb. balls were in general use, and to drag these guns within range of Russian 24-pounders was always a hazardous undertaking—hence Lord Raglan's decision to bring up two 18-pounder siege-guns during the Battle of Inkerman.

The guns were cast with extremely thick metal and had smooth bores. They were loaded from the muzzle and fired with measured charges of powder by means of a copper friction-tube, detonated by the quick jerk of a lanyard.

A burst of flame was followed by a heavy billow of smoke. The gun jumped in the air and rolled back along the battery platform, where it was cooled by a sponge fixed to a wooden stave and reloaded.

MORTARS: These were used more frequently than guns for firing shells. They had a much larger bore than modern mortars—the largest bores were of thirteen inches—and resembled immense preserving pans on hinged supports.

CASE, MITRAILLE, GRAPE, CANISTER: Although there are technical differences, these four terms were used interchangeably to describe small, loose, iron balls or bullets either clamped between metal plates or poured into cylindrical cases with thin sides. They were used against infantry and cavalry at close quarters, where the flying fragments did more damage than round shot.

BOUQUETS: A number of small shells inside a larger one. Timed to explode at varying intervals, either in the air or on falling to the ground.

CARCASS: A heavy shell filled with a combustible material which burned out of holes in its side and was used as an incendiary bomb.

ROCKETS: Rockets were fired from plain cylindrical tubes and could be used by experts with surprising accuracy. They could be adapted to carry in their nose either a round shot, a small shell or a 'carcass.'

MUSKET AND RIFLE: As explained in the text the Minié Rifle, firing a blunt lead bullet through a grooved bore, was gradually replacing the musket. Several regiments, however, left for the East equipped with antiquated muskets which fired a ball through a smooth bore with doubtful accuracy. All French regiments were equipped with rifles. Muskets were still standard equipment of Russian troops at the beginning of the war, although by its end many regiments had been issued with rifles. The superiority of the rifle over the musket was unquestionable and contributed much to the successes of the allied infantry. A Russian officer said that a single Minié bullet could kill or disable as many as six or seven men.

GABIONS: Wicker-work cylinders filled with earth, used as a protection in earthworks.

FASCINES: Bundles of long sticks used for revetting trench walls and batteries.

PARALLELS: Trenches dug parallel to the face of a besieged fortification. The trenches between parallels are known as 'approaches'; and opposing works are known as 'counter-parallels'.

MERLONS: The parts of an embattled parapet between the embrasures.

SOURCES

Manuscript

Affidavits in the action brought in the Queen's Bench against Lieutenant-Colonel the Hon. Somerset Calthorpe by James Thomas, Earl of Cardigan.

Arundel Castle Archives.

The Autobiography of William Cattell.

Confidential Report upon the Organisation and Administration of the French Army.

The Crawford Muniments.

The Crimean Papers of Field-Marshal Lord Raglan.

The Diaries of Lieutenant the Hon. Hugh Annesley, Grenadier Guards; Captain M. A. B. Biddulph, R.A.; Captain W. A. Godfrey, Rifle Brigade; Lieutenant-Colonel Frederick William Hamilton, Grenadier Guards; the Rev. Robert Hinds; Captain C. M. J. D. Shakespear, R.H.A.; and Midshipman Evelyn Wood.

The Elton Papers.

The Hickleton Papers.

The Letters of Major-General Henry Barnard; Captain M. A. B. Biddulph, R.A.; Dr. Ethelbert Blake; Sergeant Chadburn, Grenadier Guards; Colonel H. Dickson, R.A.; Paymaster Henry Dixon, Royal Fusiliers; Captain Henry Duberly, 8th Hussars; Captain Eddington, 95th Regiment; Major-General James Bucknall Estcourt; Major-General Sir George de Lacy Evans; Lieutenant-Colonel Frederick William Hamilton, Grenadier Guards; Commander Lord John Hay; Private S. R. Hudson; Ensign Robert Lindsay, Scots Fusilier Guards; John L. Lizars; Midshipman the Hon. M. A. Montagu; Cornet the Hon. Grey Neville, 5th Dragoon Guards; Captain the Hon. Henry Neville, Grenadier Guards; Captain the Hon. Henry Keppel, R.N.; Lieutenant William Powell Richards, R.A.; Major H. B. Roberts, R.M.A.; Captain J. D. Ross-Lewin, 30th Regiment; Captain C. M. J. D. Shakespear, R.H.A.; Captain R. Y. Shipley, Royal Fusiliers; Dr. Joseph Skelton; Corporal John Spurling, 63rd Regiment; Lieutenant G. W. Stacpoole, 18th Regiment; Major Clement Walker-Heneage, 8th Hussars; Private John Williams, 41st Regiment; and Midshipman Evelyn Wood.

The Medical History of the 55th Regiment during its service in Turkey and the Crimea, by Dr. Ethelbert Blake.

The Newcastle Papers.

The Notebook of Captain Hugh Hibbert.

The Pretyman Collection.

The Private Papers of Field-Marshal Lord Raglan.

Public Record Office Papers W.O. 1/379; 1/381; 3/116; 3/322; 3/500; 6/69; 6/72–80; 6/129; 28 Crimea 47–53; 56–60, 66, 68, 72, 77–81, 84, 88, 91–95, 98–100, 103, 108–109, 113–115, 118–123, 126, 133–139, 161–199, 292; 32/20; 33/1–3; 62/14; 62/17; 78/1736.

The Royal Archives.

The Russian War, 1854–1856, by Colonel James George Smith Neill.

The Verney Papers.

The Wellington Papers.

The Westmorland Papers.

Newspapers and Periodicals

Aberdeen University Review

The Army and Navy Gazette

Colburn's United Service Gazette

Courrier de l'Europe

The *Daily News*

English Historical Review

The Fortnightly Review

The Gentleman's Magazine

The Globe

The Illustrated London News

Journal of the Royal Army Medical Corps

Journal of the Royal Artillery

Journal of the Royal United Service Institution

Journal of the Society for Army Historical Research

The *Liverpool Mercury*

The *Monthly Review*

The *Morning Chronicle*

The *Morning Herald*

The *Morning Post*

SOURCES

The *North British Review*
Punch
The *Quarterly Review*
Royal Engineers Journal
Royal Military Chronicle
The *Saturday Review*
The Times
United Service Magazine

Privately Printed

Extracts from the Letters of E. R. Fisher-Rowe during the Crimean War.
Historical Record of the 7th Regiment, by W. Wheater.
The 93rd Highlanders, by Brigadier-General A. E. J. Cavendish.
Letters from the Army in the Crimea, by a Staff officer who was There.
Letters from the Crimea, by Captain Robert Portal, 4th Light Dragoons.

Published

ADYE, John
    A Review of the Crimean War (1860)
    Recollections of a Military Life (1895)
ANICHKOV, Victor Mikhailovich
    Der Feldzug in der Krim, 3tl (translated from the Russian) (1857–1860)
AIRLIE, Countess of
    With the Guards We Shall Go: A Guardsman's Letters in the Crimea (1854–1855) (1933)
ATKINS, J. B.
    The Life of Sir W. H. Russell, Vol. I (1911)
The Autobiography of Elizabeth Davis, a Balaclava Nurse (1857)
BANNATYNE, Lieutenant-Colonel Neil
    History of the 30th Regiment (1923)
BAPST, Germain
    Le Maréchal Canrobert, 6 Vols. (9th ed.) (1914)
BAZANCOURT, Baron de
    L'Expédition de Crimée (1856)
Die Belagerung von Sebastopol, von der Einschiffung der Verbündeten in Varna bis zur Einnahme von Sud-Sebastopol (1956)

BELL, H. C. F.
Lord Palmerston, Vol. II (1936)

BENSON, A. C., and ESHER, Viscount (eds.)
The Letters of Queen Victoria, Vol. III (1908)

BONNER-SMITH, D. (ed.)
The Russian War, 1854. Baltic and Black Sea Official Correspondence (1943)

BRIALMONT, Lt.-Général A.
Le Général Comte Todleben (1884)

BUCHANAN, George
Camp Life as Seen by a Civilian (1871)

Campagnes de Crimée: Lettres Addressés au Maréchal de Castellane (1878)

De CASTELLANE
Journal de Maréchal de Castellane, Vol. V (1897)

CHAPLINSKY, Georgy
Recollections of the Defence of Sebastopol (1872) (not translated from Russian)

CHENU, Jean Charles
Rapport au Conseil de Santé des Armées (1865)

Collection of Manuscripts presented to H.I.H. the Heir Apparent Czarevitch about the Defence of Sebastopol, 3 Vols. (1872–1873) (not translated from Russian)

La Conduite de la Guerre d'Orient, par un officier général (1855)

CONNOLLY, Captain T. W. J.
The History of the Corps of Royal Sappers and Miners, Vol. II (1857)

COOK, Sir Edward
Delane of "The Times" (1915)

COPE, Sir William
The History of the Rifle Brigade (1877)

The Crimean Diary and Letters of Lieutenant-General Sir Charles Ash Windham (1897)

DERRÉCAGAIX, G.
Le Maréchal Pélissier (1911)

The Diary of Sergeant William Jowett of the 7th Fusiliers (1856)

DOUGLAS, Sir George, and RAMSAY, Sir George Dalhousie (eds.)
The Panmure Papers (1908)

DUBERLY, Mrs. Henry
Journal Kept during the Russian War (1855)

DUBROVNIN, N.
History of the Crimean War, 3 Vols. (1900) (not translated from Russian)
DURANT, Horatia
The Somerset Sequence (1951)
ELPHINSTONE, H. C.
Journal of the Operations Conducted by the Corps of Royal Engineers, Part I (1859)
Expedition de Crimée. Quelques éclairissements relatifs à l'armée anglaise (1857)
FALLS, Cyril (ed.)
Diary of the Crimea: George Palmer Evelyn (1954)
FAY, C. A.
Souvenirs de la Guerre Crimée (1867)
FENWICK, Kenneth (ed.)
Voice from the Ranks. A Personal Narrative of the Crimean Campaign by a Sergeant of the Royal Fusiliers (1954)
FORTESCUE, Hon. J. W.
A History of the British Army, Vol. XIII (1930)
FULFORD, Roger, with STRACHEY, Lytton (eds.)
The Greville Memoirs, 8 Vols. (1938)
FURNEAUX, Rupert
The First War Correspondent (1944)
GERNSHEIM, Helmut and Alison
Roger Fenton: Photographer of the Crimean War (1954)
GLEASON, John Howes
The Genesis of Russophobia in Great Britain (1950)
GOOCH, Brison D.
The New Bonapartist Generals in the Crimean War (1959)
DE LA GORCE, P.
Histoire du Second Empire, Vol. I (1894)
GOWING, *see* FENWICK
GREVILLE, *see* FULFORD
HAMILTON, Lieutenant-General Sir F. W.
The Origin and History of the First or Grenadier Guards, Vol. III (1874)
HAMLEY, Sir Edward
The War in the Crimea (1891)
The Story of the Campaign of Sebastopol (1855)

HANSARD, T. C.
  Parliamentary Debates, 3rd Series (1850–1856)
  Henry Clifford, V.C., His Letters and Sketches from the Crimea (1956)
  Historical Records of the 30th Regiment (1887)
  Historical Records of the 57th Regiment (1878)
  The History of "The Times", Vol. II (1939)

HODASEVICH, Robert Adolf
  A Voice from within the Walls of Sebastopol (translated from the Russian)
  (1856)

HORSETZKY, General A. von
  The Chief Campaigns in Europe since 1792 (1909)

HUME, Major-General J. R.
  Reminiscences of the Crimean Campaign with the 55th Regiment (1894)

JOCELYN, Colonel J. R. J.
  The History of the Royal Artillery, Crimean Period (1911)

JONES, Major-General Sir Harry D.
  Journal of the Operations Conducted by the Corps of the Royal Engineers,
  Part I (1859)

KELLY, Mrs. Tom
  From the Fleet in the 50's (1902)

KENNAWAY, C. E.
  The War and the Newspapers (1856)

KINGLAKE, A. W.
  The Invasion of the Crimea, 9 Vols. (6th ed.) (1877–1888)

KRUSHCHOV, A. O.
  A History of the Defence of Sebastopol (1889) (not translated from Russian)

*Letters from Camp to his Relatives during the Siege of Sebastopol by Colin
  Frederick Campbell* (1894)

*Letters from Headquarters; or the Realities of the War in the Crimea by an
  Officer of the Staff* (1856)

Lettres du Maréchal Bosquet (1856)

Lord Raglan, a Would-be Sacrifice (1855)

LUKASEVICH, K. V.
  The Defence of Sebastopol and its Famous Defenders (1912) (not translated
  from Russian)

LYSONS, Daniel
  The Crimean War from First to Last (1895)

MAGNUS, Sir Philip
Gladstone (1954)

MAINWARING, Rowland Broughton
Historical Record of the Royal Welch Fusiliers (1889)

MARSH, C. M.
Memorials of Captain Hedley Vickers (1867)

MARTIN, Kingsley
The Triumph of Lord Palmerston (1924).

MARTIN, Sir Theodore
The Life of His Royal Highness the Prince Consort, Vol. III (6th ed.) (1878)

MARTINEAU, Harriet
England and her Soldiers (1859)

MARTINEAU, J.
Life of the Fifth Duke of Newcastle (1908)

MAURICE, Major-General Sir F.
The History of the Scots Guards, Vol. II (1934)

MAXWELL, General E. H.
With the Connaught Rangers (1883)

MAXWELL, Sir Herbert
The Life and Letters of the Fourth Earl of Clarendon (1913)

Mr. Kinglake and the Quarterlies (1863)

MITRA, S. M.
The Life and Letters of Sir John Hall (1911)

NIEL, Le Général Adolphe
Siège de Sébastopol (1858)

NOLAN, E. H.
Illustrated History of the War against Russia, 2 Vols. (1855–1857)

OLIPHANT, Laurence
The Russian Shores of the Black Sea in the Autumn of 1852 (1853)

The Opening Address of General Sir Richard Airey, K.C.B., before the Board of General Officers assembled at the Royal Hospital, Chelsea, together with his Summing-up Address (1856)

PACK, Colonel Reynell
Sebastopol Trenches (1878)

PAGET, General Lord George
The Light Cavalry Brigade in the Crimea (1881)

PEARD, Lieutenant G. S.
Narrative of a Campaign in the Crimea (1855)

PEMBERTON, W. Baring
Lord Palmerston (1954)

PIROGOV, N. I.
Letters from Sebastopol (1899) (not translated from Russian)

POOLE, Stanley Lane
The Life of Lord Stratford de Redcliffe (1888)

POWNALL, Mrs. Frederick (ed.)
At Home and on the Battlefield. Letters of Sir Frederick Stephenson (1915)

RAWTHORNE, Captain James
Descriptive Plan and Explanatory Key of the Allied Expedition from Baljik to the Crimea (1859)

REID, Douglas Arthur
Memories of the Crimean War (1911)

REILLY, W. E. M.
An Account of the Artillery Operations in 1854 and 1855 (1859)

Report upon the State of the Hospitals of the British Army in the Crimea and Scutari (1855)

Report to the Rt. Hon. Lord Panmure of the Proceedings of the Sanitary Commission Dispatched to the Seat of War in the East, 1855–1856 (1857)

First, Second and Third Report from the Select Committee on the Army before Sebastopol (1855)

Report of the Commission of Inquiry into the Supplies of the British Army in the Crimea (1856)

REVOL, J. F.
Le Vice des Coalitions: le Haut Commandement en Crimée (1923)

ROBINSON, Frederick
Diary of the Crimean War (1856)

ROSS-OF-BLADENSBURG, Lieutenant-Colonel John
A History of the Coldstream Guards, 1815–1885 (1896)

ROUSSET, Camille
Histoire de la Guerre de Crimée, 2 Vols. (3me ed.) (1894)

RUSSELL, W. H.
The War in the Crimea (1855)
The British Expedition to the Crimea (1858)
The Great War with Russia (1895)

RYAN, George
Our Heroes of the Crimea (1855)

SAYER, Frederick
Despatches and Papers Relative to the Campaigns in Turkey, Asia Minor, and the Crimea (1857)

Sebastopol and its Gallant Defenders (1867) (not translated from Russian)

Le Siège de Sébastopol, 1854–1855 (1960)

STANMORE, Lord
Life of Lord Herbert of Lea (1906)

STEEVENS, Lieutenant-Colonel Nathaniel
The Crimean Campaign with the Connaught Rangers (1878)

STERLING, Anthony
The Story of the Highland Brigade in the Crimea (1895)
Letters from the Army (1857)

STUART, Brian (ed.)
Soldier's Glory, being "Rough Notes of an Old Soldier" by Major-General Sir George Bell (1956)

TARLE, Evgeny Viktorivich
The Crimean War, 2 Vols. (2nd ed. 1950) (not translated from Russian)

TEMPERLEY, Harold
England and the Near East: The Crimea (1956)

TODLEBEN, F. E. I.
Défense de Sébastopol, 2 Vols. (1863–1870) (translated from the Russian)

TULLOCH, Alexander
The Crimean Commission and the Chelsea Board (2nd ed.) (1880)

TYRRELL, Henry
The History of the War with Russia, 3 Vols. (1855–1858)

VETCH, Colonel R. H.
Life, Letters and Diaries of Lieutenant-General Sir Gerald Graham (1901)

A Vindication of the Earl of Lucan from Lord Raglan's Reflections (1855)

VULLIAMY, C. E.
Crimea (1939)

WEIGALL, Lady Rose (ed.)
The Correspondence of Lady Burghersh with the Duke of Wellington (1903)
The Correspondence of Priscilla, Countess of Westmorland, 1830–1870 (1909)

WOLSELEY, Field-Marshal Viscount
The Story of a Soldier's Life, Vol. I (1903)

The Wonderful Adventures of Mrs. Seacole in Many Lands (1858)

WOOD, General Sir Evelyn
The Crimea in 1854 and 1894 (1895)

WOODHAM-SMITH, Cecil
Florence Nightingale (1951)
The Reason Why (1953)

WOODS, N. A.
The Past Campaign, 2 Vols. (1855)

WOOLLRIGHT, H. H.
History of the 57th Regiment (1893)
Records of the 77th Regiment (1909)

WRIGHT, H. P.
Recollections of a Crimean Chaplain (1857)

WROTTESLEY, The Hon. George
The Life and Correspondence of Field-Marshal Sir John Burgoyne, 2 Vols. (1873)
(ed.) *Military Opinions of General Sir J. F. Burgoyne* (1859)

WYLLY, Major H. C.
The 95th Regiment in the Crimea (1899)

ZHANDR, Alexsandr
Materials for a History of the Defence of Sebastopol (1859) (not translated from Russian)

REFERENCES

Abbreviations

Raglan Crimean Papers (Royal United Service Institution)—R.C.P.
Raglan Private Papers (Cefntilla Court)—R.P.P.
Sebastopol Committee Reports—S.C.R.

Chapter 1 (Page 1). LORD FITZROY SOMERSET.

1 Raglan Private Papers, A (1) 5 and Miscellaneous Papers Box 10.
2 WEIGALL, *The Correspondence of Lady Burghersh*, 216–217.
3 DURANT, *The Somerset Sequence*, 171–172.
4 Gurwood's Selections of Wellington's Dispatches, 864.
5 DURANT, 176.
6 Hoare's Bank Archives.
7 R.P.P., Miscellaneous Papers, Box 10.
8 *The Times*, 16 February 1855.
9 WEIGALL, *The Correspondence of Lady Burghersh*, 219–220.
10 *Greville Memoirs* (ed. Fulford), VI, 365.
11 BENSON and ESHER, *Letters of Queen Victoria*, II, 480.
12 R.P.P., D (1) 240.
13 R.P.P., B 188.
14 Shakespear Letters.
15 Eddington Letters.
16 Biddulph Letters.

Chapter 2 (Page 9). THE FINEST ARMY.

1 GOWING, *A Voice from the Ranks*, 6.
2 TEMPERLEY, *England and the Near East*, viii.
3 BENSON and ESHER, *Letters of Queen Victoria*, III, 14.
4 MAGNUS, *Gladstone*, 115.
5 Annesley Diary; MARTIN, III, 33–34.
6 BAPST, *Maréchal Canrobert*, II, 178.
7 Crawford Muniments; Fisher-Rowe Letters.
8 *Letters from Headquarters*, I, 87.
9 *Ibid.*, I, 88.

Chapter 3 (Page 17). SCUTARI.

1 *The Times*; Portal Letters; ROBINSON, *Diary of the Crimean War*, 33–35.
2 GOWING, 8.
3 *Henry Clifford*, 37.
4 Richards Letters.
5 RUSSELL, *The War in the Crimea*, 38 and 43.
6 Eddington Letters.
7 BAPST, II, 220.

8 RUSSELL, 53–54; *Letters from Headquarters*, I, 26.
9 RUSSELL, 61.
10 Annesley Diary; ROBINSON; Biddulph, Neville, Portal, Duberly Letters.
11 DUBERLY, *Journal*, 18–19; ROBINSON; Blake Letters; *Clifford*, 36; *Letters from Headquarters*, I, 21–22.
12 RUSSELL, 70–71; R.P.P. D (1) 193 and 194; *Letters from Headquarters*, I, 30.
13 R.P.P., D (1) 196.
14 Raglan Crimean Papers (M.M. 184 Raglan to Newcastle Private 15/5/1854).
15 R.C.P. (M.M. 192 Brown to Raglan 24/3/1854).
16 R.C.P. (M.M. 184 R. to N. Private 15/6/1854).
17 R.C.P. (M.M. 184 R. to N. Private 15/5/1854).
18 R.C.P. (M.M. 184 R. to N. Private 29/5/1854).
19 R.C.P. (M.M. 184 R. to N. Private 26/5/1854 and 29/6/1854).
20 R.C.P. (M.M. 184 R. to N. Private 5/6/1854 enclosing St. Arnaud's note 4/6/1854).
21 R.C.P. (M.M. 184 R. to N. Private 8/6/1854).
22 R.C.P. (M.M. 184 R. to N. Private 10/6/1854).
23 R.P.P. D (1) 200, 201.
24 KINGLAKE, *The Invasion of the Crimea*, II, 248–250.

Chapter 4 (Page 27). VARNA.

1 R.C.P. (M.M. 184 R. to N. Private 19/5/1854); Sebastopol Committee Report, III, 115.
2 Richards Letters.
3 Richards Letters; *The Times*; Biddulph Letters.
4 R.C.P. (M.M. 184 R. to N. Private 19/7/1854; M.M. 182 R. to N. Official 16/8/1854 and 14/11/1854).
5 Skelton; Duberly; RUSSELL, 83; AIRLIE, *With the Guards*, 40; ROBINSON, 92.
6 Richards Letters.
7 ROBINSON, 99–100; BELL (ed. Stuart), *Soldier's Glory*, 197, 201–202.
8 *Letters from Headquarters*, I, 87 and 109.
9 ROBINSON, 114.
10 ROBINSON, 115; *Letters from Headquarters*, I, 86 et seq.
11 RUSSELL, 134.
12 BELL, 203 and 204.
13 RUSSELL, 140.
14 Neville Letters; ROBINSON, 108; RUSSELL, 117–118; R.P.P. D (1) 206, 207.
15 R.C.P. (M.M. 182 R. to N. Official 14/8/1854).
16 Walker-Heneage Letters.
17 R.C.P. (M.M. 181 N. to R. Official 29/6/1854).
18 R.C.P. (M.M. 183 N. to R. Private 28/6/1854).
19 KINGLAKE, II, 254.
20 WROTTESLEY, *The Life and Correspondence of Sir John Burgoyne*, II, 31.
21 KINGLAKE, II, 271.
22 R.C.P. (M.M. 182 R. to N. Official 19/7/1854).

23 R.C.P. (M.M. 183 N. to R. Private 3/8/1854).
24 R.C.P. (M.M. 183 N. to R. Private 8/8/1854).
25 R.C.P. (M.M. 182 R. to N. Official 4/8/1854).
26 Dixon Letters.
27 RUSSELL, 144.
28 Skelton Letters.
29 Hamilton Letters; ROBINSON, 142.
30 BAZANCOURT, *L'Expédition de Crimée*, III, 160; R.C.P. (M.M. 184 R. to N. Private 11/9/1854).
31 BAZANCOURT, III, 162.
32 R.C.P. (M.M. 184 R. to N. Private 11/9/1854).
33 *Letters from Headquarters*, I, 131.
34 R.C.P. (M.M. 182 R. to N. Official and Secret 29/7/1854).
35 Westmorland Papers.
36 KINGLAKE, II, 318.
37 *Letters from Headquarters*, I, 132; EVELYN (ed. Falls), *A Diary of the Crimea*, 79.
38 Richards Letters; ROBINSON, 146–147.
39 Richards Letters; BELL, 209.
40 KINGLAKE, II, 325.

Chapter 5 (Page 39). CALAMITA BAY.

1 RUSSELL, 162.
2 BAZANCOURT, III, 180–184; FAY, *Souvenirs de la Guerre de Crimée*, 47.
3 RUSSELL, 165.
4 *Letters from Headquarters*, I, 147; KINGLAKE, II, 342–343.
5 Annesley Diary; KINGLAKE, II, 345–346.
6 WOOD, *The Crimea in 1854*, 26; Neville Letters.
7 S.C.R., III, 489–491.
8 PAGET, *Light Cavalry*, 15; Portal Letters.
9 Lyson's MS. (quoted by KINGLAKE, II, 355–356).
10 R.C.P. (M.M. 184 R. to N. Private 24/9/1854); *Royal Engineers Journal* (ELPHINSTONE), I, 8 (this gives total British forces landed as 26,800. NIEL (*Siège de Sébastopol*, 462) gives French numbers as 26,526. The Turks were 7,000 strong).
11 *Clifford*, 48.
12 RUSSELL, 170.
13 R.P.P. D (1) 215 and Miscellaneous Box 10; RUSSELL, 166.
14 BELL, 213–214.
15 WOODHAM-SMITH, *The Reason Why*, 178.
16 KINGLAKE, II, 370–372.
17 BELL, 216.
18 Richards Letters; RUSSELL, 173.
19 PAGET, 18; Westmorland Papers; Richards Letters; Annesley Journal.
20 Neville; Richards Letters.
21 Westmorland Papers; BELL, 218 (who places the incident two days later).
22 R.P.P. D (1) 197.

23 R.C.P. (M.M. 182 R. to N. 24/6/1854 official and M.M. 184 Private 4/7/1854 and 14/7/1854 and 24/7/1854).
24 KINGLAKE, II, 376.
25 KINGLAKE, II, 378.
26 WOODHAM-SMITH, 183.
27 WOODHAM-SMITH, 184.
28 Williams Letters.
29 HODASEVICH, A Voice from Within the Walls of Sebastopol, 62.

Chapter 6 (Page 53). ALMA.

1 R.C.P. (M.M. 182 R. to N. official 21/9/1854); TODLEBEN, Défense de Sébastopol, I, 173; KINGLAKE, III, 13.
2 HODASEVICH, 29–30.
3 TODLEBEN, I, 173–179.
4 Blake Letters.
5 Wood Letters.
6 ROUSSET, Histoire de la Guerre de Crimée, I, 180; FAY, 59; Lettres du Maréchal Bosquet, 344.
7 Letters from Headquarters, I, 159–160.
8 Westmorland Papers; R.C.P. (R. to N. Official 21/9/1854).
9 BAZANCOURT, III, 200–204; KINGLAKE, III, 22–27.
10 KINGLAKE, III, 33.
11 GOWING, 16.
12 Williams Letters.
13 KINGLAKE, III, 32.
14 Sir George Brown's MSS. (quoted by KINGLAKE, III, 34–35).
15 ANICHKOV, Der Feldzug in der Krim, I, 127.
16 Westmorland Papers; STERLING, The Highland Brigade, 70 (puts the remark later).
17 Shipley Letters.
18 KINGLAKE, III, 39.
19 HODASEVICH, 66.
20 Letters from Headquarters, I, 168.
21 Ibid., I, 170.
22 Biddulph Letters.
23 KINGLAKE, III, 46–48; Elton Papers.
24 KINGLAKE, III, 57.
25 FAY, 60–62.
26 HODASEVICH, 68–70.
27 ROUSSET, I, 182–183; BAZANCOURT, III, 211–213; FAY, 63.
28 HODASEVICH, 72.
29 KINGLAKE, III, 67 (quoting an unnamed French officer).
30 BAZANCOURT, III, 215–224; ROUSSET, I, 184–185.
31 KINGLAKE, III, 80–81
32 Ibid., III, 83.
33 Letters from Headquarters, I, 170.

34 GOWING, 16.
35 Biddulph Letters.
36 KINGLAKE, III, 90.
37 GOWING, 17.
38 KINGLAKE, III, 95 and 99; COPE, *History of the Rifle Brigade*, 307; WYLLY, *The 95th Regiment in the Crimea*, 11.
39 KINGLAKE, III, 105.
40 Dixon Letters.
41 Dixon Letters; WHEATER, *Historical Record of the 7th Regiment*, 177.
42 GOWING, 18.
43 HODASEVICH, 70.
44 COPE, 308.
45 FORTESCUE, *History of the British Army*, XIII, 64.
46 WYLLY, 13.
47 BROUGHTON-MAINWARING, *Historical Record of the Royal Welch Fusiliers*, 185–186.
48 *Ibid.*, 175; KINGLAKE, III, 126.
49 KINGLAKE, III, 126.
50 WOOLLRIGHT, *Records of the 77th Regiment*, 76.
51 *Clifford*, 97.
52 KINGLAKE, III, 151; BROUGHTON-MAINWARING, 176.
53 Eddington Letters.
54 KINGLAKE, III, 156.
55 KINGLAKE, III, 163; TARLE, *The Crimean War*, I, 182.
56 *Letters from Headquarters*, I, 171–172.
57 KINGLAKE, III, 166.
58 *Ibid.*, 174.
59 Dickson Letters.
60 HODASEVICH, 62.
61 ROUSSET, I, 168; BAZANCOURT, III, 224–228.
62 Westmorland Papers; KINGLAKE, III, 176–177.
63 Dixon Letters; KINGLAKE, III, 205; WHEATER, 178.
64 KINGLAKE, III, 207.
65 Gortschakoff (quoted by KINGLAKE, III, 208).
66 Biddulph Letters.
67 Hamilton Letters.
68 Annesley Diary; MAURICE, *History of the Scots Guards*, II, 67–68.
69 HAMILTON, *History of the Grenadier Guards*, III, 192; KINGLAKE, III, 239.
70 CAVENDISH, *93rd Highlanders*, 94.
71 KINGLAKE, III, 226 and 233.
72 CAVENDISH, *93rd Highlanders*, 95;
73 Biddulph Letters; CAVENDISH, 95.
74 HODASEVICH, 73.
75 *Letters from Headquarters*, I, 183; Westmorland Papers.
76 GOWING, 20.
77 Gortschakoff (quoted by KINGLAKE, III, 283).

78 HODASEVICH, 74.
79 Biddulph Letters.
80 KINGLAKE, III, 286.
81 BAZANCOURT, III, 229.
82 *Ibid.*, 237.
83 ROUSSET, 191.
84 R.C.P. (M.M. 184 R. to N. Private 24/9/1854).
85 *Letters from Headquarters*, I, 189.
86 Hospital Report, 177.
87 ROBINSON, 157.
88 PAGET, 25.
89 Wood Letters.
90 GOWING, 21.
91 Skelton Letters.
92 Biddulph Letters.
93 BELL, 220.
94 Hospital Report, 199.
95 PAGET, 26; ROBINSON, 155–159; *The Times*; TYRRELL, *The War with Russia*, II, 227.

Chapter 7 (Page 91). FLANK MARCH.

1 Memorandum of a Conversation between Sir Edmund Lyons and Mr. George Loch (1856).
2 *Ibid.*
3 TODLEBEN, I, 140.
4 R.C.P. (M.M. 181 N. to R. Official 10/4/1854).
5 R.C.P. (M.M. 184 R. to N. Private 24/9/1854).
6 BAZANCOURT, III, 243.
7 PAGET, 28.
8 BAZANCOURT, III, 243.
9 TODLEBEN, I, 222.
10 PAGET, 35; HODASEVICH, 74–80.
11 Skelton Letters.
12 BAZANCOURT, III, 249–250.
13 R.C.P. (M.M. 184 R. to N. Private 24/9/1854); R.P.P. D (1) 276.
14 Captain Drummond's Report (9/1/1854).
15 TODLEBEN, I, 230–239; Report of a Conversation between H.M. Consul in Poland and Prince Gortschakoff (P.R.O., W.O. 32/20).
16 *Royal Engineers Journal*, I, 13, and 107 Appendix 10; WROTTESLEY, *Military Opinions of Sir John Burgoyne*, 200–201.
17 WROTTESLEY, *Correspondence of Sir John Burgoyne*, II, 93–94.
18 KINGLAKE, III, 400.
19 Shakespear Letters.
20 Shakespear Diary; KINGLAKE, IV, 13.
21 KINGLAKE, IV, 14.

22 Shakespear Diary.
23 PAGET, 29.
24 *Letters from Headquarters*, I, 217.
25 Westmorland Papers; KINGLAKE, IV, 20.
26 KINGLAKE, IV, 19.
27 Godfrey Diary.
28 Biddulph Letters.
29 ROUSSET, I, 201; FAY, 73–74.
30 *Letters from Headquarters*, I, 220.
31 R.C.P. (M.M. 182 R. to N. Official 28/9/1854).
32 RUSSELL, 195.
33 Fisher-Rowe Letters.
34 ROUSSET, I, 229–230; BAZANCOURT, III, 296–299; KINGLAKE, IV, 31.
35 TODLEBEN, I, 256–257; BRIALMONT, *Le Général Todleben*, 9; Report of a Conversation between H.M. Consul in Poland and Prince Gortschakoff (P.R.O., W.O. 32/20); R.P.P., D (1) 276.
36 BAZANCOURT, III, 261.
37 Westmorland Papers.
38 R.C.P. (M.M. 184 R. to N. 8/10/1854).
39 BAZANCOURT, III, 261.
40 BAPST, II, 340.
41 KINGLAKE, IV, 181; BAZANCOURT, III, 299–301.
42 WROTTESLEY, *Military Opinions of Sir John Burgoyne*, 241; *Royal Engineers Journal*, I, 17.
43 KINGLAKE, IV, 174–175 and 189.

Chapter 8 (Page 106). SEBASTOPOL.

1 ZHANDR, *Materials for a History of the Defence of Sebastopol* (not translated from Russian), 227.
2 *Ibid.*, 228 et seq.
3 HODASEVICH, 99.
4 ZHANDR, 234.
5 TODLEBEN, I, 256.
6 HODASEVICH, 130.
7 TODLEBEN, I, 259.
8 ZHANDR, 240–244; PIROGOV, *Letters from Sebastopol* (not translated from Russian), 278.
9 ANICHKOV, *Der Feldzug in der Krim*, II, 29; TODLEBEN, I, 272.
10 ZHANDR, 243.

Chapter 9 (Page 111). BOMBARDMENT.

1 Richards Letters; ROBINSON, 170–171; Fisher-Rowe Letters.
2 ROBINSON, 169; *The Times*.
3 *Letters from Headquarters*, I, 234–236.
4 ROBINSON, 170 et seq.

5 *Clifford*, 59.
6 AIRLIE, 87; Skelton Letters.
7 *Royal Engineers Journal*, I, 26 and 282, Appendix 52.
8 R.C.P. (M.M. 184 R. to N. Private 8/10/1854).
9 WOOD, 79-80.
10 R.C.P. (M.M. 184 R. to N. 8/10/1854); WROTTESLEY, II, 99.
11 ROUSSET, I, 246-252.
12 TODLEBEN, I, 300; *Royal Engineers Journal*, I, 28.
13 Biddulph Letters.
14 R.P.P., D (1) 219.
15 BAPST, II, 247.
16 R.C.P. (M.M. 184 R. to N. Private 8/12/1854).
17 R.C.P. (M.M. 183 N. to R. Private 9/10/1854).
18 *Black Sea Correspondence* (ed. Bonner-Smith), 341.
19 *Ibid.*, 342.
20 Résolutions prises par les Amiraux des trois Escadres Alliés (15/10/1854) (quoted in *Black Sea Correspondence*, 343).
21 *Royal Engineers Journal*, I, 32; *Royal Artillery Operations*, 10-12; NIEL, *Siège de Sébastopol*, 62.
22 *Royal Engineers Journal*, I, 113, Appendix 16; *Black Sea Correspondence*, 345.
23 Dundas Journal (quoted by KINGLAKE, IV, 340).
24 TODLEBEN, I, 332-334.
25 R.C.P. (M.M. 198 Dundas to Raglan Private 17/10/1854).
26 *Black Sea Correspondence*, 339-340; TODLEBEN, I, 336; KINGLAKE, IV, 405; Diary of the Rev. Robert Hinds.
27 HODASEVICH, 88-90.
28 ZHANDR, 260.
29 *Ibid.*, 262.
30 LUKASEVICH, *The Defence of Sebastopol* (not translated from Russian), 173.
31 ZHANDR, 274.
32 TODLEBEN, I, 329.
33 ROUSSET, I, 260-261.
34 BAZANCOURT, III, 325.
35 NIEL, 62-63; BAZANCOURT, III, 326; *Royal Engineers Journal*, I, 33-34.
36 BAZANCOURT, III, 327.
37 WOOD, 100; *Royal Engineers Journal*, I, 34.
38 HODASEVICH, 143; Report of a Conversation between H.M. Consul in Poland and Prince Gortschakoff (P.R.O., W.O. 32/20).
39 TODLEBEN, I, 345.
40 Dixon Letters.
41 Wood Letters.
42 Biddulph Letters.
43 PAGET, 57.
44 Wood Letters.
45 R.C.P. (M.M. 192 Cathcart to Raglan 4/10/1854).

46 PAGET, 45.
47 *Letters from Camp*, 163.
48 Biddulph; Neville; Shipley; Skelton Letters.
49 Letters of William Charles Forrest (quoted by WOODHAM-SMITH, *The Reason Why*, 213).
50 Portal Letters.
51 Richards Letters.
52 *Greville Memoirs* (ed. Fulford), VII, 58.
53 R.C.P. (M.M. 181 N. to R. Official 13/10/1854 and 25/10/1854) and (M.M. 189 Hardinge to Raglan 9/10/1854).
54 R.C.P. (M.M. 184 R. to N. Private 23/10/1854).
55 R.C.P. (M.M. 184 R. to N. Private 24/8/1854).

Chapter 10 (Page 132). BALACLAVA.

1 PAGET, 163.
2 KINGLAKE, V, 68–70.
3 Roberts Letters; *Letters from Headquarters*, I, 306.
4 DUBERLY, 117.
5 CAVENDISH, 102.
6 STERLING, *The Highland Brigade*, 94; CAVENDISH, 100.
7 Evidence of Lt. F. W. Burroughs (quoted by KINGLAKE, V, 80).
8 CAVENDISH, 100.
9 KINGLAKE, V, 81.
10 The MS. Autobiography of William Cattell.
11 *Clifford*, 71.
12 Fisher-Rowe Letters; WOOD, 113.
13 KINGLAKE, V, 152.
14 Fisher-Rowe; *Clifford*; Cattell.
15 Westmorland Papers.
16 WOODHAM-SMITH, 231; KINGLAKE, V, 168.
17 Biddulph Letters.
18 Westmorland Papers.
19 *Letters from Headquarters*, I, 313.
20 KINGLAKE, V, 139; Cattell; Westmorland Papers.
21 KINGLAKE, V, 202–203; Hansard, 3rd Series, 136.
22 KINGLAKE, V, 211.
23 PAGET, 170.
24 KINGLAKE, V, 216.
25 KINGLAKE, V, 212.
26 KINGLAKE, V, 226.
27 *Ibid.*, 221.
28 *Clifford*, 73.
29 KINGLAKE, V, 292.
30 *Ibid.*, 259.
31 *Ibid.*, 281.

32 PAGET, 69–70; 189–191.
33 ROUSSET, I, 287–288.
34 WOODHAM-SMITH, 258.
35 KINGLAKE, V, 332.
36 Newcastle Papers.
37 WOODHAM-SMITH, 264.
38 Newcastle Papers.
39 Newcastle Papers.
40 GOWING, 38.
41 Wood; Blake; Cattell; Fisher; Portal Letters.
42 WOODHAM-SMITH, 262; KINGLAKE, V, 335–336.

Chapter 11 (Page 154). THE BEGINNING OF WINTER.

1 GOWING, 42–43.
2 BELL, 241.
3 DUBERLY, 125; Letters from Headquarters, I, 336–337.
4 WOOD, 71; Westmorland Papers.
5 PAGET, 75.
6 Opening Address of General Airey before the Board of General Officers (1856).
7 R.C.P. (M.M. 184 R. to N. Private 13/11/1854).
8 R.C.P. (M.M. 193 Raglan to Romaine 14/11/1854).
9 FURNEAUX, The First War Correspondent, 84.
10 R.C.P. (M.M. 183 Delane to Newcastle 6/12/1854).
11 MAXWELL, Life of the Fourth Earl of Clarendon, II, 101.
12 R.C.P. (M.M. 184 R. to N. Private 4/1/1855).
13 History of "The Times", II, 185 and 188.
14 R.C.P. (M.M. 184 R. to N. Private 1/5/1855).
15 The Times, 7 December 1854.
16 Dixon Letters.
17 ATKINS, Life of W. H. Russell, I, 191.
18 TODLEBEN, I, 404.
19 R.C.P. (M.M. 183 Newcastle to Raglan Private 13/10/1854) and (M.M. 184 R. to N. Private 27/10/1854).
20 The Hon. Gilbert Elliot's MS. (quoted by KINGLAKE, V, Appendix 10).

Chapter 12 (Page 163). INKERMAN.

1 KINGLAKE, VI, 35.
2 Dixon Letters.
3 R.C.P. (M.M. 184 R. to N. 3/11/1854); Royal Engineers Journal, I, 24 and 47.
4 Biddulph Letters.
5 TODLEBEN, I, 437.
6 TODLEBEN, I, 442–444.
7 Atlas de la Guerre d'Orient, 125.
8 BAZANCOURT, IV, 58.
9 Ibid., 72.

10 Elton Papers.
11 KINGLAKE, VI, 119.
12 *Clifford*, 88.
13 KINGLAKE, VI, 137; WOOLLRIGHT, *Records of the 77th Regiment*, 85.
14 Williams Letters.
15 Dixon Letters.
16 Neville Letters.
17 ROUSSET, I, 323.
18 KINGLAKE, VI, 191; HAMILTON, III, 226.
19 MAURICE, II, 98.
20 Crawford Muniments.
21 HODASEVICH, 192.
22 Williams Letters.
23 HODASEVICH, 199.
24 KINGLAKE, VI, 200.
25 *Ibid.*, 231.
26 TODLEBEN, I, 472.
27 *Ibid.*, 473.
28 KINGLAKE, VI, 261.
29 HODASEVICH, 198.
30 *The Right Flank Company at Inkerman* (quoted by KINGLAKE, VI, 238–240).
31 *Ibid.* (quoted by KINGLAKE, VI, 244).
32 KINGLAKE, VI, 266.
33 Lord Henry Percy's MS. (quoted by KINGLAKE, VI, 253); HAMILTON, III, 232
34 KINGLAKE, VI, 280.
35 *The Right Flank Company at Inkerman* (quoted by KINGLAKE, VI, 274).
36 BANNATYNE, 418.
37 WOOLLRIGHT, *History of the 57th Regiment*, 267; KINGLAKE, VI, 302.
38 Biddulph Letters.
39 ROUSSET, I, 318–319.
40 *Letters from Headquarters*, I, 375.
41 Elton Papers.
42 Shakespear Letters.
43 *Letters from Headquarters*, I, 417.
44 *Ibid.*, 418.
45 RUSSELL, 252.
46 BAPST, II, 292.
47 KINGLAKE, VI, 347.
48 Evidence of Lt.-Col. H. C. B. Daubeney (quoted by KINGLAKE, VI, 348).
49 KINGLAKE, VI, 368.
50 *Ibid.*, 372.
51 BAZANCOURT, IV, 60; FAY, 133.
52 *Journal d'Opérations de la 2me Division* (quoted by KINGLAKE, VI, 386).
53 FAY, 137.
54 *Ibid.*, 138.

55 FAY, 140.
56 *Journal d'Opérations de la 2ᵐᵉ Division* (quoted by KINGLAKE, VI, 396).
57 BAZANCOURT, IV, 73–74.
58 Dickson Letters.
59 KINGLAKE, VI, 401.
60 BAZANCOURT, IV, 77.
61 *Ibid.*, 78; NIEL, 94–95.
62 *Lettres du Maréchal Bosquet*, 349.
63 BAZANCOURT, IV, 76; FAY, 132; BAPST, II, 214.
64 *Letters from Headquarters*, I, 375.
65 KINGLAKE, VI, 414.
66 Evidence of Colonel David Wood (quoted by KINGLAKE, VI, 416).
67 WOOLLRIGHT, *Records of the 77th Regiment*, 87; KINGLAKE, VI, 430–435.
68 Dannenberg's Despatch (quoted by KINGLAKE, VI, 436).

Chapter 13 (Page 195). AFTERMATH AND STORM.

1 *Letters from Camp*, 12.
2 R.C.P. (M.M. 184 Raglan to Newcastle Private 8/11/1854 and M.M. 182 Raglan to Newcastle Official 8/11/1854); ROUSSET, I, 326, gives French losses as 1,743; Russian official returns give 11,959 killed, wounded and prisoners, but HODASEVICH puts the total at 12,300.
3 Elton Papers.
4 Roberts Letters.
5 BELL, 248.
6 R.C.P. (M.M. 182 R. to N. Official 13/11/1854).
7 R.C.P. (M.M. 204 Canrobert and Raglan to Mentschikoff 7/11/1854 and Mentschikoff to Raglan and Canrobert 9/11/1854).
8 RUSSELL, 256.
9 BELL, 248.
10 *Ibid.*, 247.
11 *Clifford*, 98–99.
12 Dixon; Fisher-Rowe; Biddulph; Richards; Shakespear; Portal Letters; Crawford Muniments.
13 *Clifford*, 93.
14 Richards; Fisher-Rowe; Dixon Letters.
15 Russell, 264.
16 Dixon Letters; ROBINSON, 210–213; EVELYN, 109–111; *Letters from Headquarters*, I, 419–421.
17 *Clifford*, 99; RUSSELL, 266.
18 RUSSELL, 265.
19 *Black Sea Correspondence*, 369 et seq.
20 R.C.P. (M.M. 182 R. to N. Official 15/11/1854 and M.M. 184 Private 16/11/1854); Diary of the Rev. Robert Hinds.
21 BELL, 253.
22 RUSSELL, 270–271.

Chapter 14 (Page 205). CHAOS.
1 *Clifford*, 105–106.
2 S.C.R., II, 159.
3 Godfrey; Robinson; Duberly; Jocelyn; *The Times*; *Clifford*; Gowing.
4 RUSSELL, 332.
5 R.C.P. (M.M. 192 Raglan to Filder 13/12/1854).
6 R.P.P., Miscellaneous, Box 10; WRIGHT, *Recollections of a Crimean Chaplain*, 30; *Letters from Headquarters*, II, 80–82.
7 Westmorland Papers; *Letters from Headquarters*, II, 62.
8 R.C.P. (M.M. 182; M.M. 184; M.M. 192: Newcastle Papers, *Opening Address of General Airey before the Board of General Officers*); Westmorland Papers; Sebastopol Committee Reports.
9 R.C.P. (M.M. 190 Filder to Trevelyan).
10 R.C.P. (M.M. 184 R. to N. Private 18/11/1854).
11 R.C.P. (M.M. 182 R. to N. Official 15/11/1854).
12 *Royal Engineers Journal*, I, Appendix 29.
13 R.C.P. (M.M. 184 R. to N. Private 18/11/1854).
14 R.C.P. (M.M. 184 R. to N. Private 18/11/1854).
15 R.C.P. (M.M. 184 R. to N. Private 6/1/1855).
16 R.C.P. (M.M. 184, R. to N. Private 26/12/1854).
17 *Royal Engineers Journal*, I, 59–60.
18 R.C.P. (M.M. 184 R. to N. Private 15/1/1855).
19 Westmorland Papers.
20 R.C.P. (M.M. 184 R. to N. Private 28/11/1854).
21 WOODHAM-SMITH, *Florence Nightingale*, 210.
22 R.C.P. (M.M. 192 Raglan to Romaine 5/12/1854).
23 Westmorland Papers; *Opening Address of General Airey before the Board of General Officers*.
24 S.C.R., IV, 32–36.
25 R.P.P., D (1) 219.
26 P.R.O. W.O. 28 Crimea.
27 R.P.P., D (1) 272.
28 *Letters from Headquarters*, II, 83.

Chapter 15 (Page 219). THE PRIVATE WAR.
1 Dixon Letters.
2 *Clifford*, 146–147.
3 ATKINS, I, 135.
4 *Ibid.*, 131.
5 *Ibid.*, 139.
6 R.C.P. (M.M. 184 R. to N. Private 14/5/1854).
7 ATKINS, I, 146.
8 *Ibid.*, 174.
9 *Ibid.*, 180.
10 *Ibid.*, 186.

11 *The Times,* 3 February 1855.
12 *The Times,* 8 February 1855.
13 *Letters from Camp,* 144.
14 *Letters from Headquarters,* II, 78.
15 WEIGALL, *Correspondence of the Countess of Westmorland,* 249.
16 R.P.P., D (1) 266.
17 *Clifford,* 163.
18 Shakespear Letters.
19 Hamilton Letters.
20 Royal Archives, G 24/73/158.
21 Royal Archives, G 24/28.
22 *Queen Victoria's Letters,* III, 221–222.
23 Royal Archives, G 28/15/21.
24 Royal Archives, G 29/99/72.
25 *Greville Memoirs,* VII, 115.
26 Elton Papers.
27 Richards Letters.
28 WEIGALL, 249–250.
29 MARTIN, III, 213.
30 Westmorland Papers.
31 WEIGALL, 252.
32 R.P.P., D (1) 225.
33 Royal Archives, G 21/65/166.
34 Royal Archives, G 22/61/162.
35 R.C.P. (M.M. 183 N. to R. 1/1/1855).
36 R.C.P. (M.M. 183 N. to R. 29/12/1854 and 29/1/1855).
37 R.C.P. (M.M. 181 N. to R. 6/1/1855).
38 R.C.P. (M.M. 184 R. to N. Private 15/1/1855).
39 R.C.P. (M.M. 184 R. to N. Private 27/1/1855).
40 Elton Papers.
41 R.C.P. (M.M. 184 R. to N. Private 20/1/1855).
42 Westmorland Papers.
43 R.P.P., D (1) 232.
44 R.P.P., D (1) 231.

Chapter 16 (Page 235). NIGHTMARE.

1 *Clifford,* 124–125.
2 RUSSELL, 314–315.
3 WOOD, 234–235.
4 GOWING, 68–69.
5 BELL, 258.
6 ROBINSON, 226.
7 BELL, 273.
8 GOWING, 68.
9 Crawford Muniments; AIRLIE, 183.

10 *Clifford*, 155.
11 BELL, 258.
12 Pretyman Collection.
13 *Clifford*, 155.
14 R.C.P. (M.M. 182 R. to N. Official 30/1/1855).
15 ROBINSON, 224 *et seq.*
16 REID, 12.
17 BELL, 265 and 270.
18 *Letters from Camp*, 204.
19 Conn Letters (*Aberdeen University Review*).
20. S.C.R., III, 67; Panmure Papers (Prince Albert to Panmure 10/2/1855).
21 Blake Letters.
22 RUSSELL, 299; Blake Letters.
23 Biddulph Letters.
24 R.C.P. (M.M. 182 R. to N. Official 13/1/1855; 20/1/1855; 23/1/1855).
25 Shakespear Letters.
26 Fisher-Rowe Letters.
27 Wood Letters.
28 *Clifford*, 162.
29 REID, 24; Richards Letters.
30 BELL, 273.
31 *Clifford*, 149.
32 REID, 35.
33 BELL, 269.
34 ROBINSON, 221.
35 Medical History of the 55th Regiment.
36 Dixon Letters.
37 BELL, 264.
38 GOWING, 67.
39 RUSSELL, 366; ROBINSON, 230.
40 R.C.P. (M.M. 182 R. to N. Official 23/1/1855).
41 Elton Papers.
42 *Clifford*, 126.
43 RUSSELL, 319.
44 BELL, 273.
45 Dixon Letters.
46 BELL, 274.
47 BELL, 256.
48 DUBERLY, 170.
49 Fisher-Rowe Letters.
50 REID, 41.
51 Stacpoole Letters.
52 WOODHAM-SMITH, *Florence Nightingale*, 193.
53 *Ibid.*, 193.
54 *The Autobiography of Elizabeth Davis.*

THE DESTRUCTION OF LORD RAGLAN

55 BELL, 257 and 265.
56 Wood Letters.
57 R.P.P., D (1) 310.
58 *Ibid.*, D (1) 267.
59 *Ibid.*, D (1) 253.
60 *Ibid.*, D (1) 259.
61 *Liverpool Mercury*, 19 January 1855.
62 R.P.P., D (1) 279.

Chapter 17 (Page 251). THE ARISTOCRATIC STAFF.

1 Hansard, 3rd Series, 136.
2 *Ibid.*
3 MAGNUS, 119.
4 PEMBERTON, 227.
5 *Ibid.*, 30.
6 Panmure Papers (Palmerston to Panmure 11/7/1855).
7 *Ibid.* (Panmure to Raglan 12/2/1855).
8 *Ibid.* (Panmure to Raglan 12/2/1855).
9 R.C.P. (M.M. 186 Raglan to Panmure 27/2/1855).
10 Panmure Papers (Queen to Panmure 13/2/1855).
11 *Ibid.* (16/2/1855).
12 *Ibid.* (24/6/1855).
13 *Ibid.* (26/3/1855).
14 *Ibid.* (undated April 1855).
15 *Ibid.* (Panmure to Queen 27/2/1855).
16 *Ibid.* (Panmure to Raglan 19/2/1855).
17 *Ibid.* (23/4/1855).
18 *Ibid.* (19/2/1855).
19 *Ibid.* (Panmure to Raglan 23/4/1855).
20 *Ibid.* (Palmerston to Panmure 15/4/1855; 1/5/1855; 8/5/1855).
21 *Ibid.* (Panmure to Raglan 1/6/1855).
22 *Ibid.* (Houston-Stewart to Panmure 24/3/1855).
23 *Ibid.* (Simpson to Panmure 16/4/1855).
24 *Clifford*, 158.
25 ROBINSON, 273–278.
26 *The Wonderful Adventures of Mrs. Seacole*; ROBINSON, 290; REID, 13; Blake Letters.
27 ROBINSON, 292–293; RUSSELL, 360; Biddulph Letters.
28 GERNSHEIM, 46.
29 Blake Letters.
30 *Ibid.*
31 *Clifford*, 193.
32 Blake Letters.
33 *Letters from Headquarters*, II, 48–49.
34 Dixon Letters.

35 *Letters from Headquarters,* II, 36.
36 *Clifford,* 185.
37 RUSSELL, 368.
38 Conn Letters.
39 ROBINSON, 272.
40 Biddulph Letters; ROBINSON, 274 and 250–251; REID, 48.
41 Panmure Papers (Panmure to Raglan 9/2/1855; 15/2/1855; 26/2/1855; 2/3/1855; 5/3/1855; 9/3/1855; May (undated) 1855; 10/6/1855; 18/6/1855).
42 Westmorland Papers.
43 Elton Papers.
44 Blake Letters.
45 Verney Papers.
46 WOODHAM-SMITH, *Florence Nightingale,* 220.
47 *Ibid.,* 221.
48 R.P.P., D (1) 310.
49 GERNSHEIM, 46.
50 R.P.P. D (1) 310.
51 *Ibid.,* Miscellaneous Box 10.
52 *Ibid.,* D (1) 310.
53 *Letters from Camp,* 214.
54 R.P.P., D (1) 251.
55 Panmure Papers (Panmure to Simpson 30/3/1855).
56 Westmorland Papers.
57 R.P.P., D (1) 235.
58 R.C.P. (M.M. 184 R. to N. 18/12/1854).

Chapter 18 (Page 270). CANROBERT AND PÉLISSIER.

1 ROUSSET, II, 30 and 128–129.
2 *Ibid.,* 27.
3 NIEL, 145.
4 BAZANCOURT, IV, 174–175.
5 ROUSSET, II, 53–54; BAZANCOURT, IV, 180.
6 ROUSSET, II, 57–61.
7 Panmure Papers (Houston-Stewart to Panmure 30/6/1855).
8 *Royal Engineers Journal,* II, 61–62; WROTTESLEY, II, 265; NIEL, 158–160.
9 ROUSSET, II, 101–105; BAZANCOURT, IV, 202–209.
10 REILLY, *Artillery Operations,* 74; ROUSSET, II, 115.
11 ROUSSET, II, 125.
12 R.C.P. (M.M. 186 Raglan to Panmure 24/4/1855).
13 *Ibid.*
14 R.C.P. (M.M. 186 Raglan to Panmure 28/4/1855).
15 *Sanitary Commission Report,* 79.
16 *Lettres du Maréchal Bosquet,* 369.
17 *Clifford,* 186.
18 *Campagnes de Crimée,* 152–155, 203.

19 Elton Papers.
20 *Letters from Camp*, 242.
21 Shakespear Letters; Biddulph Letters; Elton Papers.
22 R.C.P. (M.M. 194 Canrobert to Raglan 30/4/1855).
23 R.C.P. (M.M. 194 Raglan to Canrobert 1/5/1855).
24 Westmorland Papers.
25 R.C.P. (M.M. 199 Raglan to Lyons 4/3/1855).
26 ROUSSET, II, 138; BAZANCOURT, IV, 262-263.
27 R.C.P. (M.M. 199 Raglan to Lyons 4/5/1855).
28 BAPST, II, 309.
29 ROUSSET, II, 151; DERRÉCAGAIX, *Pélissier*, 355; DE CASTELLANE, *Journal*, V, 83.
30 BAPST, II, 316.
31 Panmure Papers (Panmure to Raglan 20/4/1855).
32 BENSON, III, 155 and 157.
33 BAZANCOURT, IV, 266-272.
34 R.C.P. (M.M. 186 Raglan to Panmure 5/5/1855).
35 DERRÉCAGAIX, 357-359, 364, 397-399, 416-419; ROUSSET, II, 163-164; BAPST, II, 468-470.
36 ROUSSET, II, 186; Westmorland Papers.
37 Hickleton Papers A4, 77.
38 Walker-Heneage Letters; GERNSHEIM, 85; RUSSELL, 459.
39 ROUSSET, II, 187; DERRÉCAGAIX, 398.
40 Panmure Papers (Panmure to Raglan 23/3/1855).
41 Panmure Papers (Granville to Palmerston 7/5/1855).
42 *Ibid.* (Palmerston to Panmure 8/5/1855).
43 *Ibid.* (Panmure to Raglan 14/5/1855).

Chapter 19 (Page 283). MALAKOFF AND REDAN.

1 DUBERLY, 200; Biddulph Letters.
2 RUSSELL, 441.
3 PAGET, 95.
4 RUSSELL, 442; Elton Papers; Wood Letters.
5 PAGET, 99-100.
6 TODLEBEN, II, 314-315.
7 *Clifford*, 221.
8 DERRÉCAGAIX, 355-413; FAY, 252-258; NIEL, 293-298.
9 TODLEBEN, II, 323-333; *Royal Engineers Journal*, II, 269-270; KINGLAKE, IX, 113-130; WOLSELEY, I, 152-162.
10 Panmure Papers (Panmure to Raglan 1/6/1855 and 11/6/1855).
11 DERRÉCAGAIX, IX, 431.
12 *Royal Engineers Journal*, II, 286; DERRÉCAGAIX, 434.
13 Hickleton Papers A4.77.
14 ROUSSET, II, 225; DERRÉCAGAIX, 435-436.
15 REILLY, *Royal Artillery Operations*.
16 BAZANCOURT, IV, 344-345.

17 KINGLAKE, IX, 151.
18 *Ibid.*, 153.
19 BAZANCOURT, IV, 347; ROUSSET, II, 231–232; DERRÉCAGAIX, 438.
20 NIEL, 314–318; ROUSSET II, 232–234; BAZANCOURT, IV. 348–365.
21 Hickleton Papers A4.77.
22 KINGLAKE, IX, 166.
23 Hugh Hibbert's MS.
24 GOWING, 86–89.
25 *Ibid.*, 87.
26 *Royal Engineers Journal*, II, 306; KINGLAKE, IX, 192–193.
27 WOOD, 320–328.
28 KINGLAKE, IX, 313.
29 WOLSELEY, I, 170.
30 WOOD, 333.
31 *Clifford*, 227–228.

Chapter 20 (Page 292). THE DYING MAN.

1 KINGLAKE, IX, 266.
2 Biddulph Letters.
3 PAGET, 103.
4 Abstract of the Case of F. M. Lord Raglan, by J. P. Prendergast, M.D. (R.C.P.).
5 R.P.P., D (1) 242.
6 Abstract of the Case of F. M. Lord Raglan, by J. P. Prendergast, M.D. (R.C.P.).
7 KINGLAKE, IX, 286.
8 Barnard Letters (evidence of Nigel Kingscote).
9 *Ibid.*
10 PAGET, 104; KINGLAKE, IX, 287.
11 *Letters from Headquarters*, II, 363.
12 REID, 76.
13 *Letters from Camp*, 209.
14 *Clifford*, 230.
15 Verney Papers.
16 GOWING, 100.

Epilogue (Page 297)

1 Panmure Papers (Simpson to Panmure 30/6/1855).
2 *Ibid.* (Houston-Stewart to Panmure 30/6/1855).
3 TYRRELL, II, 252.

INDEX

INDEX

Dumbreck, Dr., 214–15
Dundas, Admiral Sir James, 33, 36, 116–17; and plan to attack Sebastopol, 118; change of plan, 119–20; failure of attack, 120–1
Dundonald, Lord, 264 n.
Durham Light Infantry, 177–8

Egerton, Colonel the Hon. Algernon, 71, 170, 259
Ellenborough, Lord, on the mismanagement of the war, 281, 282
Elliot, Lieutenant Alexander, 137, 138–9
Elton, Captain, 169, 227
England, Major-General Sir Richard, 13; at the Alma, 59, 79; criticisms of, 126
Erminia, H.M.S., 259
Errol, Lord and Lady, 47
Estcourt, Major-General James Bucknall, 15; and the hurricane, 201; mounting criticisms of, 217; charges against, 231; Raglan's defence of, 232, 255; death, 292
Eugénie, Empress, 278
Eupatoria, 37; landing at, 38, 39, 40
Evans, Major-General Sir George de Lacy, 13, 61, 65, 72, 78, 161; illness, 169; advises Raglan to abandon Crimea, 197; dislike of Airey, 233
Ewart, Captain, 165

Federoff, Colonel, 161, 198
Fedioukine Hills, 129, 134, 145, 150
Fenton, Roger, 261, 277
Filder, Commissary-General James, 16, 208, 211, 212, 225–6
Fisher, Cornet, 35, 154, 202; on the Russians, 111; on the Turks, 214–2; criticisms of Raglan, 225; on the Army's new recruits, 269
Fisher, Lieutenant A'Court, 289
Fitzmayer, Colonel, 188
Forey, General, 63
French Army: superior army equipment at Gallipoli, 18; friendly relations with British troops, 28; landing at Eupatoria, 39, 40; methods of obtaining supplies, 43–5; lack of co-operation after the Alma, 92; discouraged by gunfire at Sebastopol, 123, 124; at Inkerman, 166, 182, 183–4, 192–3; counter-attack on Russians after Inkerman, 204; refusal to help in road construction, 212–13; superior organisation of, 240–1; indecision of, 269, 270–1; looting of Kertch, 280; attack on the Malakoff, 287

Gallipoli, 17
Gambier, Colonel, 188
Giurgevo, Battle of, 25, 130
Gladstone, W. E., 12, 25, 251, 252
Godfrey, Captain W. A., 43; on winter conditions at Balaclava, 205

Goldie, General: at Inkerman, 187–8; killed, 188
Gortschakoff, Prince, 25, 54, 96, 160, 299; at the Alma, 74, 78, 82, 85–6; and Inkerman, 167
Gough, Lord, 16
Gowing, Sergeant Timothy, quoted, 9, 41, 67–8, 88, 119, 125, 184–5, 197, 205, 242
Grant, Major, 163
Granville, Earl, 281
Grenadier Guards: at the Alma, 79; at Inkerman, 173–4, 175, 176: save their Colours, 181
Greville, Charles, 128, 227, 255
Guards, Brigade of, 21; at the Alma, 71–2, 79–80; at Inkerman 173 ff.; dissatisfaction at Raglan's mention of them, 225; losses through sickness, 237

Haines, Colonel, 187, 188, 193
Hall, Sir John, 213–14, 265
Hamelin, Admiral, 36, 117, 118; change of plan at Sebastopol, 119–20
Hamilton, Colonel Frederick, 80
Hardinge, Captain, 177
Hardinge, Lord, 6, 16, 42, 111, 128, 298
Head, Sir Francis, 5
Heavy Brigade, 15, 48; at Balaclava, 136, 137, 146, 147
Henry, Sergeant-Major, 183
Herbert, Lord, 251
Hibbert, Captain Hugh, 161, 288
Higginson, Captain, 180
Highland Regiments: at the Alma, 71–2, 83 ff.; at Balaclava, 135–6, 142
Holy Land, war in, 11
Hood, Colonel, 81, 82
Horsford, Colonel, 182
Hospital Commission, report of, 299
Hospitals: at Varna, 30–1; at Scutari, 213–14; at Balaclava, 247; improvements in, 264; Florence Nightingale inspects, 264–5
Houston-Stewart, Admiral, 258, 271, 298
Hume, Major, 80
Hussars, at Balaclava, 144–5

Ilynsky, Captain, 122
Inkerman, Battle of, 165 ff.; Russian retreat, 171–2; criticisms of conduct of, 198–9; sudden French attack, 182
Inkerman Ridge, 271, 272
Inniskilling Dragoons, 138
Istomine, Admiral, 122

Jesse, Captain, 289
Jocelyn, Major, 127; on the attacks on Raglan, 228; on losses in Guards, 237
Jones, General Sir Henry, 286; agrees to attack the Redan, 287; shot, 290

Kadiköi, 102, 129, 260
Kamiesch, 103, 240

334

INDEX

his men, 266–7; attitude to Press, 221;
The Times attacks on, 222 ff.; secret un-
happiness at criticisms, 229, 268
Redcliffe, Lord Stratford de, 9
Resolute, H.M.S., 201
Restitution, H.M.S., 202
Reynardson, Colonel, 173
Richards, Lieutenant William, 93, 111, 113,
198, 236
Richmond and Gordon, 4th Duke of, 4
Rifle Brigade, 68, 182
Rip Van Winkle, H.M.S., 202
Robinson, Dr., 44; on state of Army after
Inkerman, 197; sufferings in hurricane,
200
Rodney, H.M.S., 121
Roebuck, John, 251, 267, 281; report of his
Committee, 299
Rokeby, Lord, 241; replaces Duke of Cam-
bridge, 237
Romaine, William, 158, 214
Rooper, Major, 188
Ros, Lord de, 15, 30, 42–3
Rose, General Hugh, 24, 123
Ross-Lewin, Captain J. D., 116
Rousset, Camille, 145
Royal Artillery, 130
Royal Engineers, 289
Royal Fusiliers, 68, 77, 80, 160, 173–4, 281
Royal Horse Artillery, 240
Royal Welch Fusiliers, 68, 70, 82
Russell, Sir Charles, 179
Russell, Lord John, 252
Russell, William, 160, 245; attacks on Lord
Raglan, 218 ff.; belated tribute to him,
267–8; on the looting of Kertch, 280
Russia: at war with Turkey, 11; unpre-
paredness for war in Bulgaria, 24
Russian Army: at the Alma, 67 ff.; attacks
from Tchorgoun, 132; size of at Inkerman,
167; plan for Inkerman, 167; retreat, 171–
2; further attacks, 173 ff.; efficiency of
gunfire at Inkerman, 184; attack on French
after Inkerman, 204; defences in Sebastopol,
270–1

St. Arnaud, Marshal, 22, 28, 33; plan for
attacking at the Alma, 56–7; the battle,
62–3, 76–7, 87; unco-operativeness with
British, 91–2; illness, 95, 97; death, 103–4
St. Georges, Major Foley de, 209 n.
Sanitary Commissioners, report of, 299
Sanspareil, H.M.S., 120, 121, 230
Sapouné Hills, 167
Sardinian troops, 283
Scarlett, General Sir James, 136–9
Scots Fusilier Guards, 80 ff., 173–6
Scots Greys, 138
Scutari, base hospitals at, 213–14
Sebastopol: instructions to besiege, 32;
march around, 97; delay in attacking, 103;
Russian preparations to defend, 106–8,

270–1; Quarantine Bastion, 109; Central
Bastion, 109, 122; Flagstaff Bastion, 109,
122, 124, 271, 272; Redan, the, 109, 122,
124; British attack on, 285, failure of,
298–9; Malakoff, the, 109, 122, 271, 272,
taken by the French, 298–9; Mont Rodolphe, 115, 119, 123; Green Hill, 115;
part to be played by allied fleets in attacking, 118; change of plan, 119–20; failure of
first attack, 120–1; untouched after Inkerman, 195; the Mamelon, 272; taken by the
French, 284
Seymour, Colonel Francis, 176
Shadworth, Colonel, 288
Shakespear, Captain C. M. J. D., 99, 124,
135, 154, 195
Shewell, Colonel, 144
Shipley, Captain R. Y., 206
Silistria, 24
Simpson, Lieutenant-General James, 264 n.,
267; report from the Crimea, 258–9; on
the Army's new recruits, 269; in tem-
porary command, 297–8
Skelton, Dr. Joseph, 87–8, 119
Somerset, Hon. Arthur, 4 n.
Somerset, Hon. Charlotte, 4 n., 21, 234, 268,
293
Somerset, Hon. Katharine, 4 n.
Somerset, Hon. Richard (2nd Lord Raglan),
4 n., 28 n., 234, 277
Sonning, H.M.S., 36
Soyer, Alexis, 264–5
Spies, prejudice against use of, 33, 131
Spurling, Corporal John, on state of Army
after Inkerman, 197
Stacpoole, Lieutenant G. W., 241 n.
Star, H.M.S., 297
Star of the South, H.M.S., 201
Starling, Colonel, 276
Steele, Colonel, 36, 38, 118, 283–4
Stetzenko, Lieutenant, 109
Strangways, General, 185
Stratford, 1st Viscount, 22, 33, 227–8
Stuart, Major Ramsey, 187–8
Sutherland, Dr., 265

Tartars, the, 280
Tchernaya, river, 101, 102, 166
Tchorgoun: Russian army around, 130;
destruction of Russian camp at, 281
Thomas, Captain, 101
Times, The: quoted, 16, 17, 25, 30–1, 112,
136, 196; attacks on Raglan, 158, 218,
222 ff.; publication of military information,
158–60; protest against continuation of
war, 237–8; Army indignation against,
267
Todleben, Lieutenant-Colonel Franz; per-
sonality, 107; and the defences of Sebastopol, 96 and n.; 107–8, 110, 122, 271;
wounded, 297
Tomline, Colonel, 237

337

INDEX